Finance & Accounting for Nonfinancial Managers

4th Edition

Steven A. Finkler, Ph.D, CPA

.CCH

a Wolters Kluwer business

Editorial Staff

Production .... Christopher Zwirek, Ann Hartmann, Linda Kalteux
Cover Design .... Kathie Luzod
Index .... Deanna Leach

ISBN: 978-0-8080-2576-4

Printed in the United States of America

SFI — Certified Chain of Custody
Product Line Contains At Least
20% Certified Forest Content
www.sfiprogram.org
SFI-00756

In loving memory of my parents

About the Author

Steven A. Finkler, Ph.D., CPA, is Professor Emeritus of Accounting and Financial Management at the Robert F. Wagner Graduate School, New York University. At the Wagner School he directed the Finance Specialization for over twenty years. He holds a bachelor's degree with joint majors in accounting and finance (summa cum laude) and a master's degree in Accounting (with highest honors) from the Wharton School. His master's degree in Economics and Ph.D. in Business Administration are from Stanford University. Before joining NYU, he was on the faculty of the Wharton School.

An award-winning teacher and author, he has written nineteen other books on budgeting, cost accounting, and financial management, and over two hundred articles on financial management. He has consulted for numerous organizations around the United States and abroad. He worked for several years as a CPA with Ernst & Young.

Contents

Preface

This book is an introduction to the world of financial management. However, its intent is not to make the reader a financial manager. Rather, it is an attempt to familiarize the nonfinancial manager with what accounting and finance are all about. This book concentrates on providing a working vocabulary for communication, so that the reader can develop an ability to ask the right questions and interpret the jargon-laden answers. Any accountant can bury any nonaccountant in debits and credits. But, once you understand a few basics, you can fight back and demand information that is both useful and usefully explained.

In addition to vocabulary, this book describes a variety of methods, processes, and tools of accounting and finance. They are not described in sufficient detail for the reader to fire the treasurer or controller and take over the job (how many of you really want to do that?). Instead, there is sufficient detail so that the reader can say, "So that's what LIFO-FIFO is all about. I always wondered why we changed our inventory system," or perhaps, "Hey, we never thought about those advantages of leasing rather than buying; maybe we should give leasing a closer look!"

There's no escaping the fact that all managers are affected by the financial decisions that every firm makes. This book clarifies in the reader's mind what questions are important to the firm's financial management and why.

Who are the nonfinancial managers this book is aimed at? They are all managers except for the accountants and other financial experts in the firm. This includes all the engineers, marketing and sales personnel, and production people who have moved up within their firm to the point at which they need more financial lingo to follow what's going on in their communications with the financial officers. It includes those in law and human resources, and others throughout all areas of the firm, who have shifted career paths or who have simply grown with the firm and been promoted to more responsible positions. Sometimes managers need this book simply because the growth of their firm has been so fast that the financial complexity has increased at a more rapid rate then they have been able to keep up with.

Most of the readers of this book will not have attended business school. However, many business school graduates will pick this book up as a refresher. Frequently, business school graduates who majored in fields such as management, marketing, and industrial organization have commented years later that they would have paid far more attention to their accounting and finance course work had they realized how valuable that background is to those in responsible positions in industry.

Essentially, this book is for any manager or future manager who comes into contact with elements of the financial process and feels a need for a better understanding of what's going on. The structure of this book is such that the reader can sit down and read it in whole or in part. Although it is not a novel, the material is presented in a prose that should eliminate the need for intensive studying to understand the main points. A once-through reading should provide the reader with a substantial gain in knowledge. As specific financial questions come before the reader at times in the future, the book will serve as a good reference to brush up in a particular area.

The widespread acceptance of the first three editions of this book has been gratifying. When first published, it was selected as the book of the month by Fortune Book Club. Since then it has been featured by a number of other book clubs, and over 175,000 copies have been sold. It has been included in business CD collections, and is the basis for an on-line interactive course in accounting and finance. It has been adopted by a number of colleges and universities that wanted a less technical book for their non-accounting majors. It has been the basis for a number of executive programs as well. I am most proud of the wide number of individuals who have used it on their own, and then written to thank me because they found it so useful.

Included with this edition (on the CD that accompanies this book) are Microsoft Excel templates that will allow you to immediately apply many of the concepts and techniques discussed throughout the book. Also included in an extensive annotated list of Web sites related to accounting and finance that would be useful for nonfinancial managers.

This fourth edition has changed substantially from the prior edition. In addition to many general updates to make the book more current, this new edition includes new and expanded chapters, discussion of international accounting standards that may soon have a major impact on accounting in the United States, and a major restructuring of the order in which the material in the book is presented.

Chapter 2, new to this edition, provides a basic Excel tutorial. Many nonfinancial managers are held back in their advancement because they are not proficient in Excel. If you know how to use Excel, please skip this chapter. But if you are not currently an Excel user, you will be pleased to see how quickly and easily you can pick up the essentials.

Several of the new chapters in this edition are focused on tools and techniques. Chapter 10 focuses on Uncertainty, providing several tools to aid in making effective decisions when there is uncertainty about the future. Chapter 12 discusses the Earned Value Management technique, designed to help keep projects running on time and on budget. Chapter 17 is devoted to Variance Analysis. The chapter relies heavily on flexible budget concepts to help managers deal better with situations where actual outcomes differ from budgeted expectations.

Several discussions have been added to address some of the major financial events of recent years. In light of a rash of recent financial scandals, Chapter 18 has been refocused from accountability and internal control to a primary focus on fraud and fraud prevention. Chapter 21 now contains a discussion of mark-to-market accounting, which some believe was a major factor leading to the subprime mortgage crisis of 2008 and the subsequent Great Recession.

Chapter 14 on Leases has been substantially expanded to include information about other types of long-term financing including long-term notes, mortgages, and bonds.

As of the writing of this book, there is a movement toward requiring the use of International Financial Reporting Standards (IFRS) in the United States. A convergence committee is working on bringing U.S. generally accepted accounting principles and IFRS together. It is possible that some U.S. companies may begin using some version of IFRS as early as 2014. At this point there is no way to know what the final standards will look like if adopted in the U.S., but the reader will get a sneak peak at IFRS in a number of places throughout the book.

Some of the other new topics included in this edition include discussion of the cash versus accrual bases of accounting, cost allocation including Activity Based Costing, and the eXtensible Business Reporting Language (XBRL).

Perhaps the most dramatic change in this edition is that there has been a major restructuring of the order in which the chapters are presented. For those of you new to the book, hopefully you will just find that there is a nice flow of information from chapter to chapter. Those of you who have used earlier editions may find the restructuring somewhat jarring at first. Earlier editions of the book were written in the traditional order that accounting is generally taught. However, that order best meets the needs of future CPAs, who are primarily concerned with financial reporting to individuals outside of the firm. The new chapter order considers the needs of a nonfinancial manager, providing an emphasis on first planning, then on implementing plans, and then finally on reporting results.

Instructors using this book in a classroom setting will be pleased to see the addition of Questions for Review at the end of each chapter. The solutions to these homework questions and a set of power point class notes are available on the Instructor's Guide CD.

I would like to thank Professors Viswanathan and Alford of National University, and Professors Lange and Florence of Regis University who reviewed the book and provided helpful comments for the revisions for this new edition. My thanks go to Stewart Karlinsky for his valuable contributions to the tax sections of this book. I am also grateful for the assistance of my editor Kurt Diefenbach and also Lynn Kopon of the CCH editorial staff. I would especially like to thank Christopher Zwirek who did an outstanding job in the production of this book.

Any comments or question concerning this book may be addressed to me at *steven.finkler@nyu.edu*.

Steven A. Finkler, Ph.D., CPA
Professor Emeritus of Accounting and Financial Management
The Wagner School, New York University

List of Excel Templates

To ease your way into the application of the material in this book. a set of computer templates has been prepared. These templates, using Microsoft Excel spreadsheet software, are on the CD that accompanies this book. In each chapter where the material for a template is discussed, there is a box referring the reader to the template. The templates on the CD are:

Template 1. Balance Sheet (Simple Example)—Chapter 4

Template 2. Income Statement (Simple Example)—Chapter 4

Template 3. Statement of Retained Earnings—Chapter 4

Template 4. Income and Retained Earnings Statement (Simple Example)—Chapter 4

Template 5. Cash Flow Statement (Simple Example)—Chapter 4

Template 6. Operating Budget—Chapter 6

Template 7. Flexible Budget—Chapter 6

Template 8. Monthly Cash Budget—Chapter 6

Template 9. Present Value—Chapter 11

Template 10. Future Value—Chapter 11

Template 11. Net Present Value—Chapter 11

Template 12. Internal Rate of Return—Chapter 11

Template 13. Calculating Straight-Line and Accelerated Depreciation—Chapter 13

Template 14. Accounts Receivable Aging Schedule—Chapter 15

Template 15. Economic Order Quantity (EOQ)—Chapter 15

Template 16. Credit Terms (Calculate Implicit Interest Rates)—Chapter 15

Template 17. Computing Variances—Chapter 17

Template 18. Journal/Ledger Worksheet—Chapter 20

Template 19. Income Statement and Balance Sheet Derived from Template 18—Chapter 20

Template 20. Balance Sheet (Statement of Financial Position)—Chapter 22

Template 21. Income Statement and Analysis of Retained Earnings—Chapter 22

Template 22. Statement of Cash Flows—Chapter 22

Template 23. Common Size Ratios—Balance Sheet—Chapter 24

Template 24. Common Size Ratios—Income Statement—Chapter 24

Template 25. Liquidity Ratios—Chapter 24

Template 26. Efficiency Ratios—Chapter 24

Chapter 1

An Introduction to Financial Management

WHAT IS FINANCIAL MANAGEMENT?

Financial management is the part of management which focuses on the organization's finances. Within financial management there are two primary disciplines: accounting and finance. *See* Figure 1-1. Accounting is a system for providing financial information. It is generally broken down into two principal elements: financial accounting and managerial accounting. *Finance* is the area of financial management that supervises the acquisition and disposition of the firm's resources, especially cash.

The *financial accounting* aspect of accounting is a formalized system designed to record the financial history of the firm. The financial accountant is simply a historian who uses dollar signs. An integral part of the financial accountant's job is to report the firm's history from time to time to interested individuals, usually through the firm's annual and quarterly financial reports.

The *managerial accountant* looks forward whereas the financial accountant looks backward. Instead of reporting on what has happened, the managerial accountant provides financial information that might be used for making improved decisions regarding the future. In many small firms the same individual is responsible for providing both financial and managerial accounting information.

FIGURE 1-1
Financial Management

Finance is responsible for the organization's money. It focuses on borrowing funds and investing the cash resources of the firm. However, the finance function also involves providing financial analyses to improve decisions that will affect on the wealth of the organization and its owners. The managerial accountant provides the information for use in the analyses performed by the finance officer.

THE GOALS OF FINANCIAL MANAGEMENT

At first thought, one might simply say that the goal of financial management is to aid in the maximization of wealth, or more simply, maximization of the firm's profits. Profits are, after all, literally, the bottom line for for-profit organizations. That's true, but as all managers know, the corporate environment has many other goals—maximization of sales, maximization of market share, maximization of the growth rate of sales, and maximization of the market price of the firm's stock, for example. For not-for-profit organizations maximization of profits may not be a goal at all, although at least some profit is usually necessary to ensure the financial well-being of even not-for-profit organizations.

On a more personal level, managers are concerned with maximization of salary and perks. Such maximization is often tied in with the maximization of return on investments (ROI), return on equity (ROE) or return on assets (ROA). (*See* Chapter 24 for a discussion of these terms.) The list of goals within the organization is relatively endless, and our intention is to narrow the range rather than broaden it.

From the perspective of financial management there are two over-riding goals: profitability and viability. *See* Figure 1-2. The firm wants to be profitable, and it wants to continue in business. It is possible to be profitable and yet fail to continue in business. Both goals require some clarification and additional discussion.

FIGURE 1-2
Organizational Goals

Profitability

In maximizing profits there is always a trade-off with risk. *See* Figure 1-3. The greater the risk we must incur, the greater the anticipated profit or return on our money we demand. Certainly, given two equally risky projects, we would generally choose to undertake the one with a greater anticipated return. More often than not, however, our situation revolves around whether the return on a specific investment is great enough to justify the risk involved.

Consider keeping funds in a passbook account insured by the Federal Deposit Insurance Corporation (FDIC). The return on a bank savings account is low, but so is the risk. Alternatively, you could put your money in a nonbank money market fund where the return might be higher. However, the FDIC would not insure the investment. The risk is clearly greater. Or you could put your money into the stock market. In general, do we expect our stocks to do better or worse than a money market fund? Well, the risks inherent in the stock market are significantly higher than in a money market fund. If the expected return weren't higher, would anyone invest in the stock market?

FIGURE 1-3
Profitability Trade-Off

That doesn't mean that everyone will choose to accept the same level of risk. Some people keep all their money in FDIC insured bank accounts, and others choose the most speculative of stocks. Some firms will be more willing to accept a high risk in order to achieve a high potential profit than other firms. The key here is that in numerous business decisions the firm is faced with a trade-off—risk vs. return. Throughout this book, when decisions are considered, the question that will arise is, "Are the extra expected profits worth taking the risk?" It is, I hope, a question that you will be somewhat more comfortable answering before you've reached the end of this book.

Viability

Viability refers to the ability to continue to provide goods and services, and to not go out of business. Firms have no desire to go bankrupt, so it is no surprise that one of the crucial goals of financial management is ensuring financial viability. This goal is often measured in terms of *liquidity* and *solvency. See* Figure 1-4.

FIGURE 1-4
Viability

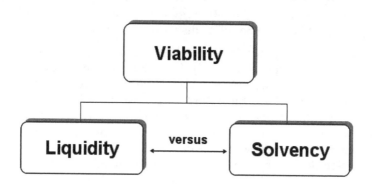

Liquidity is simply a measure of the amount of resources a firm has that are cash or are convertible to cash in the *near term,* to meet the obligations the firm has that are coming due in the near term. Accountants use the phrases "near-term," "short-term," and "current" interchangeably. Generally the near-term means one year or less. Thus a firm is liquid if it has enough near-term resources to meet its near-term obligations as they become due for payment.

Solvency is simply the same concept from a long-term perspective. *Long-term* simply means more than one year. Does the firm have enough cash generation potential over the next three, five, and ten years to meet the major cash needs that will occur over those periods? A firm must plan for adequate solvency well in advance because the potentially large amounts of cash involved may take a long period of planning to generate. The roots of liquidity crises that put firms out of business often are buried in inadequate long-term solvency planning in earlier years.

So a good strategy is maximization of your firm's liquidity and solvency, right? No, wrong. Managers have a complex problem with respect to liquidity. Every dollar kept in a liquid form (such as cash, Treasury bills (T-bills), or money market funds) is a dollar that could have been invested by the firm in some longer-term, higher yielding project or investment. There is a trade-off in the area of viability and profitability. The more profitable the manager attempts to make the firm by keeping it fully invested, the lower the liquidity and the greater the possibility of a liquidity crisis and even bankruptcy. The more liquid the firm is kept, the lower the profits. Essentially this is just a special case of the trade-off between risk and return discussed earlier.

We mentioned that profitability and viability are not synonymous. A firm can be profitable every year of its existence, yet go bankrupt anyway. How can this happen? Frequently it is the result of rapid growth and poor financial planning. Consider a firm whose sales are so good that inventory is constantly being substantially expanded. Such expansion requires cash payments to suppliers well in advance of ultimate cash collection from customers.

Consider the hypothetical firm, Expanding Growth Company, that starts the year with $40,000 in cash, $80,000 of receivables, and 10,000 units of inventory. Receivables are amounts that Expanding Growth's customers owe it for goods and services that they bought, but have not paid for yet. Its inventory units are sold for $10 each and they have a cost of $8, yielding a profit of $2 on each unit sold. During January it collects all of its receivables from the beginning of the year (no bad debts!), thus increasing available cash to $120,000. January sales are 10,000 units, up 2,000 from the 8,000 units sold last December.

Due to increased sales, Expanding Growth decides to expand inventory to 12,000 units. Of the $120,000 available, it spends $96,000 on replacement and expansion of inventory (12,000 units acquired @ $8). No cash is collected yet for sales made in January. This leaves a January month-end cash balance of $24,000.

$ 40,000 Cash, January 1
+ 80,000 Collections during January
———————
$120,000 Cash Available
− 96,000 Purchase of Inventory (12,000 units @ $8)
———————
$ 24,000 Cash Balance, January 31

During February all $100,000 of receivables from January's sales (10,000 units @ $10) are collected, increasing the available cash to $124,000. In February the entire 12,000 units on hand are sold and are replaced in stock with an expanded total inventory of 15,000 units.

$ 24,000 Cash Balance, January 31
+100,000 Collections during February
———————
$124,000 Cash Available
−120,000 Purchase of Inventory (15,000 units @ $8)
———————
$ 4,000 Cash Balance, February 28

Everyone at Expanding Growth is overjoyed. They are making $2 on each unit sold. They are collecting 100 percent of their sales on a timely basis. There appears to be unlimited growth potential for increasing sales and profits. The reader may suspect that we are going to pull the rug out from under Expanding Growth by having sales drop or customers stop paying. Not at all.

In March, Expanding Growth collects $120,000 from its February sales. This is added to the $4,000 cash balance from the end of February, for an available cash balance of $124,000 in March. During March, all 15,000 units in inventory are sold and inventory is replaced and expanded to 20,000 units. Times have never been better, except for one problem. Expanding Growth has only $124,000, but the bill for its March purchases is $160,000 (i.e., 20,000 units @ $8). It is $36,000 short in terms of cash needed to meet current needs. Depending on the attitudes of its supplier and its banker, Expanding Growth may be bankrupt.

$ 4,000 Cash Balance, February 28
+120,000 Collections during March

$124,000 Cash Available
−160,000 Purchase of Inventory (20,000 units @ $8)

$(36,000) Cash Balance, March 31

Two key factors make this kind of scenario common. The first is that growth implies outlay of substantial amounts of cash for the increased inventory levels needed to handle a growing sales volume. The second is that growth is often accompanied by an expansion of plant and equipment, again well in advance of the ultimate receipt of cash from customers.

Do growing companies have to go bankrupt? Obviously not. But they do need to plan their liquidity and solvency along with their growth. The key is to focus on the long-term plans for cash. It is often said that banks prefer to lend to those who don't need the money. Certainly banks don't like to lend to firms like Expanding Growth, who are desperate for the money. A more sensible approach for Expanding Growth than going to a bank in March would be to lay out a long-term plan for how much it expects to grow and what the cash needs are for that amount of growth. The money can then be obtained from the issuing of bonds and additional shares of stock (*see* Chapter 5), or orderly bank financing can be anticipated and approved well in advance.

Apparently, even in a profitable environment cash flow projections are a real concern. Liquidity and solvency are crucial to the firm's viability. Throughout the book, therefore, we will constantly return to this issue as well as that of profitability. In fact, the reader will become aware that a substantial amount of emphasis in financial accounting is placed on providing the user of financial information with indications of the firm's liquidity and solvency.

KEY TERMS

Financial management—management of the finances of the firm in order to maximize the wealth of the organization and its owners.

Accounting—the provision of financial information.

 a. *Financial accounting*—provision of retrospective information regarding the financial position of the firm and the results of its operations.

 b. *Managerial accounting*—provision of prospective information for making improved managerial decisions.

Finance—provision of analyses concerning the acquisition and disposition of the firm's resources.

Goals of Financial Management

 a. *Profitability*—A trade-off always exists between maximization of expected profits and the acceptable level of risk. Undertaking greater risk should only be done if there are greater anticipated returns.

b. *Viability*—A trade-off always exists between viability and profitability. Greater liquidity results in more safety, but lower profits.

QUESTIONS FOR REVIEW

1. What is the difference between accounting and finance?
2. What is the difference between financial accounting and managerial accounting?
3. What are the primary goals of financial management?
4. Explain the relationship between financial risk and financial return.
5. Explain the need for financial managers to balance liquidity and solvency.

Chapter 2

Excel Basics

Throughout this book you will find references to Excel templates that you can use to perform techniques demonstrated in the book on your own. In order to do that, you will need a basic ability to use Excel. If you are already an Excel user, it is suggested that you skip this chapter. However, if you have not used Excel or a similar electronic spreadsheet program (such as the one provided in Google Documents or Open Office), then this chapter is designed to quickly provide you with the basics you need. It will not make you an expert in Excel, but will give you all the rudiments that you need to read spreadsheets prepared by others, to work on the templates provided with this book, and do basic computations on your own.

SPREADSHEETS

A spreadsheet is a document with a grid of columns and rows. Before the widespread use of computers, financial managers used paper that was pre-lined with columns and rows for their computations. Spreadsheets have been used for hundreds of years.

In the late 1970s a Harvard Business School student, Daniel Bricklin, decided that it would be easier to do repetitive computations on a personal computer. Together with Bob Frankston of MIT, he co-invented a software program called VisiCalc. VisiCalc was a major breakthrough in personal computers, pushing them beyond their use as smart typewriters. In the early 1980s Lotus 1-2-3 added charting and database functions to the idea of an electronic spreadsheet. Lotus quickly became the dominant electronic spreadsheet. In the mid-1980s Excel was created. Excel was one of the first spreadsheets to use a mouse and pull down menus making it easier to use. When Microsoft released the Windows operating system in the late 1980s Excel was one of its primary programs, and Excel has held a dominant market position ever since.

WHAT ARE THE REASONS WE USE ELECTRONIC SPREADSHEETS?

Most computers used in business situations will have Microsoft Office software. Microsoft Office is a suite of software programs. The suite includes Microsoft Word, a word processing program, Microsoft Powerpoint, a program for making presentations, Microsoft Access, a program for working with databases, Microsoft Outlook, an e-mail program, and Microsoft Excel, an electronic spread-sheet program.

Electronic spreadsheets such as Excel are computer software programs that are used for computations and creating charts. Much of what is done using Excel could be done manually. However, the computer does computations faster and with fewer errors as compared to those done by hand or by calculator. Probably the main benefit of electronic spreadsheets is the ease with which you can rerun an analysis using a different set of assumptions. One number can be changed, and the results of the analysis can be automatically and quickly updated taking that change into account. This allows managers to do a lot of "what if" analyses, evaluating a projection under a wide range of assumptions.

Unlike a calculator, where you can only see one piece of data at a time, with a spreadsheet program you can look at the computer monitor and see a good section of your work all at once. This is helpful for organizing your approach to solving problems. It also allows you to see both the values and formulas used to derive them, making it much easier to locate and correct errors. Electronic spreadsheets can be saved and reused in the future, allowing you to save a lot of time because you don't have to recreate things from scratch. Often from one year to the next, just a few numbers have to be updated in the saved Excel file.

Once data have been analyzed in a spreadsheet such as Excel, charts or graphs can easily be created, showing the results in a way that may make them easier to comprehend. This chapter will not discuss preparation of charts, but once you have the essentials from this chapter, you will be able to go on and learn how to use charts either using the help function within Excel, or using the free on-line tutorial suggested at the end of this chapter.

Another advantage of electronic spreadsheets is the ability to link and/or share analyses. Once a computer file has been saved, it can be shared with colleagues (e.g., by e-mail or on a thumb drive). This allows them to modify your analysis without having to recreate it. Also, files can be linked, so that an analysis can draw on data in another file without having to reenter all of the information.

Although we generally think about electronic spreadsheets as being computer-based, spreadsheet software programs such as Excel are now available for download onto smart phones and other personal digital assistants (PDAs).

GETTING STARTED WITH EXCEL

In Exhibit 2-1 we see an example of an Excel spreadsheet. When you open the software program, your computer screen will look something like this. Although there are quite a few icons and menu choices on the top of the screen, the most important part for a novice to focus on now is the grid, or the columns and rows.

EXHIBIT 2-1
Excel Spreadsheet

Exhibit 2-2 zooms in on just a portion of the spreadsheet. The spreadsheet is sometimes referred to as a "worksheet." This exhibit only shows columns A through E and rows 1 through 11. Arrows in this exhibit emphasize the rows and columns, which are the critical elements of the worksheet. If you were to scroll to the right, the columns keep going. After Column Z, the next column is AA, AB, etc. And if you were to scroll down there are thousands of rows. The intersection of a column and row is called a "cell" on the spreadsheet. Each cell can be referenced by its cell name, which is its column and row. For example, in Exhibit 2-3, the cell that is highlighted is referred to as Cell A1. So if someone told you to look at Cell A1 on the spreadsheet that they just e-mailed to you, you would open the computer file, and look at the contents of the cell in Column A and Row 1.

EXHIBIT 2-2
Columns and Rows

EXHIBIT 2-3
Cell Names

The most basic operation you can perform in Excel is to enter information. If possible, as you read this chapter have a computer that has the Excel software program nearby. Open the Excel program. Use your mouse to put your pointer over the Cell A1 box, and left click the mouse. When you left click, Cell A1 will be outlined in black (as in Exhibit 2-3) to let you know, just by glancing at the spreadsheet, which cell you are currently working on. Next, hit the number 5 key, on your keyboard, and then hit the Enter key. That's it. You now know how to enter data in Excel. On your spreadsheet, in Cell A1 you should now see the number 5.

Of course, typing numbers is fine, but we are mostly concerned with doing math in Excel. All calculations in Excel start with an equals sign (=). We use the plus sign (+) sign for addition, the minus sign (–) for subtraction, the forward slash (/) for division, and an asterisk (*) for multiplication. The asterisk is used to avoid any confusion between a multiplication sign "×" and the letter "x."

Suppose that we want to add together two numbers. Let's say we want to add 5 and 5 together. We would put our cursor in a cell (move the mouse to the desired cell and then hit the left mouse button) and then type =5+5. Exhibit 2-4 shows what we would see when we type =5+5, before we hit the Enter key. Next, hit the Enter key and you should get the result we see in Exhibit 2-5. That is, as soon as you hit the Enter key, you should see 10 in Cell A1. So the result is 10. However, it is important to be aware that the formula, =5+5 has not gone away. Excel is keeping track of that formula in a "formula bar" just above columns C and D, just to the right of the letters *fx*. The formula bar shows =5+5. This is very important. As we start to develop more complex calculations, the fact that Excel keeps track of the formulas you enter is essential. To the left of the formula bar, we see A1, just above Columns A and B. This identifies the cell where our cursor is currently located. This way, we know that =5+5 which we see in the formula bar, is the formula for the data in Cell A1.

EXHIBIT 2-4
A Basic Computation

	A	B	C	D	E
1	=5+5				
2					
3					
4					
5					
6					
7					

EXHIBIT 2-5
Basic Computation after Hitting the Enter Key

Excel follows some conventions about the order in which computations are done. Suppose that we told Excel to compute =9+5-9/5. That is ambiguous. Do we mean that we want to add 9+5-9 and then divide the result by 5, which comes out to be equal to 1? Or do we mean that we want to add 9 plus 5 minus 9/5, which comes out to be 12.2? The results are very different.

Excel uses a convention that it first does multiplications and divisions and then does addition and subtraction. So Excel would look at =9+5-9/5 and first divide 9/5. If you divide 9 by 5 you get 1.8. Excel will then add 9 plus 5 and subtract 1.8 to arrive at the result of 12.2. If there are a number of multiplications and or divisions in your formula, Excel will start with the equal sign, and move to the right, performing multiplications and divisions as it comes to them.

Although you can rely on Excel to always divide and multiply first, it is always best to use parentheses to group your computations in a clear manner. Thus, you should show this computation as something such as: =(9+5)+(9/5), or as =(9+5+9)/5. By doing this, the computation you want will not only be clear to Excel, but it will also clear to you when you come back and look at your spreadsheet at a later time, or to another user, if you are sending the spreadsheet file to someone else.

ALTERNATIVE WAYS TO DO COMPUTATIONS

Excel provides a number of approaches to doing computations. Suppose that we have the following numbers that we have entered into cells. In Cell A1 we have a 5, in Cell A2 we have a 3, in Cell A3 we have a 7, in Cell A4 we have 11, in Cell A5 we have 4, and in Cell A6 we have 6. If we want to add those values, and show the total in Cell A7, we could move our cursor to Cell A7 and left click our mouse. Then we could type =5+3+7+11+4+6 and hit Enter. The total 36 would appear in Cell A7.

Another way to get that total would be to put the cursor in Cell A7 and left click. That puts the cursor firmly in Cell A7. Then type an equal sign and move the cursor up to Cell A1, left click in Cell A1 and then type a plus sign. The cursor will jump back down to Cell A7. Move the cursor up to Cell A2, left click in Cell A2, and then hit the plus sign. The cursor will jump back down to Cell A7. Repeat the process until you get to Cell A6. When you move the cursor to cell A6 and left click, instead of hitting plus, simply hit Enter. That will tell Excel you have finished adding values for the computation, and the total of 36 will appear in Cell A7.

Yet another way to do this addition would be to type cell references. That is, rather than adding the specific numbers in each cell, or moving the cursor to each cell that we want to include in the computation, we can tell Excel to add the values that appear in each cell by referring to the cell addresses. For example, we could move our cursor to Cell A7 and type =A1+A2+A3+A4+A5+A6 and then hit Enter. Again the total of 36 will appear.

However, what if you have a very long column of numbers to be added. All of the three approaches discussed above will be time consuming. A quicker way to do this would be to use the SUM function. This is one of many arithmetic formulas that are pre-programmed into Excel. To use this formula we can type the equal sign, then SUM, and then an open parenthesis, or =SUM(. Then we type the range of values. In this case since we are adding everything from Cell A1 through Cell A6, we would type =SUM(A1:A6). The colon in the formula indicates a range, and let's Excel know that we want to use all of the values from A1 through A6. Again we will see the total of 36 appear in Cell A7.

Finally, there is one more shortcut that we can use to quickly add a column or row of numbers. To do this we use the Greek letter Sigma (Σ). In mathematics, Sigma is often used to indicate that a summation is taking place. In Excel, simply move your cursor to A7, left click your mouse so that Excel knows you want to work on Cell A7, then click the Sigma icon which appears in the menus at the top of the Excel screen, and then hit Enter. *See* Exhibit 2-6. Note that when you first click on Sigma, it will show the range of numbers that Excel assumes you want to sum. When you click Enter you are accepting that range.

EXHIBIT 2-6
Using Sigma for Addition

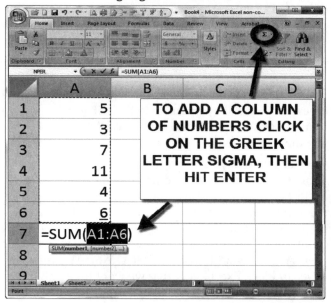

If you have a continuous column of numbers, when you click on the Sigma icon, Excel will assume you want to add that entire column. But if there is a column of numbers with a break in it, for example there are values in cells A1 and A2, but A3 is empty, and then there are values in cells A4, A5 and A6, it is not clear what you want to add. Excel will assume that you just want to add A4 through A6, and when you click on Sigma, Excel will show in Cell A7 the formula =SUM(A4:A6). If in fact you want to add all the numbers in column A, you put your cursor in A7, left click, then click on Sigma from the menu at the top. Then, when Excel shows the incorrect range, you click on Cell A6 and while holding the left mouse button down, drag your mouse up to A1, release the mouse button, and hit Enter. Excel will sum the range of cells that you indicated. After either using the SUM function or the Sigma, the total and the formula will appear as seen in Exhibit 2-7.

EXHIBIT 2-7
Excel Screen after Use of Sigma for Addition

SETTING UP THE SPREADSHEET

One of the most important aspects of Excel is how it handles computations when numbers change. To see how that works, let's first consider a traditional approach to computations on a paper spreadsheet. Exhibit 2-8 provides an example of what a spreadsheet might look like on a piece of paper.

EXHIBIT 2-8
Paper Spreadsheet Approach

Salary - Current Year		$ 38,000
Benefits – Current Year	23%	$ 8,740
Cost per employee - Current Year		$ 46,740
Projected Raise (Next Year)	4%	$ 1,520
Projected Salary (Next Year)		$ 39,520
Projected Benefits (Next Year)	23%	$ 9,090
Projected cost per employee		$ 48,610
Projected number of employees		73
Projected Total Compensation		$3,548,501

For the example in Exhibit 2-8, an organization is working on preparing a budget for labor costs for the coming year. The company is planning on giving its workers a 4% raise, and expects the cost of benefits to remain constant at 23% of salaries. The company expects to have 73 employees in the coming year.

Currently the company pays its workers an average salary of $38,000 a year, and that amount has been written on the first line of the spreadsheet. For the current year the benefits for the workers cost the organization 23%. So if you wanted to find the cost of the benefits per worker, you would take out your calculator and multiply 23% by the $38,000 wage, to find that benefits are costing you $8,740 per worker, and that could be written on the second line. If the $38,000 wage from the first line is added to the $8,740 benefits from the second line (either by hand or with a calculator), we find the total of $46,740, which can be written on the third line, to show the current cost per employee including benefits.

To find the projected raise for next year we would multiply 4% by $38,000. The resulting $1,520 raise has been entered into the worksheet in Exhibit 2-8. When the current salary of $38,000 is added to the projected raise of $1,520, a new salary for next year is determined to be $39,520, and that is put into the worksheet. Multiplying that new salary by 23% we can find that benefits are projected to average $9,090 per employee for the coming year. Adding the projected salary and benefits we get a projected cost per employee of $48,610. If that cost is multiplied by the 73 expected workers, we get a budgeted total compensation amount of $3,548,501. The old fashioned way. With paper and pencil, and maybe the assistance of a calculator. Keep in mind that this is a very simplified example. In real life if you were working on budget computations for salaries for the coming year, there would be far more computations involved.

Now let's move this onto an Excel spreadsheet so that we can see how things differ when we use Excel. In Exhibit 2-9 we see all of the same text labels from Exhibit 2-8 copied over into Column A of an Excel spreadsheet. This looks pretty much the same as the paper spreadsheet. Now let's take the percentages for benefits and put them in Column B, and all the rest of the numerical values and put them into Column C of the Excel Spreadsheet. *See* Exhibit 2-10.

EXHIBIT 2-9

Labels Copied from Paper Spreadsheet to Column A of Excel Spreadsheet

	A	B	C	D	E
1	Salary - Current Year				
2	Benefits - Current Year				
3	Cost per employee - Current Year				
4					
5	Projected Raise (Next Year)				
6					
7	Projected Salary (Next Year)				
8	Projected Benefits (Next Year)				
9	Projected cost per employee				
10					
11	Projected number of employees				
12	Projected Total Compensation				

EXHIBIT 2-10

Numbers Copied from Paper Spreadsheet to Columns B and C of Excel Spreadsheet

	A	B	C	D	E
1	Salary - Current Year		38000		
2	Benefits -	23%	8740		
3	Cost per employee -		46740		
4					
5	Projected	4%	1520		
6					
7	Projected Salary (Ne)		39520		
8	Projected	23%	9090		
9	Projected cost per er		48610		
10					
11	Projected number of		73		
12	Projected Total Com		3548501		

In Exhibit 2-10 there is a problem. Column A wasn't really wide enough for the full description or label on each line. When we dropped the numbers into Columns B and C they covered up some of the words. For example, the 23% in Cell B2 is covering some of the information about Benefits. If cells are empty, Excel lets your text from one column extend into the next. So as long as there wasn't any content in Columns B and C, the text we had typed in Column A was clearly visible. We typed it in Column A and it extended across Columns B and C (*see* Exhibit 2-9). But as soon as we enter any information into Cell B2, that information takes priority, and we no longer see the continuation of the text from Column A.

What solution can we use for this? We can adjust the width of Column A so that it is wide enough to show all of the text. Excel has a number of ways that we can change the column width. One approach is to instruct Excel to make each column wide enough to display all of the data in that column. *See* Exhibit 2-11. For the version of Excel used for these examples, you first click on the Home tab in the upper left part of the screen to make sure you can access the Format menu. Then you click your mouse in one corner of the spreadsheet, such as on Cell A1, and left click the mouse and drag the mouse (with the left button depressed) to cover all columns and rows in your spreadsheet that have data. Release the mouse button and then click on Format from the menu. A drop down menu will appear. From that menu you click on Column Autofit, or Autofit Column depending on the version of Excel you are using. Different versions of Excel will have menu bars at the top that appear somewhat differently, but the same features should exist. After you click on Autofit, the column widths will change. Exhibit 2-12 shows what the spreadsheet will look like now.

EXHIBIT 2-11
Autofit Column Width

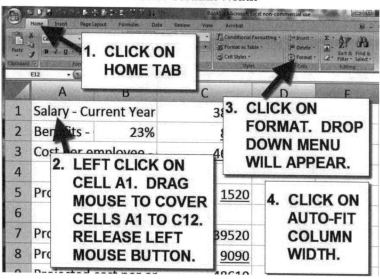

EXHIBIT 2-12
Worksheet Appearance after Autofit Column Width

	A	B	C
1	Salary - Current Year		38000
2	Benefits - Current Year	23%	8740
3	Cost per employee - Current Year		46740
4			
5	Projected Raise (Next Year)	4%	1520
6			
7	Projected Salary (Next Year)		39520
8	Projected Benefits (Next Year)	23%	9090
9	Projected cost per employee		48610
10			
11	Projected number of employees		73
12	Projected Total Compensation		3548501

In Exhibit 2-12 we can see that Column A got wider, displaying all of the text. Column B got narrower. All of the information in the spreadsheet can now be read.

There are a number of other ways to set the column width. You can click on the question mark in the menu bar at the top of the screen to access the help function. Once it opens you could type your question, such as "how do you set the column width" or simply type "set column width" and explanations of how to proceed will be shown. In fact, whenever you get stuck in Excel, the first place to go is the help function. Sometimes it can be a bit frustrating to use Excel's help, and you may have to word your question several different ways until you get the relevant response. But if you are persistent, you can usually accomplish what you want either by carefully reviewing the various menu options shown at the top of the Excel screen or by using the help function.

The next thing we would like to be able to do is to format the numbers in the spreadsheet. The numbers in Exhibit 2-12 have no dollar signs or commas to make them easier to read, and to convey the fact that they relate to currency. We can improve this appearance. For example, let's change the value in column C1 from 38000 to $38,000. See Exhibit 2-13. Start by putting the cursor in the cell to be formatted or drag the mouse to cover a range of cells to be formatted at one time. In this case, move the cursor to Cell C1. Next, right click the mouse and a drop-down menu will appear. From that menu we chose Format Cells. When we click on Format Cells a new window will open giving us choices for how we want to format the cell or cells that we have highlighted. See Exhibit 2-14.

EXHIBIT 2-13
Formatting Numbers

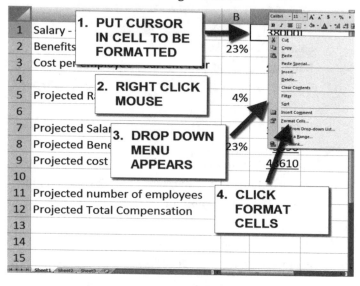

EXHIBIT 2-14
Format Cells Window

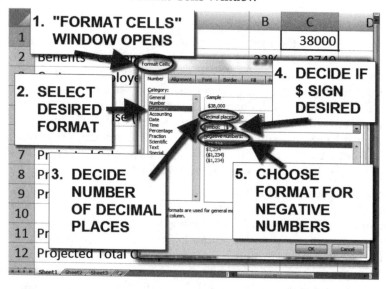

The Format Cells window gives us a variety of choices for the type of format we want the cell to have. Within the Number section of this window we can format numbers as currency, percents, fractions and so on. Once we select the format we want, such as Currency, we are given further choices, such as the number of decimal places, whether or not we want to use a dollar sign, and how negative numbers should appear. They could have a minus sign, or they could be shown within parentheses, or they could be shown in red. After making all of your formatting choices, click on OK and the spreadsheet will appear as shown in Exhibit 2-15. Note that cell C1 has now been formatted with a dollar sign and comma. We could do the same thing for all numbers in Column C by covering them all and then formatting the range of cells.

EXHIBIT 2-15
Cell C1 Formatted

	A	B	C
	C1		*fx* 38000
1	Salary - Current Year		$38,000
2	Benefits - Current Year	23%	8740
3	Cost per employee - Current Year		46740
4			
5	Projected Raise (Next Year)	4%	1520
6			
7	Projected Salary (Next Year)		39520
8	Projected Benefits (Next Year)	23%	9090
9	Projected cost per employee		48610
10			
11	Projected number of employees		73
12	Projected Total Compensation		3548501

Formatting cells can make it easier to input data. Supposed that you wanted to make a list of items, with each cell in one column showing a date, such as 10/28/11. In your mind you think of that as October 28, 2011. But without instructions, Excel may interpret that as being 10 divided by 28 divided by 11. To avoid confusion, we would format the column that will contain the dates, indicating in the Formal Cells window that the contents of this range of cells will be dates. In fact you can format it so that you could enter 10/28/11, but if you would like, have Excel automatically display October 28, 2011 in the cell. Right clicking on a cell and then choosing the Format Cells window can also be used to change the font of a cell to alter the appearance of text. You can choose different fonts, sizes, colors, and so on.

Care should be exercised in formatting. Rather than formatting one cell at a time, we often use the mouse to cover a range of cells, and then format them all at once. But when you do this, be sure that you really want the same format for all of the cells. For example, in Exhibit 2-15, do we want to change all numbers in Column C to currency? No. Row 11 refers to a number of employees rather than to an amount of money.

AUTOMATIC COMPUTATION UPDATES

Now that we know how to set up a spreadsheet, we can easily use Excel to create a document which is every bit as good as a paper spreadsheet. However, electronic spreadsheets such as Excel are a lot better than paper spreadsheets. And their most important advantage comes to light when we have to adjust our computations.

Suppose that a change is needed in the spreadsheet. Perhaps it is the result of a mistake we made. Or perhaps we were working with one assumption, but now we want to see how our results would differ under another assumption. Regardless of the cause, spreadsheet data frequently change. This requires us to re-compute calculations that have already been done. And this is where Excel shines.

Exhibit 2-16 shows the example we have been working with, with the formatting done for all numbers in Column C. Suppose that we now determine that there had been an error in the average salary for the current year. Although we showed it as $38,000 and based all of our computations on that number, in fact the salary for the current year should have been $38,800. If we were using a paper spreadsheet, we would have to go back now and manually re-compute every calculation that we had initially made. We would have to multiply the new $38,800 salary by 23% to find the benefits, and add the corrected benefits to the $38,800 to find the current cost per employee including benefits. Then we would have to compute 4% of this new current salary to find the projected raise. Then add the raise to the $38,800 to find the new salary. Then compute benefits and so on and so on. But Excel has the capability, if you set up your spreadsheet correctly, to automatically do all of the computations when you change $38,000 to $38,800. That is, you would just put your cursor in Cell C1, type 38800 and hit enter, and all the numbers in your spreadsheet would be immediately revised. The result is seen in Exhibit 2-17.

EXHIBIT 2-16
Spreadsheet with Column C Formatted

	A	B	C
1	Salary - Current Yea	**SALARY**	$38,000
2	Benefits - Current Y	**SHOULD BE** 3%	$8,740
3	Cost per employee	**$38,800**	$46,740
4			
5	Projected Raise (Next Year)	4%	$1,520
6			
7	Projected Salary (Next Year)		$39,520
8	Projected Benefits (Next Year)	23%	$9,090
9	Projected cost per employee		$48,610
10			
11	Projected number of employees		73
12	Projected Total Compensation		$3,548,501

EXHIBIT 2-17
New Budget Using Corrected Salary Information

	A	B	C
1	Salary - Current Year	➡	$38,800
2	Benefits - Current Year	23% ➡	$8,924
3	Cost per employee - Current Year	➡	$47,724
4			
5	Projected Raise (Next Year)	4% ➡	$1,552
6			
7	Projected Salary (Next Year)	➡	$40,352
8	Projected Benefits (Next Year)	23% ➡	$9,281
9	Projected cost per employee	➡	$49,633
10			
11	Projected number of employees		73
12	Projected Total Compensation	➡	$3,623,206

Notice in Exhibit 2-17 that as soon as we entered 38800, each of the numbers with an arrow next to it has automatically changed. Compare the numbers in Exhibits 2-16 and 2-17. How can Excel do that? It does it based on the use of formulas. The key is that when we create the spreadsheet in the first place, we don't manually do any of the computations. Rather, we explain to Excel the relationship between the numbers in each cell and let it do the initial computations. That will then provide it with the information needed to do re-computations.

For example, look at Exhibit 2-18. When we enter our information into the spreadsheet we don't enter numbers, we enter relationships. Originally we multiplied $38,000 from Cell C1 by 23% from Cell B2 to find that benefits were $8,740. But in constructing the spreadsheet, we should not show $8,740 in Cell C2. Instead we should enter the relationship. We should tell Excel that the value for Cell C2 should be whatever value appears in Cell B2 multiplied by whatever value appears in Cell C1. We do that by putting our cursor in Cell C2 and typing =B2 * C1 and then hitting Enter. When we do that, in Cell C2 we will see $8,740. However, in the formula bar for Cell C2, Excel will show =B2*C1. Then, when we later change the $38,000 in Cell C1 to $38,800, the value in Cell C2 will immediately change from $8,740 to $8,924. Excel knows that C2 should be whatever is in C1 multiplied by whatever is in B2. Whenever you hit the Enter key, every relationship in the worksheet is reviewed by Excel and updated. So if either C1 or B2 changes, Excel immediately makes all appropriate updates.

EXHIBIT 2-18
Using Cell Relationships and Formulas

	A	B	C
1	Salary - Current Year		$38,800
2	Benefits - Current Year	23%	=B2*C1
3	Cost per employee - Current Year		=C1+C2
4			
5	Projected Raise (Next Year)	4%	=B5+C1
6			
7	Projected Salary (Next Year)		=C1+C5
8	Projected Benefits (Next Year)	23%	=B8*C7
9	Projected cost per employee		=C7+C8
10			
11	Projected number of employees		73
12	Projected Total Compensation		=C9*C11

Similarly, for Cell C3, we wouldn't have initially entered $46,740 (the sum of $38,000 salary and $8,740 benefits). We would have typed =C1+C2 and then hit Enter. And then, if C1 or C2 or both of those values change, Cell C3 automatically is re-computed and updated. This approach is taken for all data we enter into the spreadsheet that is computed. Exhibit 2-18 shows all of the formulas for each of the cells in the spreadsheet. Note, however, that we won't see a spreadsheet with all of the formulas showing. The spreadsheet will appear as Exhibit 2-16 before we start changing any numbers. Then after we change Cell C1 from $38,000 to $38,800 all the numbers update and the numbers in the spreadsheet then appear as seen in Exhibit 2-17. The formulas for each cell just appear in the formula bar when we click on that cell.

This is an example with a very small spreadsheet. But often computations become quite complex. Yet Excel can quickly re-compute and update an entire spreadsheet, whether it is one relationship that needs to be updated or hundreds or thousands of re-computations. This capability gives Excel a tremendous advantage over doing things by hand. Further, if the original set of relationships is entered correctly, the updated results are much more reliable. If you are doing all computations by hand, there is a significant chance arithmetical errors will occur. Especially if there are a lot of computations. If you are using Excel you have to be very careful to identify all of your initial relationships correctly. But then when changes are made, as long as the revised data are input correctly, you don't have to worry about errors being made within the computations.

COPYING CELLS

You can copy and paste, just as you would in a Word document. This can be a big time saver. If you enter the formula in one cell, after you hit enter, you can put your cursor on that cell and click on the copy icon on the menu (the same icon as

Microsoft Word uses for copying). Next, move your cursor to the cell where you want to paste the information and click on the paste icon. You can also click and drag the mouse if you want to copy a range of cells. Or you can copy one cell, and then click and drag to paste the formula from that one cell into a range of cells. Rather than using the icons from the menus at the top, another way to copy is to right click your mouse and select copy. To paste you can right click your mouse and select paste.

One of the great features of Excel is that if you typed =A1 + B1 as the formula for Cell C1, then when you copy C1 and paste it into the range from C2 to C5, it will adjust automatically. That is, the formula that will paste into C2 will be =A2 + B2, and the formula that goes into C3 will be A3 + B3 and so on. Excel assumes that if you were adding across in Row 1, you probably want to do the same thing for Row 2, 3, 4, and 5, and it adjusts the formula for you. This is called copying "relatively." If you copy cell C1 and paste it into K8, the formula for K8 would be = I8 + J8. Excel would not only adjust the row, but the columns as well.

You can also copy and paste "absolutely." Sometimes you won't want Excel to adjust the formula automatically. Suppose you want the formula for cell K8 to be the same as the formula for cell C1. In that case, when you create the formula for C1 you put dollar signs before the row numbers and column letters in the formula. The formula you would type for C1 would be = \$A\$1 + \$B\$1. Now if you copy C1 to K8, the formula pasted into cell K8 will be =\$A\$1 + \$B\$1 and Excel will compute the sum of the contents of Cells A1 + B1. Sometimes you will only want to keep the row constant or the column constant. You can adjust that by choosing where to insert dollar signs in the formula. As you use Excel, you will find that you are frequently using the copy and paste commands to save time.

SUMMARY

In this chapter we have now covered everything that you must know about Excel to work with the templates in this book, and to create and/or use simple Excel spreadsheets. You now know how to enter data, perform computations, set column widths, format cells, and create formulas for computations. This is simply the tip of the iceberg. There is a huge amount of Excel that we haven't covered. But with this foundation, you should be able to go on and learn additional aspects of Excel as you go, either from the Excel help function or from an Excel how-to book, or from on-line tutorials. Those interested in going further should refer to some of the resources listed at the end of this chapter.

KEY TERMS

Spreadsheets—a document with a grid of columns and rows, often used for financial computations.

Electronic spreadsheet— a software program that allows for automatic re-computations when one number in the spreadsheet changes.

QUESTIONS FOR REVIEW

1. What is the main benefit of electronic spreadsheets?

2. How do formulas for computations in Excel begin?

3. What convention does Excel follow when doing computations?

4. What greek letter is the icon for summing a column or row of numbers?

5. Coffin Corporation is preparing a worksheet for labor. Their average starting salary is $45,000. Benefits are 25% this year. They expect them to go up to 27% next year. They are expecting to give a raise of 5% next year. Coffin has 20 employees. Prepare a formatted Excel Spreadsheet for Coffin.

ADDITIONAL RESOURCES

Tutorial: A free Excel tutorial may be found at: *http://baycongroup.com/*.

Reading: Harvey, Greg, *Excel 2010 for Dummies*, For Dummies (Computer/Tech), Apr. 26, 2010.

Frye, Curtis D., *Microsoft Excel 2010 Plain & Simple*, Microsoft Press, June 16, 2010.

Dodge, Mark and Craig Stinson Douglas, *Microsoft Excel 2010 Inside Out*, Microsoft Press, Aug. 26, 2010.

Walkenbach, John, *Excel 2010 Bible*, Wiley, May 10, 2010.

Chapter 3

Accounting Concepts

BASICS

Accounting centers on the business entity. An entity is simply the unit for which we wish to account. Entities frequently exist within a larger entity. An entity can be a department, or a project, or a firm. For example, Joe's Chili Dog Stand is a firm that is an entity. However, if it is not a corporation and Joe owns it solely, the Internal Revenue Service considers it to be part of the larger entity, Joe. That larger entity includes Joe's salary, other investments, and various other sources of income in addition to the chili dog stand.

From an accounting point of view there are two crucial aspects of the entity concept. First, once we have defined the entity we are interested in, we shouldn't commingle the resources and obligations of that entity with those of other entities. If we are interested in Joe's Chili Dog Stand as an accounting entity, we mustn't confuse the cash that belongs to Joe's Chili Dog Stand with the other cash that Joe has.

Second, we should view all financial events from the entity's point of view. For example, consider that the Chili Dog Stand buys chili dog rolls "on account." A transaction on account gives rise to an obligation or account payable on the part of the buyer and an account receivable on the part of the seller. In order for both the buyer and seller to keep their financial records, or "books," straight, each must record the event from their own viewpoint. They must determine whether they have a payable or a receivable.

We assume throughout this book that the firm you work for is the entity. Once we establish the entity we want to account for, we can begin to keep track of its financial events as they happen. There is a restriction, however, on the way in which we keep track of these events. We must use a monetary denominator for recording all financial events that affect the firm. Even if no cash is involved, we describe an event in terms of amounts of currency. In the United States, accounting revolves around dollars; elsewhere the local currency is used.

This restriction is an important one for purposes of communication. The financial accountant not only wants to keep track of what has happened to the firm but also wants to be able to communicate the firm's history to others after it has happened. Conveying information about the financial position of the firm and the results of its operations would be cumbersome at best without this monetary restriction. Imagine trying to list and describe each building, machine, parcel of land, desk, chair, and so on owned by the firm. The financial statement would be hundreds if not thousands of pages long.

Yet, don't be too comfortable with the monetary restriction either, because currencies are not stable vis-a-vis one another, nor are they internally consistent over time. During periods of inflation or deflation, the assignment of a dollar value creates its own problems. For example, the values of inventory, buildings, and equipment constantly change as a result of inflation or deflation. This problem will be discussed in Chapter 21.

ASSETS

The general group of resources owned by the firm represents the firm's assets. An asset is anything with economic value that can somehow help the firm provide its goods and services to its customers, either directly or indirectly. The machine that makes the firm's product is clearly an asset. The desk in the chief executive's office is also an asset, however indirect it may be in generating sales.

Assets may be either tangible or intangible. Tangible assets have physical form and substance and are generally shown on the financial statements. Intangible assets don't have any physical form. They consist of such items as a good credit standing, skilled employees, and patents, copyrights, or trademarks developed by the firm. It is difficult to precisely measure the value of intangible assets. As a result, accountants usually do not allow these assets to be recorded on the financial statements.

An exception to this rule occurs if the intangible asset has a clearly measurable value. For example, if we purchase that intangible from someone outside of the firm, then the price we pay puts a reasonable minimum value on the asset. It may be worth more, but it can't be worth less or we, as rational individuals, wouldn't have paid as much as we did. Therefore the accountant is willing to allow the intangible to be shown on the financial statement for the amount we paid for it.

If you see a financial statement that includes an asset called *goodwill*, it is an indication that a merger has occurred at some time in the past. The firm paid more for the company it acquired than could be justified based on the market value of the specific tangible assets of the acquired firm. The only reason a firm would pay more than the tangible assets themselves are worth is because the firm being acquired has valuable intangible assets. Otherwise the firm would have simply gone out and duplicated all of the specific tangible assets instead of buying the firm.

After the merger, the amount paid in excess of the market value of the specific tangible assets is called goodwill. It includes the good credit standing the firm has with suppliers, the reputation for quality and reliability with its customers, the skilled set of employees already working for the firm, and any other intangible benefits gained by buying an ongoing firm rather than by buying the physical assets and attempting to enter the industry from scratch.

The implication of goodwill is that a firm may be worth substantially more than it is allowed to indicate on its own financial statements. Only if the firm is sold will the value of all of its intangibles be shown on a financial statement.

Thus we should exercise care in evaluating how good financial statements are as an indication of the true value of the firm.

LIABILITIES

Liabilities, from the word *liable*, represent the obligations that a firm has to outside creditors. Although there generally is no one-on-one matching of specific assets with specific liabilities, the assets taken as a whole represent a pool of resources available to pay the firm's liabilities. The most common liabilities are money owed to suppliers, employees, financial institutions, bondholders, and the government (taxes).

OWNERS' EQUITY

Equity represents the value of the firm to its owners. For a firm owned by an individual proprietor we refer to this value as owner's equity. For a partnership we speak of this value as partners' equity. For a corporation we talk of this value as shareholders' or stockholders' equity. A not-for-profit organization refers to this as net assets. Governments call it the fund balance. This book commonly uses the term *stockholders' equity* whenever the equity of the owners is meant.

The stockholders' equity of a firm is often referred to as the "net worth" of the firm or its "total book value." Book value per share is simply the total book value divided by the number of shares of stock outstanding.

The equity of the owners of the firm is quite similar to the equity commonly referred to with respect to home ownership. If you were to buy a house for $400,000 by putting down $80,000 of your own money and borrowing $320,000 from a bank, you would say that your equity in the $400,000 house was $80,000.

If the house were a factory building owned by a firm, the $400,000 purchase price could be viewed as the value of the factory building asset, the $320,000 loan as the firm's liability to an outside creditor, and the $80,000 difference as the stockholders' equity, or the portion of the value of the building belonging to the owners.

THE ACCOUNTING EQUATION

The relationship among the assets, liabilities, and stockholders' equity is shown in the following equation and provides a framework for all of financial accounting.

$$\text{ASSETS} = \text{LIABILITIES} + \text{OWNERS' EQUITY}$$

The left side of this equation represents the firm's resources. The right side of the equation gives the sources of the resources. Another way to think about this equation is that the right side represent the claims on the resources. The liabilities represent the legal claims of the firm's creditors. The owners' equity is the owners' claim on any resources not needed to meet the firm's liabilities.

The right side of the equation is frequently referred to as the equity side of the equation because the liabilities and owners' equity both represent legal claims on the firm's assets. Therefore, both can be thought of in an equity sense. Frequently the entire equation is referred to as the firm's assets and equities.

By definition, this equation is true for any entity. Once the firm's assets and liabilities have been defined, the value of ownership or stockholders' equity is merely a residual value. The owners own all of the value of the assets not needed to pay off obligations to creditors. Therefore, the equation need not ever be imbalanced because there is effectively one term in the equation, *owners' equity*, that changes automatically to keep the equation in balance. We refer back to this basic equation of accounting throughout this book.

KEY TERMS

Entity—the unit for which we wish to account. This unit can be a person, department, project, division, or firm. Avoid commingling the resources of different entities.

Monetary denominator—All resources are assigned values in a currency such as dollars in order to simplify communication of information regarding the firm's resources and obligations.

Assets—the resources owned by the firm.

    a. *Tangible assets*—assets having physical substance or form.

    b. *Intangible assets*—assets having no physical substance or form; result in substantial valuation difficulties.

Liabilities—obligations of the firm to outside creditors.

Owners' equity—the value of the firm to its owners, as determined by the accounting system. This is the residual amount left over when liabilities are subtracted from assets.

Fundamental equation of accounting—Assets = Liabilities + Owners' Equity

QUESTIONS FOR REVIEW

    1. What is an accounting entity?

    2. Define the following:

        a. Asset

        b. Liability

        c. Owners' Equity

    3. What is the equation that provides a framework for financial accounting?

Chapter 4

An Introduction to the Key Financial Statements

This chapter is a brief introduction to the key financial statements that organizations use to convey information about their financial position and the results of their operations. We will discuss the balance sheet (or statement of financial position), the income or operating statement, and the statement of cash flows. These statements are crucial to understanding the finances of a firm.

THE BALANCE SHEET

The statement of financial position, more commonly referred to as the balance sheet, indicates the financial position of an organization at a particular point in time. Basically, it illustrates the basic accounting equation (Assets = Liabilities + Owners' Equity) on a specific date, that date being the end of the accounting period. The accounting period ends at the end of the year. Most firms also have interim accounting periods, often monthly for internal information purposes and quarterly for external reports.

By default, a firm ends its year at the end of the calendar year. Alternatively a firm may pick a financial or "fiscal" year-end different from that of the calendar year. This choice often depends on making things easier and less expensive. One factor in this decision is the firm's inventory cycle. At year-end, most firms that have inventory have to physically count every unit. If you make shipments on a seasonal basis, the low point in the inventory cycle makes a good year-end, because it takes less time and cost to count the inventory than it would at other times during the year.

Another factor in the selection of a fiscal year is how busy your accounting and bookkeeping staff is. At the end of the fiscal year, many things have to be taken care of by both your internal accountants and your external auditor. An audit must take place, with time-consuming questions and information demands by the CPA. Tax returns must be prepared. Reports to the Securities and Exchange Commission are required for publicly held companies.

Thus, if you can find a time when the accounting functions within the firm are at a slow point, it makes for a good fiscal year-end. For example, many universities end their fiscal year on June 30 because this date gives them all of July and August to get things done before the students start returning to campus.

The basic components of a balance sheet are shown in Exhibit 4-1, which uses the hypothetical Coffin Corporation as an example. The first asset subgroup is current assets, and the first liability subgroup is current liabilities. The terms *short-term*, *near-term*, and *current* are used interchangeably by accountants and usually refer to a period of time less than or equal to one year. Current assets generally are cash or will become cash within a year. Current liabilities are obligations that must be paid within a year. These items get prominent attention by being at the top of the balance sheet. Locating the current assets and current liabilities in this way ensures that the reader can quickly get some assessment of the liquidity of the firm.

EXHIBIT 4-1
Coffin Corporation
Balance Sheet
December 31, 2011

ASSETS		LIABILITIES & STOCKHOLDERS' EQUITY	
		Liabilities	
Current Assets	$ 5,000	Current liabilities	$ 3,000
		Long-term liabilities	4,000
Fixed Assets	10,000	Total Liabilities	$ 7,000
		Stockholders' Equity	
Investments	3,000	Contributed Capital	$ 5,000
		Retained Earnings	7,000
Intangibles	1,000	Total Stockholders' Equity	$12,000
TOTAL ASSETS	$19,000	TOTAL LIABILITIES & STOCKHOLDERS' EQUITY	$19,000

The long-term (greater than a year) assets are broken into several groupings. Fixed assets represent the firm's property, plant, and equipment. Fixed assets are sometimes referred to as *capital facilities*. Investments are primarily securities purchased with the intent to hold onto them as a long-term investment. Securities purchased for short-term interest or appreciation are included in the current asset category. Intangibles, although frequently not included on the balance sheet, are shown with the assets when accounting rules allow their presentation on the financial statements.

In addition to current liabilities, the firm also typically has obligations that are due more than a year from the balance sheet date. Such liabilities are termed *long-term* liabilities.

The stockholders' equity consists of *contributed capital* and *retained earnings*. Contributed capital (sometimes referred to as "paid-in capital") represents the amounts that individuals have paid directly to the corporation in exchange for shares of ownership such as common or preferred stock. Retained earnings represent the portion of the income that the firm has earned over the years that has not been distributed to the owners in the form of dividends.

Retained earnings, like all items on the equity side of the balance sheet, represent a claim on a portion of the assets and are not an asset themselves. Retained earnings of $100,000,000 does not imply that somewhere the firm has

$100,000,000 of cash readily available that could be used for a dividend. It is far more likely that, as the firm earned profits over the years, the portion of those profits that was not distributed to the owners was invested in plant and equipment in order to generate larger profits in the future. Retained earnings represents the stockholders' ownership of the plant and equipment rather than a secret stash of cash.

Excel Excercise

Template 1 provides an opportunity to prepare a simple balance sheet for your organization. The template is on the CD that accompanies this book.

THE INCOME STATEMENT

The income statement compares the firm's revenues to its expenses. Revenues are the monies a firm has received or is entitled to receive in exchange for the goods and services it has provided. Expenses are the costs incurred in order to generate revenues. Net income is simply the difference between revenues and expenses. Not-for-profit organizations generally refer to this statement as their Activity Statement, which helps to emphasize the fact that income is not their primary goal. Health care organizations (both for-profit and not-for-profit) generally refer to this as their operating statement. The simplest form of an income statement appears in Exhibit 4-2.

EXHIBIT 4-2
Coffin Corporation
Income Statement
For the Year Ending December 31, 2011

Revenues	$20,000
Less Expenses	12,000
NET INCOME	$ 8,000

Unlike the balance sheet, which is a photograph of the firm's financial position at a point in time, the income statement tells what happened to the firm over a period of time, such as a month or a year.

The income statement is frequently used as a vehicle for the presentation of changes in retained earnings from year to year. Since maximizing the wealth of the stockholders of the firm is a key goal of the firm, it is important to convey to stockholders the changes in the amount of the firm's income that is being retained for use by the firm. As noted earlier, this use may consist of purchasing buildings and equipment to increase the firm's future profits.

A combined statement of income and retained earnings might appear as in Exhibit 4-3. The year's net income is added to the beginning retained earnings. This combined amount is the total accumulated earnings of the firm that have not been distributed to its owners. Dividends declared during the year are then subtracted because they are a distribution to the owners of a portion of the accumulated earnings of the firm. The resulting balance represents the firm's retained earnings as of the end of the year. Alternatively, changes in retained earnings for the year may be presented in a separate statement of retained earnings, such as the one in Exhibit 4-4. Note that in both Exhibits 4-3 and 4-4, the retained earnings as of December 31, 2011, is the same number that appears on the Balance Sheet (Exhibit 4-1) as of December 31, 2011.

Excel Excercise

Templates 2 though 4 provide an opportunity to prepare income, retained earnings, and combined income and retained earnings statements for your organization. The templates are on the CD that accompanies this book.

EXHIBIT 4-3
Coffin Corporation
Statement of Income and Retained Earnings
For the Year Ending December 31, 2011

Revenues	$20,000
Less Expenses	12,000
Net Income	$ 8,000
Retained Earnings, January 1, 2011	4,000
Total	$12,000
Less Dividends Declared	5,000
Retained Earnings, December 31, 2011	$ 7,000

EXHIBIT 4-4
Coffin Corporation
Statement of Retained Earnings
For the Year Ending December 31, 2011

Retained Earnings, January 1, 2011	$ 4,000
Net Income for the Year Ending December 31, 2011	8,000
Total	$12,000
Less Dividends Declared	5,000
Retained Earnings, December 31, 2011	$ 7,000

Real financial statements are more complex than the examples presented in this chapter. We will take a closer look at financial statements in Chapter 22.

THE STATEMENT OF CASH FLOWS

The third major financial statement is the cash flow statement. This statement provides information about the firm's cash inflows and outflows. The current assets section of the balance sheet of the firm shows how much cash the firm has at the end of each accounting period. This can be compared from year to year to see how much the cash balance has changed, but that gives little information about how or why it has changed.

Looking only at the balance sheet can result in erroneous interpretations of financial statement information. For example, a firm experiencing a liquidity crisis (inadequate cash to meet its currently due obligations) may sell off a profitable part of its business. The immediate cash injection from the sale may result in a substantial cash balance at year-end. On the balance sheet this may make the firm appear to be quite liquid and stable. However, selling off the profitable portion of the business may have pushed the firm even closer to bankruptcy. There is a need to explicitly show how the firm obtained that cash.

The statement of cash flows details where cash resources come from and how they are used. It provides more valuable information about liquidity than can be obtained from the balance sheet and income statements. Exhibit 4-5 presents a simplified example of what a statement of cash flows would look like.

EXHIBIT 4-5
Coffin Corporation
Statement of Cash Flows
For the Year Ending December 31, 2011

Cash Flows from Operating Activities	
Collections from Customers	$19,000
Payments to Suppliers	(8,000)
Payments to Employees	(3,000)
Net Cash from Operating Activities	$ 8,000
Cash Flows from Investing Activities	
Purchase of New Equipment	$ (6,000)
Net Cash Used For Investing Activities	$ (6,000)
Cash Flows from Financing Activities	
Borrowing from Creditors	$ 2,000
Issuance of Stock	1,000
Payment of Dividends	(2,000)
Net Cash from Financing Activities	$ 1,000
NET INCREASE/(DECREASE) IN CASH	$ 3,000
CASH, BEGINNING OF YEAR	1,000
CASH, END OF YEAR	$ 4,000

Excel Excercise

Template 5 provides an opportunity to prepare a cash flow statement for your organization. The template is on the CD that accompanies this book.

CASH VERSUS ACCRUAL ACCOUNTING

You might wonder, "If we have an income statement, why would we also need a cash flow statement? Wouldn't they provide the same information?" The answer is that although revenues do generate cash inflows and expenses do require cash outflows, the income and cash flow statements often do not provide exactly the same information. This is primarily a result of the difference between the *cash* and *accrual* bases of accounting.

In some organizations, revenues are only recorded when they are collected in cash and expenses are only recorded when they have been paid in cash. Those organizations are said to be using a *cash basis* of accounting. This has the advantage of being a relatively simple approach to recording revenue and expense, but many would argue that measurement of revenue and expense on a cash basis may give a misleading idea of what happened.

Suppose that you pay labor this year to make a product, and you pay for your supplies this year, and you sell the product this year, but you don't collect any payment from your customer until next year. On a cash basis, you report expenses this year, but all of the revenue is reported next year. It will seem that you had a bad year this year since you have expense but no revenue, and it will seem like you have an outstanding year next when you have revenue but no expense. Accountants argue that this misleads people about how profitable an organization is for any one specific year, even though it all balances out in the long run.

Accountants argue that it is important for organizations to have a *matching* of revenues and expenses each year. A matching means that for a given unit of service provided, the revenues arising from providing that service and the expenses incurred in providing that service are both recorded in the same fiscal period. In that way, the organization will be able to determine if the provision of specific services results in a profit or loss.

To accomplish a matching, the *accrual basis* of accounting is usually used. Under accrual if we sell a product or provide a service this year we will record all the revenues and expenses related to that product or service this year, regardless of when we collect that revenue[1] or actually pay the expenses. Cash accounting is easier, but it does not do a good job of letting managers understand how profitable the organization's operations were for the year. Accrual accounting is more difficult, but it provides a better matching of revenues and expenses.

The accounting profession strongly endorses accrual accounting. Not only does accrual accounting better show the profits from this year's sales, but it also leaves less room for manipulation than a system based on cash. Imagine an operating statement that used cash receipts and disbursements. If one wanted to look especially well off, you could postpone paying your suppliers, thus reducing reported expenses, and increasing profits. This might mislead potential buyers of stock, vendors, or lenders. In contrast, with accrual accounting the speeding up or slowing down collection of revenues or payment of expenses will have no impact on reported profits and are therefore accrual is much less subject to manipulation.

---

[1] Most organizations do not actually collect all of the money that is owed to them for goods or services that they have provided. The amounts that are never collected are referred to as uncollectible accounts or *bad debts*. Under accrual accounting, the operating budget would show the full amount of revenue earned less the portion that it expects it will not be able to collect.

Although accrual accounting provides a better idea of how profitable the organization is expected to be based for a particular period of time, it does not give an accurate idea of how much cash it will have. Whenever organizations use accrual accounting to record revenues and expenses, they also track cash inflows and outflows using a cash flow statement. While it is important to have a clear understanding of how profitable an organization is for a period of time, such as one year, it is equally important to have an understanding of how much cash is coming and going, and the amount of cash an organization has. If you run out of cash, the continuing survival of the organization is immediately threatened. Both the income statement and the cash flow statement are essential financial statements.

KEY TERMS

Fiscal year-end—the firm's year-end should occur at a slow point in the firm's normal activity to reduce disruption caused in determining the firm's results of operations and year-end financial position.

The balance sheet—tells the financial position of the firm at a point in time.

Asset classification—assets are commonly classified on the balance sheet as current, fixed, investments, and intangibles.

Liability classification—liabilities are generally divided into current and long-term categories.

Stockholders' equity is divided into contributed capital and retained earnings.

    a. *Contributed or paid-in capital* is the amount the firm has received in exchange for the issuance of its stock.

    b. *Retained earnings* are the profits earned by the firm over its life-time that have not been distributed to its owners in the form of dividends.

The income statement—a summary of the firm's revenues and expenses for the accounting period (month, quarter, year).

Statement of cash flows—shows the sources and uses of the firm's cash.

Cash accounting—a system for recording financial events that recognizes revenue when cash is collected and expenses when cash is paid.

Accrual accounting—a system for recording financial events that recognizes revenue when goods and services have been provided and eventual receipt of payment is expected, and recognizes expenses when resources are consumed.

QUESTIONS FOR REVIEW

    1. Why is the balance sheet considered a point-in-time statement?

    2. What is a fiscal year?

    3. What does an accountant mean by short-term?

    4. Distinguish between paid-in capital and retained earnings.

    5. What does the income statement demonstrate for the organization?

    6. Why do organizations that use accrual accounting also have cash flow statements?

Chapter 5

Where Does the Organization's Money Come From? Capital Structure

Organizations typically sell goods and services, and get paid for doing so. However, before the first sale is made, they need resources to be able to buy land, buildings, equipment, and supplies. The money needed to acquire these assets is referred to as the organization's *capital*. Where does a business get the capital it needs to operate? Once the business is well established, capital can come at least partly from profits. But reinvestment of profits may not provide enough resources for everything the organization wants to do. And during the early life of any business, other sources of capital are essential.

The dominant sources of capital are from the owners of the organization, referred to as *equity financing*, and loans, referred to as *debt financing*. The choices made with respect to obtaining resources determine the *capital structure* of the firm.

PROPRIETORSHIPS AND PARTNERSHIPS

For organizations that are owned by one individual, referred to as sole proprietorships, or for partnerships, the prime source of capital is money that the owner or owners put into the organization (equity financing) in exchange for their ownership of the business. If debt financing is needed, it is generally obtained from either family and friends, or from a bank.

A partnership has a number of restrictions which make it cumbersome and complicated. It may be difficult for a partner to liquidate their interest in the partnership. Partners generally may not transfer their ownership shares to outsiders. Further, there are legal limits on the number of partners a business can have, and this can make it hard to raise a large amount of equity-financing.

NOT-FOR-PROFIT ORGANIZATIONS

Not-for-profit organizations do not have owners, but still need capital. Initially a substantial portion of that capital comes from charitable donations. Donations are considered to be equity financing because, unlike a loan, they do not need to be repaid. However, not-for-profit organizations often rely heavily on debt-financing because they are unable to generate unlimited amounts of donations. Once the organization is established, reinvestment of profits becomes another primary source of capital to allow the organization to replace facilities as they wear out, adopt new technologies, and expand.

FOR-PROFIT ORGANIZATIONS

There are several advantages to organizing a business as a corporation. Corporations provide their owners with *limited liability*. Limited liability means that if the corporation is unable to pay its bills, creditors may take all of the assets of the corporation, but may not come after the other assets of the owners of the corporation. This contrasts with proprietorships and partnerships. In those organizations, the obligations of the company may be treated as obligations of the owners. If the business fails, the creditors can pursue the owners for payment from their own resources. Because of corporate limited liability, the maximum amount that owners of a corporation stand to lose is the amount they invested in the business. It should be noted that there are some situations where partnerships may be formed in a way that does provide limited liability for the partners.

A second major advantage of corporate form is that owners can readily sell their share of ownership in the company to a third parties with very little impact on the organization. This makes it easier to raise capital. And since there can be an unlimited number of owners of a corporation, there is potential to raise a very large amount of equity capital.

Common Stock

A dominant source of capital in the early life of most corporations is the issuance of *common stock*. Common stockholders own a share of the corporation's assets, have the right to vote to elect the board of directors, are entitled to a proportionate share of distributions (such as dividends), and can freely sell their ownership interest. Common stockholders invest their money, hoping to benefit from dividends and/or increases in the value of the stock.

Once a company is well established, common stock is often issued as a result of mergers (where the acquiring organization pays for the acquired company with shares of the acquiring organization's stock) or to managers as a result of various compensation arrangements. However, common stock is not regularly used to raise capital at that point because of the potential to dilute the share of the company owned by the current owners.

Dividends are paid to shareholders of common stock if the corporation decides to distribute some of its profits directly to its owners. Alternatively, the corporation may retain some or all of its profits for reinvestment in other potentially profitable opportunities. Hopefully this will result in even greater future profits. If so, the value of each share of stock may rise, and the stockholder will be able to sell the stock for a higher price, resulting in a profit referred to as a *capital gain*.

A significant advantage the corporation gains by issuing common stock is that there are no requirements to make payments to the stockholders. If the corporation has a bad year, at least it doesn't have to worry about getting the cash to make required payments to the common stockholders. A second significant advantage gained by issuing common stock is that it creates an equity base. This provides a safety cushion for lenders and makes it possible for the company to incur debt.

Debt

Debt is a second major source of financing for corporations. Debt represents a loan. The borrower must pay interest and repay the amount borrowed. In order for a company to be stable, a substantial portion of the firm's debt will generally be in the form of long-term debt. This avoids the potential problems created if, for example, a building is financed with a one-year loan that it intends to renew each year. What if the lender decides not to renew the loan when it conies due for payment? Long-term debt also eliminates the risk of interest rates being substantially higher when it is time to renew the loan.

Long-term debt is often issued in the form of a bond. A bond is a debt instrument in which investors (bondholders) lend money to the company in exchange for the right to receive periodic (usually semiannual) interest payments of a set amount on set dates, plus repayment of principal at a maturity date. Bondholders can sell their bonds to other investors in the same way that stock may be sold. Failure to meet these obligations puts the organization at peril of bankruptcy. Interest payments on debt are tax-deductible. This tax treatment lessens the effective cost of debt to the organization. Bonds are discussed further in Chapter 14.

Preferred Stock

Preferred stock is a hybrid with characteristics of both stock and debt. It is part of stockholders' equity. However, in most respects it is like a bond. The dividends to preferred stockholders are paid at a predetermined rate, much like the interest rate on a bond. Unlike interest on a bond, the dividends are not tax-deductible to the corporation. Why include preferred stock in a corporation's capital structure if the payments are not deductible? The dividend payments may be deferred. When a corporation falls on hard times, it still must pay the interest due on bonds. It does not have to pay the dividends due on the preferred stock. However, dividends on preferred stock must be paid before any dividends may be paid to common shareholders. Some preferred stock is cumulative and some is not. With cumulative preferred stock, any dividends that have been skipped in prior years must be paid to the preferred shareholders before dividends may be paid to common shareholders.

Cost of Capital

The choice of the relative mix of stock versus debt is an important one. If the business is very profitable, greater amounts of debt result in higher earnings per share of common stock. (This is the result of something called leverage, which will be discussed in Chapter 9.) However, greater amounts of debt substantially increase risk if profits start to decline. If the company cannot meet its required payments of interests and principal on its debt, its viability may be threatened.

Managers should try to strive for a capital structure that keeps the organization's *cost of capital* low. The cost of capital is a weighted average of the cost of common stock, preferred stock, and debt. The cost of debt is the interest. The cost of preferred stock is the required dividend payment. The cost of common stock is the dividend plus the growth in the value of the stock.

A reasonable level of debt tends to reduce the cost of capital. Not only does it provide the opportunity for increased profits for common shareholders, but also the interest payments, as noted above, are tax deductible. This tax benefit substantially reduces the cost of debt relative to equity financing. On the other hand, one must always keep in mind the increase in financial risk caused by having debt. Further, if debt levels rise too high, lenders will be reluctant to provide further financing and the cost of debt will rise.

Other Elements of a Corporation's Capital Structure

In addition to common stock, preferred stock, and debt, there are several other financial instruments that have a place in the capital structure of a corporation. These include stock options, stock rights, warrants, and convertibles.

Stock Options

Stock options give option holders the right, but not the obligation, to purchase shares of stock at some predetermined price over some specified period of time. Such options are often issued to key employees in an organization to motivate them to help the organization achieve or exceed its goals. For example, suppose that the corporation's common stock is currently selling for $50 a share. The owners of the stock would certainly like that value to increase. Employees may be given options to buy shares of stock at $60 per share. The options might expire in three years.

These options give the employees a personal interest in seeing the price of the stock go up. If the stock price fails to exceed $60, the employees will just let the options expire. However, if the stock price rises to $70, they can then pay just $60 to buy a share of stock that is worth $70.

Stock Rights

At times a corporation will want to raise money through a common stock offering to the public, but avoid the high costs of hiring an underwriting firm to sell the stock. They can achieve this through a rights offering. A stock right gives the holder the right to buy a share of stock at a stated price. Usually the stated price is somewhat less than the current market price.

Stock rights are usually offered in proportion to a stockholder's current holdings. For example, suppose you owned 1,000 shares of stock in XYZ Corporation, which has 10,000 shares outstanding in total. That means you currently own 10 percent of the corporation. The corporation now plans to use stock rights to issue another 2,000 shares to raise additional capital. You would be entitled to 200 rights, or 10 percent of the total offering. If the corporation's stock is currently selling for $50 a share, and the rights allow you to buy stock at $47 a share, you would either exercise the rights, buying the 200 shares, or you could sell your rights to someone else.

Warrants and Convertibles

Warrants are similar to stock rights, but they generally have an exercise price above the level of the current market. Warrants are often given as an inducement to investors to get them to do something the organization wants. For example, a corporation may have trouble raising debt. As an inducement to lend money to the corporation, warrants may be given to the lender.

Suppose that the corporation's stock currently sells for $5 a share. Warrants may be issued to a lender allowing it to buy a certain number of shares anytime in the next five years for $10 a share. Lenders do not generally share in the extreme successes of the companies they lend to. They just get earned interest and repayment of the loan. However, if this corporation's stock shoots up to $50 a share, the lender could use the warrants to buy shares for $10 and join in the success they helped cause by financing the company.

Similarly, convertible debt or convertible preferred stock is debt or preferred stock that can literally be converted into shares of common stock. This convertible feature generally allows the corporation to borrow at a lower interest rate or issue preferred stock with a lower dividend rate. The lenders or purchasers of the preferred stock will take a lower interest or dividend rate because they have the potential for large profits if the common stock rises in value.

Dividends

Some companies hold themselves out as growth companies. Growth companies generally retain all or most of their profits to use for additional, hopefully highly profitable ventures. Other companies have a policy of paying dividends to their investors on a regular basis.

Some investors prefer growth companies. By holding stock without receiving dividends, they don't have to pay tax on the dividends. Later they will sell the stock, hopefully at a higher price, and pay tax at a lower, capital gains rate. And in the meantime, the company has invested the entire amount of retained earnings in ventures that are potentially more lucrative than might be available to the investor. If the investor had received dividends, some of them would have been paid in tax, leaving less for reinvestment.

Other investors, however, need dividends to pay for current living expenses. Although they could sell off some shares of stock from time to time to raise money for such expenses, they prefer to receive a steady, dependable flow of income. As a result, managers must decide on the dividend policy they wish to adopt. The choice will affect the potential buyers of the firm's stock.

At times, a corporation will issue a stock dividend. For example, there might be a 10 percent dividend, giving the investor one share for every ten shares currently owned. Or there might be a stock split such as a two-for-one split, in which case the investor gets two new shares in exchange for each old share owned. Such dividends and splits are not substantive. If you own 1,000 out of 10,000 shares, you own 10 percent of the company. After a two-for-one split, you own 2,000 out of 20,000 shares. You still own exactly 10 percent of the company.

Stock dividends and splits are generally done for psychological purposes. First, they make you feel like you have more, even if you don't. Second, they may bring the stock price down to a more reasonable trading range. For example, if a growth company keeps growing, its shares will get more and more expensive.

Some individuals might be tempted to buy a stock, but might decide that its price is so high that they could only afford to buy a few shares. Instead, they buy a less expensive stock so that they own more shares.

This is illogical. They should purchase the stock of the company with the greatest percentage appreciation potential. Fifty shares of a $100 stock are more valuable than 100 shares of a $50 stock, if the $100 stock has the potential to increase by a greater percentage because of the underlying profit potential of the firm. The key should not be the number of shares, but the likely percent increase in the $5,000 investment.

Nevertheless, some companies believe that if their stock is selling for $120 per share, a three-for-one split will be beneficial. It will bring the price per share down to $40 a share. That is a value that seems substantial, but not prohibitively expensive. These companies believe that this may attract more investors, causing the stock to rise by a greater percentage than it would have without the split.

Reverse splits are also possible. If a stock is selling for a very low price, investors might be skeptical of the viability of the company. A reverse split will bring the price back up to a respectable level. For example, a stock selling at $2 a share might have a one-for-ten split that would reduce the number of shares outstanding by 90 percent, but raise the price per share to $20. This latter price might be more likely to attract investor interest.

Some stock exchanges also have minimum dollar prices for the stocks on their exchange. Without a reverse split, a stock might be delisted, substantially reducing the ability of owners of the stock to find a liquid market when they wish to sell their stock.

GETTING CAPITAL

Understanding your desired capital structure is one thing. Getting the money is another. The capital to run a business is obtained by a variety of means. These include venture capital, public stock offerings, private stock placements, debt offerings, and leasing. Each of these is discussed briefly below.

Venture Capital

Start-up businesses must prove that they have a potentially viable business before the general public will be willing to invest in them. However, some investors, called *venture capitalists*, will put up money called *venture capital* or *risk capital* to help a new business get started.

If you can convince these investors that they can make a lot of money by financing your start, they can get money into your firm quickly, without the lengthy and costly process of an initial public offering (IPO) of stock. In return, they generally expect that an IPO will take place within approximately five years.

Businesses often begin with seed capital needed to do market research and product development. Seed money is often provided by the entrepreneurs starting the business themselves, or their friends and families. Businesses may typically raise up to $5 million this way with minimal government registration requirements. After this point, venture capitalists are called upon to provide the *working capital* needed to acquire supplies and hire workers to start producing the product, and in some cases the *acquisition capital* to acquire plant and equipment or a going business.

Venture capitalists rely heavily on the firm's business plan (*see* Chapter 7) in determining whether to invest in the business. Therefore the business plan may be a critical element in determining if the venture ever gets the initial capital it needs to get off the ground.

Be aware that many liken venture capitalists to the devil. The business may be something that you have conceived of and developed. It is your baby. However, not only will the venture capitalists take a substantial financial share of your business in exchange for their investment, but they will take a major share of the control of the business as well.

Public Stock Offerings

A public stock offering is one in which shares of a corporation are sold to a broad range of investors to secure capital for the organization. Issuing stock to the public is costly, time-consuming, and complicated. At times, general economic conditions or stock market conditions will have a bigger impact on the success or failure of your offering than the underlying worth of your company will have. On the other hand, to raise significant amounts of capital without incurring an unreasonable level of debt, a public stock offering may be required.

The first time a public stock offering takes place for a company, it is referred to as an Initial Public Offering (IPO). Subsequent offerings of stock to raise additional capital are referred to as *secondary issues*. Whether you are considering an IPO or a secondary offering, stock offerings to the public are expensive. The costs include payments to lawyers, accountants, printers, and *underwriters*.

Underwriters are firms that act as general contractors. They coordinate with all of the accountants, lawyers, and brokerage firms that will initially sell the stock to investors. They help prepare all of the documents that are legally required before stock can be sold, including a prospectus and registration statement. Underwriters have access to potential buyers of your stock through their networks of stock brokers.

Once you have "gone public" your organization has an equity base that makes it easier to borrow, provides you with broader public recognition, and results in increased personal net worth for the original owners of the business. On the other hand, there are ongoing reporting expenses, loss of control, and potential liability of officers for failure to comply with a complicated set of rules and regulations.

Private Placements

Given some of the complexities of public offerings, sometimes businesses issue stock through a private placement. The money received from venture capitalists is one type of private placement. Even when the amounts of capital to be raised are substantially higher—perhaps hundreds of millions of dollars or even several billion dollars—a private placement is sometimes possible. Selling stock directly to a few large investors avoids much of the cost of a public offering, and avoids the need to file certain elaborate documents with the government. Large insurance companies often participate in such placements, putting perhaps $50 million or $100 million into a company in exchange for stock.

Private placements can also raise funds much more quickly than a public offering can. However, in most cases the amount of money that can be raised from a private placement may be substantially less than the business might raise from a public offering. It should also be noted that, because of the risks involved to the investor, government regulations tend to prohibit all but sophisticated investors from participating in such placements.

Bond Offerings

Bonds can be issued through private placements or public offerings in the same way as stocks are. As with stocks, private placements are simpler and less expensive, but don't have the ability to raise as much money as a public offering.

Bonds are a particularly good alternative to bank financing because they can be for large amounts of money, they can extend for long periods of time (typically thirty years), providing stability, and they eliminate the bank intermediary. For example, a bank might pay 4 percent to a depositor and then lend the depositor's money to a corporation for 9 percent. The 5 percent difference represents the bank's costs and profits. If the corporation issues a bond at an interest rate of 6.5 percent, it will pay 2.5 percent less than the bank charges, and the ultimate investors will receive 2.5 percent more than they would have received from the bank. The investors have more risk than they would if they deposited their money in the bank. The corporation has greater costs and legal compliance issues than it would if it borrowed the money from a bank. For a large loan, it is worth paying these higher costs to get a lower interest rate. Bonds are discussed further in Chapter 14.

Leasing

Another source of financing is leasing. Someone buys an asset, such as a building, and rents it to a business that wants to use that asset. The business using the asset is a lessee and the owner of the asset is a lessor. Leasing is very similar to having borrowed money and purchased the asset directly. Therefore leases are generally considered to be a form of debt financing. Management and tax issues related to leasing are discussed in Chapter 14.

KEY TERMS

Capital—the money needed by the firm in order to acquire resources.

Capital structure—the mix of debt and equity used to finance the firm.

Equity financing—capital provided in exchange for an ownership interest, typically through the issuance of stock.

Debt financing—capital provided in the form of loans.

Stock option—security that gives the holder the right to purchase shares of stock at some predetermined price, usually above market value.

Stock right—security that gives the holder the right to buy a share of stock at a stated price, usually below market value.

Sources of capital—venture capital, public stock offerings, private stock placements, debt offerings, and leasing.

QUESTIONS FOR REVIEW

1. What are the two major sources of capital for an organization, aside from reinvestment of profits?

2. Where do sole proprietorships generally get debt funds from?

3. What is the major capital source for not-for-profit organizations, early in their existence?

4. What are two main advantages that the corporate form has over partnerships?

5. What are several advantages of common stock?

6. What is a bond?

7. What are the key characteristics of preferred stock?

8. What is the cost of capital?

9. Why would an organization issue stock options, stock rights, or warrants?

10. Do stock splits provide a direct benefit to stockholders?

11. Many companies need to get funding from venture capitalists to get their business going. What are the major negatives of using venture capitalists to finance a business?

12. What is an IPO?

Chapter 6

Strategic Planning and Budgeting

DEFINITION AND ROLE OF BUDGETS

A *budget* is simply a plan. Despite any unpleasant connotations the term may have picked up over time, a budget is simply a plan. In business budgets are formalized (i.e. written down) and quantitative (expressed in dollars and/or units).

For an organization to excel, its management needs vision. Great managers are those individuals under whose stewardship organizations make great strides forward. In some cases, vision may come from inspiration that only a few people ever have. In many cases, however, vision is a result of hard work and careful planning. What is the organization trying to achieve? Why does it want to achieve that goal? How does it intend to translate that goal into results? Successful managers and organizations specifically address these questions, rather than simply letting things happen. This is accomplished through a process of strategic planning and the development of budgets.

STRATEGIC PLAN

A *strategic plan* is a document that sets the direction the organization will take to achieve its underlying *mission*. The mission of the organization represents its primary reason for being in business. It explains in broad terms the purpose and goals of the organization. The strategic plan selects the primary approaches that the organization will take to achieve those goals. Generally, strategic plans do not have specific financial targets. However, they set the stage for specific, detailed budgets that will be established to achieve the goals.

For example, suppose that the mission of a soup kitchen was to ensure an adequate supply of nutritious food for the homeless. It could attempt to achieve that mission by any of a number of different approaches. It could be a lobbying organization, raising money and using it to lobby for legislation requiring the government to provide nutritious food for the homeless. That would be one strategy. Another strategy would be to solicit donations of food and money, and to use those resources to prepare and serve meals directly to the homeless. Suppose that the soup kitchen chose the latter strategy.

In addition to a strategy, the strategic plan should have goals. For example, given its strategy to directly provide meals, the soup kitchen might adopt the following two goals (among others):

- Increase the percentage of the target population served from 20 percent to 60 percent within five years.

- Expand funding sources to cover the cost of the increase in services.

Once you have a strategic plan that identifies your strategies and goals, the next step is to translate the goals of the strategic plan into attainable objectives.

LONG-RANGE PLAN

While the strategic plan establishes goals and broad strategies, the *long-range plan* considers how to achieve those goals. Long-range plans establish the major activities that will have to be carried out in the coming three to five years. This process provides a link between the strategic plan and the day-to-day activities of the organization.

For example, one element of the strategic plan for the soup kitchen is expansion of meals provided from 20 percent to 60 percent of the target population. This cannot be achieved by simply carrying out the existing daily routine, day after day, year after year. The managers will have to determine what must happen to attain the goals. A variety of approaches or tactics might be considered and developed into a long-range plan.

The managers decide that the most efficient way to expand from 20 percent to 60 percent coverage (the goal) would be to add three new locations and four more vehicles (specific tactics to achieve the goal). Money will be needed to buy equipment and vehicles, and to pay rent, buy food, and hire staff. The long-range plan will also have to consider how to raise the money and when to spend it (more tactics). A reasonable long-range plan for the soup kitchen might include the following objectives:

Year 1: Establish fund-raising campaign, and begin fund-raising. Raise enough money to open one new site.

Year 2: Add a food distribution/soup kitchen location. Raise additional money to acquire and operate a vehicle and open another location. Solicit more restaurants for leftover food donations.

Year 3: Add another food distribution/soup kitchen location and a new vehicle. Raise additional money to acquire and operate a vehicle and open another location. Solicit more restaurants for leftover food donations.

Year 4: Add another food distribution/soup kitchen location and a new vehicle. Raise additional money to acquire and operate two vehicles. Solicit more restaurants for leftover food donations.

Year 5: Add two new vehicles. Raise additional money to begin replacement of old kitchen equipment and old vehicles. Get enough contributions to at least reach a steady state where replacements take place as needed.

As can be seen from the above objectives, unless planning is done in year one to raise money, the organization will never be able to undertake the acquisition and expansion in years two through five. The organization cannot be satisfied with raising enough to get through the coming year. For it to thrive, rather than merely survive, it must think ahead. The long-range plan provides the opportunity to think ahead prior to making budgets for the coming year.

The objectives included in the long-range plan can be thought of as quantified targets. These targets can relate to both inputs and outputs. For example, we can think in terms of specific fund-raising objectives, specifying the total dollar amount of donations we plan to receive each year over the coming five years. We can also think in terms of the specific number of delivery vans to be purchased. These targets or objectives make it possible to create specific detailed budgets for the organization in financial terms.

ANNUAL BUDGETS

Each year the organization will prepare an operating budget, cash budget, and capital budget. These annual budgets are prepared to take the long range vision of the strategic and long-range plans and fill in the specific details of what has to happen over the coming year to keep the organization on track to accomplish its long term goals. Annual budgets provide specific itemization of resources to be used and resources to be generated over the coming year.

Budgets provide a number of benefits to organizations. They force managers to think ahead. When plans are made well in advance more choices are generally available than when decisions are made on a fire-fighting or crisis basis. Advance planning provides the necessary lead-time for effective decisions. Once decisions are made, they must be acted upon by the organization. Budgets provide the information needed for those decisions to be properly implemented. They also provide a tool to allow for effective evaluation of both departments and managers.

Another key use for a budget is as a tool of communication and coordination. Even if the Chief Executive Officer has great plans for the organization, they can only be put into operation if they are communicated to the appropriate individuals. The budget serves this purpose.

The operating budget provides all of the information necessary to prepare a budgeted income statement. It includes revenue projections, cost-of-goods-sold projections, including the projected costs of materials, labor, and overhead for a manufacturing firm, or cost of purchases for a merchandising firm; selling expenses; administrative expenses; and finally financing (interest cost) expenses. These separate elements are combined into a projected income statement. Exhibit 6-1 provides an example of an operating budget.

Excel Exercise

Template 6 may be used to prepare an operating budget for your organization. The template is included on the CD that accompanies this book.

EXHIBIT 6-1
Executive Corporation
Operating Budget
Projected Revenues and Expenditures

Revenues	
Product Sales	$14,000,000
Other	500,000
Total Revenues	$14,500,000
Expenses	
Cost of Goods Sold	
Labor	$ 5,000,000
Materials	4,800,000
Overhead	1,700,000
Selling Expenses	1,500,000
Administration	500,000
Interest	600,000
Total Expenses	$14,100,000
Profit	$ 400,000

The cash budget projects the cash inflows and cash outflows of the organization over the coming year. This budget is often broken down into monthly, or even more frequent, time periods so that the organization can assure that it will have sufficient cash balances at all time throughout the year. For example, even if cash collections from customers exceed routine day in and day out operating expenses, if we are constructing a new building, the cash outlays to pay for that construction must be taken into account in the cash budget to assure that we always have sufficient funds. Cash budgets are discussed in more detail later in this chapter.

In addition to the annual operating and cash budgets, there will be a capital budget for acquisition of capital assets. A capital acquisition is anything the organization buys that it expects will last for more than one year. Capital acquisitions often require special methods of analysis to evaluate whether they make financial sense for the organization. Capital budgeting and evaluation of proposed capital acquisitions is discussed in Chapter 11.

BUDGET PREPARATION

Preliminaries

The first step in budget preparation is the completion of an environmental statement. The firm cannot effectively plan for the coming year without a clearly stated idea of what its position is vis-a-vis its suppliers, competitors, and customers. An annual evaluation of industry trends, changes in customer base, technological changes, and so on can help the firm to better determine where it should be going.

The next step is for top management to develop a set of general objectives and policies. This statement should be a broad-based look at what the firm hopes to achieve. Is the coming year one of holding the line against competitors, or is it to be a year of rapid growth? Is the firm looking for domestic expansion, or establishment of foreign markets? Does the firm expect to increase the market share in existing products, or to be aggressive in the introduction of new products? If top management communicates the desired direction of the firm, middle management can set out to move in that direction.

Before the actual budget can be developed, a set of assumptions must be adopted. What will inflation be in the coming year? What actions do we expect competition to take that might affect our sales or the price of our product? Will suppliers be raising their prices? Will new sources of raw materials become available? Are there going to be more significant shifts in consumer demand? All of these and many more questions must be answered; but there is no way to know the answer, so assumptions must be made and communicated to those directly involved in the budget preparation process.

Finally, specific, measurable goals should be established. Here we are not dealing simply with the general direction of the firm, but with the actual operating objectives. For example, sales should increase by 10 percent and profits by 15 percent. These are two ambitious objectives—more often than not, a firm that doesn't budget, or that doesn't control the budget, will not have much success in achieving such goals.

Forecasting

A critical step in the budget process is the preparation of forecasts of what would happen under a variety of alternatives. What if we raise our price? What if we import partially assembled parts? What if we automate? In all of these cases, how much will we sell, at what price, and at what cost?

Forecasts can be quite simple, such as a projection that indicates that what happened this year will happen again next year. Or they can be based on extremely complex mathematical formulas. Most forecasting is based, to a major extent, on historical patterns. An accurate forecast must also consider any changes that may make the future different from the past. These changes can be due to various decisions we've made, improved technology, initiatives by competitors, changes in laws, world events, etc.

Computers make sophisticated forecasting techniques accessible to managers. Some software programs allow the user to select from a range of statistical forecasting methods, or to simply have the computer automatically select the best forecasting method for your data.

Some software programs can take seasonal patterns into account. If a firm has times of the year that are generally very busy or unusually slow for production, sales, or both, a forecast for the year as a whole is not fully satisfactory. A manager gains a significant advantage by knowing which months are likely to be unusually busy or slow, and how busy or slow. Such information may be used to minimize the cost of staffing and inventory throughout the year, while still allowing for adequate staff and inventory during peak periods of demand.

Data Needs for Forecasting

The forecasting process should begin with some basic assumptions about the likely future of the industry. Too often managers are myopic, looking within their own firms and missing industrywide cycles or trends. If the future sales outlook for the industry is turning negative, managers cannot ignore that information just because their own sales have historically been strong.

Working from a base of the outlook for the industry, managers can then turn their attention to a forecast of the company's sales. Sales in the future are often largely a reflection of sales in the past. Information on how many units of each product or service have been sold in the last five to ten years provides a basis for the forecast of the future. Techniques to use this historical data for the forecast are discussed below. Once the historical data for sales is used to predict future sales, that information can be used to forecast the necessary materials, labor, and other expenses.

What to Do When Historical Data Are Not Available

At times historical data may not be available. This is generally the case when a new service or program is suggested. How can forecasts be made in the absence of such data? To some extent, one can rely on engineering calculations. A determination can be made of exactly what resources should be required for each unit of the service provided. Another useful approach is to base such forecasts on the collective opinion of groups of individuals. Industrial experience has shown that when a team of experts arrives at a consensus, subjective forecasts can be reasonably accurate. There are two techniques for achieving consensus: Nominal Group and Delphi. Both approaches select a team of individuals who are likely to have reasoned insights with respect to the item being forecast.

The Nominal Group technique brings individuals together in a structured meeting. Each member writes down a forecast. The forecasts are then presented to the entire group without discussion. Once all of the forecasts have been revealed, the reasoning behind each one is discussed. Through a repetitive process, a group decision is eventually made.

There are weaknesses to this approach. In some cases it may be impossible to get the group to reach consensus. A more common problem concerns politics and personalities. As members of the group defend their forecasts, extraneous issues having to do with whose idea it is may bias the group decision. Some individuals may be reluctant to share their ideas in public for a variety of reasons.

The Delphi technique overcomes those weaknesses. In the Delphi approach, the group never meets. All forecasts are presented in writing to a group leader who provides summaries to all group members. After several rounds, a decision is made based on the collective responses. The weakness of the Delphi method is that it takes more time and is more cumbersome than the Nominal Group method. But, by avoiding a face-to-face meeting, the Delphi technique avoids confrontation. Decisions are based more on logic than on politics or personality.

Forecasts Based on Historical Data

In cases for which historical data do exist, forecasting is somewhat easier. Knowledge about the past is often an excellent starting point for predicting the future.

The simplest approach to forecasting using a series of historical data points is simply to take an average. The data for five years can be aggregated and divided by five to get an estimate for the coming year. Such an averaging approach, however, assumes that there is no underlying pattern and that results are essentially random.

A somewhat superior approach is the linear regression statistical technique. This method plots historical points and uses the information to develop a trend line. That trend is projected into the future to make a forecast. This is generally more accurate than a simple average. The limitation of regression is that it is based on a straight line. Straight lines do a poor job of forecasting seasonal patterns.

However, a number of forecasting software programs, such as SmartForecasts,[1] can produce curved-line forecasts. Such forecasts can more closely match a seasonal historical pattern. This results in a much more accurate forecast. These programs may be used to forecast overall sales or expenses, sales of a given product, expenses of a given type, and virtually anything else for which the organization has historical data.

Consider Table 6-1. This table, for simplicity, provides quarterly data. Managers can further improve the usefulness of their forecasts by using monthly data. Figure 6-1 provides a time-series forecast graph from the SmartForecasts program. Time is shown on the horizontal axis, beginning with the first quarter of 2009 and ending with the last quarter of 2012. Data from the first three years are used to forecast the fourth year. Sales in units are shown on the vertical axis.

---

[1] *SmartForecasts*. Belmont, MA: SmartSoftware, Inc. (800) 762-7899. Version 8.3 was used for the example in this chapter.

TABLE 6-1
Historical Data

QUARTER	SALES VOLUME
2009	
January—March	20,000
April—June	23,000
July—September	27,000
October—December	20,000
2010	
January—March	21,000
April—June	25,000
July—September	29,000
October—December	20,000
2011	
January—March	19,000
April—June	24,000
July—September	26,000
October—December	21,000

FIGURE 6-1
Forecast for Table 6-1 Data,
Using Curvilinear Forecasting

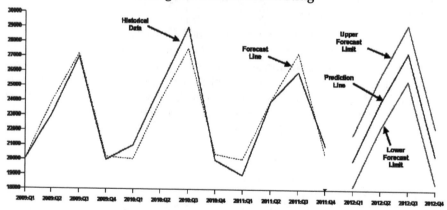

The solid line from 2009:Q1 to 2011:Q4 in the graph in Figure 6-1 represents the actual historical data points connected from quarter to quarter. The dashed line is the forecast line. For the future year being forecast, the prediction line is bracketed above and below by lines that represent a *forecast interval*. It is expected that 90 percent of the time, the actual results for the coming year will remain within that range. The forecast interval can be set at a different level if desired. For example, the range could be set at 99 percent, so that the actual result would fall outside of the predicted range in only one out of 100 predictions.

Table 6-2, generated by the computer program, provides the forecast for each of the next four quarters, along with lower and upper limits. This is extremely valuable managerial data. Not only do we have a forecast, but we also have detailed information that can be used for planning. For example, the third quarter will likely have a high rate of activity, but substantial reductions are likely in the fourth quarter. Based on the upper limit column in Table 6-2, we know that we need to plan on only enough labor and materials to make 22,248 units in the fourth quarter, at most.

TABLE 6-2
Forecast and Forecast Interval Limits for Figure 6-1

| | APPROXIMATE 90 PERCENT FORECAST INTERVAL | | |
TIME PERIOD	LOWER LIMIT	FORECAST	UPPER LIMIT
FY4:Q1	18,232	19,998	21,764
FY4:Q2	22,244	24,010	25,776
FY4:Q3	25,436	27,330	29,224
FY4:Q4	18,437	20,343	22,248

Given that software programs such as this one are extremely easy to use, one cannot help but be impressed by the potential for improvements in a wide variety of forecasts throughout the organization. Nevertheless, managers should always bear in mind that forecasts are merely educated guesses about the future. As a manager you know more about your business than any formula or mathematical technique. Managers should rely on their judgment to modify forecasts to take into account factors the computer software may not have considered. Once forecasts have been made, the budgets can be prepared.

Departmental Budgets

Having completed the preliminary budget activities, and having prepared forecasts for the key elements of the budget, the next step is the actual preparation of the budget. The organizational budget consists of a compilation of the operating and capital budgets for the various departments. Based on the total requirements for each department, cash flow projections can also be made.

Each department must compile its budget based on the specific costs that it expects to encounter and, if it is a revenue center, the revenues that it projects as well. Budgets should be as detailed as possible, to ensure that all relevant items have been included. The budgeting task sometimes seems very complicated because of the specific forms that any given organization requires to be completed. However, the essential process is not complicated. Each organization strives to get an itemization of the various costs that it will encounter for the coming year, and the associated revenues.

Once these itemizations are completed, there is a process of evaluation. Are the requests reasonable? Do the departments need all of the resources they are requesting, or are they building fat into the budget? If the budget is carried out as specified, will it result in a satisfactory outcome for the organization? Will the sales be high enough? Will costs be low enough?

Even if a department's budget is reasonable, there may still be limitations on what the organization can, or will, approve. It is possible that a series of capital expenditures, even if profitable in the long term, will require more cash than the organization believes will be available. Thus, there is an interplay between the operating and capital budgets prepared by departments, and the resulting projections of cash flows prepared by the financial office. All of the elements of the budget must come together to result in a satisfactory outcome for the organization before the individual components can be approved.

FLEXIBLE BUDGETING

Preparing a budget requires many assumptions and predictions. One of the most prominent of these involves the *workload* level. *Workload* refers to the volume of goods or services that the organization will produce. If the volume of services, cost of services, and revenues related to services all rose and fell in equal proportions, this might not create a significant problem. However, that is generally not the case. Revenues may change in a sharply different proportion than costs. Managers need to be able to anticipate such variations. A *flexible budget* is a tool to aid managers in this area.

A flexible budget is an operating budget for varying workload levels. For example, suppose that Finkler Corporation expects to sell 40,000 units of its product. Its budget for the coming month appears in Table 6-3. A surplus of $1,000 is projected. But what will happen if the number of units sold were to turn out to be 25% more or less than we had budgeted? Will profit rise to $1,250 or fall to $750?

TABLE 6-3
Operating Budget
for Next Month

Revenues	
Sales of Goods	$165,000
Total Revenue	$165,000
Expenses	
Salaries	$136,000
Supplies	10,000
Rent	12,000
Other	6,000
Total Expense	$164,000
Surplus	$ 1,000

If the number of units of its product that are sold increases or decreases, revenue will change proportionately. However, some of the expenses are *fixed costs*; that is, they will not change as the volume of work changes. For example, if the volume of units sold goes up or down, rent will remain the same. For most organizations, however, at least some costs are *variable*; they vary as the volume of sales goes up or down. Finkler will have to buy more supplies if it gets busier.

A flexible budget takes the basic operating budget and adjusts it for the impact of possible workload changes. Assume revenue changes as units sold change, and supply expenses change as volume changes, but all other expenses are fixed. A flexible budget for Finkler, assuming a budget of 40,000 units sold, but considering the possibility of unit sales of 30,000 or 50,000 is shown in Figure 6-4. This flexible budget shows that if the number of units of service provided drop by 25% from 40,000 to 30,000, a loss of $37,750 is likely to occur. This information can serve as a warning to the managers. If they start seeing demand and the number of units sold decrease, they can anticipate the likely financial shortfall without waiting until the end of the month or later to find out. Actions can be taken to increase sales or find ways to cut costs. On the other hand, managers also see that if they can boost sales by 25%, there would be a substantial increase, well more than 25%, in the amount of profits earned.

TABLE 6-4
Finkler Corporation
Operating Budget
for Next Month

	Units Sold		
	30,000	40,000	50,000
Revenues			
Sales of Goods	$123,750	$165,000	$206,250
Total Revenue	$123,750	$165,000	$206,250
Expenses			
Salaries	$136,000	$136,000	$136,000
Supplies	7,500	10,000	12,500
Rent	12,000	12,000	12,000
Other	6,000	6,000	6,000
Total Expense	$161,500	$164,000	$166,500
Surplus	($ 37,750)	$ 1,000	$ 39,750

The key to preparing a flexible budget is determining which numbers in the budget are likely to change and which are likely to remain the same. Will the costs that vary change in direct proportion to volume changes, or will their change be more or less than proportional? Management must work to understand revenue and cost structures enough to be able to anticipate the changes caused by volume variations.

Excel Excercise

See Template 7 for a worksheet that you may use to develop a flexible budget for your organization. The template is on the CD that accompanies this book.

THE CASH BUDGET

The *cash budget* is a plan for expected cash receipts and payments. For organizations using an accrual basis of accounting (*see* Chapter 4), the cash budget provides vital information. The operating budget focuses on revenues and expenses, regardless of when revenue is collected in cash or expenses are paid. However, organizations cannot afford to run out of cash, even if they are making profits! The cash budget provides the information needed to know if there will be adequate cash on hand at all times.

The cash budget allows the organization either to arrange for sources of cash to alleviate an expected shortage (such as a loan from the bank) or to change the organization's planned revenues and expenses to avoid the shortage.

Monthly cash budgets are typically prepared for the coming year. Cash flow forecasting is complicated by the fact that collections and payments are not constant throughout the year. Monthly cash budgets assist in planning for short-term investments and loans during the year.

Cash budgets start with the cash balance expected to be on hand at the beginning of the month. The expected cash receipts for the month are added to this beginning balance to find the expected available cash for the month. Expected payments are subtracted to find the anticipated balance at the end of each month. Surpluses can be invested and are subtracted from the balance. Deficits require borrowing. The amount to be borrowed is added to the balance. The final projected balance for each month becomes the beginning balance for the next month. The general format for cash budgets is as follows:

> Beginning Cash
> + Cash Receipts
> _____
> Subtotal: Available Cash
> − Less Cash Payments
> _____
> Subtotal
> + Borrowing or − Investments
> _____
> Ending Cash Balance
> _____

Excel Excercise

See Template 8 for a worksheet you may use to develop a detailed monthly cash budget for your organization. The template is on the CD that accompanies this book.

ZERO-BASED BUDGETING

Zero-based budgeting (ZBB) is an approach that requires evaluation of all proposed spending. It gets its name from the fact that each department or program starts with a zero base of justified costs. All spending from zero on up must be explained and justified. ZBB helps to keep budgets from developing "fat." No expenditure is automatically accepted without some explanation of why the organization is better off with that expenditure.

This contrasts with the more typical *incremental budgeting* that focuses on just the increase in a budget. With incremental budgeting, there is negotiation over how large an increase will be authorized. While incremental budgeting implicitly assumes that every department can spend what they spent the prior year and then some, ZBB requires justification of all spending, not just the increase from one year to the next.

ZBB argues that some departments might have a need for a 10 percent budget increase, while another might not need any increase at all. Some departments should even be cut, because they no longer have needs that justify the budget level of the previous year. As a result of this philosophy, ZBB is better at allocating an organization's resources to the areas that have the greatest needs.

However, the evaluation of each and every item in each budget is a very time-consuming process. Some organizations use a rotating approach, with each department receiving a thorough ZBB review every three (or four or five) years, and incremental budgets in the intervening years.

ZBB not only requires justification of all costs in the budget, but it also focuses on alternatives. Information is collected into a decision package. This package provides the analysis of the program or department being evaluated. It contains broad information about why something is being done, the negative effects of not doing it, and the costs and benefits. One of the key elements of a decision package is a statement of alternatives.

ZBB requires evaluation of alternatives in a variety of ways. Different programs aimed at the same goal should be compared. Different ways of performing each given program should be compared. Different quality and quantities of each program should be compared. For example, if we could buy a top-model machine to make our product, or a middle-of-the-road model, ZBB requires explicit evaluation of the extra costs and extra benefits related to the top-model machine. By examining alternative approaches and the costs and benefits of each approach, managers are placed in a better position to make informed choices when allocating limited resources. Each alternative is ranked, with the manager giving consideration to the costs and benefits of the differing approaches. As a result, ZBB is a valuable budget technique.

KEY TERMS

Budget—a formalized (written), quantitative (in dollars) plan.

Uses of budgets—set goals; evaluate results; improve the effectiveness of decision making by planning ahead; improve communication and coordination.

Budget Preparation

Preliminaries—an environmental statement should be developed to determine the position of the firm relative to customers, suppliers, and creditors. General objectives should be set, specific assumptions made, and measurable goals established.

Forecasts—the essential ingredient for compilation of budgets is a set of forecast information. Generally, forecasters use such mechanical means as statistics and computers to project the past into the future. Managers must be aware that judgment should be used to modify forecast results.

Departmental budgets—the organization budget consists of the aggregation of budgets from each department. The departmental budgets itemize revenues and expenses in detail.

Workload level—volume of goods or services that the organization provides.

Flexible budget—an operating budget for varying workload levels.

Fixed costs—cost that do not change as volume changes.

Variable Costs—costs that change in proportion to changes in volume.

QUESTIONS FOR REVIEW

1. What is a strategic plan?
2. What is a long-term plan?
3. What types of budgets are prepared annually?
4. What are some of the benefits of operating budgets?
5. What are the preliminary steps in budget preparation?
6. How can forecasting using curved lines help an organization keep inventory levels low?
7. What does workload refer to?
8. What is a flexible budget?
9. Using the assumptions in the chapter, prepare a flexible budget for the coming month for Finkler Corporation assuming that sales are either 36,000 or 44,000 units.
10. Assume that Finkler Corporation is budgeted to begin its year with $25,000 of cash. Further assume that revenues for the coming month (on an accrual basis) are budgeted to be $160,000. However collections from customers only expected to be $140,000. Expenses on an accrual basis are budgeted to be $164,000. The company expects to actually make payments of $150,000. Prepare a cash budget for Finkler Corporation for the coming month.
11. What is Zero-based budgeting?

Chapter 7

Business Plans

One of the ways that organizations prosper is through the introduction of new programs, projects, and other ventures. A business plan is a document that provides the information needed to determine whether the venture is likely to fail or to succeed. A business plan should help you assess whether the proposed venture is sensible, whether it fits the organizational mission, and whether it will be financially viable.

WHY DEVELOP A BUSINESS PLAN?

The more time and effort managers put into a project, the more committed they become to it, and the harder it becomes to recognize the project's limitations. So the first and foremost reason for developing a business plan is to discover weaknesses and eliminate bad proposals at an early stage.

If the plan provides evidence that the proposed venture is a good one, then the plan becomes a vital tool in a number of ways. It provides the details of why the idea is a good one, supporting the idea with evidence instead of merely opinion. It helps to clarify what we do and don't know about the venture. It provides a basis to identify and analyze elements of a proposal that are critical to its success. And finally, it is the primary tool for convincing others (e.g., our boss or investors) that the idea is a good one, worthy of financial support.

A business plan also serves other purposes. First, it communicates the purpose of the project to everyone throughout the organization. The plan also provides a road map for the future, laying out the steps that will be needed to fully implement the new venture. It should include a formal statement of both financial and nonfinancial goals for the project, and forecasts of what resources will be needed and how they will be obtained. These resources are not only financial, but also include elements such as management talent that will be needed to implement and run the new program. Finally, we prepare a plan so that we will have a basis for assessing and controlling organizational performance once the venture is fully operational.

QUESTIONS THAT DRIVE A BUSINESS PLAN

A business plan document represents an effort to provide answers to many questions:

- What is the venture that is being proposed?
- Why would our organization want to do it?

- Who will we provide products or services for?

- How much will potential customers pay?

- How many potential customers are there?

- What will our share of the market be?

We must be as clear as possible in defining the business concept. To make an evaluation of a project, we need to know whether we are responding to an opportunity or a competitive threat, or simply following the next logical step in achieving the organization's mission. We must clearly identify the customer for the products or services that will be provided. Understanding the likely possible pricing and demand for the product or service is critical. Similarly, we must address questions related to marketing approaches.

There are also many questions about specific operating issues that need to be addressed. Where will we do it? Location may be a critical factor in the success of any venture. How will we do it? That is, we need to have some information about the specific operating elements. Who will do it? We need to know both the specific individuals and the organizational elements. Will someone try to stop us from doing it? We cannot consider only our plans without considering the likely response from our competitors.

Four final questions are critical. What resources will we need? If we cannot obtain adequate financing, it is often best not to try to undertake the project. A good idea may waste an incredible amount of time if there is no mechanism that can result in sufficient funding to get the project off the ground. Can it sustain itself? Even if the project fills a tremendous need, we must evaluate whether it can be financially viable. If it can't be, then we need to directly address the question of where a sustaining subsidy might come from. What can go wrong and what will we do if it does? We can never anticipate all problems that may arise. However, the biggest problem with most new plans is that there are risks of failure. To the extent possible we must try to anticipate those risks so that we can evaluate whether the potential payoff justifies taking those risks. Finally, if it's such a good idea, why isn't someone already doing it? This is a tough question, but it is one that is worth thinking about.

THE PLANNING PROCESS

The first step in the process of developing a business plan is to define the business concept. Make it extremely clear what the project will be all about. Next, gather the data we need to answer the questions posed above. As the data is collected, focus and refine the concept. In other words, the project we wind up proposing in a finished business plan is likely to be very different from the one we started with. As we learn more about what might or might not work, the plan should evolve. If, after gathering all the data, things still look positive, put the plan in a ''high-impact'' format. Remember, you likely will be competing for resources.

THE ELEMENTS OF A BUSINESS PLAN

What does a business plan look like? There is no standard document that fits all projects. Make the plan fit the project, not the reverse. Bear in mind that different projects call for different amounts of detail. Essentially, a plan should be complete enough to make a decision about whether to go forward with the project, and yet as concise and easy to read as possible.

In writing a plan, try to aim its contents at the intended audience, be it a supervisor, board members, bankers, venture capitalists, etc. It may be necessary to have different versions of the plan prepared for different readers. It is quite important that we try to assess their knowledge of our project. The document should meet the reader's information needs. The goal is not to show how much we know, but rather to provide the information the reader needs to know. For example, providing a three-page background on our organization may be useful to a venture capitalist, but is just excess baggage if we are asking our own CEO to review and approve the plan.

Maintain a consistent voice and tense throughout the document. Don't shift between the third person (the organization) and the first person (I or we) and between the present (the clinics see 1,000 clients each year) and the future (the clinics will see 1,000 clients each year).

Although each business plan document will be unique, there are some elements that are typically included. The plan should have a cover memo. Next comes a title page, followed by a table of contents, executive summary, description of the initiative, proposed organizational structure, market analysis and marketing plan, financial/resource requirement plan, financial feasibility analysis, implementation and operating plan, key performance measures, and summary of strengths and weaknesses, including risks. If we need to say more—add a topic!

Cover Memo

This memo, sometimes in the form of a letter, should be a brief explanation of what the business plan document is and the specific action that is requested. That action will vary from a request for funding to simply a request for permission to move forward with implementation. For example, a cover memo might appear as in Exhibit 7-1.

Title Page

The body of the plan should have a title page. This may seem pretty obvious, but it is a simple element that is often forgotten. The title page might appear similar to Exhibit 7-2.

Table of Contents

A table of contents should be provided next. This table should provide page numbers for easy reference. Many readers will choose to skip around, and this table should help keep them from getting frustrated.

EXHIBIT 7-1
Cover Memo

Doc in a Box Clinics (DBC)
Internal Communication

To: C. Eeo
From: Steven Finkler
Date: October 31, 2012
Re: Business Plan for Stress/Anxiety Reduction Clinics

Attached is a copy of the business plan for a proposed chain of Stress/
Anxiety Reduction Clinics. The plan describes the clinical, operating,
and financial impacts of adding a national chain of clinics focusing on
stress reduction.

The new clinics are consistent with the Doc in a Box Clinic mission
statement, in that they meet an important health care need, while also
being likely to add substantially to the overall profits of the company.
The first new clinic in the chain can be operational within six months.

I hope that you will review this plan for our upcoming meeting. It is my
recommendation that DBC make a financial and operating commitment
to go forward with this clinic

EXHIBIT 7-2
Title Page

A Proposal
To Establish
A National Chain of
Stress/Anxiety Reduction Clinics

Submitted by
Steven Finkler
Doc in a Box Clinics
Planning Department
October 2012

Executive Summary

Next comes a brief executive summary. Depending on how extensive a project is
being proposed, this summary may range anywhere from one to three pages. **It
should not be longer**. The summary is written last. Everything else in the plan
should be completed before the summary is written. It should give the reader an
overview of the entire project.

It is critical to make your points quickly and clearly in this summary. Pique
the readers' interest, or they may not go any further. Start quickly, with no more
than one or two sentences describing the project, and immediately follow with
the financial benefit. If profits are expected, tell the reader right away.

Then summarize all key points and critical numbers from the document. Provide the essence of why the project will succeed. Establish the approach to be taken, the timing, the management and structure of the project, the costs, revenues, and financial viability. Finally, be clear about what you want from the reader. If you grab the readers' attention, they will move into the document to get the details.

Description of the Initiative

The next section should provide a description of the initiative in some detail. The first sentence should define the business concept. The rest of that paragraph should explain the project's importance. The remainder of the section can lay out the proposed venture in somewhat more detail, giving the project's history, current status, and other information. Try to explain why this is different from what others are already doing, and why it isn't already being done by someone else.

Organizational Structure

Management and organizational structure may be critical to a venture's success. The document must clearly explain who will manage both the initial implementation and the ongoing project once it is up and running. Brief bios should be provided for each member of the project management team.

It would be nice to be able to identify each member of the management team, but it is not uncommon for there to be positions listed as "to be announced" in the early stages of planning. Realize, however, that this weakens the plan. You must convince the reader that the management team is capable and can make the plan succeed. If there are too many gaps in the management team, it will erode the reader's confidence.

Market Analysis

The greatest product or service will not be a financial success if no one is interested in buying it. Market analysis must be conducted to assure that there is, in fact, some demand for the product or service. We must also know if the existing or potential competition will make it too difficult to gain adequate market share. The business plan should identify the target market and its scope (local, regional, national, or worldwide).

Will potential customers pay the price we want to charge? How do we know? Is there competition now? If yes, who? What does their company look like—what products or services do they offer? Where? When? What quality? If there isn't any current competition for the product or service, why isn't there? Will competition arise after others see our successful venture? What are our strengths and weaknesses relative to competitors? Can the market bear both companies, or will we have to force them out of the business in order to succeed? How likely are we to be able to do that?

Marketing Plan

Assuming that our market research indicates that there is a potential market for our product at the price we want to charge, how will we gain our desired market share? We will need to inform customers of the availability of our product or service. How do we intend to do that? Will we advertise on the radio, on television, or in newspapers? Will we put flyers on car windshields? Once we let customers know about us, how will we motivate them to buy from us? It is wishful thinking to assume that "if we will build it, they will come." A proactive marketing plan is essential.

Financial/Resource Requirement Plan

The business plan should identify all resources needed for the start-up of the venture, as well as the expected revenues and expenses related to the project. In some cases this may not be very difficult. For example, if the proposal is to replace an existing facility or expand capacity of a successful activity, we may have excellent historical information to use as a guide.

In many cases, however, the project is new, and the financial estimates are more difficult to make. The manager needs to be careful to find out as much as possible about the resources that are likely to be needed and their cost. Any assumptions made should be listed explicitly. As people read the plan, they can add their insights as to the likely accuracy of those assumptions, and help make refinements that will shape a more accurate plan. The plan should include a contingency fund. This represents an extra amount of money that will be raised in advance and will be available to meet unexpected needs during the implementation and early stages of operation.

Financial Feasibility Analysis

A key element of most business plans is the determination of whether the proposed venture is expected to be financially feasible. Usually this requires forecasts of both the future profits and cash flows of the venture.

Forecasting is as much art as science. If possible, before using any method, test its forecasting accuracy over time. Look at past periods, apply the technique retrospectively, and see how well it would have predicted what we now know actually happened. Consider seasonal factors. If possible, look at industry data or comparable ventures. Forecasts used for financial feasibility are largely based on the marketing analyses and implementation plans. The manager must exercise thought and judgment to make the forecast as accurate as possible.

Financial feasibility analysis is often done with a very rough first pass, and then revised over and over as more information is incorporated. Doing all of the analysis on a computer spreadsheet program such as Excel is highly recommended.

Anticipating the revenues and expenses will be critical to the financial feasibility analysis. Revenue forecasts require that we anticipate both demand and prices. Discounts that will be offered and a likely rate of bad debts must be considered. Growth rates from month to month must also be factored in as new ventures rarely reach a steady state of sales right from the start. Revenue projections must also consider how long the business will take to get organized before it can begin to see sales. Delays in collecting payments from customers must also be anticipated.

The business plan must document the expected start-up costs, capital equipment needs, and ongoing operating costs. Managers must be careful to include both direct production costs and also indirect costs such as marketing and administration. This information should be fairly detailed. For example, the capital costs should include the amount and cost of equipment and facilities, location, timing of acquisition, and estimated useful life.

Focus on Cash Flow

Profits compare revenues and expenses. Do we sell the product or service for more than it costs us to provide it? If so, then we earn a profit. However, in a world in which we often have to buy and pay for supplies, buildings, and equipment well in advance of when our customers ultimately pay us for the goods and services that they buy from us, cash flow is as critical as profits. Recall from the discussion in the viability section of Chapter 1 that it is possible for a profitable venture to go out of business because it runs out of cash. In fact, the more successful the new venture is, the more likely it is to fail because of the growing needs for cash investment as expansion takes place.

Therefore, the business plan must 1) anticipate how long it will take the organization to achieve profitability, and 2) estimate how long it will take until it achieves a level of positive cash flow.

Pro Forma Financial Statements

Most business plans include a set of *pro forma* income and cash flow statements. Pro forma statements are financial statements that provide projections or forecasts of the future. Generally the business plan will include three years of projections, although five years of pro formas are sometimes provided. Income or cash flow statements that only project each year as a whole don't show the tremendous variability in resource needs and in organizational results within each year. Therefore, pro forma statements often show each month, or at least each quarter, for the first year or two, and sometimes for three to five years. Exhibit 7-3 provides an example of a pro forma cash flow statement for one year.

If a venture is not projected to achieve a positive cash flow position within the first three years, it is unlikely to gain much support from venture capitalists or internal managers who have to make funding decisions. There is a great deal of uncertainty in the world, and it turns out that managers are better at predicting the things that might go right than they are at predicting all of the possible things that might go wrong. Given the unexpected, it is risky to commit to a project that will require cash subsidy far into the future, unless the potential rewards are truly lucrative.

EXHIBIT 7-3
Pro Forma Cash Flow Statement for One Year
DBC Stress/Anxiety Clinics
For the Period Beginning January 1, 2013

MONTH	JAN	FEB	MAR	APR	MAY
Beginning Cash Balance	$ 10,000	$ 10,000	$ 10,000	$ 10,000	$ 10,000
Cash Receipts					
Product Sales	$ 4,500	$ 4,600	$ 4,800	$ 5,000	$ 5,200
Services	5,000	6,000	7,000	8,000	9,000
Royalties	—	—	—	500	1,000
Total Cash Receipts	$ 9,500	$ 10,600	$ 11,800	$ 13,500	$ 15,200
Total Cash Available	$ 19,500	$ 20,600	$ 21,800	$ 23,500	$ 25,200
Cash Disbursements					
Labor	$ 24,000	$ 24,533	$ 25,600	$ 26,667	$ 27,733
Supplies	16,600	16,969	17,707	18,444	19,182
Rent	24,000	24,000	24,000	24,000	24,000
Interest Expense	—	1,891	2,799	3,722	4,455
Marketing	30,000	30,000	30,000	10,000	10,000
Capital Acquisitions	100,000	—	—	—	—
Other	4,000	4,000	4,000	4,000	4,000
Total Disbursements	$198,600	$101,393	$104,106	$ 86,833	$ 89,371
Subtotal	−$179,100	−$ 80,793	−$ 82,306	−$ 63,333	−$ 64,171
+Borrowing/−Loan Payments	189,100	90,793	92,306	73,333	74,171
Ending Cash Balance	$ 10,000	$ 10,000	$ 10,000	$ 10,000	$ 10,000
Cumulative Outstanding Loan	$189,100	$279,893	$372,199	$455,532	$519,703

JUN	JUL	AUG	SEP	OCT	NOV	DEC	YEAR
$10,000	$ 10,000	$ 10,000	$ 10,000	$ 10,000	$ 10,000	$ 10,000	$ 10,000
$ 5,400	$ 5,600	$ 5,800	$ 6,000	$ 6,200	$ 6,400	$ 6,600	$ 66,100
10,000	11,000	12,000	13,000	14,000	15,000	16,000	126,000
1,500	2,000	2,500	3,000	3,500	4,000	4,500	22,500
$ 16,900	$ 18,600	$ 20,300	$ 22,000	$ 23,700	$ 25,400	$ 27,100	$ 214,600
$ 26,900	$ 28,600	$ 30,300	$ 32,000	$ 33,700	$ 35,400	$ 37,100	$ 224,600
$ 28,800	$ 29,867	$ 30,933	$ 32,000	$ 33,067	$ 34,133	$ 35,200	$ 352,533
19,920	20,658	21,396	22,133	22,871	23,609	24,347	243,836
24,000	24,000	24,000	24,000	24,000	24,000	24,000	288,000
5,197	5,947	6,656	7,373	8,098	8,831	9,573	64,542
10,000	5,000	5,000	5,000	5,000	5,000	5,000	150,000
—	—	—	—	—	—	—	100,000
4,000	4,000	4,000	4,000	4,000	4,000	4,000	48,000
$ 91,917	$ 89,472	$ 91,985	$ 94,506	$ 97,036	$ 99,573	$ 102,120	$1,246,911
–$ 65,017	–$ 60,872	–$ 61,685	–$ 62,506	–$ 63,336	–$ 64,173	–$ 65,020	–$1,022,311
75,017	70,872	71,685	72,506	73,336	74,173	75,020	1,032,311
$ 10,000	$ 10,000	$ 10,000	$ 10,000	$ 10,000	$ 10,000	$ 10,000	$ 10,000
$594,720	$665,591	$737,276	$809,782	$883,118	$957,291	$1,032,311	

Return on Investment Analysis

The pro forma income statements must also show that the venture will begin to be profitable within a reasonable period of time. But how much profitability is necessary? Suppose that Doc in a Box Clinics (DBC) puts up $10 million for the construction of new stress/anxiety reduction clinics around the country. Assume that the pro formas show that by the second year the clinics start to turn a profit, and by the third year they become self-sufficient from a cash flow basis. Is that enough to warrant going ahead? No.

The two main elements that we have not yet considered are the rate of return on the investment and the element of risk. DBC is contemplating an investment of at least the $10 million to construct the new clinics. That money is spent before the first patient is seen, but the profits earned on providing care will occur in the future. Collection of the revenues earned will occur even farther in the future. The business plan must assure DBC that it will eventually recover its up-front cash investment to build the clinics, as well as the cash subsidy to operate the clinics for the first two years, plus a return on that investment, with an adequate reward for having taken the risk that everything might go wrong and all of the investment might be lost. Chapter 11 discusses investment analysis techniques available for making this type of calculation.

Break-Even Analysis

Another tool often employed to evaluate a new project's potential for profitability is break-even analysis. This technique evaluates the volume necessary for a venture to at least break even. At higher volumes the project will be profitable and at lower volumes losses would be incurred. The reason for this is that virtually all projects have some costs that do not vary as the activity level varies.

For example, once we acquire a machine, we can use it to make a few units each year, or many units. If the annual depreciation on the machine is $10,000 and we use it to make 500 units a year, part of the cost of each unit is a $20 pro rata share for using the equipment ($10,000 ÷ 500 units = $20). If the same equipment is used to make 1,000 units a year, the cost for the equipment is only $10 per unit. The higher the volume (within the capacity of the machine), the lower the cost per unit. Therefore we become more profitable as volume increases. In Chapter 9, the break-even analysis technique is discussed further.

"What-If" Analysis

Finally, a "what-if" sensitivity analysis should be undertaken. This analysis assesses what would happen if the plan's assumptions turn out to be incorrect. For example, what if the volume of sales is 10 percent below expectations? How about 20 percent? What if operating costs are 15 percent higher than planned? If such events mean the project would fail, the reader must know that. The size of the planned contingency fund may be adjusted accordingly.

The financial feasibility analysis can become quite lengthy. It is usually best to summarize all of the financial feasibility information in the body of the business plan, and put most of the detailed calculations, statements, and tables into an appendix.

Implementation/Operating Plan

The implementation plan needs to address the who, what, where, when, and how questions: Who will do the implementation? Exactly what will they do? Where will they do it? When? How? The plan needs to have timetables for hiring various personnel, buying and constructing facilities, and purchasing equipment and supplies, and a complete schedule of the start-up resources that will be needed. In many cases the plan needs to address coordination issues relative to the existing organization.

Clearly the activities that have to take place first can be predicted with a greater degree of accuracy and described in more detail. However, an overall plan is necessary. The plan should include the likely impact of delays. It should distinguish among resources needed right away, those not needed until operations begin, and those not needed until operations are well under way. It is particularly helpful to use a timeline in developing the plan, showing the various activities that will occur at different points in the timeline.

The operations portion of the plan must be as specific as possible about how this organization will operate. It must convince the reader that you have anticipated all of the elements of running the business on an on-going basis.

Key Performance Measures

The financial profitability of the venture, discussed earlier, is one of the most important performance measures. However, for most ventures it is not the only key measure. The plan should consider other outcome measures as well. Targets for sales and market share are often critical. Quality measures of the product or service are essential. Early achievement of customer satisfaction targets may also be a key to long-term success of the venture.

Summary of Strengths and Weaknesses, Including Risks

It is important to itemize not only the positive elements of the venture, but also the business risks and strategies for offsetting them. What might go wrong? What are the implications if those things do go wrong? What can we do to try to avoid those problems? What can we do to minimize the impact if they do occur anyway?

Most implementation plans at some point indicate what will happen "if everything goes according to plan." However, it is rare that at the time operations finally commence, anyone says, "Well, everything went according to plan." Unexpected things always seem to happen. What things? Well, if we could say, then they wouldn't be unexpected! But we must still make our best attempt to say what will happen to the proposed venture if everything does not go according to plan.

HOW A BUSINESS PLAN IS READ

Most readers review the executive summary first. After that, the reader will often jump to an area of concern or an area that the reader has the most familiarity with. If the reader has great expertise in marketing, then the marketing plan may be reviewed first. If the reader concludes the plan is naive with respect to market analysis or the marketing plan, that may be as far as he or she goes. Another reader might believe that, ultimately, if the management team is inadequate no idea can succeed. So the first section reviewed might be the organizational structure and management team. Others will jump to the financial statements first.

The writer of a business plan has relatively little control over the way that the reader moves through the document. Therefore the writer should just ensure that, as the readers ask the following questions, there are satisfactory answers in the plan:

- Does the business concept make sense?
- Can and will the market support the business?
- Can the management team do the job?
- Are the financial projections realistic?
- Has management realistically assessed the risk in the venture?
- Do the economics justify the investment?

If the document cannot provide satisfactory answers to these questions, then the person preparing the plan should be the first to argue that it doesn't pay to proceed. If the answers to these questions indicate that the project is a good one, then the document should be designed to convince someone to provide the needed approvals and resources.

A SUCCESSFUL BUSINESS PLAN

Many business proposals are never implemented. How many times is that because the idea just wasn't any good, and how often because the plan document was not compelling enough? What does a successful business plan do that an unsuccessful one does not do? First, a successful plan gets to the point quickly. Second, it brings together all data needed to make a decision in one document. However, it does not overwhelm the reader with detail. Most of the technical details can be relegated to appendices and supplements. The main document need not be more than twenty to thirty pages long. Third, it clearly defines the reason for the proposal—the business strategy. Fourth, it evaluates the strengths and weaknesses of the proposed venture or project. Fifth, it includes satisfactory consideration of implementation, operations, marketing, and financial issues. Sixth and finally, it makes a strong case that the venture is likely to be successful if implemented.

KEY TERMS

Business plan—a document that provides the information needed to determine whether a proposed new business, program, or project will probably succeed or fail, and the resources needed to implement the project.

Critical questions—What is the venture? Why would we want to do it? How much profit will we make? What are the risks?

Elements of a business plan—cover memo, title page, table of contents, executive summary, description of the initiative, organizational structure, market analysis and plan, financial/resource requirement plan, feasibility analysis, implementation/operating plan, key performance measures, and a summary of strengths and weaknesses, including risks.

Financial feasibility analysis—pro forma income statements, pro forma cash flow statements, return on investment analysis, and break-even analysis.

QUESTIONS FOR REVIEW

1. What is the first and foremost reason for developing a business plan?

2. What are some questions that drive a business plan?

3. What are the elements of a business plan document?

4. What is wrong with listing roles in the business plan organization structure section as "to be announced"?

5. For a complex project, would it be reasonable to have a 5 page executive summary?

6. What are some critical elements of a financial feasibility plan?

7. In order to undertake a proposed project, the reader must feel comfortable with the business plan document's answers to what key questions?

Chapter 8

Cost Accounting

This chapter focuses on the terminology of cost accounting and how cost information can be used for improved managerial decisions. The role of cost accounting is to collect cost information to report what costs have been and to use that information for making decisions about the future. We must know how much our product costs us to make so that we can charge a high enough price to make a profit.

AVERAGE VS. MARGINAL COSTS

Very often we hear someone speak of the average cost or "cost per unit" of a product. However, short-term decisions should be based on marginal costs, rather than on average costs. To understand this we first need to discuss *fixed* and *variable* costs. Fixed costs are those that do not change with changes in the volume of production. Variable costs change in direct proportion to production. For example, if we produce more units in our existing factory, the rent wouldn't rise, so rent would be a fixed cost. The amount of raw materials we use would increase, thus being a variable cost.

Suppose we currently are manufacturing 10,000 units at a cost of $10,000. Our cost per unit is $1. Suppose further that the variable costs for the 10,000 units are a total of $2,000, while the fixed costs are $8,000. If we are selling our units for 80 cents each, and they have a cost per unit of $1, then we are losing 20 cents on each unit we sell. We've all laughed at the story of the individual, faced by such a situation, who decided to increase production and make it up on volume! However, that is exactly the correct strategy. This is because our cost per unit is $1 *at a volume of* 10,000 units.

What happens to our cost per unit if we produce and sell 20,000 units? Our variable cost of $2,000 for 10,000 units doubles to $4,000 for 20,000 units, but the fixed cost remains $8,000. Thus the total cost for 20,000 units is $12,000, and the cost per unit is 60 cents. Suddenly our loss of 20 cents per unit becomes a profit of 20 cents per unit! This assumes that we could sell 20,000 units at the same price of 80 cents. The key is that, because some costs are fixed, the cost per unit declines as volume increases. Thus, some products that look unprofitable at certain volumes might be very profitable at higher volumes. Of course, this only helps if you can sell the higher volume of units.

We can go even one step further. What if we were making 10,000 units at a cost of $1 per unit at that volume. However, now suppose that we were selling them for $1.20, so we are making a profit. Along comes a potential high-volume customer who offers to buy 10,000 units for 50 cents per unit. We assume that this additional sale of 10,000 units does not affect our original sales at $1.20. Should we take the offer?

First we must understand how it might be possible for this new order not to affect our current sales. In order for this to be possible, we must be able to segment the market we face into distinct groups. This task generally belongs to the marketing department. The airlines have commonly charged several distinct prices for the same product. However, the lower super-saver fares usually have restrictions that make them undesirable to business traffic. Another form is separation by wholesale and retail or by purchase volume. For example, a firm normally selling a cleaner for home use might sell the same product at a substantially different price to a high-volume industrial user.

Assuming that we can segment our market adequately to prevent our current customers who are paying $ 1.20 from demanding and receiving a 70-cent discount, should we sell an extra 10,000 units at 50 cents each? At first thought, we might say no. Even if we double our production from 10,000 units to 20,000, our average cost only falls to 60 cents. We would lose 10 cents on every unit sold. Or would we?

We are already making and selling 10,000 units. What will happen to the firm if it accepts this order, versus what would happen if it rejects the order? For every extra unit produced, we are going to generate an additional 50 cents of revenue. For every extra unit we make, we are going to spend an extra 20 cents on variable costs. How about fixed costs? How much extra fixed cost will we have for each extra unit we make? By definition, fixed costs are fixed in total. Assuming that we have sufficient excess capacity of plant and equipment to make the extra 10,000 units without incurring any additional fixed cost, our total fixed costs will not change. In that case, the total extra cost of producing an extra unit is only 20 cents. This cost is often referred to as the out-of-pocket, or incremental, or *marginal cost*. As long as the extra revenue received from each unit sold exceeds the extra cost, we are better off to make the additional sales.

Basically this constitutes a short-run strategy. In the long run, the firm cannot survive unless it has some sales that not only cover variable cost, but also pay for the fixed costs. However, once the firm has committed itself to its fixed costs, all of the short-term decisions should consider those costs to be irrelevant. This is frequently referred to as marginal or incremental costing.

Thus, it should not be surprising that financial managers sometimes make decisions that seem perverse on the surface. They insist on allocating costs, even if those costs exist anyway. This is done because the financial reporting for historical purposes requires that total costs be shown. On the other hand, the same financial officers may require that you offer a product, even at a loss, because its revenue exceeds its marginal cost. Such marginal cost pricing will increase firm profits.

COST VS. EXPENSE: THE INVENTORY PROCESS

The words *cost* and *expense* are often casually used interchangeably. However, they are very distinct in their underlying meaning. From an accounting perspective, the cost of an item is what is paid to acquire it. Expense refers to resources that have been used up. In essence, an item is a cost before it becomes an expense. If we purchase clay to make statuettes, we can refer to the cost of the clay. However, if we have not yet used the clay to make the statuettes, nor sold any statuettes, then the matching principle of accounting does not allow us to consider that cost to be an expense. Using generally accepted accounting principles (GAAP), we can only treat a cost as an expense in the period in which we record the revenues associated with that cost. Until a cost becomes an expense, it is generally treated as an asset, such as inventory.

This creates some rather interesting problems. Assume that we started the hypothetical Statuette Corporation on the last day of 2011. The owners purchased common stock in exchange for $1,000 cash. Statuette purchased 100 pounds of clay in 2012 for $1 per pound. Each statuette it makes requires one pound of clay. By the end of 2012, it had started 80 statuettes and had 20 pounds of unused clay. Only 70 of the statuettes had been completed, and of those 70, a total of 60 statuettes had been sold for $2 each. What was the expense for clay for 2012?

EXHIBIT 8-1
The Inventory Process

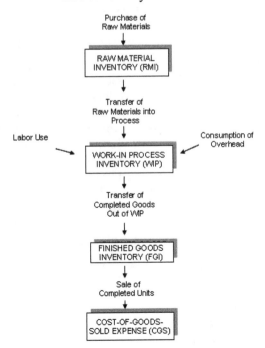

The answer to this question requires an understanding of the inventory process. See Exhibit 8-1. When Statuette initially bought the clay, it was recorded as $100 of raw materials inventory (RMI). The 20 pounds that were not used remain as a $20 inventory balance for the raw materials account at the end of 2012. When we started to make statuettes, the clay was transferred from the raw materials inventory into production. From an accounting point of view, the cost of that portion of clay was transferred from the RMI account into a separate work-in-process (WIP) account. Thus, during 2012, $80 was transferred from RMI into the WIP account. Other production costs, such as labor and the various elements of overhead, also go into the WIP account and ultimately become expenses. Here, however, we are focusing only on how much of the cost of clay ultimately becomes an expense this year.

Of the clay put into production, work was finished on 70 pounds, causing a transfer from WIP into a finished goods inventory (FGI) account. Then 60 units were sold, so they were transferred into a cost of goods sold (COS) expense account. It is the $60 related to the final transfer that becomes an expense. At the end of 2012, $40 of cost is still in the raw materials, work in process, and finished inventory accounts.

This process represents a manufacturing operation. For a wholesale or retail company, goods enter a merchandise inventory account when they are acquired. Their cost is transferred to cost of goods sold expense when the units are sold.

PERIOD COSTS VS. PRODUCT COSTS

In the previous example, we looked only at the cost of direct materials. In fact, there is a wide variety of costs. We must be concerned with labor, rent, administration, and marketing. We divide all costs into two broad categories: period costs and product costs. All costs directly associated with the product itself are considered to be product costs. All other costs are period costs.

For a merchandising firm that simply buys and sells, the cost of the units purchased is the product cost. In a manufacturing firm, all costs associated with the manufacture of the product are considered to be product cost. This means that materials, labor, and factory rent are all treated as part of the cost of the product. Consider the implications of this for labor or factory rent. When we pay our factory workers, we cannot directly charge labor as an expense. That would imply that the labor generated revenue this period. However, it might be that the workers made units of product that have not yet been sold. To charge labor costs to expense directly would violate the matching principle. Instead, we add the cost of the labor to the WIP inventory account. Similarly, the factory rent will be added to WIP. In this way, only a proportionate share of the labor and rent winds up being an expense this period. This proportion depends on how much of the product that we work on this period is finished and sold. The remainder of these costs reside in the WIP and FGI accounts until all of this year's production is finally sold.

Any costs that are not product costs are automatically period costs. For all period costs, such as selling, general, and administrative costs, there is no matching. These costs are charged to expense in the year incurred. Generally this is because it would be too difficult to determine which future sales result from bookkeeping, administrative, and selling efforts of this year. Thus, all depreciation on an office machine is an expense in the year the depreciation is incurred.

But not all of the depreciation on a factory machine is an expense this year, unless all of this year's production is sold. When we see cost of goods sold on an income statement, it represents all elements of product cost: direct labor (the hands-on labor in the production process), direct materials (the raw materials used to make the product), and factory overhead (all other elements of the production process such as supervisory labor, electricity, rent, depreciation, etc.).

COST SYSTEMS: PROCESS, JOB-ORDER, AND STANDARD COSTS

The main focus of cost accounting is to be able to come up with a figure for the cost of each unit produced or acquired. The two most rudimentary systems for calculating this cost per unit are process and job-order actual costing. In both of these methods, we collect actual cost information and assign it directly to the units. Standard costs are the next step in the costing picture. Standard costs can simplify the costing process substantially.

Let's first consider process costing. This approach represents one extreme costing method. Under this approach, a firm that makes a large quantity of an individual product keeps track of both the cost of the various components of the production process, and the number of units made. For example, an aspirin manufacturer could keep track of the total amount of acetylsalicylic acid, labor, and so on used for a batch, and the number of bottles of aspirin produced in that batch. By dividing the total costs by the number of units, we find the cost per unit. This calculation can be done on a batch basis, or for continuous operations, on a monthly basis.

At the opposite extreme is the job costing or job-order costing approach. Consider the manufacturer of customized items, such as furniture. We can think of a custom furniture house receiving an order for six rosewood tables and another order for six knotty pine tables. The rosewood lumber is far more expensive than the knotty pine lumber. We might use skilled workers on the rosewood tables and apprentices on the knotty pine tables. Clearly, the firm cannot get a good estimate of costs if it simply adds the total lumber and labor costs for the month and divides by twelve tables. Because each job is different, we need to gather information separately for each job.

Job-order costing is inherently more expensive from a bookkeeping standpoint than process costing. We need to keep track of how much of each type of lumber was used for each job. We need time cards to keep track of how much time each type of worker spent on each job. Pricing decisions cannot effectively be made without this information if the labor and materials truly are different for each job.

Many hybrid methods are possible. For example, it might well be that our furniture manufacturer has substantially different material costs depending on whether tables are oak, rosewood, or knotty pine. But if all tables are alike from the point of view of labor, then regardless of which lumber we use, the labor requirements are identical. In that case, we could use job-order cost accounting to keep specific track of the materials used on each job, but we could use process-cost accounting for labor. We could simply total our labor cost and divide by the number of tables to get the labor cost per table.

What about standard costs? In using process and job-order accounting, one approach is to collect costs as you go and assign them periodically (often monthly) to the units produced. This provides very accurate information. Information, however, is costly. Managerial accountants are always attempting to find ways to provide an adequate amount of information at a lower cost. Do we really need the accuracy gained from actual process or actual job-order costing? Standard costs are a simplification that often provide enough information, but at a lower cost.

Suppose that our aspirin manufacturer produces a wide variety of pharmaceuticals, and the workers are used interchangeably among the various products. Further, there are materials that are used in common by many of the products. Process costing is no longer reasonable because there are so many different products using the same resources. Job-order costing is expensive because of the extra detail of material records and time cards. The standard costing alternative uses industrial engineering estimates and past experience to determine how much of our various resources we expect each unit of each product to consume, and what we expect those resources to cost.

For example, we have a standard cost card for aspirin showing how much of each material and how much labor we expect each bottle (or hundred bottles or thousand bottles) to consume, and the price we expect to have to pay for each material, type of labor, and so on. At the end of any month, as long as we know the number of units we have produced, we can multiply the standard cost per unit times the number of units produced to get our total estimated production costs.

COST ALLOCATION

How do we assure that when we determine the cost to make a unit of our product or service, that cost includes a share of all the overhead costs? We do it through a process called cost allocation.

Production costs are classified as being either *direct* or *indirect*. The direct costs generally consist of direct labor and direct materials. Direct labor is the labor directly associated with the production of a specific product or service. Direct materials are the materials specifically used to make a product. Anything that does not fall into a direct category is indirect, and is considered to be overhead. Examples of overhead costs include the maintenance staff, administrative offices, utilities such as heat and electric, legal department, security guards, the company cafeteria, and so on.

Direct costs for each product or service are measured and assigned directly to that product or service on a cause-and-effect basis. That is, because we produce a product or service we consume specific direct resources. Then, cost allocation takes the costs of the overhead departments and allocates them first to the production departments and then to the units of each product. When we combine the direct costs assigned to a unit and the overhead costs allocated to that unit we come up with the total cost of producing that unit of product or service.

The first step in the cost allocation process is to determine an allocation base. For example, suppose that there is a Cleaning Department whose employees go through all areas of the business washing the floors, emptying waste baskets, and doing whatever cleaning is required in each department. That Cleaning Department might incur costs of $100,000. In order to allocate that cost to the departments that produce the organization's goods or services, we need to decide what the cost will be allocated based on. We might decide to allocate it based on square feet. The more square feet of building space a department occupies, the greater the share of the cost that will be assigned to it.

Once we know the base, we can compute an overhead allocation rate. We find the rate by dividing the overhead cost by the rate. For example if the Cleaning Department incurred $100,000 of cost and if there are 50,000 square feet in the building, then the Cleaning Department overhead allocation rate would be $2 per square foot, computed as follows:

$$\frac{\$100,000}{50,000 \text{ square feet}} = \$2 \text{ per square foot}$$

If one particular production department, e.g. Department C, had 5,000 square feet, it would be assigned $10,000 of cleaning department cost (5,000 square feet × $2 per square foot = $10,000).

The next step would be to allocate the overhead cost to individual products. For example, if Department C produced 50,000 units of product, we could assign 20 cents of Cleaning Department overhead to each unit of product as follows:

$$\frac{\$10,000 \text{ overhead}}{50,000 \text{ units}} = \$.20 \text{ per unit}$$

Overhead allocation is not perfect. Just because a department has a certain percentage of the square feet in a building, that doesn't mean that it necessarily consumes that percentage of the resources of the Cleaning Department. Some departments might well require more cleaning per square foot than other departments. Also, it is not clear that every product made within a department consumes an equal amount of overhead.

In determining the cost of a product, we would like to directly associate with the product all of the costs it is responsible for causing to be incurred. That would increase accuracy. More accurate costs provide managers with better information for pricing and other product decisions.

Activity-Based Costing (ABC)

One method commonly used to improve overhead allocations, making them more accurate, is Activity-Based Costing (ABC). ABC examines the drivers of overhead costs to see whether they can be directly related to specific activities. That is, rather than arbitrarily assigning the overhead cost based on an arbitrary base such as square feet, ABC focuses on assessing the activities that are taking place that cause overhead resources to be consumed, and then allocates the overhead cost based on the usage of those activities.

For example, suppose the Cleaning Department in the above example sends workers to clean different production departments as needed. Some departments work on processes that need frequent cleanups. Other departments don't have processes that require those cleanups. All departments, however, do need regular cleaning. ABC would argue that we have two activities: regular cleanups, and process cleanups.

A study might reveal that regular cleanups depend on space. The bigger the department, the longer it takes the cleanup staff to clean it, and the more supplies they use. So allocation based on square feet is reasonable for allocating the cost of regular cleanups. But process cleanups take about $10 of Cleaning Department resources for each cleanup. Whatever costs the Cleaning Department incurs that are not related to process cleanups are for the regular cleaning of each department.

Let's consider the cost allocation under a non-ABC approach and under an ABC approach. We'll start with a non-ABC approach. Assume that there are three production departments, and that their square feet are as follows:

Department A	35,000 square feet
Department B	10,000 square feet
Department C	5,000 square feet
Total	50,000 square feet

Using the overhead rate of $2 per square feet that was computed above, the $100,000 overhead cost of running the Cleaning Department would be allocated to these departments as follows:

Department A	35,000 square feet × 2 = $ 70,000
Department B	10,000 square feet × 2 = $ 20,000
Department C	5000 square feet × 2 = $ 10,000
Total Cost Allocated	$100,000

For an ABC allocation, we would also need to know how many times cleaning had to come to each department to clean up related to processes. Assume that each department required cleaning after the completion of each process, and that the following information is available:

Department A	1,000 process completions
Department B	1,000 process completions
Department C	5,000 process completions

Given this information, using ABC we would allocate the Cleaning Department costs to the production departments, as shown in Exhibit 8-2.

EXHIBIT 8-2
Allocation of Cleaning Department Overhead Costs to Production Departments Using ABC Approach

Part I. Allocation Based on Processes Completed	
Department A: 1,000 process completions × $10	$ 10,000
Department B: 1,000 process completions × $10	10,000
Department C: 5,000 process completions × $10	50,000
Total cost allocated based on process completions:	$ 70,000
Part II. Cleaning Department Costs for Regular Cleaning	
Total Cleaning Department Cost	$100,000
Less portion allocated based on process completions (Part I)	(70,000)
Remaining portion to be allocated based on square feet:	$ 30,000
Part III. Computation of Allocation Rate per Square Foot	
$30,000 cost (from Part II) ÷ 50,000 square feet base = $.60 per square foot	
Part IV. Allocation of Regular Cleaning Based on Rate per Square Foot	
Department A: 35,000 square feet × $.60	$ 21,000
Department B: 10,000 square feet × $.60	6,000
Department C: 5,000 square feet × $.60	3,000
Total cost allocated based on square feet:	$ 30,000
Part V. Total Cleaning Department Cost Allocated to Each Department	
Department A: $10,000 (Part 1) + $21,000 (Part IV)	$ 31,000
Department B: $10,000 (Part 1) + $6,000 (Part IV)	16,000
Department C: $50,000 (Part 1) + $3,000 (Part IV)	53,000
Total Cleaning Department Cost Allocated	$100,000

In Exhibit 8-2, Part I determines the portion of the Cleaning Department overhead cost allocated based on the number of process completions. It is determined that those cleaning activities consume $70,000 of resources. In Part II, we find that since the overall cost of running the Cleaning Department was $100,000 and $70,000 of that went for cleaning after process completions, the balance to be allocated based on square feet is $30,000. Part III divides that $30,000 (the overhead cost) by the total number of square feet (the base), to find the overhead allocation rate, which is $.60 per square foot. In Part IV of the exhibit, that rate is used to determine the Cleaning Department overhead cost allocated to each production department based on square feet. Finally in Part V, the overhead allocations from Parts I and IV are used to determine the total amount of Cleaning Department overhead cost allocated to each production department.

Notice how dramatic the differences are between the cost allocation with and without the use of ABC. For example, If we were not using the ABC approach, then Department C would only have been allocated $10,000 (5,000 square feet × $2 per square foot) of Cleaning Department overhead cost. However, when ABC is used, the large demands Department C places on the Cleaning Department for cleaning after processes are completed is taken into account. Using ABC, we see in Exhibit 8-2 that Department C is really responsible for $53,000 of the Cleaning Department cost.

ABC would then push further and examine the activities within each department, so that when this overhead is allocated to products, it isn't divided evenly based on the number of units produced in each department, but also takes into account whether some types of units produced require activities that really consume more of the cleaning than others.

For example, suppose that Department C produces 50,000 units. If we only used square feet, we would have allocated $10,000 of Cleaning Department cost to Department C, and then would have divided that $10,000 by 50,000 units, coming up with an overhead cost of $.20 per unit. Now with ABC we see that the Cleaning Department cost for Department C was $53,000, and if we divide that by 50,000 units we would come up with a Cleaning Department cost allocation of $1.06 per unit.

But what if Department C makes 10,000 units of Product 1 and 40,000 units of Product 2. Product 1 requires many processes along the way, while Product 2 requires only a few. ABC would argue that in that case it doesn't make sense to allocate the overhead cost simply on a per unit basis, with the same cost to every unit. Somehow we must take into account the fact that Product 1 units requires more processes, and therefore more cleaning than Product 2 units. Assume that an ABC study determines that the most reasonable way to allocate the entire overhead cost within Department C is based on processes completed. It further determines that the 10,000 units of Product 1 required 4,000 process completions, while the 40,000 units of Product 2 required only 1,000 process completions. Exhibit 8-3 shows the computations for the allocation of the Cleaning Department overhead cost to each unit of Products 1 and 2.

In Part I of Exhibit 8-3 the total Cleaning Department cost allocated to Department C is divided by the number of process completions (the base) to find the overhead rate per process completion. Then in Part II of the exhibit, the rate is multiplied by the number of process completions for each of the Department C products. In Part III the cost determined in Part II is then divided by the number of units of each product produced, to find the amount of Cleaning Department cost that should be appropriately allocated per unit of each product.

As you can see in Exhibit 8-3, the Cleaning Department allocation would come out to be $4.24 per unit of Product 1 and $.265 per unit for Product 2. This is very different than the original $.20 per unit computed without considering ABC at all, or even very different from the $1.06 per unit for all units in Department C, if we used ABC to allocate to Department C, but didn't use ABC to allocate the Department C overhead to individual units produced in Department C.

EXHIBIT 8-3
Allocation of Cleaning Department Overhead Costs Within
Department C to Product 1 and Product 2 Using ABC Approach

Part I. Determine Cost per Process Completion

Cleaning Department Cost Allocated to Department C	$53,000
Divided by Department C Process Completions	÷ 5,000
Overhead Cost per Process Completion	$10.60

Part II. Allocation to Products Based on Processes Completions

Product 1	4,000 Process completions × $10.60	= $42,400
Product 2	1,000 Process completions × $10.60	= $10,600
Total cost allocated based on process completions:		$53,000

Part III. Allocation of Cost Per Unit of Product 1 and 2

Product 1	$42,400 (Part II) ÷ 10,000 units of Product 1	= $4.240
Product 2	$ 10,600 (Part II) ÷ 40,000 units of Product 2	= $ .265

Think of the managerial implications of inexact allocations. Before we considered using ABC, we were assigning only $.20 of cost per unit of product for all units produced by Department C. ABC has shown that some of the units produced should have been assigned $.265 and some should have been assigned $4.24. Suppose that the direct labor and material costs of Product 1 were $12.00. Before using ABC, we thought it cost $12.00 of direct cost and $.20 of overhead, or $12.20 to produce Product 1. We might have sold that product for $15 thinking we were making a nice profit of nearly $3 a unit. In fact, if the direct costs were $12.00 and a more accurate measure of overhead per unit was $4.24, then the cost of a unit of Product 1 is $16.24 and at a price of $15 we would have been losing money. Clearly, efforts such as ABC, intended to improve the accuracy of cost allocations, can provide managers with the information they need to make better decisions.

KEY TERMS

Cost accounting—the collection of information related to the costs incurred for the acquisition or production of a product or service, and for making decisions regarding future production and product strategy.

Marginal costing—additional cost incurred to produce an additional unit; the appropriate cost measure for short-term decision making.

The manufacturing inventory process—when inventory is acquired, its cost is recorded as raw materials inventory (RMI). The costs of RMI that enter into the production process are transferred into the work-in-process inventory account (WIP). Other production costs are also added to WIP. When production is completed, the costs in WIP related to that production are transferred to the finished goods inventory account (FGI). When goods are sold, their cost is transferred from FGI to the cost-of-goods-sold (CGS) account.

Product cost vs. period cost—product costs are all of the costs of manufacturing or acquiring the product. These costs become an expense only in the year in which the units of product are sold. Period costs are all costs that are not product costs. They become expenses in the year in which they are incurred.

Cost systems:

Process costing—the determination of unit costs by comparing the number of units made to the total cost for large amounts of production, such as an entire month's output.

Job-order costing—the costs of each particular job are accumulated separately, and the cost per unit is assessed based on resources consumed for each particular job.

Standard costing—use of a predetermined estimate of the cost per unit for each product.

Cost allocation—the process of determining a base for allocation of overhead costs, and using the base to determine an overhead allocation rate, and then using the rate to assign overhead cost to departments and units of product or service.

Activity-based costing (ABC)—a method of examining overhead costs to see whether they can be related to specific activities. If so, then they can be assigned to products as direct costs, rather than being arbitrarily allocated as part of general overhead.

QUESTIONS FOR REVIEW

1. For most prospective decision making should we rely on average costs?

2. Cost varies as volume changes because of what type of cost?

3. What is the difference between cost and expense?

4. What are the stages of inventory once we acquire it, up until we sell a finished product?

5. Are general administrative expenses considered to be product or period expenses?

6. Explain the three major approaches to product costing.

7. What is the basic approach to cost allocation in a non-ABC system?

8. What is the focus of the ABC approach to cost allocation?

Chapter 9

Leverage

A fundamental decision made by any business is the degree to which it incurs *fixed costs*. A fixed cost is one that remains the same regardless of the level of operations. As sales increase, fixed costs don't increase. The degree to which a firm locks into fixed costs is referred to as its *leverage position*. The more highly leveraged a firm, the riskier it is because of the obligations related to fixed costs that must be met whether the firm is having a good year or not. At the same time, the more highly leveraged, the greater the profits during good times. This presents a classic problem of making a decision whereby there is a trade-off between risk and return.

There are two major types of leverage, financial and operating. *Financial leverage* is specifically the extent to which a firm gets its cash resources from borrowing (debt) as opposed to issuance of additional shares of capital stock, reinvested profits, or donations (equity). The greater the debt compared to equity, the more highly leveraged the firm, because debt legally obligates the firm to annual interest payments. These interest payments represent a fixed cost.

Operating leverage is concerned with the extent to which a firm commits itself to high levels of fixed costs other than interest payments. A firm that rents property using cancelable leases has less leverage than a firm that commits itself to a long-term noncancelable lease. A firm that has substantial vertical integration has created a highly leveraged situation. Consider what happens if Executive Corporation vertically integrates by acquiring its raw materials supplier, Embiay, Inc. Raw materials will now cost the company less, because it doesn't have to buy them from an outside firm. But when times are bad, the firm will have to bear the fixed costs associated with the Embiay subsidiary. Had there still been two separate companies, Executive could have simply slowed its purchases of raw materials from Embiay without having to bear Embiay's fixed costs. In the cases of both financial and operating leverage, the crucial question is, how much leverage is appropriate?

FINANCIAL LEVERAGE

Let's start our discussion of financial leverage with an example. Assume you were to buy a small building as a piece of investment property. You buy the building for $100,000 and pay the full amount in cash.

Suppose that a year later you sell the building for $130,000. Your pretax profit is $30,000. This is a 30 percent pretax return on your original investment of $100,000.

As an alternative to paying the full $100,000 cash for the investment, you might put $10,000 cash down and borrow $90,000 from the bank at 15 percent interest. This time when you sell the property for $130,000, you repay the $90,000 loan to the bank, plus $13,500 interest. After deducting your original $10,000 investment, $16,500 is left as a pretax profit. This is a pretax return of 165 percent on your $10,000 investment. Compare the 30 percent we calculated earlier to this rate of return of 165 percent. That's leverage!

Note that we had a net profit of $30,000 without leverage, but only $16,500 in the leveraged case. Although we earned a higher return in the latter case, we had less profits because of the interest we had to pay. In the unleveraged case we had invested $100,000 of our money, but in the leveraged case we had invested only $10,000. If we have additional investment opportunities available to us, we could have invested our full $100,000, borrowed $900,000, and had a pretax profit of $165,000 on the same $100,000 investment that yields $30,000 in the unleveraged situation. Financial leverage can not only increase your yield from investments, but can also allow you to consider projects that are much larger than would be feasible without borrowing.

Suppose, however, that the property was sold after one year for $70,000 rather than $130,000. On a $100,000 unleveraged investment, the loss would be $30,000 before taxes. This would be a 30 percent loss on our original $100,000 investment.

In the leveraged case, the loss will be magnified. We would have to repay the bank the $90,000 loan plus $13,500 of interest. These payments total $103,500, which is $33,500 greater than the $70,000 proceeds from the sale. Further, we've lost our initial $10,000 investment. The total loss is $43,500 before taxes. On our initial investment of $10,000, this constitutes a loss of 435 percent. That's leverage too!

Clearly the firm must decide if the 165 percent possible gain is worth the risk of a 435 percent loss. Whether it is or not depends on the likelihood of the increase in value versus the probability of a decline. If the project really were a sure thing, leverage would certainly make sense. Rarely are projects sure things. Yet, managers should try to decide how confident they are of the success of a project, and weigh that confidence against the implications for the firm if the project does indeed fail.

Some managers and firms tend to be more averse to risk than others. Usually stockholders align themselves with a firm that they feel does things the way they want them done. A person dependent on a steady level of income from stock dividends might prefer to buy the stock of a firm that shuns leverage and prefers a steady, if lesser, income. A person looking for large potential appreciation in stock price might prefer the stock of a firm that is highly leveraged.

The Rule of OPM

In making a decision regarding whether additional funds should be raised by debt or equity, there are several factors to be considered. The first rule of financial leverage is that it only pays to borrow if the interest rate is less than the rate of return on the money borrowed. We can refer to this as the "rule of OPM"—other people's money. If your firm can borrow money and invest it at a high enough rate so that the loan can be repaid with interest and still leave some after-tax profit for your stockholders, then your stockholders have profited on OPM. They have made extra profit with no extra investment. This greatly magnifies the rate of return on the amount they invested.

Stability of Earnings

What factors should you consider in trying to arrive at a reasonable level of leverage? To a great degree, your desired leverage position depends on the degree to which your sales and profits fluctuate. The greater the fluctuation in sales and profits, the less leverage you can afford. If your firm is a stable, noncyclical firm that makes money in good times and bad, then use of OPM will help improve the rate of return earned by your shareholders. If cyclical factors in your industry or the economy at large tend to cause your business to have both good and bad years, then debt entails a greater risk.

For example, the airline industry, with its huge capital requirements for jet purchases, has traditionally been highly leveraged. The results have been very large profits during the good years, but substantial losses during periods when air traffic falls off or competition is particularly intense. As a result, a number of airlines have gone out of business.

Cyclical factors shouldn't scare companies away from having any debt at all. The key is to accumulate no more interest and principal repayment obligations than can reasonably be met in bad times as well as good. Ultimately, considering the variability of your profit stream, a decision must be made regarding the level of extra risk you are willing to take to achieve a higher potential rate of return on stockholder investments.

OPERATING LEVERAGE

While financial leverage is an issue that is almost strictly the domain of the firm's highest levels of management together with its financial officers, operating leverage is an issue that directly affects the line managers of the firm. The level of operating leverage a firm selects should not be decided without input from the managers directly involved in the production process. For example, one of the most significant operating leverage issues is the choice of technology levels. Selection of the highest level of technology available is not always in the best interests of the business.

Suppose that we are opening a chain of copy centers. We are faced with the choice of renting a relatively slow copy machine, or the newest technology machine, which is considerably faster. The faster machine is also considerably more expensive to lease. It will generally be the case that newer technology has a higher fixed cost and lower variable cost than the older technology. Variable costs are those that vary directly with volume. If we double the number of copies made, we double the amount of paper, printing ink toner, and labor time needed for making the copies. One of the principle functions of new technology is to reduce the variable costs of production.

It may turn out that a machine that can reduce the variable costs is more expensive to make, and thus has a higher purchase or lease price than the older generation machine. However, even if it doesn't cost more to make, its manufacturer will charge more for the new machine than for the older machine. Intuitively, if the new machine is in some respect better than the old machine and doesn't cost more to buy, then no one will buy the older machine. Thus, anytime we see two technologies being sold side by side, such as slow and fast copy machines, we can expect the faster machine to have a higher rental fee or purchase price, and therefore a higher fixed cost.

Let's assume that we could lease the slower, older technology copy machine for $10,000 per year, or a faster, newer technology copy machine for $25,000 per year. Both produce photocopies of equal quality. Both use the same quantities of paper and ink toner, but the faster machine requires less operator time. Therefore, the labor cost is much lower for the faster machine. As a result, the variable cost of copies on the slow machine is 6 cents each, while the variable cost of copies from the fast machine is only 3 cents each. Is the faster machine the better bet?

That depends. Suppose we sell each copy we make for 10 cents. Then, for each copy we sell we receive 10 cents and spend an extra 6 cents or 3 cents (depending on our choice of machine) for the variable costs. The difference between the price and the variable costs is referred to as the *contribution margin*.

CONTRIBUTION MARGIN = PRICE – VARIABLE COST

This margin represents the amount of money available to be used to pay fixed costs and provide the firm with a profit.

If we use the slower machine, we receive 10 cents and spend 6 cents, leaving 4 cents to be used toward paying the rent on the copy machine. If we sell enough copies, there will be enough individual contributions of 4 cents apiece to pay the full $10,000 rent and leave some receipts for a profit.

Break-Even Analysis

How many copies must we make before we "break even?" Break-even analysis requires dividing the fixed costs by the contribution margin per unit. This is equivalent to saying, "How many times do we have to get a contribution of 4 cents before we have covered our fixed cost of $10,000?" The break-even point can be computed using the following formula:

$$\text{Break-Even Quantity} = \frac{\text{Fixed Costs}}{\text{Price} - \text{Variable Cost}}$$

or

$$\text{Break-Even Quantity} = \frac{\text{Fixed Costs}}{\text{Contribution Margin}}$$

For the slower machine, $10,000 divided by 4 cents equals 250,000. We need to make and sell a quarter of a million copies to break even. For the faster machine, the contribution margin is 7 cents per unit, because the price is 10 cents and the variable costs are only 3 cents. The $25,000 rental fee for the fast machine, divided by a 7-cent contribution margin per unit, results in a break-even point of 357,143 copies. Apparently, we can make a profit on the slower machine at a lower output level than we can with the faster machine.

If we sell more copies than the break-even point for the machine we have, we make a profit. If we sell fewer copies than the break-even point, we lose money. Consider sales of 300,000 copies per year. Our revenue would be $30,000 at 10 cents per copy. For the slow machine, our costs would be $10,000 fixed rental cost, plus $18,000 of variable cost (300,000 copies at 6 cents). The total cost would be $28,000 and we would have a pretax profit of $2,000. For the fast machine, the fixed rental cost is $25,000. The variable cost would be $9,000 (300,000 copies at 3 cents). The total cost would be $34,000 and we would have a loss of $4,000. We are above the break-even point for the slow machine, but below the break- even point for the faster machine.

If we sell 400,000 copies, we might expect the faster machine to come out better than the slower machine. After all, both are operating at a level above their break-even point. The faster machine is earning a profit of 7 cents for every extra copy above the break-even point, while the slower machine is only earning a profit of 4 cents a copy. While there is some truth to this reasoning, we must be careful. The slower machine has been earning profits, albeit not much per copy, ever since the 250,000 copy point was passed. The faster machine has been earning profits, albeit a larger amount per copy, only since passing 357,143 copies. You can't assume that the faster machine is better for us as long as our volume exceeds its break-even point. In this case, our revenue is $40,000 (400,000 copies at 10 cents). The slow machine has costs of $10,000 rental plus $24,000 variable (400,000 copies at 6 cents), leaving a pretax profit of $6,000, while the fast machine has a $25,000 rental plus $12,000 of variable cost (400,000 copies at 3 cents). The faster machine is making a profit of $3,000 now, but that's only half as much the slow machine.

At 500,000 copies, the two machines produce an equal pretax profit of $10,000. Above that point, the faster machine generates a higher profit because every extra copy yields a 7-cent profit as compared to the 4 cent profit from the slower machine. On the other hand, for each copy less than 500,000, the slower machine has a higher profit, because its profits go down only 4 cents per copy, while the faster machine's profits fall off at a rate of 7 cents per copy.

Which machine should we lease? That depends on our expected volume and how sure we are of our projections. If we expect to always make more than 500,000 copies, the fast machine is preferred. If we will always make fewer than 500,000 copies, the slow machine is preferred. If we expect to make fewer than 250,000 copies, we should get out of the business.

The problem of operating leverage that faces us is what to do if we expect to make more than 500,000 copies, in general, but sometimes it may be less than that. We can play it safe with the slower machine and be sure of a profit, or at least not a huge loss. We have a lower fixed cost (rent of $ 10,000) and therefore a lower operating leverage. On the other hand, we can get the faster machine that produces a much higher profit if sales are good. In that case we take a chance. We have a higher fixed cost (rent of $25,000) and therefore a higher operating leverage. If sales fall off, profits will decline much faster, and any loss will be much larger than it would have been.

Again, as in the case of financial leverage, we are trading off risk and return. The less the variability in our production volume, the lower the risk associated with incurring the larger fixed costs in order to achieve a higher profit.

Technology is only one example. Should we buy our buildings and equipment or rent them? If we buy them, we incur fixed charges even if volume falls off. If we rent with relatively short leases, the annual cost is likely to be greater, but it is easier to terminate the fixed costs in the face of business downturns. Another operating leverage decision is whether to acquire plant and facilities and manufacture all components of our product or to subcontract the manufacturing and merely do assembly. With subcontracting, we can terminate contracts when demand declines. If we buy the plant and equipment, the fixed costs remain even when demand falls off.

Ultimately, these decisions fall into management's lap. Once managers consider the likelihood of sales variability, a decision has to be made as to whether the risks associated with the fixed costs of financial and operating leverage are worth the higher potential return. Issues of vertical integration, buying versus renting, and choice of technology can have vital competitive implications.

Both these financial decisions—how much financial leverage and how much operating leverage the firm should have—are fundamental to the firm. We can simply let things develop, handling items on a crisis basis, or we can make such decisions on a rational, planned basis. In Chapter 24, one of the topics examined is the solvency of the firm. Is the firm able to meet its interest costs and other fixed obligations? More often than not, the firms that have solvency problems are the ones that didn't formally address the leverage issues head on.

KEY TERMS

Leverage—Represents locking in a set level of fixed cost. As revenues rise, these costs don't rise, so profits rise rapidly. As revenues decline, these costs remain, so profits fall rapidly.

Financial leverage—the degree to which the firm chooses to finance its operations by borrowing money, thus locking in fixed interest charges.

The rule of OPM—If the return from invested capital exceeds the current interest rate on borrowed funds, then the firm's owners benefit if the firm borrows, thus allowing the owners to profit from the use of other people's money.

Operating leverage—the degree to which the firm chooses to lock in fixed costs other than interest in order to leverage profits during good times. Examples of high operating leverage are vertical integration and the use of new technology.

Stability of earnings—the less variable the firm's earnings, the lower the risks and the greater the advantages of being highly leveraged.

QUESTIONS FOR REVIEW

1. What is leverage?

2. What are the two major types of leverage? Define each.

3. When does it make the most sense to have high leverage?

4. Assume that you can invest $50,000 for one year in a project that is expected to have a 20% profit. You can borrow money at a 12% interest rate. If you borrow $40,000 and invest $10,000 of your own money, what will your rate of return be if things go as expected?

5. Considering the information in question 4 above, what would be your rate of return on your investment if the project winds up with a 15% loss instead of a 20% profit?

6. What is the rule of OPM?

7. If you have a choice of leasing a machine that you can return after each month, or buying the machine, if you buy it, that would be an example of what type of leverage?

8. What is contribution margin?

9. What are two forms of the formula to find the break-even quantity?

Chapter 10

Dealing with Uncertainty

Managers often make decisions using uncertain data. Expected revenues and expenses are predicted based on a number of calculations, and decisions are made based on the results of those calculations. There is a high degree of uncertainty inherent in such estimates. A number of decision analysis techniques are available to improve the predictions made and used for decisions under uncertainty. This chapter addresses two prominent approaches: *expected value* and *network cost budgeting*.

THE EXPECTED VALUE TECHNIQUE

Expected value analysis is a technique that estimates the costs or revenues based on the likelihood of each possible outcome. The focus of expected value analysis is on the possible events that might occur. Management can take actions to affect outcomes, but events are defined as occurrences that are beyond the control of managers. For that reason, events are sometimes referred to as *states of nature*.

An Expected Value Example

Suppose a company is planning for a new service, without knowing for sure how many customers the service will attract. For example, perhaps the company is considering buying an expensive new machine. Based on marketing estimates of demand, it expects to use the machine to produce 1,000 units per year. Calculations based on industry prices for the product and operating costs indicate that the service would be profitable at that volume. However, there is the possibility that a competitor will buy a similar machine. In that event, the demand for our product would probably be only 500 per year. At that lower volume, the company would lose a lot of money. We are only interested in the project if it will make money, and there is only enough demand to support one profitable company.

Should the manager assume 500 units will be sold each year or 1,000? Some managers might be conservative, calculating based on the worse event occurring, and, therefore, use the 500 estimate. Other managers might look to the most likely result. What if there is only a 25 percent chance that the other company will buy the machine? In that case, the manager might use the 1,000 for the calculation, if that is what will probably happen. Neither of these approaches is optimal.

The Expected Value Concept

Expected value is a methodology that finds a middle ground between the two extremes. It does not rely on either event but rather on a combination, or weighted average, of the two. The weighted average to be used must be based on a combination of the likely gain or loss in each event and the probability of that gain or loss occurring.

At first, one might object to this. We are fairly certain that one or the other event will occur, not something in between. Either the competitor will buy the machine, or it will not. Volume will be very close to 1,000, or close to 500, not somewhere in between. That is true. However, from the viewpoint of maximizing the financial results of decisions, in the long run it still makes sense to undertake the weighted average approach. The reason is that over the course of time, any organization will make a large number of decisions. It can never predict totally what events will occur, but it must make decisions anyway. The best strategy is to approach the decisions so that on average, over the long run, the financial results are maximized.

An expected value is a weighted average of the possible outcomes. The weights of each value is based on the likelihood, or probability of that event being the actual state of nature. To compute the expected value, it is first necessary to make your best estimate, using as much available data as possible, of the probability that each possible state of nature will occur.

For example, suppose that we believe there is a 25 percent chance that the competitor will buy the machine, and a 75 percent chance that it will not, assuming that we buy one. Further, suppose that the profits from 1,000 patients are expected to be $50,000, whereas the loss related to 500 patients will be $150,000. The expected value of this proposed project can be measured by multiplying each probability by the expected payoff and summing the results as shown in Exhibit 10-1.

EXHIBIT 10-1
Expected Value of Purchase Alternatives

	Probability	Payoff	Expected Value
Competitor buys one	25% ×	–$150,000	= –$37,500
We buy machine			
Competitor does not buy	75% ×	$50,000	= $37,500
		Expected Value	$ 0

Over the long run, across a large number of projects, if we were to undertake projects like this, we would expect neither a profit nor loss from them, on average.

Taking Risk into Account

One problem with this approach is that it assumes investors are risk-neutral. Essentially there are two components to this issue. One is that it assumes that the potential size of the loss is not a major concern to investors. The second is that it assumes that investors do not mind losing if they are likely to win an equal amount.

Consider the size of the potential loss first. In the preceding example, the potential loss is $150,000, whereas the potential gain is only $50,000. Some managers may be reluctant to risk such a large potential loss for such a small potential reward. Even though the gain is more likely than the loss, and even though mathematically there will be no loss on average, managers may reject any projects that bear the potential of a large loss.

Next consider the notion that investors do not mind losing if they are likely to win an equal amount. The risk-neutral perspective is that in the long run, with enough projects, one should come out even. Many managers might argue, however, that there is no assurance that will happen. And even if it does, they may be fired before the laws of chance turn their way. Given that perspective, it makes sense to demand a risk premium. That is, rather than being neutral, one might decide that a project must have a positive expected value to be accepted. Why undertake projects that you don't expect to make a profit on? A positive expected value represents a reward for being willing to accept the risk of losses. The size of the risk premium should be determined after considering the magnitude of the potential loss in comparison with the magnitude of the potential gain.

The Full Range of Possible Events

In making decisions, one should also attempt to consider all possible states of nature that might occur. In our example, we have treated the problem as if the only possible events are that we buy the machine or not, and that if we buy the machine, the competition may or may not buy it. We have evaluated only two options: We buy it, and they do not, or we buy it, and they also buy it (*see* Exhibit 10–1). We have implicitly assumed that if we do not buy the machine, there is no change from our current status.

However, there is a flaw in the logic. If we does not buy the machine, there are still two possible outcomes: (1) we do not buy, and the competition does not buy; and (2) we do not buy, but the competition does buy. All possible events must be considered in the expected value analysis.

What are the chances that the other company will buy a machine even if we do not? We can only guess at that. However, we have also guessed at the probability that they would buy one if we did. We must recognize the fact that all of these estimates are based on *subjective probability*. When we roll a die, we know that there is a 1/6 chance of each side coming up. Assuming it is a fair die, the probabilities are known with certainty. In situations facing managers, we often do not know with certainty what the probabilities are. There may be situations in which we know with a high degree of confidence what will happen. History may provide information that convinces us there is a 30 percent chance of one event and a 70 percent chance of another. More often than not, however, managers must use their knowledge, experience, and judgment to make a best guess about the likelihood of each event, without a high degree of confidence.

One reason that risk aversion is common, and managers demand a risk premium—a positive rather than zero expected value—is the nature of subjective probabilities. We might have the odds wrong. It is true that having the odds wrong can work for you as well as against you. However, there is always the risk that unknown negative factors not taken into account will determine the probabilities. Therefore, many organizations demand a substantial positive expected value to move forward with a project.

In the machine example, suppose we believe that if we do not buy a machine, there is a 50 percent chance that the other company will. Why might we believe that there is a higher likelihood that they will buy the machine if we do not, then there was if we did buy it? Before we only estimated 25 percent, whereas now we estimate 50 percent. Perhaps we think that they might buy it to compete directly with us, but there is a low chance (25 percent) of that occurring because then we would both lose money. However, if they have the market to themselves, it is more likely to be profitable. Therefore, they are more likely to make the investment.

Suppose we calculate that if they buy the machine and we do not, we will lose some of our current market share for our other products. As a result, our current profits will decline by $30,000. On the other hand, if neither buys the machine, there will be no financial effect. In that case, the options and expected values would appear as in Exhibit 10–2. Note that this exhibit provides a more comprehensive look at all of the possible events that might occur. In looking at Exhibit 10–1, we ignored an event that might occur if we do not buy.

Exhibit 10–1 indicates there is no expected profit or loss from buying a machine. Based on that, without any risk premium, we would be unlikely to buy the machine. However, the expected value analysis in Exhibit 10–2 reveals that the company may still have a clear financial interest in buying it. It turns out that the company has a negative expected value if it does not buy the machine!

In other words, if we buy it, we might make money or lose money and the expected value is zero. If we do not buy it, Exhibit 10–2 reveals, we will either have no financial effect or a loss, and the expected value is a loss of $15,000. This is based on the 50 percent chance that the competitor will buy the machine, inflicting a $30,000 loss on our company. It is easy to see why it is necessary to be inclusive in considering all alternative events that might occur. Preparing a decision tree of the possible outcomes, such as appears in Exhibit 10–2, can help us visualize whether all alternative possibilities have been considered.

EXHIBIT 10-2
Expected Value of Expanded Purchase Alternatives

		Probability	Payoff	Expected Value
	Competitor buys machine	25% ×	−$150,000	= −$37,500
We buy machine	Competitor does not buy machine	75% ×	$50,000	= $37,500
We do not buy machine	Competitor buys machine	50% ×	−$30,000	−$15,000
	Competitor does not buy machine	50% ×	$0	$0

Expected Value −$15,000

NETWORK COST BUDGETING

Network analysis is a popular management tool used primarily for planning and controlling nonroutine, complex projects. It also may be beneficial for some ongoing activities in many organizations. Using arrow diagrams, a *critical path* is found that determines the least amount of time for project completion. It is possible to enhance the value of network analysis by connecting it directly to costs and budgeting. Network cost budgeting refers to combining the techniques of network analysis with cost accounting to generate the most cost-effective approach to the project.

In network analysis, it is often assumed that the network is laid out in an optimal fashion. However, it is clear that networks do not indicate the only possible timelines. By using overtime or extra staff, it is often possible to reduce the amount of time needed. Such time reductions are often associated with extra cost, but that cost may be justified if other benefits result.

For example, suppose that a company plans to construct and open a new facility. Once opened, it is expected to yield profits for the company. Each day of delay in opening the unit means lost profits. If the unit can be opened earlier by adding extra construction crews, it may be worth the extra cost.

Therefore, a technique is needed to match the potential benefits of shortening the project time with the additional costs that would create. Network cost budgeting, sometimes referred to as program evaluation and review technique (PERT) cost budgeting, is a technique designed for working out those calculations.

Network Analysis

A network uses a diagram to show the relationships in a complex project. Arrows represent specific activities that must be done. It is possible to have many activities all begin from one point and take place at the same time. The crucial aspect of network analysis is identifying those activities that must be completed before some other activity or activities can commence.

Exhibit 10–3 presents an example of a simple network diagram. For the example, assume that a company has determined midway through a construction project that it might benefit from earlier completion. There are eight major components of construction that remain to be completed. Some steps can occur while other activities are occurring, while others cannot. In Exhibit 10–3, each activity starts at a numbered point. Each activity has a number at its start and at its completion, and the activity can be identified by those two numbers, such as Activity 1-2 or 2-4, or they can be given names such as Task A, Task B, Task C, etc. An alternative presentation is to place each activity in a "node" as in Exhibit 10–4, and refer to it by the name or description in the node.

EXHIBIT 10-3
Network Analysis

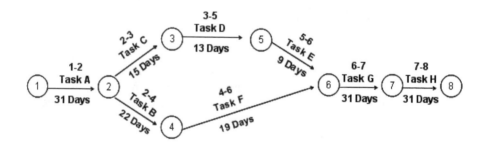

EXHIBIT 10-4
Network Analysis Using Nodes

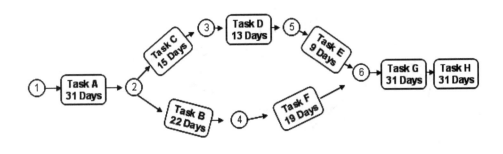

The Critical Path Method

A critical path is always found as an element of network analysis. In fact, one widely used network approach is called the *critical path method (CPM)*. To find the critical path, it is necessary to determine the expected length of time for each activity. In this example, it is assumed that an initial plan was developed as follows:

- Task A or Activity 1-2: 31 days.
- Task B or Activity 2-4: 22 days.
- Task C or Activity 2-3: 15 days.
- Task D or Activity 3-5: 13 days.
- Task E or Activity 5-6: 9 days.
- Task F or Activity 4-6: 19 days.
- Task G or Activity 6-7: 31 days.
- Task H or Activity 7-8: 31 days.

Note that all days are shown, including weekend days. In this plan, however, it was not assumed that any work would take place on weekends.

The critical path for the project is shown in bold in Exhibit 10–5. One route or path through the network is 1-2-3-5-6-7-8. The total days for that path are 130. In this simple example, there is only one other path through the network. That is 1-2-4-6-7-8. Adding up all of the days along that path comes to a total of 134 days. The critical path is determined by totaling the days required for each possible route through the network and finding the longest one. Recall that all of the tasks must be undertaken. Therefore, the project can be achieved in no less time than the time it takes for the longest path.

EXHIBIT 10-5
Critical Path

Working Time vs. Slack Time

Some time allocated to a project is actual working time. However, much of the time in any project is waiting time. Waiting time between activities is clearly identified in network analysis. For example, in Exhibit 10–5, Activities 2-3-5-6 take 37 days, whereas Activities 2-4-6 take 41 days. That means that if 2-3-5-6 are done as expeditiously as possible, at the end there will be a 4-day wait while 2-4-6 catches up. Those 4 days are referred to as *slack time*. A delay in the completion of 2-3-5-6 would have no impact in delaying the overall project. However, even a one-day delay in 2-4-6 would delay the project. That is why the critical path line goes through those activities.

Consideration of Costs

To get the project done in an extremely short time period may require very high costs. These often appear in the form of labor costs for extra workers or for overtime. An underlying assumption of network analysis is that finding the critical path and minimizing it also minimizes costs. Further, knowing which paths have slack and allowing that slack also keeps costs down—no overtime should be spent to complete an activity in the minimal number of days if that activity has several slack days. If the activity falls a day or two behind, it will reduce the amount of slack, but won't delay completion of the project.

However, cost minimization is not necessarily optimal. It may be beneficial to push a project through faster, even if at a higher cost. The enhancement that network cost budgeting adds to network analysis is determination of the optimal time and cost budget for the project. The first step in this process is to determine the "least cost, least time" to complete each activity. That is, first one must determine the lowest cost for an activity, and then one must determine the fewest possible days for the activity within that cost. In many cases, there is only one number of days for which the least cost is attainable. In other cases, however, it may be possible to do an activity at the lowest cost over a range of possible days. In those cases, we want to find the fewest possible days for accomplishing the activity at the lowest cost. We will assume that the example shown in Exhibit 10–5 presents the least cost, least time for each activity. The project can be shortened only by decreasing the time required for an activity on the critical path. The critical path 1-2-4-6-7-8 was indicated in Exhibit 10–5.

Next, the accountant must determine how much extra it would cost to shorten each activity by one day. In most of the activities, such cost will represent the cost of additional personnel or the cost of weekend or other overtime work. Recall that the days shown in this network include weekends, but assume they are not worked. By working a 6- or 7-day week during the project, or by working 12 hours a day instead of 8, or by hiring additional staff, some activities (perhaps most activities) can be completed in a shorter number of calendar days.

The Network Cost Calculation

To carry out this process, the organization will have to review each activity and the various individuals involved. There must be consideration of which employees are paid an annual salary with no overtime, and which individuals will be paid overtime. What is the extra cost per overtime hour? How much overtime would have to be worked to reduce the activity required time by one day? This process must be done for each activity.

Once that is completed, we can determine which activity is the least costly to shorten by one day. For example, suppose that the following information was calculated for Activities 1-2 and 2-4 on the Exhibit 10–5 critical path:

Activity 1-2
Original days: 31
Extra cost to go from 31 to 30 days: $800
Extra cost to go from 30 to 29 days: $1,100
Extra cost to go from 29 to 28 days: $1,100
Extra cost to go from 28 to 27 days: Not feasible to go below 28 days

Activity 2-4
Original days: 22
Extra cost to go from 22 to 21 days: $400
Extra cost to go from 21 to 20 days: $400
Extra cost to go from 20 to 19 days: $400
Extra cost to go from 19 to 18 days: $400
Extra cost to go from 18 to 17 days: $600
Extra cost to go from 17 to 16 days: $600
Extra cost to go from 16 to 15 days: Not feasible to go below 16 days

Once the cost per day reduction is known for each activity, the next step would be to determine the benefits of a shortened project and compare the costs of the least costly way to reduce one day with the benefits of such a reduction.

The Network Benefit Calculation

To compare the costs of a faster project with its benefits, we need to know the benefits. What are the benefits of shortening a project? If we are planning to open a facility, benefits would be the daily profits once it is opened. Suppose it is hoped that the facility will generate profits of $1,200 per day, and that we expect at least $1,000 per day can be earned. The sooner the project is completed, the sooner the company will begin earning at least $1,000 per day.

Each day that the critical path can be reduced produces an anticipated benefit of $1,000 to $1,200. Therefore, overtime and other measures should be used to reduce the critical path, as long as the extra cost for each day the project is reduced is less than $1,000. In Activity 1-2, one day can be saved for $800. The time for that activity should therefore be reduced by one day. However, reducing that activity by another day would cost an additional $1,100. Therefore, the activity should not be reduced by two days.

In Activity 2-4, there could be a reduction of up to six days. The first four cost an extra $400 each, and the next two cost an extra $600 each. However, it is important to remember that reductions in days are effective only as long as they are on the critical path. The first four days that Activity 2-4 is shortened will make the total number of days for both Paths 1-2-3-5-6-7-8 and 1-2-4-6-7-8 equal. There will no longer be any slack in the 1-2-3-5-6-7-8 path. The implication is that before one shortens Activity 2-4 by a fifth day, the extra cost of reducing Path 2-3-5-6 by one day must be considered. It will be necessary to reduce both 2-4-6 and 2-3-5-6 by one day to save a day on the total project. You would not reduce activity 2-4 by a fifth day if the combined cost of that reduction plus a reduction of one day in the 2-3-5-6 activities would exceed the $1,000 benefit.

Further Complications

Another problem to consider is the selection of which activities to shorten. For instance, does it make more sense to shorten 2-4 or to shorten 4-6 by a day? In certain areas of the network, this is not a problem. If only one path is over part of a network, we want to shorten all activities along that part of the path as long as the benefit exceeds the extra cost. Therefore, Activities 1-2, 6-7 and 7-8 should all be shortened as much as possible. Each of those activities is on the critical path, and each one occurs at a point in the network where there is only one activity at a time. The case of Activities 2-4 and 4-6 is more complicated. Before deciding to reduce 2-4 by four days, as we did above, we must consider whether it would have been cheaper to reduce Activity 4-6 instead.

The concept of network cost budgeting has significant potential benefit for bringing the length of projects under control. The introduction of computer software that makes network analysis on personal computers possible has increased the accessibility and usefulness of this technique.

KEY TERMS

Expected value—a technique that estimates the costs or revenues based on the likelihood of each possible outcome. It utilizes a weighted average of the possible outcomes.

Network analysis—a management tool that finds the *critical path* to achieve the least amount of time for project completion.

Critical path—the set of activities which total to the longest overall time to complete the project. A delay in any task in the critical path will delay project completion. Speeding up any task in the critical path can speed completion of the entire project.

Network cost budgeting—combines the technique of network analysis with cost accounting to generate the most cost-effective approach to the project, often recommending extra spending in order to reduce the time to accomplish the critical path.

QUESTIONS FOR REVIEW

1. Can managers take actions that affect events?
2. Does an expected value represent the most likely outcome?
3. True or false: A rational decision maker would always want to undertake a proposed project with a positive expected value.
4. In expected value calculations, how reliable are the probabilities used?
5. What is network analysis?
6. What is network cost budgeting?
7. Design a network cost budget. Show an initial plan, and then revise it to reduce the period of time needed. Explain how each time savings is achieved. Show the critical path. Show slack. Prepare a separate calculation that shows a cost-benefit analysis for reducing the time to accomplish the task.
8. We are planning the staff level for a company. The managers want to know what it will cost for labor for each unit made. They have decided to staff for a moderate number of units. If volume is low, staff will be sitting around with nothing to do and cost per unit will be high. If volume is high, they will have to pay overtime rates and cost per unit will be high. Based on the table below, what is the expected cost per unit for labor?

Units Sold	Probability	Labor Cost Per Unit
20,000—25,000	.10	$60
25,001—30,000	.40	50
30,001—35,000	.35	50
35,001—40,000	.15	60

Chapter 11

Capital Budgeting

Analysis of investments in long-term projects is referred to as *capital budgeting*. Long-term projects are worthy of special attention because of the fact that they frequently require large initial investments, and because the cash outlay to start such projects often precedes the receipt of cash inflows by a significant period of time. In such cases, we are interested in being able to predict the profitability of the project. We want to be sure that the profits from the project are greater than what we could have received from alternative investments or uses of our money.

This chapter focuses on how managers can evaluate long-term projects and determine whether the expected return from the projects is great enough to justify taking the risks that are inherent in long-term investments. Several different approaches to capital budgeting are discussed: the payback method, the net present value method, and the internal rate of return method. The latter two of these methods require us to acknowledge the implications of the *time value of money*.

The time value of money refers to the fact that money received at different points in time is not equally valuable. To give a rather elementary example, suppose that someone offered to buy your product for $250, and that they are willing to pay you either today or one year from today. You will certainly prefer to receive the $250 today. At the very least, you could put the $250 in a bank and earn interest in the intervening year.

Suppose, however, that the buyer offered you $250 today or $330 in twenty-two months. Now your decision is much more difficult. How sure are you that the individual will pay you twenty-two months from now? Perhaps he or she will be bankrupt by then. What could we do with the money if we received it today? Would we put the $250 in some investment that would yield us more than $330 twenty-two months from today? These are questions that we have to be able to answer in order to evaluate long-term investment opportunities. But first let's discuss some basic issues of investment analysis.

INVESTMENT OPPORTUNITIES

The first step that must be taken in investment analysis is to identify the investment opportunity. Such opportunities fall into two major classes: new project investments, and replacement or reinvestment in existing projects. New project ideas can come from a variety of sources. They may be the result of research and development activity or exploration. Your firm may have a department solely devoted to new product development. Ideas may come from outside of the firm. Reinvestment is often the result of production managers pointing out that certain equipment needs to be replaced. Such replacement should not be automatic. If a substantial outlay is required, it may be an appropriate time to reevaluate the product or project to determine if the profits being generated are adequate to justify continued additional investment.

DATA GENERATION

The data needed to evaluate an investment opportunity are the expected cash flows related to the investment. Many projects have a large initial cash outflow as we acquire plant and equipment and incur start-up costs prior to actual production and sale of our new product. In the years that follow, there will be receipt of cash from the sale of our product (or service) and there will be cash expenditures related to the expenses of production and sales. We refer to the difference between each year's cash receipts and cash expenditures as the net cash flow for that year.

You're probably wondering why we have started this discussion with cash flow instead of net income for each year. There are several important reasons. First, net income, even if it were a perfect measure of profitability, doesn't consider the time value of money. For instance, suppose that we have two alternative projects. The first project requires that we purchase a machine for $10,000 in cash. The machine has a ten-year useful life. Depreciation expense is $1,000 per year.

A totally different project requires that we lease a machine for $1,000 a year for ten years, with lease payments at the start of each year. Are the two alternative projects equal? No, they aren't. Even though they both have an expense of $1,000 per year for ten years, one project requires us to spend $10,000 at the beginning. The other project requires an outlay of only $1,000 in the first year. In this second project, we could hold on to $9,000 that had been spent right away in the first project. That $9,000 can be invested and can earn additional profits for the firm before the next lease payment is due.

The data needed for investment or project analysis includes cash flow information for each of the years of the investment's life. Naturally we cannot be 100 percent certain about how much the project will cost and how much we will eventually receive. There is no perfect solution for the fact that we have to make estimates. However, we must be aware at all times that, because our estimates may not be fully correct, there is an element of risk. Project analysis must be able to assess whether the expected return can compensate for the risks we are taking. It should also include consideration of any taxes that will have to be paid.

THE PAYBACK METHOD

The payback method of analysis evaluates projects based on how long it takes to recover the amount of money put into the project. The shorter the payback period, the better. Certainly there is some intuitive appeal to this method. The sooner we get our money out of the project, the lower the risk. If we have to wait a number of years for a project to "pay off," all kinds of things can go wrong.

Exhibit 11-1 presents an example of the payback method. In the exhibit, four alternative projects are being compared. In each project, the initial outlay is $400. By the end of 2014, projects one and two have recovered the initial $400 investment. Therefore, they have a payback period of three years. Projects three and four do not recover the initial investment until the end of 2015. Their payback period is four years, and they are therefore considered to be inferior to the other two projects.

EXHIBIT 11-1
Payback Method—Alternative Projects
PROJECT CASH FLOWS

	ONE	TWO	THREE	FOUR
January 2012	$(400)	$(400)	$(400)	$ (400)
2012	0	0	399	300
2013	1	399	0	99
2014	399	1	0	0
2015	500	500	500	5,000
TOTAL	$500	$500	$499	$4,999

It is not difficult at this point to see one of the principal weaknesses of the payback method. It ignores what happens after the payback period. The total cash flow for project four is much greater than the cash received from any of the other projects, yet it is considered to be one of the worst of the projects. In a situation in which cash flows extend for twenty or thirty years, this problem might not be as obvious, but it could cause us to choose incorrectly.

Is that the only problem with this method? No. Another obvious problem stems from the fact that according to this method, projects one and two are equally attractive because they both have a three-year payback period. Although their total cash flows are the same, the timing is different. Project one provides $1 in 2013, and then $399 during 2014. Project two generates $399 in 2013 and only $1 in 2014. Are these two projects equally as good because their total cash flows are the same? *No.* The extra $398 received in 2013 from project two is available for investment in other profitable opportunities for one extra year, as compared to project one. Therefore, it is clearly superior to project one. The problem is that the payback method doesn't formally take into account the time value of money.

This deficiency is obvious when looking at project three as well. Project three appears to be less valuable than projects one or two on two counts. First, its payback is four years rather than three, and second, its total cash flow is less than either project one or two. But if we consider the time value of money, then project three is better than either project one or two. With project three, we get the $399 right away. The earnings on that $399 during 2013 and 2014 will more than offset the shorter payback and larger cash flow of projects one and two.

Although payback is commonly used for a quick and dirty project evaluation, problems associated with the payback method are quite serious. There are several methods commonly referred to as discounted cash flow models that overcome these problems. Later in this chapter, we will discuss the most commonly used of these methods, net present value and internal rate of return. However, before we discuss them, we need to specifically consider the issues and mechanics surrounding time value of money calculations.

THE TIME VALUE OF MONEY

It is very easy to think of projects in terms of total dollars of cash received. Unfortunately, this tends to be misleading. Consider a project in which we invest $400 and in return we receive $520 after three years. We have made a cash profit of $120. Because the profit was earned over a three-year period, it is a profit of $40 per year. Because $40 is 10 percent of the initial $400 investment, we have apparently earned a 10 percent return on our money. While this is true, that 10 percent is calculated based on simple interest.

Consider putting money into a bank that pays a 10 percent return "compounded annually." The term compounded annually means that the bank calculates interest at the end of each year and adds the interest onto the initial amount deposited. In future years, interest is earned not only on the initial deposit, but also on interest earned in prior years. If we put $400 in the bank at 10 percent compounded annually, we would earn $40 of interest in the first year. At the beginning of the second year we would have $440. The interest on the $440 would be $44. At the beginning of the third year, we would have $484 (the $400 initial deposit plus the $40 interest from the first year, plus the $44 interest from the second year). The interest for the third year would be $48.40. We would have a total of $532.40 at the end of three years.

The 10 percent compounded annually gives a different result from the 10 percent simple interest. We have $532.40 instead of $520 from the project. The reason for this difference is that in the case of the project, we did not get any cash flow until the end of the project. In the case of the bank, we were given a cash flow at the end of each year. We reinvested that cash to earn additional interest.

Consider a cash amount of $100 today. We refer to it as a present value (PV). How much could this cash amount accumulate to if we invested it at an interest rate (i) of 10 percent for a period of time (N) equal to two years? Assuming that we compound annually, the $100 would earn $10 in the first year (10 percent of $100). This $10 would be added to the $100. In the second year our $110 would earn $11 (that is, 10 percent of $110). The future value (FV) is $121. That is, two years into the future we would have $121.

Mechanically this is a simple process—multiply the interest rate times the initial investment to find the interest for the first period. Add the interest to the initial investment. Then multiply the interest rate times the initial investment plus all interest already accumulated to find the interest for the second year.

While this is not complicated, it can be rather tedious. To simplify this process, mathematical formulas have been developed to solve a variety of time value of money problems. The most basic of these formulas states that:

$$FV = PV (1 + i)^N$$

This formula has been built into both business calculators and computer spreadsheet programs. If we supply the appropriate raw data, the calculator or spreadsheet software performs all of the necessary interest computations.

For instance, if we wanted to know what $ 100 would grow to in two years at 10 percent, we would simply tell our calculator that the present value, PV, equals $100; the interest rate, i, equals 10 percent; and the number of periods, N, equals 2. Then we would ask the calculator to compute FV, the future value.

Can we use this method if compounding occurs more frequently than once a year? Bonds often pay interest twice a year. Banks often compound monthly to calculate mortgage payments. Using our example of $100 invested for two years at 10 percent, we could easily adjust the calculation for semiannual, quarterly, or monthly compounding. For example, for quarterly compounding, N equals 8 (four quarters per year for two years) and i equals 2^1/2 percent (10 percent per year divided by four quarters per year). For monthly compounding, N equals 24 and i equals 10/12. Thus, for monthly compounding, we would tell the calculator that PV = $100, i = 10/12, and N = 24. Then we would tell the calculator to compute FV. We need a calculator designed to perform present value functions in order to do this. Note that most calculators will interpret 10 input as i to be 10%. Computer spreadsheet programs require that you include the % sign.

If we expect to receive $121 in two years, can we calculate how much that is worth today? This question calls for a reversal of the compounding process. Suppose we would normally expect to earn a return on our money of 10 percent. What we are really asking here is, "How much would we have to invest today at 10 percent, to get $121 in two years?" The answer requires unraveling compound interest. If we calculate how much of the $121 to be received in two years is interest earned on our original investment, then we know the present value of that $121. This process of removing or unraveling the interest is called *discounting*. The 10 percent rate is referred to as a discount rate. Using the calculator, this is a simple process. We again supply the i and the N, but instead of telling the calculator the PV and asking for the FV, we tell it the FV and ask it to calculate the PV.

Earlier in this chapter, we posed a problem of whether to accept $250 today or $330 in twenty-two months. Assume that we can invest money in a project with a 10 percent return and monthly compounding. Which choice is better? We can tell our calculator (by the way, if you have access to a business-oriented calculator, you can work out these calculations as we go) that FV = $330, N = 22, and i = 10/12. If we then ask it to compute PV, we find that the present value is $275. This means that if we invest $275 today at 10 percent compounded monthly for twenty-two months, it accumulates to $330. That is, receiving $330 in twenty-two months is equivalent to having $275 today. Think of the problem as "would you prefer to have $250 today or $275 today?" Clearly you would prefer $275. Well, in that case you should choose the alternative of waiting twenty-two months for the $330, because $330 in twenty-two month is worth the same to us as $275 today. This assumes there is no risk of default. Looking at this problem another way, how much would our $250 grow to if we invested it for twenty-two months at 10 percent? Here we have PV = $250, N = 22, and i = 10/12. Our calculation indicates that the FV = $300. If we wait, we will get $330 twenty-two months from now. If we take $250 today and invest it at 10 percent, we only have $300 twenty-two months from now. Twenty-two months from now would you rather have $300 or $330? Clearly, $330. So, we find that we are better off waiting for the $330, assuming we are sure that we will receive it.

Are we limited to solving for only the present or future value? No, this methodology is quite flexible. Assume, for example, that we wish to put $100,000 aside today to pay off a $1,000,000 loan in fifteen years. What rate of return must be earned, compounded annually, for our $100,000 to grow to $1,000,000? Here we have the present value, or $100,000; the number of periods, fifteen years; and the future value, or $1,000,000. It is a simple process to determine the required rate of return. If we simply supply our calculator with the PV, FV, and N, the calculator readily supplies the i, which is 16.6 percent in this case.

Or, for that matter, if we had $100,000 today and knew that we could earn a 13 percent return, we would calculate how long it would take to accumulate $1,000,000. Here we know PV, FV, and i, and we wish to find N. In this case, N = 18.8 years. Given any three of our four basic components, PV, FV, N, and i, we can solve for the fourth. This is because the calculator is simply using our basic formula stated earlier and solving for the missing variable.

So, far, however, we have considered only one single payment. Suppose that we don't have $100,000 today, but we are willing to put $10,000 aside every year for fifteen years. If we earn 12 percent, will we have enough to repay $1,000,000 at the end of the fifteen years? There are two ways to solve this problem. We can determine the future value, fifteen years from now, of each of the individual payments. We would have to do fifteen separate calculations because each succeeding payment earns interest for one year less. We would then have to sum the future value of each of the payments. This is rather tedious. A second way to solve this problem is by using a formula that accumulates the payments for us. The formula is:

$$FV = PMT \left[\frac{(1 + i)^N - 1}{i} \right]$$

In this formula, PMT represents the payment made each period, or annuity payment. Although you may think of annuities as payments made once a year, an annuity simply means payments that are exactly the same in amount, and are made at equally spaced intervals of time, such as monthly, quarterly, or annually.

To solve problems with a series of identical payments, we have five variables instead of the previous four. We now have FV, PV, N, i, and PMT.

Annuity formulas are built into business calculators and computer spreadsheet programs such as Excel.

Annuity formulas provide you with a basic framework for solving many problems concerning receipt or payment of cash in different time periods. Keep in mind that the annuity method can be used only if the amount of the payment is the same each period. If that isn't the case, each payment must be evaluated separately.

Using Computer Spreadsheets for TVM Computations

As noted above, electronic spreadsheet software programs can be used to solve TVM problems. Excel has TVM formulas built into the program.[1] Excel uses the following abbreviations for the variables:

PV—Present Value

FV—Future Value

Rate—Interest rate

Nper—Number of periods

PMT—Periodic or annuity payment

Consider the problem of finding the future value of $100 invested for two years at 6 percent. Using Excel, begin clicking on a cell where you want the FV to appear. Then type:

$$=FV($$

As soon as you do that, Excel will show the variables that should be inserted, and the order in which they have to entered. *See* Exhibit 11-2.

EXHIBIT 11-2
Using Excel to Solve for FV. Initial View.

	A	B	C	D	E
1	=FV(				
2	FV(rate, nper, pmt, [pv], [type])				
3					
4					
5					
6					

Note that we are trying to solve for the FV in Cell A1. When we start the formula in A1, just below it we see the full set of variables Excel needs: FV(rate, nper, pmt, [pv], [type]). The brackets around "pv" and "type" indicate that those variables are optional. We can sometimes ignore them and still be able to compute the FV.

The next step in using Excel to find the FV, is to type the interest rate into the formula. In this case we would type 6%. Be sure to include the percent sign, or alternatively type .06. If you simply use 6 without the percent sign, Excel will interpret that as 600% and badly throw off the answer. After typing 6% type a

---

[1] The Excel approach used in this chapter is based on Microsoft Excel 2007. Other versions of Excel may differ somewhat in minor respects.

comma to separate the rate from the next variable. Since we are investing for 2 years, we would next type a 2 followed by a comma. In this problem there is no repeating periodic payment, so we have no value for the PMT. However, it is necessary to add another comma. That is, after the 2 there will be two commas in the formula. This tells Excel that there is no value for the PMT. If we didn't put the second consecutive comma, when we enter the value for the PV, Excel would interpret that value as being a value for a PMT. Next we enter -100. The PV is entered as a negative number because you are paying out money now, so that you will receive money in the future. We can ignore the Type variable for now. *See* Exhibit 11-3 to see what the Excel spreadsheet would look like at this point. We can then simply hit the Enter key at this point and Excel will solve for the FV and the spreadsheet will appear as seen in Exhibit 11-4.

EXHIBIT 11-3
Data Inserted to Solve for FV

	A	B	C	D	E
1	=FV(6%,2, , -100				
2	FV(rate, nper, pmt, [pv], [type])				
3					
4					
5					
6					

EXHIBIT 11-4
FV Result

	A	B	C	D	E
1	$112.36				
2					
3					
4					
5					
6					

Similarly, we can compute any of the other variables. Suppose that you want to borrow money from a bank for a mortgage on your new factory building. You need to borrow $1,000,000 today. The bank is willing to lend to you for 30 years at 8%, with payments each month at the end of the month. How could we solve for the monthly mortgage payment that we will have to make? Type:

=PMT(

and you will see something that looks like Exhibit 11-5. Next we will provide the rate by typing 8%/12 followed by a comma. It is important to let Excel do all the computations. There is a temptation to simply divide 8% by 12 to find the monthly interest rate of .67%. The problem is that is rounded off. 8%/12 is closer to .666666666666666667% than to .67%. While this might not seem to be a big deal, with monthly compounding over a 30 year period, it can have a significant impact on the result. So if we insert the interest rate as "8%/12" we are taking much less risk of rounding errors impacting our final result. *See* Exhibit 11-6.

EXHIBIT 11-5
Excel Formula for PMT

	A	B	C	D	E
1	=pmt(				
2	PMT(rate, nper, pv, [fv], [type])				
3					
4					
5					
6					

Next we can insert 30*12 followed by a comma. This represents 30 years with 12 monthly compounding periods each year. Next we have to enter the amount of money that we will be receiving today. We show that as 1000000 followed by a comma. Note, it is very important that the PV not be entered with commas. That is, if you show the PV as 1,000,000, Excel will interpret the first comma in that number as separating one variable from another. So it would interpret the PV as being 1 if you entered 1,000,000, and then will interpret the value for FV as being 000 and the value for type as being 000. So be careful to enter the number simply as 1000000 followed by a comma. There is no value for FV in this problem, so we would next enter another comma. The two commas in a row lets Excel know there is no FV value.

EXHIBIT 11-6
Excel Formula for PMT with Variables Inserted

	A	B	C	D	E
1	=PMT(8%/12,30*12,1000000, ,0				
2					
3					
4					
5					
6					

This brings us to the "type" variable. This variable examines whether periodic payments come at the beginning or end of each period. Lease payments, for example, typically are made at the beginning of each month. You lease an office and pay for the first month prior to use. For mortgages, in contrast, you generally borrow the money and don't make the first payment until the end of the first month. If payments come at the end of each period, that is referred to an annuity in arrears or an ordinary annuity. The value for the "Type" variable in Excel for an ordinary annuity should be 0. You can either enter a 0 or just ignore the variable and Excel will default to an ordinary annuity. If payments come at the beginning of each period that is referred to as an annuity in advance, and the Type variable must be shown in Excel as a 1.

Exhibit 11-6 shows the PMT formula with the values for the rate, nper, pv, and type variables inserted. If you were to hit the Enter key at that point, the solution would appear as in Exhibit 11-7. If you borrowed the $1 million today, you would have to make monthly payments of $7,337.65 for 30 years.

EXHIBIT 11-7
PMT Result

	A	B	C	D	E
1	($7,337.65)				
2					
3					
4					
5					
6					

This $7,337.65 result shows as a negative number because you would have to pay that amount, so the cash is flowing out each month. In general, there has to be at least one positive cash flow and one negative cash flow in each TVM problem. If you were to try to solve for the Rate or the Nper and you showed both the PV and FV as positive numbers, Excel would give an error message. It would not be able to solve the problem. Excel assumes that either money is paid now and received later, or vice versa. If all dollar amount are shown as positive numbers or all dollar amounts are shown as negative number, Excel cannot compute a solution.

If the values for the variables are shown elsewhere in the spreadsheet, then rather than typing values into the Excel formula, we can just use cell references. For example, in Exhibit 11-8, note that the Excel formula for the PMT appears as =PMT(A4,A5,A3, , 0. The advantage of using cell references is that if any of the variables change, the PMT would automatically be updated. For example, if we want to compare the monthly payments for this loan to a 20 year loan, we can just replace the 360 value in Cell A5 with 240 (i.e. 20 years × 12 months a year = 240) , and the monthly payment will automatically be recomputed.

Note in Exhibit 11-8 that the $1 million amount of the loan is formatted with commas. If you are using cell references, Excel understands that the value in Cell A3 is just one variable, so the commas within the number are not a problem. Also, although it looks like the rate has been rounded off in Cell A4, the formula for A4 was =8%/12. That means that the actual number that Excel will use for the computations will be computed by Excel and will carried out far more decimal places than are shown in the computer display.

EXHIBIT 11-8
Computing PMT Using Cell References

◢	A	B	C	D	E
1	**Computation of Monthly Mortgage Payment**				
2					
3	$1,000,000	Amount of Loan			
4	0.67%	Rate			
5	360	Nper			
6					
7	=PMT(A4,A5,A3, ,0|				
8	PMT(rate, nper, pv, [fv], **[type]**)				
9					

In a similar manner, Excel can be used to compute the PV, Rate, or Nper. The Formulas that Excel will display for each variable are:

PV =PV(rate,nper,pmt,[fv],[type])

FV =FV(rate,nper,pmt,[pv],[type])

Rate =Rate(nper,pmt,pv, [fv],[type],[guess])

Nper =NPer(rate,pmt,pv,[fv],[type])

PMT =PMT(rate,nper,pv,[fv],[type])

In the Excel formula for Rate, note that you are asked for a guess. Sometimes if you have a rough idea of the approximate rate Excel can compute the result faster than if it has to compute the rate without a rough starting point. So you can put your rough guess at the answer in this spot of the formula. However, inserting a guess for the rate will rarely speed up the computation by even one full second, so any time savings will not be noticeable. Given that, most Excel users don't bother entering a guess.

THE NET PRESENT VALUE (NPV) METHOD

The net present value (NPV) method of analysis determines whether a project earns more or less than a stated desired rate of return. The starting point in the analysis is determination of that rate.

The Hurdle Rate

The rate of return required in order for a project to be acceptable is called the *required rate of return* or the *hurdle rate*. An acceptable project should be able to hurdle over, that is, earn a higher rate of return than this rate.

The rate must take into account two key factors. First, we require a base profit to compensate for investing money in the project. We have a variety of opportunities for which we could use our money. We need to be paid a profit for foregoing the use of our money in some alternative venture. The second element concerns risk. Any time we enter a new investment, there is an element of risk. Perhaps the project won't work out exactly as expected. The project may turn out to be a failure. We have to be paid for being willing to undertake these risks. The two elements taken together determine our hurdle rate.

There is no one unique, standard required rate of return that is used by all companies. Different industries tend to have different base rates of return. Further, within an industry one firm may have some advantage over other firms (for example, economies of scale) that allow it to have a higher base return. On top of that, different firms, and even different projects for one firm, have different types and degrees of risk. Buying a machine to use for putting Coca-Cola in bottles involves much less risk than developing new soft drink products.

One of the most prevalent risks that investors take is loss of purchasing power. That is, price-level inflation makes our money less valuable over time. Suppose we could buy a TV for $100, but instead we invest that money in a business. If the firm uses that money to generate a pretax profit of $4 in a year when the inflation rate is 4 percent, did we have a good year, bad year, or neutral year? Because we have to pay some taxes to the government on our $4 pretax profit, we had a bad year. After paying taxes we have less than $104 at the end of the year. But, due to inflation, it costs $104 to buy a TV set. This means that in deciding if a project is worthwhile, we have to consider whether the rate of return is high enough to cover our after-tax loss of purchasing power due to inflation.

We must also consider a variety of business risks. What if no one buys the product, or he or she buys it, but fails to pay us? If the product is made or sold internationally, we incur foreign exchange risk and foreign political risk. The specific types of risks faced by a company depend on its industry. The company's past experience with projects like the one being evaluated should be a guide in determining the risk portion of the hurdle rate.

When we add the desired return to all of the risk factors, the total is the firm's hurdle rate. In most firms, the top financial officers determine an appropriate hurdle rate or rates and inform nonfinancial managers that this hurdle rate must be anticipated for a project to receive approval. Therefore, you will not usually have to go through a calculation of the hurdle rate yourself.

NPV Calculations

Once we know our hurdle rate, we can use the NPV method to assess whether a project is acceptable. The NPV method compares the present value of a project's cash inflows to the present value of its cash outflows. If the present value of the inflows is greater than the outflows, then the project is profitable because it is earning a rate of return that is greater than the hurdle rate. For example, suppose that a potential project for our firm requires an initial cash outlay of $10,000. We expect the project to produce a net after-tax cash flow (cash inflows less cash outflows) of $6,500 in each of the two years of the project's life. Suppose our after-tax hurdle rate is 18 percent. Is this project worthwhile?

The cash receipts total $13,000, which is a profit of $3,000 overall, or $1,500 per year on our $10,000 investment. Is that a compounded return of at least 18 percent? At first glance it would appear that the answer is "no" because $1,500 is only 15 percent of $10,000. However, we haven't left our full $10,000 invested for the full two years. Our positive cash flow at the end of the first year is $6,500. We are not only making $1,500 profit, but we are also getting back half ($5,000) of our original investment. During the second year, we earn $ 1,500 profit on a remaining investment of only $5,000. It is not simply how much money you get from the project, but when you get it that is important.

The present value of an annuity of $6,500 per year for two years at 18 percent is $10,177 which can be computed in Excel using the following formula: = PV (18%, 2, –6500). The present value of the initial $10,000 outflow is simply $10,000 because it is paid at the start of the project. The NPV is the present value of the inflows, $10,177, less the present value of the outflows, $10,000, which is $177. This number is greater than zero, so the project does indeed yield a return greater than 18 percent, on an annually compounded basis.

It may not be intuitively clear why this method works, or indeed, that it works at all. However, consider making a deal with your friend who is a banker. You agree that you will put a sum of money into the bank. At the end of the first year, the banker adds 18 percent interest to your account and you then withdraw $6,500. At the end of year two, the banker credits interest to the balance in your account at an 18 percent rate. You then withdraw $6,500, which is exactly the total in the account at that time. The account will then have a zero balance. You ask your friend how much you must deposit today in order to be able to make the two future withdrawals. He replies, "$10,177."

If we deposit $10,177, at an 18 percent rate, it will earn $1,832 during the first year. This leaves a balance of $12,009 in the account. We then withdraw $6,500, leaving a balance of $5,509 for the start of the second year. During the second year, $5,509 earns interest of $991 at a rate of 18 percent. This means that the balance in the account is $6,500 at the end of the second year. We then withdraw that amount.

The point of this bank deposit example is that when we earlier solved for the present value of the two $6,500 inflows using a hurdle rate of 18 percent, we found PV to be $10,177. We were finding exactly the amount of money we would have to pay today to get two payments of $6,500 if we were to earn exactly 18 percent. If we can invest a smaller amount than $10,177, but still get $6,500 per year for each of the two years, we must be earning more than 18 percent because we are putting in less than would be needed to earn 18 percent, but are getting just as much out. Here, we invest $10,000, which is less than $10,177, so we are earning a rate of return greater than 18 percent.

Conversely, if the banker had told us to invest less than $10,000 (that is, if the present value of the two payments of $6,500 each at 18 percent was less than $10,000), then it means that by paying $10,000 we were putting in more money than we would have to in order to earn 18 percent; therefore we must be earning less than 18 percent.

The NPV method gets around the problems of the payback method. It considers the full project life, and considers the time value of money. Clearly, however, you can see that it is more difficult than the payback method. Another problem with it is that you must determine the hurdle rate before you can do any project analysis. The next method we will look at eliminates the need to have a hurdle rate before performing the analysis.

THE INTERNAL RATE OF RETURN METHOD (IRR)

One of the objections to the NPV method is that it never indicates what rate of return a project is earning. We simply find out whether it is earning more or less than a specified hurdle rate. This creates problems when comparing projects, all of which have positive net present values. Alternatively we can determine the rate of return the project earns, called the Internal Rate of Return (IRR). For example, consider our project discussed earlier that requires a cash outlay of $10,000 and produces a net cash inflow of $6,500 per year for two years.

Excel has a formula built into the program to solve for the IRR. The formula is:

$$=IRR(values, guess)$$

It is not important to enter a value for the guess. One way to approach this formula is to enter the individual values into a set of contiguous cells in the spreadsheet (either in a column or row), and then use cell references, as shown in Exhibit 11-9. Here we see that the initial cash flow and the two annual cash inflows have been put into Cells A1 through A3. In the IRR formula in Cell A5, the cash flow values for the IRR computation are shown as the cell range "A1:A3". If you then hit the Enter key you will see the result, which is 19.4%, as seen in Exhibit 11-10.

EXHIBIT 11-9
Using Cell References Range to Solve for IRR

	A	B	C	D	E
1	(10000)				
2	6500				
3	6500				
4					
5	=IRR(A1:A3				
6	IRR(**values**, [guess])				
7					

EXHIBIT 11-10
IRR Result

	A	B	C	D	E
1	(10000)				
2	6500				
3	6500				
4					
5	19.4%				
6					

If you try to duplicate this example, and don't see 19.4% in the cell where you are computing the IRR, the most likely problem is that your cell is not formatted to display your result as a percentage. You can fix this by first moving your cursor to the cell where your result is shown. Then right-click your mouse (i.e. click on the button on the top right side of the mouse, as opposed to the more frequently used button on the left). A drop-down menu will appear. Select the Format Cells choice. The Format Cells window will then open. Choose the Numbers tab at the top of this window. Then choose Percentage and choose 1 decimal place. Then click OK. Your result should now appear as 19.4%.

As an alternative to showing a cell range, you can enter the values directly into the formula. However, you must show all the values within a set of squiggly brackets { }. Your Excel formula would appear as:

$$=IRR(\{-10000,6500,6500\})$$

Note that the inner set of brackets needs to be squiggly brackets as shown. Other types of brackets will not work.

PROJECT RANKING

Often, we may be faced with a situation in which there are a greater number of acceptable projects than the number that we can afford to finance. In this case, we wish to choose the best projects. A simple way to do this is to determine the internal rate of return on each project and then to rank the projects from the project with the highest IRR to the one with the lowest. We then simply start by accepting projects with the highest IRR and go down the list until we either run out of money or reach our minimum acceptable rate of return.

In general, this approach allows the firm to optimize its overall rate of return. However, it is possible for this approach to have an undesired result. Suppose that one of our very highest-yielding projects is a parking lot. For a total investment of $50,000, we expect to earn a return of $20,000 a year for the next forty years. The internal rate of return on that project is 40 percent. Alternatively, we can build an office building on the same site. For an investment of $10,000,000 we expect to earn $3,000,000 a year for forty years, or an IRR of 30 percent. We can either use the site for the parking lot or the building, but not both. Our other projects have an IRR of 20 percent.

If we build the parking lot because of its high IRR, and therefore bypass the building, we will wind up investing $50,000 at 40 percent and $9,950,000 at 20 percent instead of $ 10,000,000 at 30 percent. This is not an optimal result. We would be better off to bypass the high-yielding parking lot and invest the entire $10,000,000 at 30 percent. Our decision should be based on calculating our weighted average IRR for all projects that we accept.

Excel Excercises

Templates 9-12 may be used to calculate present values, future values, net present values, and internal rates of return, respectively, using your data. These templates are on the CD that accompanies this book.

SUMMARY

Capital budgeting represents one of the most important areas of financial management. In essence, the entire future of the company is on the line. If projects are undertaken that don't yield adequate rates of return, they will have serious long-term consequences for the firm's profitability—and even for its viability.

To adequately evaluate projects, discounted cash flow techniques should be employed. The two most common of these methods are NPV and IRR. The essential ingredient of both of these methods is that they consider the time value of money. A nonfinancial manager doesn't necessarily have to be able to compute present values. It is vital, however, that all managers understand that when money is received or paid can have just as dramatic an impact on the firm as the amount received or paid.

KEY TERMS

Capital budgeting—analysis of long-term projects with respect to risk and profitability.

Net cash flow—the difference between cash receipts and cash disbursements. Cash flow is more useful than net income for project evaluation because net income fails to consider the time value of money.

Time value of money—Other things being equal, we would always prefer to receive cash sooner, or pay cash later. This is because cash can be invested and earn a return in exchange for its use.

    Compounding—calculation of the return on a project, including the return earned on cash flows generated during the life of the project.

    Discounting—a reversal of the compounding process. Discounting allows us to determine what a future cash flow is worth today.

    Present Value (PV)—the value of an amount of money at the start of a project or investment after discounting any future cash flows.

    Future Value (FV)—the amount of money to be paid or received at some future time including the impact of compound interest.

    Number of Compounding Periods (Nper)—the number of compounding periods between the beginning and end of a time value of money computation.

    Rate—the discount rate used in a time value of money computation, adjusted for the number of compounding periods per year.

    Annuities—cash flows of equal amounts, paid or received at evenly spaced periods of time, such as weekly, monthly, or annually.

Project Evaluation

    Payback—a method that assesses how long it will take to receive enough cash from a project to recover the cash invested in that project.

    Discounted cashflow (DCF) analysis—methods that consider the time value of money in evaluating projects.

        a. *Net present value*—method determining whether a project earns more than a particular desired rate of return, also called the hurdle or required rate of return. The hurdle rate is based on a return for the use of money over time, plus a return for risks inherent in the project.

b. *Internal rate of return*—method that finds the specific rate of return a project is expected to earn.

QUESTIONS FOR REVIEW

1. Why does investment analysis focus on cash flow rather than revenue and expense?

2. Suppose that two projects each cost $10,000. The first project returns $3,000 a year for 7 years. The second project returns $5,000 a year for two years. Which has the better payback period? Is that the better project to invest in?

3. Explain compounding and discounting.

4. How much will $8,000 invested at 3 percent simple interest be worth in three years? What will it be worth if the interest rate is 5 percent?

5. How much will $8,000 invested at 3 percent interest be worth in three years if it is compounded annually? Quarterly? How much if the interest rate is 5 percent?

6. If someone offered to pay you $5,000 a year for five years and you could earn 6 percent interest per year, how much would that be worth today?

7. Suppose that you have $50,000 and need to invest it so that you will have $1,000,000 twenty years from now to repay a debt. What interest rate do you have to earn, assuming monthly compounding?

8. Suppose that you have $50,000 available today and can invest it at 7% per year. How long will it be before you have accumulated $500,000 in the investment?

9. Coffin Corporation wants to buy a new hearse for $60,000. It will last for five years. They expect to make 100 trips per year. Coffin uses a discount rate of 6 percent. If they charge $150 per trip, will they have a positive net present value for the investment?

10. Assume that Executive Corporation is considering investing $5,000 today in a new piece of equipment that will provide a service they can charge for. The annual cash profits from the machine will be $600, $700, $800, $900, $1,000, $1,100, $1,200 for each of the seven years of its useful life. What is the IRR on the investment?

Chapter 12

Earned Value Management

Earned Value Management is a technique used to improve the management of *projects*. A project is a limited effort by an organization, having a clear beginning and an end. For example, an old hospital might decide that it needs to totally renovate and update its elevators. However, the renovation is not a simple problem. Considerable logistics will be required for the multi-million dollar project. The elevators are currently quite busy, and although the renovation will increase the speed of the old elevators, taking any elevators out of service for renovations will exacerbate the problem in the short-term. The project must be undertaken in a way that assures safe movement of patients, without excessive inconvenience to staff and visitors. Getting the project done in a planned manner to achieve all projects goals, on time and on budget, will be a challenge. Such a project will be a unique event for the organization, and therefore they will be working without the benefit of a great deal of history and experience in that specific type of project. It is common for projects to have unique elements that increase the uncertainty that surrounds their execution.

Due to the level of uncertainty surrounding projects, as well as the intricate complexities of some projects, the Earned Value Management (EVM) technique was developed to assure that projects could be adequately planned and resources appropriately used. EVM evaluates progress during the life of a project. EVM helps keep track of whether your spending is getting out of control. For example, consider Boston's Central Artery/Tunnel Project, one of the most ambitious public works projects in the history of the United States. The project, generally referred to as the "Big Dig" rerouted a key highway through the city of Boston into a 3.5 mile tunnel running under the city, constructed a tunnel from the city to the airport, included a bridge and other elements. When the project was started in 1985 it was estimated that it would cost just under $3 billion.[1] However, when all was said and done, the total cost of the project reached $22 billion.[2] This kind of project overrun can have disastrous financial consequences for many organizations.

Earned Value Management (EVM) is a technique that provides us with a tool to address this issue. EVM consists of four critical elements:

---

[1] Steve LeBlanc *"On December 31, It's Official: Boston's Big Dig Will Be Done."* The *Washington Post.* http://washingtonpost.com/wp-dyn/content/arti-cle/2007/12/25/AR2007122500600.html?nav=hcmoduletmv, December 26, 2007.

[2] *Big Dig's red ink engulfs state*, Boston Globe, July 17, 2008.

- A plan for the project. This plan needs to specifically identify the work that will be done to make up the project.

- A way to value the elements of the project. This valuation is generally referred to as the Planned Value (PV)[3] or the Budgeted Cost of Work Scheduled (BCWS).

- Metrics that clearly identify how elements of the project will be valued as completed.

- Ongoing progress monitoring.

These metrics allow for measurement of Earned Value (EV) or Budgeted Cost of Work Performed (BCWP) as the work progresses. The PV is the budgeted total cost of the work that has been scheduled. The EV is the budgeted total cost of the work that has been completed. Rather than waiting till 100% of the funds are used up before you find that a project is only 15% complete, use of PV and EV allow you to track how much of the project work is completed concurrently with how much of the money budgeted for the project has been spent.

QUANTIFYING PLANNED VALUE (PV) AND EARNED VALUE (EV)

EVM has elements for the assessment of cost performance (i.e. whether a project is over budget or under budget), the assessment of schedule performance (behind schedule or ahead of schedule), and the quantification of progress (by comparing PV and EV). Let's consider this by examining several charts. In Figure 12-1, we see the planned value (PV) for the life of the project. PV is an upward sloping line, showing the expected accomplishment of the project over time. It is essentially a budget. PV converts project elements into dollar terms, so if the project went right on schedule, accomplishing each phase exactly on time and exactly on budget, the expenditure of money and the accomplishment of work would match this line exactly. In real life, however, that is rarely the case.

FIGURE 12-1
Graph of Planned Value (PV)

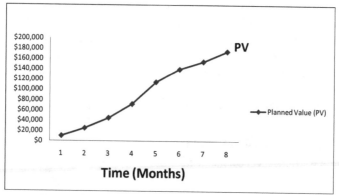

Time (Months)

---

[3] Be careful not to confuse PV as used in this Chapter for Planned Value with PV as commonly used in time value of money computations to refer to the Present Value. They are not the same concept.

In Figure 12-2, we see the cumulative actual cost (AC) that has been incurred over the life of the project to date, plotted along with the planned value (PV) for the project. We can see that for the first several months of the project we were spending more than the budgeted amount, but then our spending fell below budget. It seems as if initially our spending was out of control, but then we acted to clamp down on that, and in recent months have reached a point where we are nicely under budget. However, this simply tracks spending over time as compared to budget, without any sense of what we have accomplished over that time period.

FIGURE 12-2
Graph of Actual Cost (AC) and Planned Value (PV)

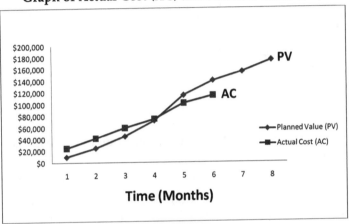

If we replace the AC line showing the amount we spent, with the EV line showing what we have accomplished, we can get a better sense of what is happening. To plot EV on the graph, the plan for the project must be prepared in a way that allows for dollar quantification of each element of the work. At the end of each time period for the project (shown in the figures as months, but depending on the project could be daily, or weekly) the project manager will have to review the portion the PV (budgeted amount) of work that has been accomplished and compute the total of EV for each element. The cumulative EV would be:

$$EV = \sum_{\text{Start}}^{\text{Current}} PV(\text{Completed})$$

or, simply, the EV is equal to the sum of the PV of each completed element from the beginning of the project to the current point in time.

In Figure 12-3 the EV is shown instead of the AC. In Figure 12-2 we were concerned that costs were over PV in the early months of the project. But here we see that the EV was also over budget in those early months. So although we were spending faster than expected, we were not necessarily spending too much money in those months, as the work was getting done faster than expected as well. But we also see that in months 5 and 6, the work accomplishment slowed down. Now, we are not only under PV in terms of cost for months 5 to 6 (as seen in Figure 12-2); we are also below PV in terms of EV accomplished during those months. Clearly, comparing actual cost to the PV did not tell the entire story.

FIGURE 12-3
Graph of Earned Value (EV) and Planned Value (PV)

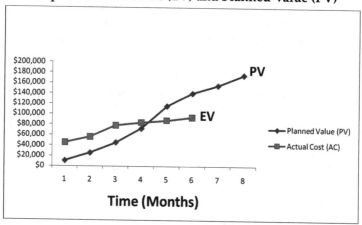

A difference between the PV and the EV at a point in time is referred to as a schedule variance.

Earned Value - Planned Value = Schedule Variance (SV)

Schedule variances are measured in dollars (the vertical amount the PV line is above or below the EV line at a specific point in time) and also in time (the horizontal difference between the EV line at a point in time, and the PV time point for that level of accomplishment). The schedule variances can be seen in Figure 12-4. The schedule variance in dollars shows that we have completed work that should require less spending through the 6th month than planned, because EV at month 6 is below PV at month 6 on the graph. The schedule variance, measured in terms of time, shows that the EV accomplished through month six is at a horizontal level relative to what had been planned to accomplish between months 4 and 5. The project is running about a month and a half behind schedule.

FIGURE 12-4
Schedule Variance

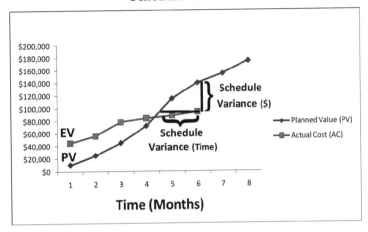

We can see from Figures 12-2 to 12-4 that early on we are spending more than PV and accomplishing more, and later we are spending less and accomplishing less. One thing we are really interested in, however, is relative to what we have accomplished (i.e., the cumulative EV), have we spent more or less than we would have expected to spend for the amount of completed work. In Figure 12-5 we compare the EV and AC over time. Any difference between EV and AC is called a cost variance.

Earned Value - Actual Costs = Cost Variance (CV)

FIGURE 12-5
Cost Variance

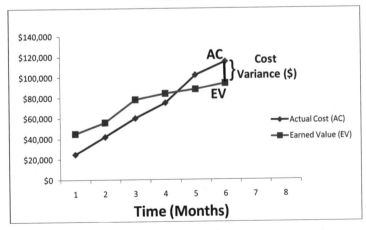

In Figure 12-5 we can see that early in the project, even though we were spending more than PV (*see* Figure 12-2), our EV was running ahead of our spending. We were actually under budget for the amount of work accomplished. In the two most recent months of the project, however, our cumulative actual costs have risen above EV. That means that we now have spent more than budget for the total amount of work we have done. This is a sharp contrast to

Figure 12-2, that might have led you to believe just the reverse. The cost variance in Figure 12-5 is unfavorable, because we have spent more than budgeted for the amount of work performed.

In Figure 12-6 we present the PV, AC, and EV information all in one chart. This is a common format for an EVM time-line chart. Generally, one first focuses on the EV, to see what has really been accomplished. Comparing the EV to the PV gives us a sense of where we are with respect to scheduled performance. Is the project proceeding on time or not? We can see here that everything was going okay at the start of the project. We were spending faster than expected (AC > PV), but we were completing elements of the project even faster (EV > AC). Through month four our results looked good. But in months five and six problems arose. Our EV has fallen not only below PV, but also below AC, both undesirable results. If this were to continue, we would likely complete the project late and over budget. Fortunately, by having an EVM analysis, we are at least alerted to the situation promptly so that any possible corrective actions can be taken on a timely basis.

FIGURE 12-6
EVM Time-Line Chart

THE METHOD

Let's now turn our attention back to the four key elements to the EVM method that were cited earlier:

- A plan for the project.
- A way to value the elements of the project.
- Metrics that identify how elements will be valued.
- Ongoing progress monitoring.

Let's consider each of these in turn.

A Plan for the Project

A key starting point is to identify the various elements of work that make up the project. Unless we can segment the overall project down into a set of measurable tasks or activities, EVM will not be possible. Although one can develop formalized approaches to defining the elements of work, all that is really essential is to at least have a list of all of the activities or tasks that, when combined, make up the entire project. It is, however, essential that the listing of individual elements is comprehensive and in total makes up all of the elements of the project, without overlap or duplication.

A Way to Value the Elements of the Project

Next, once we have identified each task or activity that combine to make up the project, we need to assign a planned value (PV) to each of them. When you add up the planned value for each work element, task or activity, the sum should be equal to the total budget for the project. Although PV is often done in terms of currency, (e.g. dollars), it can also be measured in some other unit such as labor hours. Sometimes PV is measured in terms of both currency and labor hours.

This is not a simple or obvious activity, and requires thought and careful analysis. Once the values have been assigned, they should be reviewed to get a better understanding of the entire project. A careful review of the PV for all the tasks can result in a rethinking and improvement of some aspects of the project.

Metrics That Identify How Work Elements Will Be Valued

Next, we need to have a way to determine when work has been accomplished. For example, do we assign EV to a task or activity only when it is fully completed? That may be fine for activities that start and end the same day or week. A so-called 0/100 rule argues that 0 EV is assigned to an activity until it is 100% done, at which point 100% of the EV for that task is recorded.

Another relatively simple decision rule would be to assign 50% of the EV to an activity once it has been started and the remaining 50% EV once the activity has been completed. The benefit of 0/100 or 50/50 rules is that they are relatively simple. In order to assign EV, we simply need to know when an activity is finished in the case of the 0/100 rule, or started and finished in the case of the 50/50 rule.

Other rules such as 20/80, assigning 20% when the activity is started and 80% when it is finished are also sometimes used. However, if we are dealing with activities that take a longer period of time from start to finish, and are costly, it is desirable to come up with metrics that will allow a finer level of measurement based on the degree to which the activity has really been accomplished at any point is time. Such measurements tend to be unique to each activity and specific to each project.

Ongoing Progress Monitoring

Once we have defined the work elements of the project, assigned a PV for each task or activity, and defined the way that we will measure accomplishment of each activity, we are in a position to implement EVM monitoring as the project is carried out. As each activity is started, progresses, and is finished, we need to record the EV that has been accomplished.

Although some managers may chose, for simplicity, to do periodic updates (weekly or monthly) of where we stand with respect to each task and how much EV we should record, computerized systems make it possible to track at least the start and end of individual tasks on a near real-time, basis. It is important to bear in mind the reason we are doing EVM. We want to learn as promptly as possible of deviations of EV from the PV so that corrective actions can be taken when needed.

LIMITATION OF EVM

Perhaps the biggest concern regarding EVM is that it does not explicitly include an evaluation of the quality of the work on the project. Even after the Big Dig was completed, cost over-runs did not prove to be the only problem. On July 10, 2006, a concrete ceiling panel weighing 3 tons fell on a car injuring the driver a killing a passenger.[4] While EVM would have provided more information about the schedule and cost variances, it would not have provided information about the quality of work performed. That means EVM is just one of a number of techniques that project managers need to employ.

BENEFITS OF EVM

If EVM is employed and data is generated on a timely basis, there are a number of benefits that may be realized. First, EVM helps provide a forecast of the project and its expected outcome. The close examination of work elements often helps an organization to see missing pieces and come up more a more inclusive plan that has fewer missing elements that may wind up adding cost while the project is underway.

Second, EVM reduces risk. Quickly becoming aware of variances is one of the best ways to bring an out-of-control process back under control. Cost over-runs are also less likely because there is a better focus on what is happening, why cost over-runs are happening, and a better ability to predict the likely extent of such over-runs.

Next, EVM improves communication. If in fact a project does start to vary from expectations, the sooner this information is relayed to key decisions makers, the easier it is for them critical decisions. Should the project be scaled back, or the budget increased? Where can additional resources come from? What will be the implications of downsizing the project to stay within budget? Such questions are difficult to deal with, and the sooner a problem is identified and communicated, the better.

EVM also provides for better accountability. We can see problems as they are developing, and assure that the appropriate people have the information they need to make critical decisions. Then those people can be held accountable for outcomes.

---

[4] Sigmund, Pete (2007-06-06). *"Triumph, Tragedy Mark Boston's Big Dig Project "*. Construction Equipment Guide. *http://cegltd.com/story.asp? story=8751&headline=Triumph, %20Trag-edy%20Mark% 20Boston%E2% 80%99s%20Big% 20Dig%20Project.*

Finally, with EVM we have much better information about how the project is adhering to all the various aspects of the budget—the identification of schedule variances in terms of time and money, as well as cost variances, gives the manager a powerful set of data.

KEY TERMS

Project—a limited effort by an organization, having a clear beginning and an end.

Earned Value Management—a technique that assure that projects are adequately planned and resources appropriately used by evaluating progress during the life of a project.

Planned Value (PV) or Budgeted Cost of Work Scheduled (BCWS)—the budgeted total cost of the work that has been scheduled.

Earned Value (EV) or Budgeted Cost of Work Performed (BCWP)—the EV is the budgeted total cost of the work that has been completed.

Schedule Variance—the difference between the PV and the EV at a point in time.

Cost Variance—any difference between EV and AC is called a cost variance.

QUESTIONS FOR REVIEW

1. What is earned value management?

2. How much did the Big Dig go over budget?

3. What are the four critical elements of Expected Value Management?

4. What is the PV? What other name is it known by?

5. What is the EV? What other name is it known by?

6. What information does a comparison of Actual Costs and Planned Value fail to capture?

7. What is a schedule variance? What are the two ways a schedule variance is measured?

8. What is a cost variance?

9. If the AC line is lower than the EV line on a cost variance graph, would that indicate a favorable or unfavorable variance?

10. What is the essential part of creating a plan for the project in EVM?

11. What do the planned value for the work elements add up to? How is it measured?

12. What is needed in order to make a determination that work had been accomplished?

13. What is perhaps the biggest limitation of EVM, according to this chapter?

Chapter 13

Depreciation: Having Your Cake and Eating It Too!

Depreciation refers to the allocation of the cost of a capital acquisition over the years that the organization expects to use it. Suppose we buy a machine with a ten-year useful life. This machine will produce products over its entire ten-year lifetime. Therefore, it will be generating revenues in each of those ten years. The matching principle of accounting requires organizations to record expenses in the same year as the revenues they help to generate. According to the matching principle, we would be distorting the results of operations in all ten years if we considered the entire cost of the machine to be an expense in the year in which it was acquired. We would be understating income in the first year and overstating it in subsequent years.

Instead of expensing the equipment, we consider it to be a long-term asset when it is acquired. As time passes and the equipment becomes used up, we allocate a portion of the original cost as an expense in each year. Thus, the revenue each year from the sale of the machine's output that year is matched with some of the machine's cost.

Okay, if we have to do it that way, there is some intuitive rationale. But where is the financial decision? It seems as if there is little choice left for the financial manager. In fact, that is not true. There are several complicating factors. First we must determine the valuation to be used as a basis for determining each year's depreciation. Next we must consider whether the asset really does get used up proportionately throughout its life. Perhaps it gets used up to a greater extent in some years than in others. Finally, what are some of the tax implications of the depreciation methods we decide to use? These issues make up the topic of this chapter.

AMORTIZATION

Amortization means the spreading out of a cost over a period of time. It is a generic term used for any type of item that is being prorated over time. The term *depreciation* is a specialized subset of amortization. Depreciation refers to the wearing out of a tangible asset such as a building or piece of equipment.

Some items don't wear out per se, and we don't refer to them as depreciating over time. For example, natural resources such as oil, gas, and coal are said to deplete. Deplete means to empty out and this is essentially what happens to a coal mine or oil well. Finally, some items neither deplete nor depreciate. For example, a patent loses its value over time. It doesn't break down, wear out, or empty out—it simply expires with the passage of time. When neither of the terms *depreciation* or *depletion* is applicable, we refer to the item as amortizing. Therefore, for a patent, the annual reduction in value is referred to as amortization expense. This chapter speaks exclusively of depreciation, even though the principles generally apply in a similar fashion for assets to be depleted or amortized.

ASSET VALUATION FOR DEPRECIATION

Asset valuation for depreciation is based on the cost of the asset, including costs incurred to put the asset into service. For example, suppose that we purchase a machine for $20,000, and the machine cannot be used by us without modification of our electrical system. If we pay an electrician $1,000 to run a heavy-duty power line to the spot where the machine will be located, is that a current period expense? No; the cost of the electrical work provides us with benefits over the entire useful life of the machine. Therefore, matching requires that we spread the cost of the electrical work over the same period as the life of the machine. The way that is handled is by adding the cost of the electrical work to the cost of the equipment. Instead of our equipment showing a cost of $20,000, it will have a cost of $21,000 and we will depreciate that amount over its lifetime.

In fact, all costs to put an item into service will be added to the cost of that item so that they can be matched with the revenues over the useful life of the asset. This would include freight on the purchase, insurance while in transit to our factory, new fixtures, plant modifications, etc.

Further, while repairs and maintenance are current period expenses, replacements and improvements to an asset must be added to the cost and depreciated over the life remaining at the time of the replacement or improvement. Replacements and improvements are simply expenditures that extend the useful life of the asset, improve its speed or quality, or reduce its operating costs.

If a motor burns out, is its replacement a routine repair or a *capitalizable* (capitalize means to add to the cost of a long-term item shown on the balance sheet) event? That depends on the circumstances. Do motors burn out quite regularly, or is it a rare event? Regular replacement may well be a repair, but infrequent major overhauls lead to treatment as a replacement. However, there is no clear right or wrong answer in many instances.

The Depreciable Base

Our problems are not yet over. How much of the asset's cost do we depreciate? Your first reaction may well be to say the entire cost, including the various additions to the purchase price that we have just discussed. This is basically true, except that there is still a matching problem. We wish to depreciate property that wears out in the productive process in order to get a portion of its cost assigned to each period in which it helped generate revenues. However, we only want to match against revenues those resources that actually have been used up. We don't necessarily consume 100 percent of most assets.

Suppose that we bought a machine with a ten-year expected life at a cost of $20,000, including all of the costs to put it into service. Suppose further that after ten years we expect to be able to sell the machine for $2,000. Then we really have not used up $20,000 of resources over the ten years. We have used up only $18,000 and we still have a $2,000 asset left over. This $2,000 value is referred to as the machine's *salvage value*. Therefore, from an accounting perspective, we depreciate a machine by an amount equal to its cost less its anticipated salvage value. That difference is referred to as its *depreciable base*.

The salvage value will have to be estimated—at best, it will be an educated guess. Your accountant reviews the reasonableness of your salvage value estimates for financial statement preparation.

Accumulated Depreciation

The full amount of depreciation that has been taken on a piece of depreciable property over all the years you have owned it is called *accumulated depreciation*. It is important to distinguish between each year's depreciation expense and the accumulated depreciation.

Suppose that we have a piece of equipment that cost $20,000, has a $2,000 salvage value, and has an $ 18,000 depreciable base. Assume that we plan to depreciate it at a rate of $1,800 a year for ten years. The first year that we own it, $1,800 of depreciation expense is shown on the income statement. The same is true each year for ten years.

How does the equipment appear on the balance sheet? We report capital assets net of (after subtracting) accumulated depreciation. At the end of the first year, it will appear as $18,200, net. This is the $20,000 cost, less the first year's depreciation expense. By the end of the second year, we will have taken a total of $3,600 of depreciation expense (i.e., $1,800 per year x 2 years). That $3,600 is referred to as the accumulated depreciation for that piece of equipment. The net value of the equipment is now shown on the balance sheet as $16,400 (i.e., the $20,000 cost, less the $3,600 of accumulated depreciation). *See* Exhibit 13-1.

Asset Life

How long will a machine last? We attempt to depreciate an asset over its useful life. If we depreciate it over a period longer or shorter than its useful life, we won't obtain an accurate matching between revenues and the expenses incurred in order to generate those revenues. However, we can only guess an asset's true useful life. Often we see equipment that lasts well after the estimated useful life. Accountants tend to be conservative is estimating the asset life, and more often will underestimate rather than overestimate its useful life. This helps prevent the asset from being overvalued on the balance sheet and helps prevent profits from being overstated.

EXHIBIT 13-1
Book Value

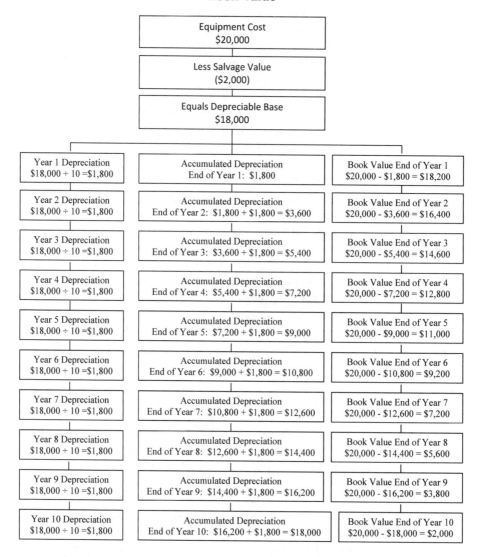

What happens if we are still using the asset after its estimated useful life is over? We stop taking further depreciation. The role of depreciation is to allocate some of the cost of the asset into each of a number of periods. Once we have allocated all of the cost (less the salvage value), we simply continue to use the asset with no further depreciation. That means we will have revenues without depreciation expense matched against them. One could argue that profits should have been reported as being higher in the earlier years. By taking too much depreciation we understate profits in the earlier years and overstate profits in the later years when the asset has already been fully depreciated. That is simply a result of a matching based on estimates instead of perfect foreknowledge, combined with a conservative approach.

What if we sell the asset for more than its salvage value? That presents no problem—we can record a gain for the difference between the selling price and the asset's *book value*. The book value of an asset is the amount paid for it, less the amount of depreciation already taken. Thus, if we bought our machine for $20,000, and sold it after ten years during which we had taken $18,000 of depreciation, the book value would be $2,000. According to our financial records, or books, its value is $2,000. If we sold it for $5,000, there would be a gain of $3,000.

What if the asset becomes obsolete after three years due to technological change and it is sold at that time for $500? Assuming we were depreciating it at a rate of $1,800 a year, then we would have $5,400 of accumulated depreciation (3 years at $1,800 per year). *See* Exhibit 13-1. The book value is $14,600, and at a sale price of $500, we would record a loss of $14,100.

STRAIGHT-LINE VS. ACCELERATED DEPRECIATION

In the previous example we noted that $5,400 of depreciation had been taken over three years, if we assumed depreciation of $1,800 per year. The $1,800 figure is based on *straight-line* depreciation. It assumes that we take an equal share of the total depreciation each year during the asset's life.

In fact, we have choices for how we calculate the depreciation. The straight-line approach is just one of several methods available to us. Not all equipment declines in productive value equally in each year of its useful life. Consider a machine that has a capacity of one million units of output over its lifetime. If it is run three shifts a day, it will be used up substantially quicker than if it is run only one shift a day. The *units of production* or *units of activity* method of depreciation bases each year's depreciation on the proportion of the machine's total productive capacity that has been used in that year. For instance, if the machine produces 130,000 units in a year, and its estimated total lifetime capacity is one million, we would take 13 percent (130,000 divided by 1,000,000) of the cost less salvage value as the depreciation for that year. Of course, this method entails substantial extra bookkeeping to keep track of annual production.

Two other methods exist that are commonly used—the *declining balance method* (really this is a group of similar methods as discussed below) and the *sum-of-the-years digits* method. These are called accelerated methods. The basic philosophy behind these methods is that some assets are likely to decline in value more rapidly in the early years of their life than in the later years. A car is an excellent example. If we consider the decline in value for a car, it is largest in its first year, not quite as large in the following year, and eventually tails off to a point where there is relatively little decline per year in the latter part of its life.

COMPARISON OF THE DEPRECIATION METHODS

We will use an example to demonstrate the principal depreciation methods and to allow us to compare the results using each method. Assume that we buy a machine for $20,000 and we have $4,000 of costs to put the machine into service. We expect the machine to have a useful life of six years and a salvage value of $3,000.

The straight-line method (STL) first calculates the depreciable base, which is the cost less salvage. In this case, the cost is the $20,000 price plus the $4,000 to put the machine into service. The salvage value is $3,000, so the depreciable base is $21,000 ($20,000 + $4,000 - $3,000). The base is then allocated equally among the years of the asset's life. For a six-year life, the depreciation would be $1/6$ of the $21,000 each year, or $3,500 per year. The straight-line method is rather straightforward.

The declining balance method accelerates the amount of depreciation taken in the early years and reduces the amount taken in the later years. When someone refers to accelerated depreciation, he or she is not referring to a shortening of the asset life for depreciation purposes. The life remains six years under the accelerated methods. Declining balance represents a group of methods. We will start with double declining balance (DDB), also referred to as 200 percent declining balance. We will discuss the other declining balance methods later.

The DDB approach starts out with a depreciable base equal to the asset cost ignoring salvage value. The cost is multiplied, not by $1/6$ as in the STL method, but by a rate that is double the STL rate. In this case we would multiply the depreciable base by 2 times $1/6$, or by $2/6$. Hence the word double in the name of this method. If we take $2/6$ of $24,000 (remember that cost includes the various costs to get the machine into service, and that this method ignores salvage value), we get $8,000 of depreciation for the first year. At that rate, the asset will be fully depreciated in just three years, and we've said that accelerated methods generally do not shorten the asset life!

Therefore, we need some device to prevent the depreciation from remaining at that high level of $8,000 per year. This device is the *declining balance*. Each year we subtract the previous year's depreciation from the existing depreciable base to get a new depreciable base. In this example, we start with a base of $24,000 and take $8,000 of depreciation in the first year. This means that in the second year there will be a new depreciable base of $16,000 ($24,000 - $8,000). In the second year, our depreciation would be $2/6$ of $16,000 or $5,333. For year three, we will determine a new base equal to $16,000 less year two's depreciation of $5,333. Thus we have a new base of $10,667, and so on.

However, there is one caveat to this process. We cannot take more depreciation during the asset's life than the asset's cost less its salvage value. In this problem, we can take no more than $21,000 of depreciation, regardless of the method chosen. We have achieved our goal of having higher depreciation in the early years and less in each succeeding year. The method, which simply doubles the STL rate, does have some intuitive appeal as an approach for getting the desired accelerated effect.

The declining balance family also includes 150 percent declining balance and 175 percent declining balance. In each of these methods, the only difference from the 200 percent, or DDB, is that the STL rate is multiplied by 150 percent or 175 percent instead of 200 percent to find the annual rate.

Sum-of-the-years-digits (SYD) is a similar accelerated method. SYD takes the cost less salvage, that is, $21,000, the same as STL, and multiplies it by a fraction that consists of the life of the asset divided by the sum of the digits in the years of the life of the asset. That sum simply consists of adding from one to the last year of the asset's life, inclusive. In our example, we would add 1 +2 + 3 + 4 + 5 + 6, because the asset has a six-year life. The sum of these digits is 21. Therefore, we would multiply $21,000 by 6/21 (the life of the asset divided by the sum). This gives us first-year depreciation of $6,000.

In each succeeding year, we would lower the numerator of the fraction by one. That is, for year two the fraction becomes 5/21 and the depreciation would be $5,000 ($21,000 × 5/21). For year three the fraction becomes 4/21 and the depreciation $4,000, and so on. It is hard to find any intuitive appeal to this manipulation. All we can say is that it does achieve the desired result of greater depreciation in the early years, and it does account for the proper amount of total depreciation.

Exhibit 13-2 compares the three methods for this piece of equipment for its entire six-year life. It is especially important to note that all three methods produce exactly the same total depreciation over the life of the asset.

EXHIBIT 13-2
Comparison of Depreciation Methods

YEAR	STRAIGHT-LINE (STL)	DOUBLE DECLINING BALANCE (DDB)	SUM-OF-THE-YEARS-DIGITS (SYD)
1	$ 3,500	$ 8,000	$ 6,000
2	3,500	5,333	5,000
3	3,500	3,556	4,000
4	3,500	2,370	3,000
5	3,500	1,607	2,000
6	3,500	134	1,000
Total	$21,000	$21,000	$21,000

Ideally, in choosing a depreciation method for your firm, you would select from among STL, declining balance, and SYD based on the method that most closely approximates the manner in which your particular resources are used up and become less productive. You need not use the same method for all of your depreciable property.

Many firms simply choose the STL approach for reporting depreciation on their financial statements to be issued to their stockholders. The apparent reason for this is that it tends to cause net income to be higher in the early years than it would be using the accelerated methods and their high charges to depreciation expense. Reporting a high net income is likely to please the organization's owners.

Excel Excercise

Template 13 may be used to calculate straight-line and accelerated depreciation using your firm's data. The template is included on the CD that accompanies this book.

Up until now, we have been speaking strictly in terms of recording information for financial statements. It is now time to consider the special tax treatment of depreciation.

MODIFIED ACCELERATED COST RECOVERY SYSTEM (MACRS)

The first and most important point that the reader should be aware of is that this is one place where you can actually have your cake and eat it too! It is not required that firms use the same method of depreciation for reporting to the Internal Revenue Service (IRS) as they use for reporting to their stockholders. The implications of that are enormous. We can use straight-line depreciation on our financial statements, thus keeping our depreciation expense relatively low, and be able to tell our stockholders that we had a very fine year. Then we can use the IRS accelerated depreciation system, called the Modified Accelerated Cost Recovery System (MACRS), which accelerates depreciation, lowering income and taxes in the early years of an asset's life.

The IRS' MACRS system uses shorter asset lives than companies generally use in their financial reporting system for the useful life of the asset. MACRS also ignores salvage value until the organization disposes of the asset. And MACRS uses an accelerated (declining balance) system for computing depreciation. All of these factors result in high depreciation in the early years of an asset's life. This causes the organization to have a higher reported deduction for depreciation expense on the organization's tax return. Higher deductions result in lower taxable profits, and therefore lower taxes. However, this may only be a temporary result, as the MACRS system results in higher depreciation expense in the later years of an asset's life.

At the same time, many organizations, for their internal financial records, will use straight-line depreciation over the full useful life of the asset, taking salvage value into account. The result is a dichotomy in which depreciation expense reported to a company's owners is lower and profits are higher in the early years of an asset's useful lifetime, as compared to what is reported on the company's tax return. Thus companies get the benefit or reporting higher income to their owners, while reporting lower income and paying lower taxes to the government.

It is important to note that tax law is a complex, ever-changing field. Tax laws change constantly because of new laws, changes in IRS rulings and interpretations of law, and as a result of court decisions. No decisions should be made as a result of tax implications without first consulting a qualified tax expert.

DEPRECIATION AND DEFERRED TAXES: ACCOUNTING MAGIC

Does MACRS actually reduce your tax payments, or just shift them to the future? That is a very interesting question. The fact that we can tell different depreciation stories to our stockholders and the IRS has interesting ramifications for the firm and its financial statements. It creates something called a *temporary difference*. Our financial records record taxes in a different year than our tax return does.

If we tell our stockholders that we had a good year, then they expect the firm to pay a lot of taxes on the profits we are currently making. Even if we don't pay those taxes now, but instead defer payment to the future, the matching principle would seem to require that we record the tax expense based on our depreciation in our financial records, rather than when the IRS calculates the depreciation and taxes. In fact, that is exactly the case. Taxes are recorded on the firm's financial statements as tax expense and a liability, called a *deferred tax liability*. However, the implications of this deferred tax are quite unusual—almost magical.

Generally, if we can postpone payment of taxes, with no other change in the operation of our business in any respect, we should do so. For any one asset, the deferred tax liability represents an interest-free loan that will eventually be repaid to the government. However, what is true for one asset is not necessarily true for the entire firm. For many companies the balances in the deferred tax account will not become zero, but rather will grow continuously into the future.

This rather amazing result is simply explained. If we had one depreciable asset, over its lifetime we would first defer some tax and later repay it. But if we are constantly replacing equipment—buying new equipment as old equipment wears out—the deferral increase on the new assets will offset the deferral reduction on the old assets, often causing the deferral to effectively become a permanent interest-free loan. However, the magic of deferred taxes is not yet fully apparent.

Consider what happens for a firm that is growing. Such a firm is not only offsetting higher taxes on older equipment with deferred taxes on an equal amount of new equipment. The expansion in fixed assets will cause the deferred liability to grow each year. For growing companies, the startling result is that deferred taxes represent both a growing and permanent interest-free loan as long as the company continues to grow. A bit of accounting magic.

KEY TERMS

Matching—Depreciation is an attempt to match the cost of resources used up over a period longer than one year with the revenues those resources generate over their useful lifetime.

Amortization—a generic term for the spreading out of costs over a period of time. Depreciation is a special case of amortization.

Amounts to be depreciated—The cost of an asset, less its salvage value, is depreciated over the asset's useful life. The cost is the fair market value at the time of acquisition, plus costs to put the asset into service, plus the costs of improvements made to the asset.

Depreciation methods—The asset may be depreciated on a straight-line basis, taking equal amounts in each year, or by an accelerated method, which results in greater depreciation in the earlier years of the asset's life. Two common accelerated depreciation methods are double declining balance and sum-of-the-years-digits.

Modified Accelerated Cost Recovery System (MACRS)—the depreciation method used for tax reporting.

Deferred taxes—If the pretax income reported to stockholders is more than that reported to the IRS, then a tax deferral will arise; that is, some of our current tax expense becomes a liability to be paid at some unstated time in the future, rather than being paid currently.

QUESTIONS FOR REVIEW

1. What is depreciation?

2. What accounting principle requires the use of depreciation?

3. What is the difference between depreciation and amortization?

4. Are costs to get an asset into service, such as the delivery cost we pay when we buy equipment, treated as current expense, or depreciated?

5. What must be subtracted from the cost of a building or equipment to find its depreciable base?

6. Assume that a piece of equipment is purchased for $100,000. It costs $5,000 to install the equipment. We expect it to last for 5 years, and believe that we will be able to sell it for $25,000 at the end of that five year period of time.

   A. What is the depreciable base for the equipment?

   B. Using straight-line depreciation, what is the annual depreciation?

   C. After 3 years, how much accumulated depreciation will there be?

   D. After 2 years, what is the net or book value of the equipment?

   E. If we sell it after 3 years for $50,000 will we have to record a gain or a loss? How much?

   F. If we were using double declining balance instead of straight line depreciation, how much depreciation would there be in each year of the asset's five year life?

7. What are the main elements of the MACRS system for depreciation for tax reporting that causes it to result in high depreciation in the early years of an asset's lifetime?

Chapter 14

Long-Term Financing

In Chapter 5 it was noted that long-term debt is one primary source of the money that organizations need to fund their operations. This chapter takes a closer look at the primary sources of long-term debt: long-term notes, mortgages, bonds, and leases. Debt financing represents money the organization borrows that will be repaid in the future, usually with interest. It is referred to as long-term debt if it will be paid back more than one year into the future.

LONG-TERM NOTES

One form of long-term debt occurs when an organization borrows money and signs a note promising repayment. The note indicates the specific terms under which the money has been borrowed, such as the interest rate and timing of payments. Long-term notes are often *unsecured loans*. This means that the organization as a whole owes the money, but there is no one specific asset that the organization pledges as collateral to ensure repayment. Thus, the lender is considered to be an "unsecured" creditor. If the organization has problems making payments on its obligations, all unsecured creditors share whatever resources are available to repay the organization's various unsecured obligations.

In contrast, a lender can ask for *collateral*. Collateral is a specific asset the lender can claim if the borrower fails to make payment of amounts due. For example, if the organization has made an investment buying 10,000 shares of Microsoft stock, it may offer that stock as collateral when it later borrows money. When there is specific collateral associated with a loan the creditor is considered to be a *secured creditor*. The collateral is used to repay the secured creditor.

By providing the lender with specific valuable collateral, the loan is less risky. Therefore, the lender is more likely to be willing to make the loan and to charge a lower interest rate. In general, the greater the likelihood that a borrower will not be able to repay a loan, the higher the interest rate charged unless there is adequate collateral.

MORTGAGES

Mortgages are loans secured by real property. Real property is land and anything attached to it. That means a building is real property, but equipment within the building is not. There are different possible types of payment arrangements for mortgages. Some do not require any repayment of principal for a number of years, and then a large "balloon" payment is made. It is more common, however, for a mortgage to require equal payments at the end of each month throughout the term of the loan. The equal mortgage payments each include some interest and some principal repayment.

The portion of each monthly payment that is interest and the portion that is principal changes from payment to payment. Why is that the case? Since each mortgage payment repays part of the loan, after the payment the organization owes the lender less money. Interest is a payment on the amount of money that is owed. As the amount owed declines, the required interest payment declines as well. Since the monthly mortgage payment is calculated as a constant monthly payment, the same each period, the repayment portion increases as the interest portion of the payment declines.

For example, suppose that Coffin Corporation took out a $500,000 mortgage loan to build a new structure. The terms of the loan were 12 percent interest, with equal monthly payments for 3 years. How much would the annual mortgage payment be? We can use Excel to solve this as follows:

=PMT(rate, nper, pv, fv, type)

=PMT(12%/12, 3*12, 500000, ,0)

=$16,607.15

You can get a good idea of the relationship between interest and principal on a mortgage by looking at a mortgage repayment schedule, such as the one in Exhibit 14-1. In that Exhibit, the loan amount at the beginning of each month is in a column labeled A. The monthly payment is in the column labeled B. Note that this payment is the same each month. The interest is 12% per year, or 1% each month (12% divided 12 months = 1% per month). The interest amount (Column C) is found by taking the amount owed (from Column A) and multiplying it by 1%. The portion of the monthly payment (Column B) which is a repayment of part of the loan principal (Column D) is found by subtracting the interest in Column C from the monthly payment in Column B. The principal amount of the loan still owed at the end of the month (Column E) is the starting balance from Column A, less the amount of loan repayment from Column D. That ending balance for the month, then transfers over to Column A to become the beginning loan balance for the start of the next month. Notice how the interest portion of the monthly payment declines over time, and the amount of monthly loan repayment of principal rises over time. At the end of the three year life of the mortgage loan, the loan balance just reaches zero.

EXHIBIT 14-1
Mortgage Repayment Schedule

Month	Principal Owed at Beginning of Month (A)	Monthly Payment (B)	Interest at 1% Per Month (C=1%×A)	Repayment of Principal (D=B–C)	Principal Owed at End of Month (E=A–D)
1	$500,000	$16,607	$5,000	$11,607	$488,393
2	$488,393	$16,607	$4,884	$11,723	$476,670
3	$476,670	$16,607	$4,767	$11,840	$464,829
4	$464,829	$16,607	$4,648	$11,959	$452,870
5	$452,870	$16,607	$4,529	$12,078	$440,792
6	$440,792	$16,607	$4,408	$12,199	$428,593
7	$428,593	$16,607	$4,286	$12,321	$416,271
8	$416,271	$16,607	$4,163	$12,444	$403,827
9	$403,827	$16,607	$4,038	$12,569	$391,258
10	$391,258	$16,607	$3,913	$12,695	$378,563
11	$378,563	$16,607	$3,786	$12,822	$365,742
12	$365,742	$16,607	$3,657	$12,950	$352,792
13	$352,792	$16,607	$3,528	$13,079	$339,713
14	$339,713	$16,607	$3,397	$13,210	$326,503
15	$326,503	$16,607	$3,265	$13,342	$313,161
16	$313,161	$16,607	$3,132	$13,476	$299,685
17	$299,685	$16,607	$2,997	$13,610	$286,075
18	$286,075	$16,607	$2,861	$13,746	$272,329
19	$272,329	$16,607	$2,723	$13,884	$258,445
20	$258,445	$16,607	$2,584	$14,023	$244,422
21	$244,422	$16,607	$2,444	$14,163	$230,259
22	$230,259	$16,607	$2,303	$14,305	$215,955
23	$215,955	$16,607	$2,160	$14,448	$201,507
24	$201,507	$16,607	$2,015	$14,592	$186,915
25	$186,915	$16,607	$1,869	$14,738	$172,177
26	$172,177	$16,607	$1,722	$14,885	$157,291
27	$157,291	$16,607	$1,573	$15,034	$142,257
28	$142,257	$16,607	$1,423	$15,185	$127,073
29	$127,073	$16,607	$1,271	$15,336	$111,736
30	$111,736	$16,607	$1,117	$15,490	$96,246
31	$96,246	$16,607	$962	$15,645	$80,602
32	$80,602	$16,607	$806	$15,801	$64,801
33	$64,801	$16,607	$648	$15,959	$48,841
34	$48,841	$16,607	$488	$16,119	$32,723
35	$32,723	$16,607	$327	$16,280	$16,443
36	$16,443	$16,607	$164	$16,443	$0

BONDS

When organizations borrow large amounts of money, they often issue a bond. Bonds are agreements to borrow and repay money with specific *stated*, *face* or *maturity* values. The stated, face, or maturity value is the amount that will be repaid at the end of the loan period, called the maturity date. Suppose that Coffin Corporation wishes to borrow $100 million for 20 years for a major expansion. That $100 million is the maturity value and 20 years from now is the maturity date. Bonds typically pay interest every six months, in which case they are referred to as semiannual bonds.

Many individuals each lend a portion of the total amount to the organization in exchange for the organization's promise to repay the loan. That promise is evidenced by a formal document called a bond. For example, one person might lend money to the organization in exchange for a $5,000 bond. The organization promises to make regular interest payments and to repay the full $5,000 face value at the maturity date. Although we are lending money to the organization, we often speak of buying and selling bonds. This is because the bond obligation is often transferable. After lenders lend money to the organization and receive bonds in exchange, they can wait until the maturity date to get their money back. However, they do not have to wait. They can sell the bond to someone else. Then the borrowing organization will pay interest and principal to the person who purchased the bond obligation.

Organizations issue bonds rather than simply borrowing money from a bank for three major reasons: to spread risk, to eliminate a middleman, and in some cases to obtain a lower rate due to tax issues. First, if one lender were to lend a very large amount of money to one borrower, the lender would be taking a tremendous risk. No one bank would want to lend $100 million to Coffin. The firm's failure to repay the loan could have a devastating impact on the bank. Lenders would prefer to lend smaller amounts to a larger number of borrowers. Second, lenders such as banks are lending other people's money. People put money in bank accounts, and the bank lends the money to the borrower. The bank acts as an intermediary or middleman between the individual with the money and the borrower who needs the money. If the borrower can eliminate that middleman, it can save that cost. Finally, in the case of governments or not-for-profit organizations, bonds can sometimes be issued that pay interest which is tax-exempt. That means the recipient of the interest doesn't have to pay federal and possibly state tax on that interest income. These so-called municipal bonds often are issued at a lower interest rate because of the tax benefit to the lender. That lower rate potentially saves the borrower a lot of money.

Why not use bonds for all loans? Why would we ever borrow from a bank if we are then paying an extra middleman? Issuing a bond is costly. It is expensive to find individual investors who are willing to lend money to the borrower. A large sales force is needed, and commissions must be paid. Lawyers are needed to protect the interests of the lender and borrowers. Accountants are needed to track the bond payments. Investment banking firms undertake and coordinate this costly process. It generally does not pay to incur all the costs related to issuing a bond if only a relatively small amount of money is borrowed. The lower interest on the bonds would not offset the high issuance costs.

Call Provisions

Many issuers of bonds are concerned by the long time-frame involved. If a corporation issues a bond for thirty years when interest rates are high, it would be obligated to pay those high interest rates for the full term of the loan, even if subsequent changes in the economy result in falling interest rates. To deal with this, many bond issuers insert a clause in their bond agreements that allows them to repay the bond early. This is called a *call provision*. When a bond is called, that means that the borrower chooses to repay the bond early.

Suppose that 10 years have gone by, and the borrowing rate for Coffin has fallen from 8 percent to 4 percent. The corporation might borrow money at 4 percent and use it to call in and pay off the outstanding 8 percent bond. This puts lenders in an unfavorable position. If market interest rates go up, lenders will not benefit from that rise because they have lent money for a long period at a fixed rate. But if market interest rates drop, the bond will be called and the lenders will be repaid at a time when they can only reinvest their money at a lower rate. Therefore, to make up for this unbalanced situation, lenders demand a higher interest rate payment for a bond with a call provision than for one without such a provision.

Calculating Bond Payments and Values

Bonds have a specific *stated interest rate*, such as 10 percent. The organization promises to pay interest at that rate on the bond obligation. Therefore, a 10 percent, $5,000 bond with annual interest payments would pay $500 of interest every year until the bond matures. At that point, the organization would make the last interest payment and also repay the $5,000 face value. Usually, interest payments on bonds are made semiannually. In that case, this bond would make a payment of $250 every six months until the maturity date.

However, bonds are not always issued or sold at their maturity value. In fact, they are usually issued and also subsequently bought and sold for a higher or lower price, because interest rates are constantly fluctuating. For example, assume a 20-year, 10 percent, semiannual bond. What if the bond is about to be issued, but interest rates rise in the general economy? No one will be willing to lend money to get 10 percent if they can get 12 percent elsewhere. The organization must offer to sell (issue) the bonds at a *discount*. (If interest rates have instead decreased, then the organization will be able to charge a *premium* for the bond, and will receive more than its face value.)

The actual amount to be paid for a bond is calculated using time value of money (TVM) computations. A bond represents a promise to make periodic interest payments and a repayment of principal. If we know the current interest rate in the marketplace, the number of compounding periods, and the future interest and principal payments, we can find the PV, which is the amount an investor would give to get the bond, and its promised payments.

What would Coffin receive today if it issued a $100 million bond offering at a 10 percent stated interest rate with interest paid semiannually and the maturity in 20 years? Assume that interest rates in the general marketplace have risen to 12 percent.

First, since the bond pays interest semiannually, there are two compounding periods per year. A 20-year bond would have 40 compounding periods. Bonds typically pay interest semiannually, and semiannual compounding is the usual convention. The number of compounding periods is used to compute the PV of both the interest and the principal payments.

Second, note that the stated interest rate is used to determine the interest payments that will take place over time. A $100 million bond at 10 percent would pay interest of $10 million per year, or $5 million every six months.

Next, we need to find the PV of an annuity of $5 million each period for 40 periods at a current market interest rate of 6 percent per period (i.e. 12% per year divided by two compounding periods per year = 6% per half year period), plus the PV of the single future payment of $100 million paid 40 periods from now with an market interest rate of 6 percent. The value of the bond is determined by the current market rate rather than the stated rate. The stated interest rate only is used to determine the specific amount of the semiannual interest payments.

By taking the PV of the periodic interest payments and the future principal payment, we find the value of the bond today at current interest rate conditions. For the Coffin bond mentioned previously, the future value, FV, is the $100,000,000 maturity payment; the periodic interest payments, PMT, are the semiannual $5,000,000 payments; the number of compounding periods is 40 six-month periods; and the interest rate is the 6 percent semiannual current market rate:

$$=PV(rate, nper, pmt, fv, type)$$

$$=PV(6\%, 40, 5000000, 100000000, 0)$$

$$= (\$84,953,703.13)$$

Coffin will receive $84,953,703.13 from the lenders when they issue the bond. Note that this is shown as a negative number in the computation because it is the amount that lenders would be willing to pay (cash outflow) in order to later receive (cash inflow) the interest payments of $5 million every six months and the maturity payment of $100 million at the end. Notice that even though the lenders are only lending about $85 million, they will receive $100 million at maturity. That is because the $5 million interest payments are inadequate to provide a 12% yield on the money they lent. By paying $5 million every six months *and* $100 million at the end it works out that the lenders are just earning exactly 12% on the $84,953,703.13 that they are lending to Coffin.

Note that the difference in the interest rates in this example are extreme. Interest rates vary by one 100th of a percent. A 10 percent face value bond might be issued when interest rates are 10.02 percent or 9.97 percent. A jump from 10 percent to 12 percent is fairly large. Thus, the value of a bond at the time of issuance is not likely to vary nearly as much from the face value as in this example. Over time, however, after 5 or 10 years have passed, wider variations in interest rates are common. If the bond is sold by the original lender to a different investor, a new PV calculation is essential to determine a price for the bond that will yield the current market rate at the time the bond is being sold.

Keep in mind one critical point. The stated interest rate on a bond is only used to compute the interest payments that will be made. So if a bond is an 8%, $5,000, semiannual bond, we use the 8% to find the interest per year of $400 (i.e. 8% × $5,000 = $400), then divide that by 2 since it is a semiannual bond. We now know the interest to be paid every six months is $200. We do not use the 8% to find the PV of the bond. A bond's value is determined using the current market interest rate.

LEASES

A lease is an arrangement where the owner of an asset, called the lessor, allows someone else (the lessee) to use the asset for a period of time in exchange for monthly payments, called lease payments.

Operating vs. Capital Leases

Leases are classified as either *operating leases* or *capital leases*. Operating leases are treated by the lessee on a strictly rental basis. Rental payments are expenses. The asset is not considered to be owned by the lessee and it doesn't show up on the balance sheet. In contrast, a lessee treats a capital lease as if the property was bought and financed with a mortgage. The leased property appears as an asset on the balance sheet. There is also a liability on the balance sheet to account for future payments to be made on the lease.

Short-term leases are always treated as operating leases. This stems from the fact that there is no strong ownership displayed by someone who leases the property for only a short period of time. In contrast, if there appears to be a significant ownership interest in the property on the part of the lessee, it is usually treated as a capital lease.

Many firms make covenants, or agreements, with lenders that restrict management from taking certain risky actions. A common type of covenant is to agree to maintain a certain amount of assets relative to the amount of liabilities. For instance, a firm may agree that it will always have two dollars of assets on the balance sheet for every dollar of liabilities. This reduces risk because if the firm does get into financial difficulty, creditors will be fully protected if the firm can get at least 50 cents for every dollar of assets it owns.

Suppose a firm had made such an agreement, and that it currently has $20,000,000 in assets and $10,000,000 in liabilities. At this point, the president of the company sees a building that is the perfect building for the firm. The firm has been looking for a building like this one for years. The price is $5,000,000, which it plans to pay by borrowing $4,000,000 from a bank on a twenty-year mortgage, and paying $1,000,000 in cash. Unfortunately, that would result in assets of $24 million (the original $20 million + $5 million building - $1 million cash down payment), and liabilities of $14 million (the original $10 million + $4 million mortgage). But to sustain $14 million of liabilities, the firm would need $28 million in assets. The firm cannot buy the building without defaulting on the loan agreement.

However, what if the firm merely rents the building? What if the firm takes out a twenty-year lease, with a provision that the property automatically becomes the firm's at the end of the twenty years? In that case, if the lease were an operating lease, the firm wouldn't be in violation of the letter of its agreement with the bondholders! It would, however, certainly be violating the spirit of the agreement. Leasing property rather than buying it, with the main purpose being to avoid showing the asset and liability on the balance sheet, is referred to as "off-balance-sheet financing." It gets that name because you have effectively financed a purchase without explicitly showing the long-term commitment the firm has made.

Criteria for Capital Leases

As one might suspect, lenders weren't too pleased with this type of behavior. Ultimately, the accountants modified their generally accepted accounting principles (GAAP) to handle this type of situation. Current GAAP specify that long-term, noncancelable leases must be treated as capital leases if they were entered into with the lessee intending to have an ownership interest in the property. A technical set of rules is used by the CPA to assess whether a lease must be treated as a capital lease. If it is a capital lease, then an asset and a liability appear on the balance sheet. This eliminates most opportunities for off-balance-sheet financing.

International Financial Reporting Standards and Leasing

This discussion reflects accounting principles in effect as of the writing of this book. However, a current movement toward adoption of International Financial Reporting Standards (IFRS) would likely impact the treatment of leases. If IFRS becomes required for financial reporting in the United States, it is possible that the operating lease category would be eliminated. If so, then any time there is any lease, the lessee would have to show both and asset and liability for the lease on their balance sheet. This could affect whether the organization remains in compliance with its debt covenants. In anticipation of adoption of IFRS, companies should be starting to review all of their legal contracts that depend on balance sheet values, and where necessary take actions to prevent a change in generally accepted accounting principles from having an adverse impact on the organization. Such steps could range from simply rewriting debt covenants to be less stringent to selling off assets and using the proceeds to reduce debt.

Management Considerations for Leasing

Many financial managers are strong supporters of leasing due to the added flexibility it provides. If you know you'll need a piece of equipment for only half of its useful life, a lease can eliminate the effort required to dispose of the asset after you no longer need it. If you're afraid that technology will make the item obsolete, a cancelable lease can protect you.

A lease also provides a greater degree of financing. Purchases financed by a mortgage typically require a down payment of perhaps 20 percent or more. Banks are quite reluctant to lend 100 percent of the cost for any item they use as collateral. Therefore, the firm with a great idea but no cash may not be able to get started. A lease provides an alternative way to start production with less equity financing.

Leases, however, tend to cost more than mortgages. We would expect that, considering the risk and return issues. Certainly the leasing company bears more risk than a mortgagor does, if only because it bears all of the normal risks of ownership, such as assuring that fire insurance is maintained. Further, while the lessee has more flexibility to avoid technological obsolescence, the lessor charges a higher rent because of added risk. The same thing is true with respect to 100 percent financing. The potential loss due to lessee default is greater to the lessor than to the mortgagor because there is no sizable down payment to absorb losses on foreclosure sales.

In some cases, leasing may be more efficient. Consider the firm that needs two autos. If it leases the autos, it may pay more for the autos than if it bought them outright, but it might get a wholesale service contract with the lease. The leasing company is willing to give a discount on service to get the lease. On the other hand, if the firm needs 2,000 autos, all in one geographic area, it might pay to buy them and open its own auto repair shop, thus maintaining the autos at cost, rather than wholesale or retail rates.

One final consideration: Who owns the property at the end of the lease? Well, unless it is specified one way or the other in the lease contract, the property belongs to the lessor. The lessor stands to gain from any increase in the value of the property. Frequently, the right of ownership upon termination of the lease is given to the lessee for "free." In such leases, the monthly or annual lease payments are higher than they would have to be if the lessor retained ownership of the property.

None of these managerial considerations provide absolute weight in favor of or against leasing. There are some benefits for the lessee, but they tend to raise the risk to the lessor, who therefore charges a higher price. Clearly, by adding a lessor instead of buying direct, we have brought in a participant who will want to earn a profit. This profit must come from the lease payments. As we turn to our next section, however, it will become apparent that tax considerations can provide a situation in which the lessor and the lessee may both clearly benefit from a lease arrangement.

Tax Considerations for Leasing

Tax Bracket Shifting

Suppose that a taxpayer in a low tax bracket—perhaps 15 percent—was anticipating buying a machine directly versus leasing it from a taxpayer in the 35 percent tax bracket. Every dollar of depreciation taken as a deduction by the taxpayer in a 15 percent tax bracket would reduce taxes paid by him or her to the government by 15 cents. If the taxpayer in the 35 percent bracket takes that same dollar of depreciation as a tax deduction, it will reduce his or her taxes by 35 cents. Therefore, there is a tax savings if a high tax bracket taxpayer buys property and leases it to a lower tax bracket taxpayer. The high tax bracket taxpayer gets the depreciation deduction, and can share the benefit with the low tax bracket payer through lower lease rental charges. (Note that the value of this approach has been lessened substantially by IRS Passive Activity Loss rules, which limit allowable deductions.)

Sale and Leaseback

Developed real estate is commonly sold and then leased back by the seller. This "sale and leaseback" technique allows for effective depreciation of land for tax purposes. If we simply own an office building, we can depreciate the building, but not the land it sits on. If we sell the building and lease it back, all of the lease payments are deductible. In areas where land is expensive, this can result in substantial tax savings.

Care must be exercised, however. First, if the real estate is sold at a profit, taxes are paid on the gain. Second, once sold, any subsequent increases in value belong to the new owner.

Alternative Minimum Tax

The Alternative Minimum Tax (AMT) also has interesting implications for leasing. The AMT is designed to ensure that taxpayers pay at least some minimum tax on their income. Deductions, which may be generated by leases, can trigger the AMT. However, it is an extremely complicated area, and is beyond the scope of this book. In general, tax issues with respect to leasing are extremely complex. There are a number of potential pitfalls. The discussion here should alert you to the fact that even if a lease doesn't have strong managerial rationale, the tax consequences may make it attractive. However, you must seek out the advice of a tax expert to review the specifics of any potential lease. The tax law in this area is extremely volatile. Congress closes loopholes as fast as it opens them. You cannot be advised strongly enough that a lease should not be undertaken without a tax expert specifically reviewing the tax consequences of the lease.

KEY TERMS

Unsecured loans—a loan where the organization owes the money, but there is no one specific item that the organization pledges as collateral to ensure repayment.

Collateral—a specific asset the lender can claim if the borrower fails to make payment of amounts due.

Secured creditor—a creditor whose loan to the organization is secured by collateral.

Mortgage—loans secured by *real property*.

Real property—land and anything attached to it.

Bond—agreement to borrow and repay money with specific *stated, face* or *maturity* values and a specific interest rate.

Stated, face or *maturity value of a bond*—the amount that will be repaid at the end of the loan period, called the maturity date.

Call provision—a clause in the bond contract between the borrower and the lender that allows the borrower to repay (call in) the bond early.

Discount—the amount a bond sells for below its face value because the market place demands a higher interest rate than the bond's stated interest rate.

Premium—the amount a bond sells for above its face value because the market place is willing to accept a lower interest rate than the bond's stated interest rate.

Operating leases—leases treated as rental arrangements in which no asset or liability appears on the balance sheet of the lessee.

Capital lease—leases treated as if the lessee had acquired the property. An asset and liability appear on the lessee's balance sheet.

QUESTIONS FOR REVIEW

1. What is the difference between a secured and unsecured loan?
2. Over time, does the interest portion of each mortgage payment go up or down?
3. How would you find the amount that would be paid monthly on a 30-year mortgage?
4. What is the stated rate of interest on a bond used to compute?
5. Assume that a 30 year, 5%, semiannual, $10,000 bond was issued ten years ago. Today current market rates are 4.5%. How much could that bond be sold for today?
6. What are the two types of leases, from an accounting perspective? What is the difference between them?
7. What are some of the non-tax related advantages of leasing?
8. What are some disadvantages of leasing?
9. What are some tax considerations of leasing?

Chapter 15

Working Capital Management and Banking Relationships

WORKING CAPITAL MANAGEMENT

An organization's *net working capital*, or simply working capital, is its current assets less its current liabilities. This chapter focuses on *working capital management*: techniques and approaches designed to maximize the benefit of short-term resources and minimize the cost of short-term obligations.

Working capital is based on a cycle of outflows and inflows. For example, Coffin Corporation might use cash to buy raw materials inventory. The inventory is used to construct coffins. The employees making the coffins must also be paid. The coffins can then be sold to funeral homes, resulting in receivables. Once those receivables are collected, the cycle starts over, as that money can be used to buy more inventory and pay workers to construct more coffins.

The cycle may be delicately balanced. At the beginning of the cycle, Coffin Corporation may have just enough to pay for inventory and wages if it receives payments promptly from its customers. If Coffin issues bills once a month instead of weekly or daily, it may be more convenient for the bookkeeper, but it postpones collection of cash from customers. That cash is needed as soon as possible so that Coffin can cover its expenses.

In performing working capital management, it is the role of the manager to ensure that there is adequate cash on hand to meet the organization's needs and also to minimize the cost of that cash. To do this, the manager must carefully monitor and control cash inflows and outflows. Cash not immediately needed should be invested, earning a return for the organization. Excess inventory should not be kept by the organization. The money spent to pay for inventory that is not yet needed could be better used by the organization for some other purpose. At a minimum, the money could be earning interest. Similarly, if the organization pays its bills before they are due, it will also lose interest it could have earned if it had left the cash in its savings account for a little longer.

SHORT-TERM RESOURCES

The most essential element of working capital is cash. When accountants refer to cash they mean both currency on hand and also amounts that can be withdrawn from bank accounts. A second type of short-term resource is *marketable securities*. These are investments such as stock and debt that can be bought and sold in financial markets, such as the New York Stock Exchange. In most organizations, accounts receivables and inventory are also important parts of working capital. These short-term resources are discussed in this section.

Cash

There are three principal reasons that organizations want to keep some cash on hand or in their bank accounts. First, cash is needed for the normal daily transactions of any activity. For example, cash is needed to pay employees and suppliers. Second, although many activities can be anticipated, managers can never foresee everything that might happen. Experience has shown that it makes sense for organizations to have a safety cushion available for emergencies. A third reason for holding cash is to have it available if an attractive investment opportunity arises.

Given these three reasons to hold cash, one might think that the more cash we have, the better. That is not the case. Cash earns a very low rate of return (e.g., bank savings account interest) at best. If we use our cash to buy buildings and equipment we can probably earn higher profits. But then we wouldn't have cash for transactions and emergencies. At the other extreme, we can keep all our resources in cash, but then we wouldn't earn much of a profit. In practice, managers must find a middle role, trying to keep enough cash available, but not too much.

Short-Term Cash Investments and Marketable Securities

Cash should be earning a return whenever possible. Organizations should have specific policies that result in cash and checks received being deposited promptly into interest-bearing accounts. In fact, even after a check is written to make a payment, it is possible to continue to earn interest on the money. The period from when you write a check until it clears your bank account is called the *float*. Many banks have arrangements that allow money to be automatically transferred from an interest-bearing account to a checking account as checks are received for payment.

Although interest-bearing accounts are better than noninterest accounts, they pay relatively low rates of interest. There are a variety of alternative short-term investments that have the potential to earn a higher rate of return. In a world of no free lunches, however, there is generally a trade-off when one obtains a higher rate of return. The two most common trade-offs are decreased liquidity and increased risk. Decreased liquidity means that the money is not immediately accessible. For example, *certificates of deposit (CDs)* pay higher interest rates than savings accounts, but there is often a penalty for early withdrawal.

Although CDs may tie up money for a period of time, they are generally quite safe. Other investments hold promise of even higher rates of return, but entail greater risks. Marketable securities can be sold almost immediately and cash from the sale can be received within a few days. However, such investments are subject to market fluctuations. The prices of stocks and bonds may go up and down significantly, even on a daily basis.

Other Short-Term Investment Options

Other options exist for short-term investments of cash. A *Treasury bill* (often called "T-bill") is a debt security issued by the U.S. government. Maturities range from four weeks to one year. If the bill is held until it matures, the federal government guarantees to pay the maturity value. It is possible to sell a T-bill prior to its maturity date.

Another alternative is money market funds. These investments tend to pay a rate below that of CDs, but competitive with Treasury bills and higher than the rate paid on a bank savings account. Interest is earned daily and money can be deposited or withdrawn at any time. Although the investment has no guarantee, money market funds are generally considered to be reasonably safe investments and they are very convenient to use.

The next type of money market instrument is a *negotiable certificate of deposit* issued by a U.S. bank. A negotiable CD can be sold to someone else, just as a bond can be sold. Sales commissions will be incurred and the value of the CD at the time of sale will depend on what has happened to market interest rates and the creditworthiness of the lender during the time since the investment was made.

Another type of money market instrument is *commercial paper*. Commercial paper generally represents a note payable issued by a corporation. Typical maturities are less than one year, and the interest rate is higher than a Treasury bill. The buyer of the paper is lending money to a corporation. There is a risk, albeit small, that the corporation will not repay the loan.

Repurchase agreements, or *repos*, are types of short-term investments that are collateralized by securities. Repos may be for as short a period of time as overnight. The organization with idle cash provides it to the borrower at an agreed-upon interest rate, which may fluctuate daily. Although repos are quite liquid, they do have a variety of risks. For example, if the borrower defaults, the collateral may turn out to be insufficient to cover the full investment.

Another option is *derivatives*. Derivatives are securities whose value is derived from the value of something else. For example, we could establish a security that will have as its value the average value of the stock price of five large corporations. Derivatives can be designed to reduce risk by allowing an investor to have the average gain or loss from a large number of securities, without having the expense of investing in all of those securities.

However, derivative securities often allow investors to enter into an investment without paying the full cost of that investment. This concept, called leverage, was discussed in Chapter 9. Leverage offers the potential for much higher returns if the investment performs the way that the investor would like it to, or much greater losses if it does not.

Commercial paper, negotiable CDs, repos, and derivatives would generally be suitable only for organizations that have substantial amounts of cash (perhaps over a million dollars) available for short-term investment. These investments can be quite complicated and should be used only by organizations that employ competent advisors knowledgeable in their intricacies and potential risks.

Accounts Receivable

One should always attempt to collect accounts receivable as quickly as possible. The sooner we collect all of our receivables, the sooner the organization has the cash available for its use, at least for investment in an interest-bearing bank account. Also, the longer we allow an account receivable to be outstanding, the lower the chances that it will ever be collected.

Accounts receivable are collected as a result of a cycle of activities, as shown in Exhibit 15-1. The faster and more accurately we compile the information needed to issue an invoice, and the sooner we actually issue the invoice, the faster payment can be expected.

EXHIBIT 15-1
Accounts Receivable Collection Cycle

However, management of accounts receivable does not stop when we issue an invoice. We need to establish credit policies that reduce the amount of money lost because customers fail to pay the amounts they owe us. We also need to monitor unpaid receivables to minimize such losses. An aging schedule, showing how long our receivables have been outstanding, is a very helpful device. When receivables are collected, there should be specific procedures to safeguard the cash until its ultimate deposit in the bank.

Credit Policies

Credit policies relate to deciding which customers will be allowed to make purchases on account. Organizations require some (or all) customers to pay cash at the time of purchase if there is a high risk that payment would not be received later. However, by excluding individuals or organizations from buying our goods or services on account, we may lose their business. You want to give credit terms that are as good as the competition, but don't want to give credit to customers who wind up never paying their bills. This requires a skillful credit manager to weigh the risks versus the benefits of extending credit to specific customers.

The Billing Process

The activities concentrated around issuing bills are critical. They must be done quickly, but also correctly. Something as minor as a missing zip code in the billing address could lead to a payment delay of several months or more. When we have gathered all necessary information and reviewed the information for both completeness and accuracy, a bill should be issued promptly. Even speeding up collections by two or three days can have a significant impact. For any one bill, it does not seem to matter if there are a few delays. However, when all bills are considered, the impact of prompt billing is significant.

Electronic Billing and Collections

One method to speed collections is electronic billing. In addition to allowing faster collection, electronic billing may prove to be less expensive to process than paper billing because it uses less labor. Electronic billing also allows for quicker communication of problems. The sooner we know that a customer has a problem with an invoice, the greater the likelihood that the organization can still gather any data needed to correct the invoice, and the more likely it is that it will ultimately be paid.

Many businesses now use electronic transfers to collect payment from their customers. Clearly, if your organization can draw money directly from its customers' bank accounts, it can increase the speed of collections and reduce the amount of bad debts.

Aging of Receivables

Once bills have been issued, it is important for the organization to monitor receivables and to follow up on unpaid bills. A useful tool for this process is an accounts receivable *aging schedule*. An aging schedule shows how long it has been between the current date and the date when uncollected bills were issued. For example, at the end of July, a summary aging schedule for the Coffin Corporation might appear as the example in Exhibit 15-2.

In Exhibit 15-2, we notice that the largest share of Coffin's receivables is from independent funeral homes. Coffin also has several large funeral home chains as customers: Mortuaries, Inc., In Your Time of Need, and Undertakers of America. Because those three chains are much larger than Coffin's other customers, they are listed individually. We can see from the bottom half of the aging schedule that 81 percent of Coffin's receivables have been outstanding for less than one month. Less than 1 percent of its receivables are outstanding for more than ninety days. In the period shortly after invoices are issued, Undertakers of America is the slowest customer to pay, with only 60 percent collected in the first month. In the longer period, the independent homes lag with 7 percent being collected in the 61-90 day period and 1 percent still outstanding after ninety days.

EXHIBIT 15-2
Coffin Corporation
Receivables Aging Schedule
As of July 31, 2012

PAYER	1-30 DAYS	31-60 DAYS	61-90 DAYS	>90 DAYS	TOTAL
By Total Dollars					
Independent Homes	$ 8,052,342	$ 995,028	$702,556	$ 93,050	$ 9,842,976
Mortuaries, Inc.	3,250,000	475,000	56,000	22,000	3,803,000
In Your Time of Need	861,232	223,637	27,333	2,222	1,114,424
Undertakers of America	538,474	389,640	4,500	2,760	980,374
Total	$12,747,048	$2,083,305	$790,389	$120,032	$15,740,774
By Percentage					
Independent Homes	81.8%	10.1%	7.1%	1.0%	100.0%
Mortuaries, Inc.	85.5%	12.5%	1.5%	.5%	100.0%
In Your Time of Need	77.3%	20.1%	2.5%	.1%	100.0%
Undertakers of America	59.5%	39.7%	0.5%	.3%	100.0%
Total	81.0%	13.2%	5.0%	.8%	100.0%

Excel Excercise

You may use Template 14 to prepare an aging schedule for your organization. The template is on the CD that accompanies this book.

The aging schedule is a valuable tool because problem areas can be quickly identified. Efforts to collect payment should begin as soon as the invoice is issued. If anything goes beyond the current column (i.e., 1-30 days), there should be a formal procedure, such as the issuance of a reminder statement. If an account exceeds sixty days, there should be procedures such as mailing another statement, often colored pink to get greater attention. The "over-ninety-day" category in an aging schedule is a particular concern, even though it may be a small part of the total. Amounts in that category probably reflect problems encountered in processing the bills or else an inability or unwillingness to pay. All organizations should have specific follow-up procedures for accounts that fall into this category. These procedures should include not only monthly statements, but also late charges and telephone calls to determine why payment has not been made. The longer an invoice goes unpaid, the less likely it will ever be paid.

In some cases, it is necessary to use a collection agency if other efforts have failed. This is a costly approach, since collection agencies retain as much as half of all amounts that they are successful in collecting.

Lockboxes

Some organizations have payments sent directly to a lockbox rather than to the organization itself. Lockboxes are usually post office boxes that are emptied by the bank rather than the organization. The bank opens the envelopes with the payments and deposits them directly into the organization's account.

One advantage of this approach is that the bank will empty the box and deposit the money daily. This gets the money into interest-bearing accounts faster than if it had to go through the organization. Secondly, use of a lockbox tends to substantially decrease the risk that receipts will be lost or stolen.

Inventory Management

Careful management of inventory can also save money for the organization. The lower the level of inventory kept on hand, the less you have paid out to suppliers, and the greater the amount of money kept in your own interest-bearing savings accounts. On the other hand, for many organizations, there are uncertainties that require inventory both for current use and as a safety measure. Management must develop systems to ensure adequate availability of inventory when needed while keeping overall levels as low as possible.

Centralized storing of inventory should be used if possible. If separate locations for inventory are created, convenience rises but so do costs. The more separate storage sites, the greater the amount of each inventory item the organization is likely to have. The ordering process should also be as centralized as possible to minimize employee time spent processing orders, and maximize the possibility of volume discounts.

Economic Order Quantity (EOQ)

There are a variety of costs related to inventory in addition to the purchase price. We must have physical space to store it, we may need to pay to insure it, and there are costs related to placing an order and having it shipped. A method called the *economic order quantity* (EOQ) considers all of these factors in calculating the optimum amount of inventory to order at one time.

The more inventory ordered at one time, the sooner we pay for inventory (taking money out of our investments or interest-bearing accounts) and the greater the costs for things such as inventory storage. These are called *carrying* or *holding* costs. On the other hand, if we keep relatively little inventory on hand to keep carrying costs low, we will have to order inventory more often. That drives *ordering* costs up. EOQ balances these two factors to find the optimal amount to order.

There are two categories of carrying costs. These are *capital cost* and *out-of-pocket costs*. The capital cost is the cost related to having paid for inventory, as opposed to using those resources for other alternative uses. At a minimum this is the foregone interest that could have been earned on the money paid for inventory. Out-of-pocket costs are other costs related to holding inventory, including rent on space where inventory is kept, insurance and taxes on the value of inventory, the cost of annual inventory counts, the losses due to obsolescence and date-related expirations, and the costs of damage, loss, and theft.

Ordering costs include the cost of having an employee spend time placing orders, the shipping and handling charges for the orders, and the cost of correcting errors when orders are placed. The more orders, the more errors.

There is an offsetting dynamic in inventory management. The more orders per year, the less inventory that needs to be on hand at any given time, and therefore the lower the carrying cost. However, the more orders per year, the greater the amount the organization spends on placing orders, on shipping and handling costs, and on error correction. The total costs of inventory are the sum of the amount paid for inventory, plus the carrying costs, plus the ordering costs.

Total Inventory Cost = Purchase Cost + Carrying Cost + Ordering Cost

The goal of inventory management is to minimize this total without reducing the quality of services the organization provides.

We will use N for the total number of units of inventory ordered per year, C for the annual cost to carry one unit of inventory, and O for the costs related to placing one order. The EOQ represents the optimal number of units to order at one time.

Suppose that Coffin pays $10 per gold-plated coffin handle. They buy 2,000 handles per year. Each time they place an order, it takes a paid clerk $5 worth of time to process the order. The delivery cost is $ 10 per order. The $15 is the total of ordering costs. Coffin earns an average of 6 percent interest on invested money. Therefore, the capital part of the carrying cost is 60 cents per handle per year (6% × $10 price = $.60). Other carrying costs (such as storage and insurance) are estimated to be $2.40 per handle per year. Therefore the total carrying costs are $3 per handle per year.

The formula to determine the optimal number to order at one time is:

$$EOQ = \sqrt{\frac{2\,ON}{C}}$$

where EOQ is the optimal amount to order each time.

$$EOQ = \sqrt{\frac{2 \times \$15 \times 2,000}{\$3}}$$

$$= 141$$

This result indicates that we should order 141 handles at a time, to minimize costs related to acquiring and holding inventory.

Excel Excercise

Template 15 may be used to calculate the Economic Order Quantity for your organization. The template is on the CD that accompanies this book.

The basic EOQ model, as presented here, makes a number of assumptions that are often not true. For example, it assumes that any number of units can be purchased. In some cases an item might only be sold in certain quantities, such as hundreds or dozens. Another assumption is that the price per unit does not change if we order differing numbers of units with each order. It is possible that we might get a quantity discount for large orders. Such a discount could offset some of the higher carrying cost related to large orders. Managers should adjust the EOQ based on the impact of these issues.

Another assumption is that we use up our last unit of an item just when the next shipment arrives. A delay in processing, however, could cause inventory to arrive late, and we might run out of certain items. To avoid negative consequences of such stock outs, we might want to keep a safety stock on hand. How large should that safety stock be? That will depend on how long it takes to get more inventory if we start to run out, and on how critical the consequences of running out are.

Just-in-Time Inventory

One aggressive approach to inventory management is called *just-in-time (JIT) inventory*. This method argues that carrying costs should be driven to an absolute minimum. This is accomplished by having inventory arrive just as it is needed for production. The advantages are obvious: no storage costs, reduced handling costs, minimum breakage, and no need to pay for inventory before you need it. However, there are clear disadvantages as well: increased ordering and shipping costs, and the risk that it will be necessary to stop production lines if inventory doesn't arrive as it is needed.

The application of JIT really centers on how close one can come to the ideal. There will invariably be problems when implementing a JIT system. For any organization, workflow will not necessarily proceed in an orderly manner. There will be peaks and valleys in demand. Such variability creates major challenges for the implementation of a JIT system.

SHORT-TERM OBLIGATIONS

To this point, this chapter has focused on short-term resources. We now turn our attention to management of short-term obligations, or current liabilities. Careful management of such obligations can save a substantial amount of money. Some short-term obligations that need management attention are *accounts payable, payroll payable, notes payable,* and *taxes payable.*

Accounts payable represents amounts that the organization owes to its suppliers. Payroll payable is an amount owed to employees. Notes payable represents an obligation to repay money that has been borrowed. Taxes payable includes income, sales, real estate, payroll, and other taxes.

As a general rule, managers should try to delay payment of short-term obligations in order to keep resources in the organization available to earn interest, or to avoid unnecessary short-term borrowing and related interest expenses. However, this must be balanced against any negative consequences related to delayed payments.

Accounts Payable

Accounts payable is often called *trade credit*. In most cases, there is no interest charge for trade credit, assuming that payment is made when due. For example, Coffin might order and receive a shipment of mahogany lumber. Shortly afterward, it receives an invoice from the supplier. The invoice will generally have a due date.

Some suppliers charge interest for payments received after the due date. Others do not. A common practice in many industries is to offer a discount for prompt payment. On an invoice, under a heading called *terms*, there may be an indication such as: 2/10 N/30. This would be read as "two ten, net thirty." A discount of 2/10 N/30 means that if payment is received within ten days of the invoice date, the payer can take a 2 percent discount off the total. If payment is not made within ten days, then the full amount of the bill is due thirty days from the invoice date. Some companies state their terms in relation to the end of the month. Terms of 2/10 EOM (two ten, end of month) mean that the buyer can take a 2 percent discount for payments received by the company no later than ten days after the end of the month in which the invoice is issued.

One confusing element is that if you don't take the early payment discount, you pay the "net" amount, which is the full amount on the invoice. Usually net refers to a number after a subtraction has been made. The reason for this strange terminology is that many times organizations negotiate a discount from the full price at the time an order is placed. For example, suppose that the regular wholesale price for silver-plated coffin handles is $2.50 each. However, Coffin successfully negotiated a 20 percent discount off the official or "list" price. Perhaps this is a volume discount. Alternatively, it may be a discount that the handle manufacturer offers to meet a competitor's price. From the seller's viewpoint, $2.50 is the list or gross price, $2.00 is the invoice or *net price*, and $ 1.96 is the net price less a discount for prompt payment (the $2.00 negotiated price less the 2 percent discount = $1.96).

Does it make sense to take advantage of discounts for prompt payment? A formula can be used to determine the annual interest rate implicit in trade credit discounts:

$$\text{Implicit Interest Rate} = \frac{\text{Discount}}{\text{Discounted Price}} \times \frac{\text{365 Days}}{\text{Days Sooner}} \times 100\%$$

For example, suppose that Coffin purchased $5,000 of casket liners with payment terms of 2/10 N/30. A 2 percent discount on a $5,000 purchase would be $100. This means that if the discount is taken, only $4,900 would have to be paid. By taking the discount, Coffin must make payment by the tenth day rather than the thirtieth day. This means that payment is made twenty days sooner than would otherwise be the case.

$$\text{Implicit Interest Rate} \ = \ \frac{\$100}{\$4,900} \ \times \ \frac{365 \text{ Days}}{20 \text{ Days}} \ \times 100\% \ = 37.2\%$$

While the stated discount rate of 2 percent seems to be rather small, it is actually quite large on an annualized basis. Gaining a 2 percent discount in exchange for paying just twenty days sooner represents a high annual rate of return. Suppose that the organization has $4,900 of cash available to pay the bill on the tenth day. In order for it to make sense not to pay the bill promptly and take the discount, it would have to invest the money for the next twenty days in an investment that would earn at least $100 over that period. Any investment that could give us that return would be earning profits at a rate of at least 37.2 percent per year. Since most organizations do not have access to short-term investments that are assured of earning such a high rate, it pays to take the discount and pay promptly. Even if you have to borrow money to take the discount you should, as long as you can borrow at an interest rate of less than 37.2 percent per year.

This assumes, of course, that the invoice will be paid on time if the discount is not taken. Suppose, however, that Coffin often pays its bills late. Sometimes, it pays after three months. Would it make sense to take the discount and pay in ten days, or to wait and pay the bill after ninety days? Paying after ten days is eighty days earlier than if we normally wait for ninety days before making our payment.

$$\text{Implicit Interest Rate} \ = \ \frac{\text{Discount}}{\text{Discounted Price}} \ \times \ \frac{365 \text{ Days}}{\text{Days Sooner}} \ \times 100\%$$

$$\text{Implicit Interest Rate} \ = \ \frac{\$100}{\$4,900} \ \times \ \frac{365 \text{ Days}}{80 \text{ Days}} \ \times 100\% \ = 9.3\%$$

If Coffin can earn more than 9.3 percent on its investments, or if Coffin does not have enough money to pay the bill and a bank would charge more than 9.3 percent to lend the money, then Coffin is better off waiting. However, that assumes its suppliers are willing to wait and will not charge interest for late payments. Otherwise, Coffin should pay promptly and take the discount.

Excel Excercise

   Use Template 16 to calculate the implicit interest rate for any discount for prompt payment. The template is on the CD that accompanies this book.

Payroll Payable

Each organization must decide upon a number of general policies, such as how many holidays, vacation days, and sick days employees get. Most new organizations are well advised to be fairly conservative to start. It is much easier to later decide that you can afford to give employees more vacation than it is to reduce the vacation allowance. The benefits of employee morale from a more liberal policy must be weighed against the cost of paying for days not worked.

Another policy decision relates to whether employees will receive pay for sick days in cash if they do not use them. If employees are allowed to accumulate sick days and know they will get paid eventually whether they take them or not, then they are more likely to accumulate a substantial bank of sick leave for a serious illness. When sick leave is lost each year if it is not used, employees are more likely to take sick days when they are not sick. This encourages a culture whereby employees lie to the organization.

Although it is costly to pay employees for accumulated sick leave, it is important to bear in mind that for many employees it will be years or decades before that payment is made. In the intervening time the employer has had the benefit of earning interest on that money. If sick leave can't be accumulated, most of it will be used and paid for currently. So it may actually turn out to be less costly to allow accumulation than to enforce a "use it or lose it" policy.

Each organization must also decide on the length of the payroll period, and how soon payment is made to employees once the payroll period ends. Employees could be paid daily, weekly, biweekly, or monthly. They could be paid on the last day of the payroll period, or a few days or a week later. The less frequently you pay, the fewer checks that must be written, reducing bookkeeping costs. Further, paying less frequently and later means that the employer holds onto the cash for a longer period, earning more interest. On the other hand, employees obviously prefer to be paid more often and sooner. Poor morale can turn out to be more costly than the benefits that the organization may have accrued in the form of extra interest.

Payroll policy must also focus on other *fringe benefits*. The organization must decide what fringes to offer, and how much will be paid by the employer versus the portion paid by the employee. Other fringes (in addition to vacation, holidays, and sick leave) include items such as health and dental insurance, life insurance, child care, car allowances, parking, and pensions.

Accounting and Compliance Issues

Payroll accounting is complicated by the various deductions that must be made from wages. The most prominent reason for payroll deductions relates to tax compliance issues. It is necessary to withhold income taxes, Social Security (PICA) taxes, unemployment insurance, and disability insurance. Most states also have state income taxes that must be withheld, and some localities have payroll or income taxes.

Calculating taxes can be complicated. At times the government changes the tax rates or the amount of income subject to tax. It is also critical to submit payments to the various governments on a timely basis. We don't want to pay early, because we are better off holding the money in our interest-bearing account for as long as possible. On the other hand, there are costly penalties for late payment that should be avoided.

In addition to taxes and other government-required deductions, there are a number of other types of deductions from payroll. These include amounts for health and dental insurance, pensions, life insurance, and other similar items. Often the employer pays for part or most of these benefits, and the employee makes a lesser contribution. Payroll can be further complicated if your organization pays bonuses, overtime, or piecework pay, or if your employees receive tips.

It is probably inadvisable for nonfinancial managers to attempt to take on too much of the payroll process themselves. Either the organization needs to have a payroll department that can specialize in this process, or an outside payroll vendor should be used.

Notes Payable

Notes payable are short-term loans evidenced by a written document signed by all parties that specifies the amount borrowed, the interest rate, and the due date for repayment. Often such notes are *demand notes*. This means that the lender has the right to call for immediate payment of the full amount borrowed, plus accrued interest, at any time.

The interest on a note or loan is equal to the amount of the loan, multiplied by the annual interest rate, multiplied by the fraction of the year that the loan is outstanding:

$$\text{Interest} = \text{Loan Amount} \times \text{Interest Rate per year} \times \text{Fraction of Year}$$

For example, the interest on an 8 percent, six-month note for $10,000 would be:

$$\text{Interest} = \$10,000 \times 8\% \times 1/2 = \$400$$

For organizations that have limited financial resources, another approach for obtaining short-term financing is to borrow money from an organization that specializes in financing and factoring receivables. A *factoring* arrangement is one in which we sell our receivables. The buyer is called a factor. The right to collect those receivables then belongs to the factor. In most cases, if receivables are factored, the organization receives less than it would have received but it gets the cash sooner. Alternatively, a financing arrangement is one whereby money is borrowed with the receivables being used as collateral in case we cannot repay the loan.

Taxes Payable

Taxes payable represents a short-term obligation. As with other short-term obligations, these should not be paid before they are due. However, since there are often penalties in addition to interest for late payment, managers must have a system in place to ensure that taxes are paid on time.

BANKING RELATIONSHIPS

Working capital management often requires a good working relationship with one or more banks. A system of checking and savings accounts will be required by most organizations. Many short-term investments are made with one of the organization's banks. And, of course, money is often borrowed from banks.

Many people think of banks as a place to go when you need a loan. However, you are much more likely to get a loan if you establish a long-term relationship with a bank. Let the bank get to know your organization. Use the bank for some of your investment needs. Teach the bank about the cyclical patterns in your business that are likely to generate cash surpluses at some times of the year, and cash deficits at other times.

It is important to be able to show banks that your organization has thought through its working capital situation. How much money do you expect to borrow over the next year? When? What for? How long will you need the money? Banks are more likely to lend to organizations that can anticipate temporary cash needs long before the cash is needed, especially if you can show when you expect to be able to repay the loan. In Chapter 6 we discussed the cash budget. Such a budget is very important when the time comes to approach a bank about a loan.

Some organizations borrow specific amounts on short-term *commercial* loans. Such loans, often called commercial paper, were discussed earlier in the short-term investment section of this chapter. If your needs are intermediate-term, then a *term* loan, typically from one to five years, can be arranged. Such commercial loans and term loans can be arranged at the time the money is needed. However, many organizations arrange for a line of bank credit at a time when they currently have more than adequate cash.

For example, Coffin Corporation might arrange for a $10 million line of credit at the bank where it handles most of its routine financial transactions. The arrangement would typically include repayment terms and interest rates tied to some benchmark rate that may vary over time. The *prime rate* is the interest rate banks charge their most creditworthy clients. Coffin Corporation might negotiate for a loan at 2 percent over prime (referred to as "2 OP") at a time when the prime rate is 7 percent. Suppose that Coffin doesn't need to borrow any of its $10 million credit line for six months. At that time the prime has fallen to 5.5 percent. The interest rate on money borrowed against the line of credit would be 7.5 percent, which is 2 percent over the then-current prime. If the prime rate changes again, the interest rate on the outstanding portion of the loan will change as well. A common alternative to the prime rate, especially for companies with international operations, is the London Interbank Offered Rate (LIBOR). The LIBOR rate represents the rate that banks charge each other in the London Eurocurrency market. Having a credit line allows the organization to hold lower cash reserves than it might otherwise need.

In exchange for credit arrangements, many times banks require the organization to keep *compensating balances* in the bank. That is, the organization must always keep a certain amount of money in the bank. Why agree to a compensating balance arrangement? Because the line of credit greatly exceeds the compensating balance and provides a level of cash safety that the organization might not otherwise have. Will the bank make a loan to your organization, or offer it a line of credit? The bank will look for things such as positive cash flow from your operations, a strong management team, and adequate collateral. The weaker your position in these areas, the higher the rate of interest you will be charged. If you are too weak, the bank will not make the loan.

However, this is a two-way street. You don't want to borrow from just any bank. You need to pick the right bank for you. You need a big enough bank to meet all your needs, but not such a big bank that you are irrelevant to them. You need a bank that has experience serving businesses in your industry. Such a bank will better understand your problems and needs. Does your business have international operations? If so, you may want to chose a bank that has an international department. You need a bank with a range of services to meet your needs now, and as you grow. Banks can be useful in many ways, sometimes offering advice on how to run your business better, or even linking you with potential customers.

Concentration Banking

Although many companies deal with more than one bank, they often maintain a significant presence at one or more banks, which are referred to as *concentration banks*. Arrangements can be made with the concentration bank to *sweep* or transfer money into and out of accounts automatically.

For example, suppose that a nationwide company has many individual locations around the country that collect cash from customers, and deposit that cash in local banks. The company wants to have access to those deposits to make disbursements for various purposes. An arrangement may be made in which the concentration bank transfers balances from these other feeder accounts to a master account at the concentration bank. There could be daily, weekly, or monthly transfers, depending on the expected balances in the accounts.

The process can also be reversed with *zero-balance accounts*. An organization can write checks on an account that has a zero balance. When the checks are presented for payment, the bank keeps a tally of the total amount disbursed. That amount is then automatically transferred from one central account at the concentration bank into the zero-balance account.

This type of automatic transferring of funds back and forth allows the organization to have quicker access to its cash resources for payment needs. It also allows it to maintain less cash in total than it would if it had cash balances in many different accounts. The excess cash can be invested and may enable the organization to earn a higher yield on investments by purchasing securities in larger denominations.

KEY TERMS

Working capital management—management of short-term resources and short-term obligations to maximize financial results.

Short-term resource management:

> *Cash* is kept for transactions, safety, and investment opportunities.

> *Short-term investments*—bank deposits, certificates of deposit, money market funds, T-bills, unsecured notes, commercial paper, repurchase agreements (repos), derivatives, and similar securities.

Accounts receivable aging schedule—management report that shows how long receivables have been outstanding.

Inventory management—Inventory levels should be kept as low as possible, while allowing for adequate inventory for current use and as a safety measure.

    a. *Economic order quantity (EOQ)*—technique used to calculate the optimal amount of inventory to purchase at one time.

    b. *Just-in-time (JIT)*—inventory management approach that calls for the arrival of inventory just as it is needed, resulting in zero inventory levels.

Short-term obligation management:

Trade credit and terms—payables to suppliers. Terms represent the payment agreement, sometimes including a discount for prompt payment.

Payroll payable—amount owed to employees. Payroll policy must consider payroll benefits, and also when and how often payroll is paid.

Notes payable—short-term loans that may be unsecured or secured by collateral.

Banking relationships—needed for transactions (e.g., checking), short-term investments, and borrowing.

Concentration bank—bank where an organization keeps a significant presence.

Short-term loans—*commercial* loans, *term* loans and *lines of credit*. The interest rate may be a specific set rate, or may vary with a benchmark such as the prime rate.

Compensating balances—balances that must be maintained on deposit at all times in exchange for a line of credit (prearranged loan to be made when and if needed in an amount up to an agreed-upon limit.)

QUESTIONS FOR REVIEW

1. What is net working capital, or simply working capital?
2. What is working capital management?
3. What are the most common types of short-term investments?
4. What are the three principal reasons that organizations keep cash?
5. What is the period of time from which you write a check until it clears your bank account called?
6. When cash is invested to earn a higher return than a bank savings account, what are the two primary tradeoffs?
7. What are the steps from issuance of a bill until we collect payment from a customer and have access to the funds? What role do managers play, aside from issuing the bill?
8. Why would you want to keep inventory levels low?

9. What are the variables that have to be considered in the EOQ system for inventory?

10. Suppose that you need 5,000 units of inventory over the course of a year. Each unit costs $1. The costs related to placing each order are $20. Your cost of capital is 8%. Other carrying costs are estimated to be $.10 per unit. What is the EOQ for this inventory?

11. Account payable are sometimes referred to as _____ _____.

12. If you are buying something for $50,000 and are offered terms of 1/10, N/30 should you take the discount if you normally earn a return of 15% on your money? Show your work.

13. What are some issues that must be considered regarding payroll policy?

Chapter 16

Inventory Costing: The Accountant's World of Make-Believe

THE INVENTORY EQUATION

Inventories are merely a stock of goods held for use in production or for sale or resale. Retailers and wholesalers have merchandise inventory. They buy a product basically in the same form as that in which it is sold. Manufacturers have several classes of inventory—raw materials that are used in the manufacturing process to make a final product; work in process that consists of goods on which production has begun that has not yet been finished; and finished goods that are complete and awaiting sale.

Just as there is a basic equation of accounting, there is a basic equation for keeping track of inventory and its cost.

Beginning Inventory (BI)	+	Units Purchased (P)	−	Units Sold (S)	=	Ending Inventory (EI)

This equation can be understood from a reasonably intuitive point of view. Consider a firm selling clay statuettes. At the start of the year, it has 1,000 statuettes. During the year, it buys 4,000 statuettes. If it sells 3,000 statuettes, how many will be left at the end of the year?

BI	+	P	−	S	=	EI
1,000	+	4,000	−	3,000	=	2,000

We can readily see that there should be 2,000 statuettes on hand at year-end.

PERIODIC VS. PERPETUAL INVENTORY METHODS

Firms must make a major decision about the fashion in which they intend to keep track of the four items in the inventory equation. This year's beginning inventory is always last year's ending inventory. All accounting systems are designed so as to keep track of purchases. A problem centers on the cost of goods sold and ending inventory.

If we wish, we can keep track of specifically how much of each of our products is sold. However, this requires a fair amount of bookkeeping. Certainly we keep track of the total dollars of sales from each transaction, but that in itself does not tell which goods (if our firm has more than one product) or how many are sold. Consider a hardware store that stocks thousands of small items. To record which items and how many of each are being sold could more than double the time it takes to ring up each sale. This could mean paying for at least twice as many cash register clerks.

A far simpler approach is to simply wait until year-end and then count what is left. Once we know the ending inventory, we can use our inventory equation to determine how many units of each product were sold. For example, if we started with 1,000 statuettes and purchased 4,000, then a year-end count of 2,000 on hand would indicate that we had sold 3,000 during the year.

	BI	+	P	–	S	=	EI
If:							
	1,000	+	4,000	–	S	=	2,000
then					S	=	3,000

This method is called the *periodic method of inventory*. It requires us to take a physical count to find out what we have on hand at any point in time. It gets this name because we keep track of inventory from time to time, or periodically.

A major weakness of the periodic system is that, at any point in time, we don't know how much inventory we've sold and how much we have left. Therefore, our control over our inventory is rather limited. If running out of an item creates a serious problem, this method is inadequate. There are several easy solutions to that problem in some situations. If parts are kept in a bin or a barrel, we can paint a stripe two-thirds of the way down the bin or barrel. When we see the stripe, we know it's time to reorder.

The periodic method has other weaknesses as well. Although we calculate a figure for units sold based on the three other elements of the inventory equation, we don't know for sure that just because a unit of inventory isn't on hand, it was sold. It may have broken, spoiled, evaporated, or been stolen.

An alternative to periodic inventory accounting is the *perpetual method* for keeping track of units of inventory. Just as the name implies, you always, or perpetually, know how much inventory you have, because you specifically record each item.

Which of the two methods is considered more useful? Clearly the perpetual method gives more information and better control. However, it also adds substantial bookkeeping cost. Most firms would choose perpetual if they could get it for the same money as periodic, but typically they can't. The result is a management decision as to whether the extra benefits of perpetual are worth the extra cost.

Computers have made significant inroads in allowing firms to switch to perpetual inventory without incurring prohibitively high costs. For example, supermarkets were a classic example of the type of firm that couldn't afford perpetual inventory. Imagine a checkout clerk in the supermarket manually writing down each item as it's sold. The clerk rings up one can of peas, and then turns and writes down "one 6-ounce can of Green Midget peas." Then the clerk rings up one can of corn, and turns and writes down, "one 4-ounce can of House Brand corn," and so on. At the end of the day, another clerk would tally up the manual logs of each checkout clerk. The cost of this would be enormous. In such a situation, a firm would just keep track of total dollars of sales, and would take periodic inventories to see what is still on hand. Yet supermarkets run on extremely tight margins, so they can ill afford to run out of goods, nor can they afford the carrying cost of excess inventory.

Supermarkets were among the leaders in adopting use of bar codes. These computer-sensitive markings allow the store to save the cost of stamping the price on goods. The computer that reads the bar code knows how much the price of each item is, so the clerk no longer needs to see a stamped price. It also allows the clerk to ring up the goods at a much faster pace. Finally, it automatically updates the inventory. In many of the supermarkets using this system, the cash register tape gives you more information than just the price. Not only does it tell you that you bought a 4-ounce container of yogurt, but also that it was blueberry yogurt. That detailed information tells the purchasing department specifically the size, brand, and flavor of yogurt to be restocked. The potential time saved in stamping prices on goods and in the checkout process can offset much of the cost of the computerized system.

It should be noted that even on a perpetual system there is a need to physically count inventory from time to time (typically at least once a year). The perpetual method keeps track of what was sold. If there is pilferage or breakage, our inventory records will not be correct. However, when we use a perpetual system, we know what we should have. When we count our inventory, we can determine the extent to which goods that have not been sold are missing.

THE PROBLEM OF INFLATION

The periodic and perpetual methods of inventory tracking help us to determine the quantity of goods on hand and the quantity sold. We must also determine which units were sold and which units are on hand. Consider the following situation:

	Quantity	Cost
Beginning Inventory	10,000	$100 Each
Purchase March 1	10,000	$110 Each
Purchase June 1	10,000	$120 Each
Purchase September 1	10,000	$130 Each
Sales during Year	30,000	

How many units are left in stock? Clearly from our basic inventory equation the answer to that is 10,000. Beginning inventory of 10,000, plus the purchases of 30,000, less the sales of 30,000 leaves ending inventory of 10,000. What is the value of those 10,000 units? Here a problem arises. Which 10,000 units are left? Does it matter? From an accounting point of view it definitely does matter. Generally accepted accounting principles require us to value items on the balance sheet at their cost. In the case of inventory, its reported value is the lower of its cost or its market value. In order to know the cost of our remaining units, we must know which units we sold and which are still on hand. This requires the manager to make some assumptions, referred to as *cost-flow assumptions*.

This is particularly important during periods of high inflation. Recently inflation has been modest, but at some point in the near future the rate of inflation may accelerate. Therefore managers need an understanding of the impact of the cost-flow assumptions that they make.

COST-FLOW ASSUMPTIONS

The methods for determining which units were sold and which are on hand are referred to as cost-flow assumptions. There are four major alternative cost-flow assumptions.

Specific Identification

This is the accountant's ideal. It entails physically tagging each unit in some way so that we can specifically identify the units on hand with their cost. Then we can deduce the cost of the units sold since we keep track of the sale of each item.

As you might expect, for most businesses such tagging would create a substantial additional bookkeeping cost. Think of the supermarket not just trying to keep track of how many cans of peas are sold, but also the specific cans. Can any type of business go to this effort? Certainly some can—typically those firms that keep close track of serial numbers for the items sold. For example, a car dealership buys only a few units at a time. The invoice the dealership receives for each car indicates a serial number. When the dealership sells a car it also records the serial number. At the end of the accounting period, it is not overly burdensome for the dealership to determine specifically which units are on hand and which were sold.

First-In, First-Out (FIFO)

The second cost-flow approach is called first-in, first-out, and is referred to by the shorthand acronym FIFO. This method allows you to keep track of the flow of inventory without tagging each item. It is based on the fact that, in most industries, inventory moves in an orderly fashion. We can think of a factory or a warehouse as a building with a front door and a back door. Raw materials or new deliveries of merchandise are received at the back door and put on a conveyor belt. They move along the conveyor belt and right out the front door. We would never have occasion to skip one unit ahead of the other items already on the conveyor belt ahead of it.

A good example of FIFO is a dairy. It is clear that the dairy would always prefer to sell the milk that comes out of the cow today, before they sell the milk that the cow produces tomorrow. We've all seen in the supermarket that the fresh milk is put on the back of the shelf so that we will purchase the older milk from the front of the shelf first. Of course, we know the fresh milk is in the back so we sometimes reach back to get it. But then, they know we know so they sometimes.... Nevertheless, the point is clear—the supermarket's desire is for us to buy the oldest milk first; they want to sell the milk in a FIFO fashion.

In most industries there is a desire to avoid winding up with old, shopworn, obsolete, dirty goods. Therefore, FIFO makes reasonable sense as an approach for processing inventory.

Weighted Average (WA)

The weighted average approach to inventory cost-flows assumes that our entire inventory gets commingled and there is no way to determine which units we are selling. For example, consider a gas station that fills up its underground tanks with gasoline costing $2.20 per gallon. A week later when the tanks are half full, they are refilled with additional gasoline costing $2.40 per gallon. When we now sell gasoline to a customer, are we selling gallons that cost the gas station $2.20 or $2.40? Because there is really no way to know, the WA method assumes that all of the gasoline has been thoroughly mixed, and therefore the gas being sold cost $2.30 per gallon. This method would be appropriate whenever the inventory gets stirred or mixed together and it is physically impossible to determine what has been sold.

Last-In, First-Out (LIFO)

The last of the four methods of cost-flow for inventory is last-in, first-out. The LIFO method is just the reverse of the FIFO method. It assumes that the last goods we receive are the first goods we ship. In the case of the dairy it would mean that we always would try to sell the freshest milk first and keep the older, souring milk in our warehouse.

Does the LIFO method make sense for any industries at all? Yes. In fact it is the logical approach to use for any industry that piles their goods up as they arrive, and then sells from the top of the pile. For example, a company mining coal or making chemicals frequently piles them up and then simply sells from the top of the pile. However, for most firms it doesn't provide a very logical inventory movement. Nevertheless, a large number of firms use the LIFO method. Why? The answer to this question will be addressed in the next section of this chapter.

COMPARISON OF THE LIFO AND FIFO COST-FLOW ASSUMPTIONS

Financial statements are not ideally suited for inflationary environments. During inflation we have problems trying to report inventory without creating distortions in at least one key financial statement.

Consider an example in which we buy one unit of inventory on January 2 for $10 and another unit of inventory on December 30 for $20. On December 31, we sell a unit for $30. What happens to the financial statements if we are using the FIFO method of inventory tracking? The FIFO method means that the inventory that is first-in is the inventory that is the first-out. The January 2 purchase was the first one in, so the cost of the unit sold is $10 and the cost of the unit remaining on hand is $20 (the December purchase). Is the balance sheet a fair representation of current value? It says that we have one unit of inventory that cost $20. What would it cost to buy a unit of inventory near year-end? Well, we bought one on December 30 for $20, so the balance sheet seems pretty accurate.

However, consider the income statement under FIFO. We presumably sold the first-in, which cost $10, for a selling price of $30, leaving us with a $20 profit.

Is that a good indication of the profit we could currently earn from the purchase and sale of a unit of inventory? Not really. At year-end we could have bought a unit for $20 and sold it for $30, leaving a profit of only $10. Thus, during periods of rising prices, the FIFO method does not give users of financial statements a current picture of the profit opportunities facing the firm.

We do not have that problem with LIFO. Under LIFO, the last-in is the first-out, which means that we sold the unit that was purchased on December 30. That unit had cost us $20, and by selling it for $30 we realize a profit of $10. When we tell our stockholders that our profit was $10, we are giving them a reasonably current picture of the profit we can currently make by buying and selling a unit.

Unfortunately this gives rise to another problem. Under LIFO, we have sold the unit that cost $20, so we must have held onto the unit that cost $10 to acquire. Therefore, the inventory number to be shown on the balance sheet is $10. Is it true that we could currently go out and buy more inventory for $10 a unit? No, by year-end the price we paid was already up to $20. So, under LIFO, the value of inventory on the balance sheet is understated.

There is no readily available solution to this problem. The weighted average method simply leaves both the balance sheet and income statements somewhat out of whack, instead of causing a somewhat bigger problem with respect to one or the other, as results under LIFO and FIFO. In the face of this problem, some firms have shifted to LIFO for a very simple reason: to save taxes.

Let's take a second to consider the implications of our example. If we use a FIFO system during inflationary periods, we report a pretax profit of $20 because we have sold a unit that cost $10 for $30. Under LIFO, we report a pretax profit of only $10 because we have sold a unit that cost $20 for $30. Therefore, by being on the LIFO system, we can reduce our tax payments. Are the tax savings worth the fact that we will be reporting lowered profits on our financial statements? Absolutely. If we can lower our taxes by using allowable GAAP, we should take advantage of that opportunity.

However, it gets even better. Suppose we purchased a unit on January 2 for $10. On July 1 we sold that unit. On December 30 we buy a unit for $20. Which unit did we sell? You probably think we sold the unit we paid $10 for. However, you are now entering the accountant's world of make-believe.

Inventory accounting make-believe is played this way. Under FIFO we record $10 of expense and $20 of inventory as an asset. But under LIFO we record $20 of expense on the income statement and $10 as an asset on the balance sheet! That implies that we sold the unit we acquired on December 30, even though the sale took place six months earlier.

The accountant knows that obviously this can't physically be so. But that's okay. We'll just make believe that that's what happened. Under LIFO there is no need for us to actually move our inventories on a LIFO basis. We don't have to throw our conveyor belt into reverse, or keep milk on hand until it turns sour. If our product is dated, there is no need to feel we can't be on a LIFO system because we can't afford to keep stock on hand past the expiration date.

The firm on LIFO can continue to behave all year long as if it were on FIFO. Your managers should continue to make their product decisions based on the current cost of inventory items—and that usually requires a FIFO-type approach. However, your accountant at year-end will make adjustments to your financial records to calculate your income *as if* you were shipping on a LIFO basis.

Assume the following:

Beginning Inventory	$0
January 3, Purchase 1 Unit @	$10
July 1, Sell 1 Unit @	$30
December 1, Purchase Sell 1 Unit @	$20

Under either method, the first unit purchased was physically shipped and the second unit purchased was physically on hand at the end of the year. From a standpoint of physical movement of goods, the FIFO income statement tells the truth. However, by making believe that we shipped a unit that we hadn't even received by the shipping date, we can report a higher cost of goods sold expense, and therefore report a lower profit and pay the government less tax.

The LIFO Conformity Rule

When we talked about depreciation in Chapter 13, we noted that we could have our cake and eat it too. We could tell our stockholders what a good year we had, but we could also tell the government how miserable things had really been. This is not true with LIFO. The government requires that the firm use the same method of inventory reporting to stockholders as it uses to report to the government.

Who Shouldn't Use LIFO

Many, many firms could benefit from LIFO during inflationary periods, but there are some that would not. LIFO is not necessarily advantageous if the cost of your inventory is highly uncertain, and veers downward as often as upward. For many firms dealing in commodities, WA remains a better bet. Firms whose inventory costs are actually falling (electronics, for example) will have lower taxes by staying on FIFO.

LIFO AND IFRS

There is currently a movement in the United States toward adoption of International Financial Reporting Standards (IFRS). IFRS do not allow the use of the LIFO inventory cost flow assumption. Generally Accepted Accounting Principles in the United States are undergoing a period of transformation in preparation for movement to IFRS. This could result in the LIFO method of inventory costing no longer being allowed for financial reporting.

If LIFO is disallowed for financial reporting purposes, then it is likely that companies also will not be able to use LIFO for tax purposes because of the LIFO conformity rule. This could have significant reporting and tax consequences. This will be somewhat softened by an Internal Revenue Service rule that would allow the tax impact of a shift away from LIFO to be spread out over a four year period. Nevertheless, the impact could be dramatic. Inventory carried at purchase values from decades earlier would have to be treated as being sold at potentially enormous profits. Managers should plan ahead for this potential transition.

KEY TERMS

Periodic vs. perpetual inventory—different methods for keeping track of how many units have been sold, and how many units are on hand.

> *Periodic*—goods are counted periodically to determine the ending inventory. The number of units sold is calculated using the inventory equation.

> *Perpetual*—the inventory balance is adjusted as each unit is sold so that a perpetual record of how many units have been sold and how many are on hand is maintained at all times.

Cost-flow assumptions—inventory is valued at its cost. Therefore, it is necessary to know not only how many units were sold and how many are left on hand, but specifically which were sold and which are left. This determination is made via one of four different approaches.

> *Specific identification*—We record and identify each unit as it is acquired or sold.

> *First-in, First-out (FIFO)*—We assume that the units acquired earlier are sold before units acquired later.

> *Weighted average (WA)*—We assume that all units are indistinguishable and assign a weighted average cost to each unit.

> *Last-in, First-out (LIFO)*—We assume that the last units acquired are the first ones sold, even if this implies sale of a unit prior to its acquisition. During periods of inflation there are tax savings associated with LIFO.

QUESTIONS FOR REVIEW

1. Explain the difference between periodic and perpetual inventory systems.

2. How does periodic inventory work? If you don't keep track of units when you use them, how do you figure out how much you consumed?

3. What are the four basic cost flow methods for inventory valuation?

4. How does inflation impact the valuation of an organization's inventory?

5. Assume your organization has the following inventory changes during the year:

Beginning Inventory	20 units valued at $7,500 each
January purchases	10 units at $8,500 each
April purchases	15 units at $8,750 each
Total Units Used	30

Calculate the value of the ending inventory and the value of the inventory used (the inventory expense) for the year using both the FIFO and the LIFO methods.

Chapter 17

Variance Analysis: Using Budgets for Control

Even if budgets are prepared carefully, actual results often differ from the budget. The difference between the budget and the actual results is called a *variance*, that is, the amount by which the results *vary* from the budget. A variance may result if the budget is not implemented properly, or if actions are not taken to keep the organization running according to the plan. But variances may also be the result of factors beyond the control of the organization. Organizations need to determine if variances have occurred, and take corrective actions when needed.

Variances are calculated for three primary reasons. One reason is aid in controlling results throughout the current year. By understanding why variances are occurring, actions can be taken to avoid additional unfavorable variances over the remaining months of the year. A second reason is to aid in preparing the budget for the coming year. By understanding why results were not as expected, the budget process can be improved and be more accurate in future planning. Finally, variance analysis may be used to evaluate the performance of departments and their managers. However, it should be stressed that the main reason for investigating why variances have occurred is not to assign blame; crying over spilt milk is not the primary goal. Rather, the focus is to determine where and how remedial actions can be taken to avoid spilling any more milk in the future.

Variance analysis can help managers locate the cause of inefficiencies and help organizations avoid waste. In addition, variance analysis can also help managers explain why variances have arisen when they are due to neither inefficiency nor other controllable events.

UNDERSTANDING WHY VARIANCES OCCURRED

Organizations should generally provide each manager with a monthly variance report indicating budgeted expectations, actual results, and the variance for each item in the budget. In order for variance reports to be a valuable managerial tool, managers must be able to determine and understand the causes of the variances. This requires investigating why each *substantial* variance occurred.

Generally, small variances are assumed to be the result of uncontrollable, random events. A manager would not spend much time investigating a $20 variance. Only variances that are either large in dollar amount or as a percentage of the budgeted amount are investigated. Determination of whether an amount is large enough to warrant investigation requires both skill and judgment, and no easy rules of thumb exist. Many organizations will use institutional history as a guide to determine what size variances should be investigated. Others use control charts, with upper and lower limits above and below the budgeted amount. If the limits are exceeded the variance must be investigated.

Chart 17-1 presents an example of a control chart for variance analysis, showing annual staffing costs by month. The chart shows both budgeted and actual costs for each month. The key to a control chart is that a determination is made of how far actual costs can be from budget before we are concerned and believe investigation is necessary. In this chart, we have used plus or minus 20%, but that range is up to the manager and organization. Statistical measures such as standard deviations can be used to determine the limits, or they can be simple dollar or percent amounts. The upper and lower limits are plotted on the chart. Each month we review the chart to see if spending has gone above or below the lower limit. In the months that actual results are either above the upper limit or below the lower limit, that indicates to the manager that the variation is great enough to require investigation.

CHART 17-1
Control Chart
Budget and Actual Labor Costs by Month

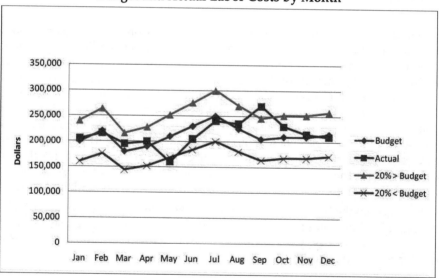

In Chart 17-1, we see that in May actual spending dipped slightly below the lower limit. Even though spending was less than budgeted, this should still receive investigation. If spending is so far from budget because there is something wrong, we need to know about it. If there is nothing wrong, then we want to understand the variance so we can learn how to duplicate that lower spending. From May to September spending steadily increased, and in September exceeded the upper limit and required investigation.

Often, only the person who has supervised a department has enough actual knowledge of that department to effectively determine why it spent more or less than expected. As a result, finance officers often generate variance reports, but each department manager is required to prepare an analysis of why variances occurred in their department.

If variances arose as a result of inefficiency (e.g., unduly long lunch breaks), then the process of providing cost-effective services is out of control. By discovering this inefficiency, actions can be taken to eliminate it and to bring the process back under control. In this case, future costs will be lower because of the investigation of the variance.

In many cases, however, variances are caused by factors outside of the control of managers. For example, the cost of an essential raw ingredient may unexpectedly rise. Blaming a manager for increased spending that results from things that are outside of his or her control can only result in poor morale and even worse future performance.

Nevertheless, even if the cause of a variance is something outside the control of the manager, the variance should be investigated and its cause determined. The impact of such variances on total costs should not be ignored. If the increase in the price of the raw ingredient is likely to persist, then the organization will continue to go over budget. Eventually this may cause the organization to run out of money. This could threaten its continued existence. Decisions will have to be made. Should the organization continue to make the product that uses this ingredient? Should (can) it raise the price of the finished product? Can the organization survive with the losses? Can the organization cut back on other resource costs? Whether variances are controllable or not, they set into motion a number of actions and decisions that are necessary in order for the organization to achieve its best possible overall result and ensure its continued existence.

STATIC BUDGETS

The typical operating budget is sometimes referred to as a "static" budget. The static budget is used to compare expected results with actual results. Any difference is called a variance. If the amount actually spent on an expense item is greater than the budgeted amount, it is considered to be an unfavorable variance. On the other hand, if less was spent than anticipated, it is a favorable variance.

Within this framework, the more detailed the budget is, the greater the amount of control we can exercise. For example, if we know only the total budget, we have very little information. Consider the case of hypothetical Bud Jet Corporation. In Exhibit 17-1 we see that Bud Jet had total manufacturing costs of $200,000 more than expected for a particular month. Why? From the information in this exhibit it is hard to tell. If we had information by department, we would have a better idea of what has occurred.

EXHIBIT 17-1
Total Manufacturing Variance
Bud Jet Corporation

BUDGETED TOTAL COSTS	ACTUAL TOTAL COSTS	VARIANCE FAVORABLE/ (UNFAVORABLE)
$2,000,000	$2,200,000	$(200,000)

From Exhibit 17-2, we can see that although the Polishing department had a good year, the Processing, Assembly, and Packing departments were substantially over budget. This is the first step toward discovering what has happened. Now we can begin to investigate why cost overruns occurred so that we can hopefully avoid them in future months. Specifically, we can focus our attention on the departments where the largest variances occurred.

EXHIBIT 17-2
Manufacturing Variances by Department
Bud Jet Corporation

DEPARTMENT	BUDGETED COSTS	ACTUAL COSTS	VARIANCE
Purchasing	$1,000,000	$1,010,000	$ (10,000)
Processing	200,000	280,000	(80,000)
Assembly	400,000	460,000	(60,000)
Polishing	100,000	90,000	10,000
Packing	300,000	$60,000	(60,000)
TOTALS	$2,000,000	$2,200,000	$ (200,000)

Yet, we still don't really have adequate information. Consider the large Processing Department variance. We want the manager of the Processing Department to explain what happened. But the financial officers haven't given the manager of that department much to go on. The manager simply knows the department was $80,000 over budget. If the static budget is broken down even further by line item for each department, such as personnel cost, materials, and overhead, it becomes easier to determine why excess costs occurred. Exhibit 17-3 presents such an analysis for the Processing Department at Bud Jet.

EXHIBIT 17-3
Processing Department Line-Item Variances
Bud Jet Corporation

	BUDGETED COSTS	ACTUAL COSTS	VARIANCE
Processing Dept.			
Personnel	$ 80,000	$ 80,000	$ 0
Materials	100,000	180,000	(80,000)
Overhead	20,000	20,000	0
TOTALS	$200,000	$280,000	$ (80,000)

Note that the entire variance occurred in the area of materials. Investigation might show that this was unavoidable due to a significant unexpected rise in the price of raw materials used. On the other hand, we might find that employees had been quite careless in the use of materials, resulting in significant waste. This latter possibility makes clear the fact that budget variances should be calculated and investigated frequently. We should catch waste and correct it long before year-end.

Line-item analysis of variances can, of course, be quite detailed. We can calculate the variance with respect to each type of labor or raw material input. However, even that still does not help us to isolate the cause of the variance as much as we would like. Did the processing department go over on its materials budget because it wasted materials or because the price of materials had risen? We have gone as far as we can with the static budget. In order to gain additional information about the cause of variances, we now have to turn our attention to flexible budgeting.

FLEXIBLE BUDGETING

The key problem with static budgets is that they provide an expected cost for one particular volume, hence the name static. At the end of a reporting period such as a month or a year, it is highly unlikely that we will have attained exactly the expected output level. If we produce more units than we had planned because sales are up substantially over our expectations, then it is logical to assume that we will have to go over our budget. On the other hand, if volume is down, then costs should be under budget. Flexible budgets provide an after-the-fact device to tell what it should have cost for the volume level actually attained. Adjusting the static budget for the actual production volume achieved results in the flexible budget.

Flexible Budget Variance and Volume Variance

Suppose we expect the variable cost per unit to be $10. If we expect to produce 100,000 units, then we expect a total variable cost of $1,000,000. What if we only produced 85,000 units, and we had a total variable cost of $900,000? The static budget comparison would be that we had a budgeted variable cost of $ 1,000,000, and we only spent $900,000, so we had a favorable variance of $100,000. But it should have cost only $850,000 to produce 85,000 units. We actually spent more than we should have, given the level of actual production. In this example, the actual cost was $900,000, the static budget was $1,000,000, and the flexible budget was $850,000.

The total variance between the actual cost of $900,000 and the static budget of $1,000,000 is a favorable variance of $100,000, as noted earlier. Exhibit 17-4 shows that we can decompose this total variance into two parts. The first part, on the right side of the exhibit, is the difference between the static budget and the flexible budget. This is a $150,000 favorable variance. However, by favorable we simply mean we spent less than expected. This variance is called a volume variance: it is caused because our volume varied from what was expected. It is likely that, because volume was below that expected, this was an unfavorable event, even though the accountant called it a favorable variance.

On the left side of Exhibit 17-4 is the difference between the actual cost and the flexible budget, which gives rise to an unfavorable flexible budget variance of $50,000. That is, we actually spent $50,000 more than we would have budgeted for the level of production attained. The flexible budget variance and the volume variance in total are equal to the total variance.

EXHIBIT 17-4
Flexible Budget Variance and Volume

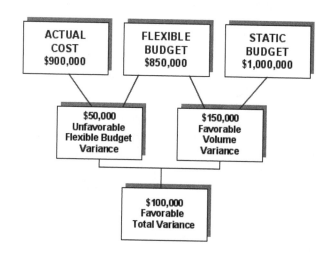

Price and Quantity Variances

We can get still more information from variance analysis. For each variable cost item, we can calculate not only the volume and flexible budget variances, but also a price and a quantity variance.

The difference between the flexible budget and the actual costs incurred makes up the flexible budget variance. The accountant may then break down this flexible budget variance into two components: 1) the part of the total variance caused because we paid a different price for our inputs, and 2) the part of the difference caused because we used more or less of an input than expected for the actual volume of production. See Exhibit 17-5. The total of the price, quantity, and volume variances makes up the total variance between actual costs and the original static budget for any budget line item.

Excel Excercise

Template 17 may be used to calculate price, quantity, volume, and total variances. The template is on the CD that accompanies this book.

EXHIBIT 17-5
Price, Quantity, and Volume Variances

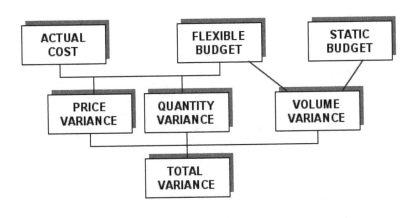

When we consider materials, we refer to the price variance simply as a price variance, and we refer to the quantity variance as a use variance. While the term *price* is adequately clear, the word use allows us to visualize that the variance refers to how much material we used to make the amount of product. With respect to variances in the cost of labor, we generally refer to these variances as rate and efficiency variances. The term rate is based on the rate we pay labor. The term *efficiency* is based on the fact that frequently, when we consume more labor than expected to produce a given level of output, inefficiency exists. However, this may not always be the case.

We should be especially careful in interpreting variances. The accountant uses the word *favorable* to imply that less money was spent than was expected. The term *unfavorable* is used to mean that more money was spent than was expected. There is no sense of good, bad, efficient, or inefficient implied by the terms *favorable* and *unfavorable* in an accounting context. If we have an unfavorable labor efficiency variance, this doesn't necessarily imply that labor worked inefficiently. There may have been a machine breakdown or a stockout of a key material. It is possible the purchasing department bought inferior materials that required more labor input.

The benefit of using price and quantity variances is that it can help to very narrowly pinpoint the specific areas where we went over or under budget. However, the variances themselves should not be considered causes for punishment or congratulations. All that variances can do is point the direction for investigations to take to determine the underlying causes for variances. But by undertaking such investigations on a timely basis, we can better control results, so that we come as near to achieving or surpassing the plan as possible.

Those individuals who would like more detailed information about the computation of price, quantity and volume variances should see the Appendix to this chapter.

KEY TERMS

Static budget—a budget prepared before the year begins, establishing what it should cost for the anticipated output level.

Flexible budget—an after-the-fact budget establishing what it should have cost for the actual attained output level.

Variance—the difference between an actual result and a budgeted amount.

    Volume variance—the difference between the static budget and the flexible budget. The amount of the total variance caused by having a higher or lower output volume than had been expected.

    Price variance—the portion of the difference between the flexible budget and actual costs caused by paying a different price for each unit of raw material or hour of labor than had been anticipated.

    Quantity variance—the portion of the difference between the flexible budget and the actual costs caused by using more raw materials or labor for each unit produced than had been anticipated.

    Total variance—the volume variance, plus the price variance, plus the quantity variance make up the total variance for the variable inputs. This is equal to the difference between the static budget and the actual costs.

QUESTIONS FOR REVIEW

1. What are some uses of budgets for control?
2. Why is a variance analysis performed?
3. What is meant by favorable and unfavorable variances?
4. What are some possible causes of variances?
5. What is the essence of flexible budget variance analysis?
6. Does flexible budget variance analysis explain the cause of variances observed?
7. The following are the department labor costs for the month of March:

Actual	Budget	Variance
$22,815	$17,250	$5,565 U

Budgeted volume	= 1,250
Actual volume	= 1,500
Budgeted labor hours per unit	= .60
Actual labor hours per unit	= .65
Budgeted pay rate	= $23.00/hr
Actual pay rate	= $23.40/hr

Calculate the price, quantity, and volume variances. (See Appendix).

APPENDIX—COMPUTING VARIANCES

Suppose that the Bud Jet Corporation expected to spend $1,000,000 on labor for a particular product they manufacture. It turned out that the cost of production was $968,000 for labor. There is an favorable variance of $32,000 because we spent less than the original, or static, budget. However, that doesn't tell us the full story. In order to compute rate (or price), efficiency (or quantity or use), and volume variances, we need to have six pieces of input information:

- bQo: the budgeted quantity of output
- aQo: the actual quantity of output
- bQi: the budgeted quantity of input needed per unit of output
- aQo: the actual quantity of input used per unit of output
- bPi: the budgeted price of input per unit of input
- aPi: the actual price of input per unit of input

For example, suppose that we expected to produce 10,000 units of a product. That would be a bQo of 10,000. We refer to the product we are making as output. Suppose that we actually produced an aQo, or actual quantity of output, of 11,000 units. We planned to use 5 hours of labor for each unit of output produced. The labor is referred to as the input, and in this case the bQi, or budgeted amount of input needed put unit of output, would be 5. In fact, however, it turned out that we only used 4 hours of labor for each unit of product we made. So our aQi, or actual quantity of input used per unit of output, was 4. We expected to pay our labor $20 per hour. Actually, labor cost us $22 per hour. So the bPi, or budgeted labor per hour was $20, and the aPi, or actual price of labor per hour was $22. We can summarize the information we have as follows:

- bQo: 10,000 units of output
- aQo: 11,000 units of output
- bQi: 5 hours of labor per unit of output
- aQo: 4 hours of labor per unit of output
- bPi: $20 per labor hour
- aPi: $22 per labor hour

Variances are computed in a certain order, by convention. If the order of computation is changed, it will affect the result somewhat. Generally, we first compute the volume variance by comparing all budgeted information to the budgeted price of inputs, budgeted quantity of input per unit of output, but actual quantity of output, as follows:

$$bPi \times bQi \times bQo$$

vs

$$bPi \times bQi \times \mathbf{aQo}$$

or

$$\$20 \times 5 \times 10{,}000 = \$1{,}000{,}000$$

vs

$$\$20 \times 5 \times 11{,}000 = \$1{,}100{,}000$$

Volume Variance $ \underline{100,000}$ Unfavorable

The volume variance is unfavorable because we made more units than expected. More units require more labor. If we have more labor we spend more. Spending more results in an unfavorable variance. That doesn't mean it is a bad outcome. Perhaps we sold the extra units at a profit. An unfavorable variance only means spending more; it does not imply a bad outcome for the organization.

We would next compute the efficiency (or quantity or use) variance. This computation compares the budgeted price of inputs, budgeted quantity of input per unit of output, and actual quantity of output to the budgeted price of inputs, actual quantity of input per unit of output, and actual quantity of outputs. Note that we do not go back and keep everything budgeted except for the quantity of input per unit of output. The reason for this is that we need a mathematical approach that will assure that the price, quantity, and volume variances add up to the total variance, and the approach demonstrated here will assure that occurs. We compute the efficiency variance as follows:

$$bPi \times bQi \times aQo$$
vs
$$bPi \times \mathbf{aQi} \times aQo$$

or

$$\$20 \times 5 \times 11,000 = \$1,100,000$$
vs
$$\$20 \times 4 \times 11,000 = \$\ \ 880,000$$

Efficiency Variance $ 220,000 Favorable

The efficiency variance is favorable because we used less labor per unit of output than expected. If we use less labor we spend less. Spending less results in a favorable variance. That doesn't mean it is a good outcome. Perhaps with less labor we made a shoddy product that we won't be able to sell. A favorable variance only means spending less than budgeted.

We would next compute the rate (or price) variance. This computation compares the budgeted price of inputs, actual quantity of input per unit of output, and actual quantity of output to all actual values. We compute the rate variance as follows:

$$bPi \times aQi \times aQo$$
vs
$$\mathbf{aPi} \times aQi \times aQo$$

or

$$\$20 \times 4 \times 11,000 = \$880,000$$
vs
$$\$22 \times 4 \times 11,000 = \$968,000$$

Rate Variance $ 88,000 Unfavorable

The rate variance is unfavorable because we paid more per hour for labor than was budgeted. If we pay more per hour for labor we spend more. Spending more results in an unfavorable variance.

Note that the three variances when combined total to a variance of $32,000 favorable (i.e. $220,000 favorable less $100,000 unfavorable less $88,000 unfavorable = $32,000 favorable). Although the total variance is favorable, these three sub-variances: rate, efficiency, and volume, are each sufficiently large that they should be investigated. The causes for the variances should be determined, and appropriate actions taken to improve future outcomes for the organization.

Chapter 18

Fraud

WHAT IS FRAUD?

There are many types of fraud, but most fraud consists of an intentional deception for the purpose of a financial gain. For example, suppose that you take your car for service and the mechanic says you need a new carburetor that will cost $1,000. You agree and pay for the new carburetor. In fact, the mechanic just performs a minor adjustment to your fuel-injection system. It has been quite a while since cars had carburetors. You have been defrauded. Fraud is not uncommon and the amount of the fraud might be quite small, or enormous, such as Madoff's $65 billion Ponzi scheme (i.e. a fraud in which one takes money from new investors to make payments to earlier investors, making it appear that the money has been profitably invested, when in fact the money often is never invested at all).

Some types of fraud are well-known and commonplace, such as embezzlements, bribes, and writing bad checks. Additional acts that constitute fraud include bait and switch tactics, making false statements, acting in conflict of interest, extortion, mail wire fraud, failure to report a felony, false advertising, over-billing, filing false insurance claims, forgery, and breach of fiduciary trust.

Although no statistics exist, it is likely that discovered embezzlements amount to only the tip of the iceberg of what is really occurring. It is usually the greedy embezzlers that are caught. The modest embezzlers have an excellent chance of going undetected, especially if collusion among several employees exists. A common misperception is that embezzlement leaves a large cash shortage which is eventually discovered. We go to withdraw money from our bank account and find that a million dollars is missing. This sort of open embezzlement is really the exception, not the rule.

Consider an individual whose job is to approve bills for payment. Suppose he were to print up stationery for Bill's Roofing Repair and send an invoice for $400 to his employer. What happens? He will receive the invoice at work and will approve it for payment. Large payments may require a second approval. Therefore, larger embezzlements may require a partner if they are to go undetected.

Doesn't this type of embezzlement cause a cash shortage? No! We record the roofing repair expense and reduce the cash account by the amount of the payment. The money paid is being correctly reported as an expense. From the auditor's viewpoint, there is a misclassification of expense. We are calling the expense a roofing repair expense when, in fact, it should be called miscellaneous embezzlement expense. However our cash balance isn't overstated because the cash account was appropriately reduced when we paid the expense. The income isn't overstated because we did record an expense, even if we didn't correctly identify its cause. Nevertheless, money has been stolen from the company.

How can the fraud be detected? If we send a letter to Bill's Roofing Repair and ask if their invoice was a bona fide bill, we will likely get an affirmative response, albeit coming from the embezzler himself. If we directly ask the employee if he approved the bill for payment, he will say yes, because he did approve it for payment to himself. In order to really see if this type of embezzlement is going on, we would have to trace each bill back to the individual in the organization who originally ordered the work done or the goods purchased. Unfortunately, the cost of the audit work involved to double check every accounting transaction is likely to far exceed the amount likely to have been embezzled.

The result is that it is possible for numerous small frauds to go undetected. Since it is so hard to catch all small embezzlements, the need for an approach to prevent fraud, discussed below, is of particular importance.

The internet has created an environment which creates increased risk of frauds. Many readers of this book have received an e-mail from someone who needs your assistance liquidating their fortune and will pay you a handsome commission. Hopefully you delete such e-mails. However, if you were to followup on such requests, generally you would wind up having to provide some of your own money at some point. You may even receive a large check from the perpetrator of the fraud which you can deposit in your bank account before you have to pay out any money. The problem is that long after your money has left your account and can't be retrieved, the check you received and deposited comes back unpaid. This can happen even weeks after your bank has indicated that the check has "cleared" your account.

BUSINESS FRAUD

In addition to the typical frauds that the lay person is likely to be aware of, there are frauds that take place within businesses that the nonfinancial manager should know about. Specifically, it is important to focus on frauds that:

- overstate revenue
- understate expense
- overstate assets, or
- understate liabilities.

Some of the biggest frauds in history, such as the Enron scandal, revolved around actions to manipulate the organization's reported profits and resources.

Overstating revenues makes the organization look better than it otherwise would. Overstating revenues results in profits being overstated. Overstated profits will lead to a higher than warranted stock price. Sometimes revenues are overstated by management in an effort to keep their jobs by leading the Board of Directors to think that things are going better than they are. How might this occur? One way is to simply record fictitious revenues. Order forms can be filled out representing orders by companies that don't even exist. This will increase both reported revenue and also accounts receivable. Or revenues might be recorded before they are earned. Perhaps a client pays for services in advance. That money is not supposed to be recorded as revenue until service is provided. However, if it is immediately shown as revenue, the organization's profits will be overstated.

Expenses can be understated. Some items that should be an expense may be recorded as capital, with the expense spread out of a period of years in the future. For example, rather than treating routine equipment repairs as expenses, they may be added to the value of the repaired equipment, and depreciated over the remaining life of the equipment. Or expenses may simply not be recorded. Employee work done near the end may not be recorded as labor expense. This results in an understatement of the true costs of operating the business, and therefore overstates profits.

Assets can be overstated in a number of different ways. An organization could simply list assets that either don't exist at all, or exist, but are not owned by the organization. One would hope that an independent auditor would uncover such frauds. However, asset overstatements are difficult to uncover. Suppose an employee records fictitious accounts receivable. When the auditor sends a letter to confirm the accuracy of the accounts receivable balance, the perpetrator of the fraud will receive that letter at the fictitious company's post office box, and will complete and return it indicating that the receivables balance is correct.

Lastly, liabilities may be understated. This can be done by simply omitting obligations from the financial records of the organization, or by understating the amount of a liability. For example, when the bills are received, they can be thrown away. This will temporarily avoid not only recording the account payable liability, but also the related expense.

Manipulation of revenue, expense, assets, and liabilities tends to eventually come to light. But often the individual defrauding the organization will have benefited (perhaps by selling stock at an inflated price, or by getting a new job elsewhere based on outstanding performance at their current job) and may have disappeared before the fraud is detected.

WHY DOES FRAUD HAPPEN?

Although fraud is illegal, our society tends to glamorize it. In movies and TV shows the acts of con men are often viewed in a positive light. The con man is sometimes portrayed as a Robin Hood stealing from the rich and giving to the poor, or as a lovable rogue committing a victimless crime. Such a perception makes it easier to rationalize committing fraud. Many people who commit fraud contend that "they were unfair to me—I was just taking what I deserved." However, once started, frauds often continue with the total amount stolen being much greater than the perpetrator could contend they deserved. Once started, it is hard to stop.

Often frauds take place as a result of pressure. "I needed money because the bank was going to foreclose on my house." However, while there are often external needs, sometimes fraud occurs in an effort to please the boss. "We hadn't been doing well, and there was a lot of pressure from the boss to show better results. So I fudged the numbers a bit so things would look good."

To protect the organization, managers need to find ways to prevent fraud from occurring. One approach is to focus on ethical behavior, educating employees that fraud is wrong—it is not a glamorous thing that is okay if you can get away with it. Another approach is to enact legislation focusing on fraud, creating severe enough penalties to dissuade individuals from committing fraud. A third approach to prevent fraud is for organizations to assure that they have adequate management control systems to discourage and discover frauds. Each of these approaches will be discussed below.

PREVENTING FRAUD BY FOCUSING ON ETHICS

There are mixed views on the role that a focus on ethics can have on fraud. Some argue that there are people who would commit fraud and people who would not, and that their personalities have been formed long before they take their first full-time job. However, there are those who argue that even if that is true, organizational culture can have a big impact on employee actions. At least on the margin, a strong organizational emphasis on what is okay and what is not okay can affect the decisions that employees make.

It has become common for organizations to have ethics programs. Such programs can communicate a set of policies related to ethics and make sure that all employees are made aware of those policies. The policies of some organizations are very general statements, while other organizations have policies that are more detailed and provide a specific codes of ethics. Detailed policy statements sometimes indicate potential ethical dilemmas that might arise and how they should be addressed. This hopefully will lead to both employee awareness of ethical issues and also employee awareness that the organization focuses on ethics and is likely to be vigilant in finding unethical behavior.

Some characteristics of a well-developed ethics program are:

- a written statement
- a strong statement of support from top management
- public disclosure of examples of actions management has taken which indicate adherence to, and support of, the policy
- periodic occasions when ethics is discussed in seminars that focus specifically on ethical corporate behavior
- periodic occasions where ethical considerations are discussed in meetings where the primary focus of the meeting was not ethics, so that ethics become a part of the day in and day out business of the organization
- a plan for monitoring compliance
- clearly stated consequences for failure to adhere to the policies

- a policy that is perceived as being attainable within the corporate culture of the organization.

One concern is the extent to which corporate ethics programs are simply lip service. There may be great pressure on employees to perform no matter what, regardless of ethical concerns. And yet those same companies, whether to maintain a good image or to protect themselves from lawsuits, may have an active ethics program.

It is also important for each business to examine the unintended incentives that the business model creates that might push people toward unethical behavior. Are there unreasonable expectations that cause employees to feel they must act in an unethical manner in order to keep their job? A survey of managers would likely show that they support ethical behavior. Yet, managers often come under severe financial performance pressures that can lead them to make improper decisions in an effort to help their organizations.

Overcharging for services, charging for services that have not been provided, paying bribes or improper referral fees, and similar practices are not new. These types of activities have occurred and, realistically, likely will continue to occur. However, we must be careful to avoid thinking that such activities are acceptable. "Everyone does it" is just as incorrect a generalization as "no one cheats." Both represent extreme and unrealistic positions. By conveying by action and word that "everyone does it" is not acceptable, an organization can change culture toward more ethical behavior.

Being ethical may seem to be clear-cut in the abstract, but in practice it often becomes hard to draw the line between the clearly acceptable and the clearly unacceptable. Things that are within the letter of the law may not be in the spirit of the law. Things that may be correct in principle may not be legal. Therefore the organization's ethics policies should be as specific as possible in explaining the ethical behavior expectations and should provide examples to help managers deal with some difficult realities that confront them.

PREVENTING FRAUD THROUGH LEGISLATION

Fraud is a crime, and people convicted of fraud are subject to criminal penalties including jail time. Fraud is also a violation of civil law. Generally the laws covering fraud vary by state. However, a number of large corporate scandals from 1998 through 2002 led the federal government to take a close examination of governance and internal control of organizations. Perhaps the most notable of those scandals was the Enron bankruptcy in 2001. In 2002 the Public Company Accounting Reform and Investor Protection Act, commonly referred to as the Sarbanes-Oxley Act (SOX), was passed.

The Sarbanes-Oxley Act

SOX requires more rigorous internal control systems, reporting of financial transactions, and disclosure of conflicts of interest in an effort to prevent fraudulent activities. It specifically identifies corporate fraud as a crime and contains specific criminal penalties for records tampering, destruction, or alteration.

The law also creates a greater level of responsibility for managers and board members, and requires senior executives to take individual responsibility for the accuracy and completeness of corporate financial reports. The CEO and CFO of organizations required to comply with SOX have to certify that they have reviewed the annual financial report, that it does not contain any untrue statement of a material fact, and that the statements fairly present the financial condition of the organization.

Furthermore, the CEO and CFO will have to certify that internal control systems are in place to ensure awareness of material misinformation, and that any known deficiencies in control, or any known frauds involving key personnel, have been disclosed to both the outside auditors and to the audit committee. As a result of this greater reliance on internal control, all organizations are making an effort to upgrade their internal control systems. Managers need to know that they really can rely on their control systems to catch problems as they arise. Control systems are discussed later in this chapter.

SOX requires organizations to have a mechanism for claims of improper behavior to be reported anonymously and followed up on. It also provides significant protections for whistle-blowers, and severe penalties to those who retaliate against them.

Furthermore, the law lays out harsh penalties (up to 10 years in prison) for inadequate internal documentation. Policies must be developed to determine which documents must be preserved (paper or electronic), for how long, and how they should be stored and retrieved.

The Board of Directors' audit committee has an enhanced role under SOX, so that it becomes easier to determine if top management is acting inappropriately. Instead of managers hiring the independent auditor, the audit committee retains and supervises the outside auditors so that there is a decreased chance of top management exerting influence over the auditor. Key executives, such as the CEO and CFO, are excluded from the committee, to reduce their influence over its work and also so that whistle-blowers will be less inhibited from approaching the committee to report problems. To avoid conflicts of interest, audit committee members are not be allowed to be consultants paid by the firm, and audit committees are required to have some members with financial expertise.

For many organizations, the outside auditor has also served as the primary financial consultant. To try to ensure more independence on the part of the auditor, SOX explicitly lists a number of different types of consulting activities that may not be provided by the accounting firm that is conducting the annual audit of the organization's financial statements. These prohibited areas include bookkeeping, information systems design, appraisal services, actuarial services, internal audit outsourcing, human resources, investment advising, and legal or expert service unrelated to the audit.

Another primary focus of the act is to create more oversight over the public accounting firms that audit organizations. The law requires periodic audit partner rotation and places limits on the services that can be provided by auditors. Unfortunately, such provisions are still inadequate measures if the audit firm is not truly independent of the client being audited. One option would be to require companies to change the independent accounting firm that audits them on a regular basis, rather than just rotating the audit firm's partner who is in charge of the audit. Some argue further that it might make sense to have the government assign the auditor rather than allowing the company to select and hire the auditor. SOX did not go that far. But one has to wonder if the Madoff scheme could have been perpetrated for such a long period of time without the collusion of their audit firm. So despite some strong anti-fraud measures contained in SOX, at least one serious weakness remains.

USING CONTROL SYSTEMS TO PREVENT FRAUD

In order for a fraud to take place, there must be opportunity. If it is easy to commit and get away with fraud, it is more likely to take place than if it is difficult. A management control system (MCS), or set of internal controls, is a set of policies and procedures designed to keep operations going according to plan. Such systems detect variations from plans and provide managers with information needed to take corrective actions when necessary. One aspect of MCS' is that they deter fraud by making it difficult to commit the fraud and by making it more likely that the person committing the fraud will be caught. MCS' also serve the function of keeping the organization on track to assure that it has the best possible chance to attain its budgeted goals.

Management control systems have often been compared to thermostats. We might set a thermostat for 70 degrees. That is our plan. It is the temperature that we hope will exist in a room. However, a thermostat does more than just establish the desired temperature. It also monitors the existing temperature in the room. Similarly, an MCS assesses the actual *outcomes* for the organization. If the temperature in the room varies from the desired 70 degrees, the thermostat activates the furnace to send heat if it gets too cold, or turns off the furnace if it gets too hot. Similarly, the MCS must set in motion actions that are needed if it determines that there are variations from the plan.

Further, management control systems establish an environment in which it is likely that the organization will come as close to its plans as possible. This means that MCS' are proactive as well as reactive. They are reactive to the extent that they monitor, detect if something is going wrong, and then initiate actions to correct the problem. However, they are also proactive in that they put in place a set of incentives and controls that help the organization avoid having bad outcomes in the first place.

As part of an overall management control system, organizations develop a set of internal controls that play an essential role in safeguarding resources. The first step in safeguarding resources is to hire ethical people and create a culture that rewards ethical behavior and condemns unethical behavior. Unfortunately, no matter how hard you try to do that, it is still necessary to take additional steps to protect the resources of the organization. These include having an audit trail, separation of duties, proper authorization, adequate documentation, proper procedures, physical safeguards, bonding, vacations, rotation of duties, independent checks, and cost-benefit analysis. Each of these elements is discussed in turn.

Audit Trail

It is important for organizations to have an *audit trail*. An audit trail refers to the ability to trace each transaction in an accounting system back to its source. For example, suppose that the Coffin Corporation spent $50,000 on travel expenses for the year. That might seem to be an inordinately large amount. Documentation should exist that would allow us to determine exactly what that $50,000 was spent on. Perhaps the expenses were legitimate approved expenses. But they might represent unauthorized travel.

The existence of the audit trail serves as a preventive device. If people knew that we did not have good audit trails, they might feel safer in misappropriating money. They might assume that we would never be able to backtrack and find where the money went. When people recognize that all spending is carefully documented and that an audit trail will allow the organization to retrace the steps in the accounting process back to the source of unusual expenditures, it serves to inhibit inappropriate spending.

In order for an audit trail to be effective, there must be regular use of the trail to identify and examine discrepancies or unusual spending patterns. If employees knew that a trail was kept, but investigations never took place utilizing that information, it would not have as strong a preventive influence as if it were used on a regular basis.

Separation of Functions

Activities that relate to the disbursement of resources should be separated so that no one individual controls too much of the process. The individual who approves bills for payment should not be the same person who writes checks, and the person who writes checks should not be the same person who signs the checks.

The benefit of such separation is that each individual may catch a problem that is missed by another. If a bill is not correct, the person approving payment should catch it. If that person doesn't, the person writing the check for payment may find the problem. Even if neither of them finds the problem, the person signing the check may raise a question about the payment, which leads to discovery of the problem. This system of separation is also an especially powerful tool for reducing the potential for embezzlement.

If the same person authorizes payments, writes checks, and signs them, that person has the ability to steal money with a minimum likelihood of detection. By separating functions, we make such activity more likely to be discovered and therefore less likely to occur.

Another example of separation is keeping operations separate from accounting. For example, Coffin Corporation has a central inventory department that tracks all of the coffin inventory. This department should not be the one responsible for making periodic checks of the number and models of coffins on hand (called "taking an inventory"). The members of that department have access to these coffins, and there is the potential for theft. If the same individuals are responsible for counting them, they can falsify records to hide the theft. If they know that independent individuals from elsewhere in the organization will count them, they know there is a high likelihood of the theft being discovered, so theft is less likely to occur.

However, any control system can be defeated. Separation of functions will not protect resources if several individuals collude to steal from the organization. If the person approving payment, the person writing checks, and the person signing checks all agree to steal money and share it, it will be hard for the control system to prevent such actions. That is why hiring ethical individuals and having a corporate culture that stresses ethical behavior are critical elements of a control system.

Proper Authorization

Another control element is related to proper authorization. A system of authorization for spending helps the organization to set spending policies, and then adhere to them. For example, a policy decision might be that all air travel is done in coach. But the organization may have thousands of employees. What is to stop one of them from buying and using a first-class air ticket and charging the organization for the higher first-class airfare?

Organizations accomplish this by establishing formal authorization mechanisms. Expenditures will be reimbursed only if they have received the proper authorization. This can be stifling if every individual has to go through an elaborate process to get authorization to spend any amount on any item. Therefore, some items can qualify for *general authorization*. General authorization is a standing approval of certain spending. Items under a certain dollar limit or for certain purposes may fall under that general authorization. For example, air travel at the coach airfare rate for valid business reasons may fall under general authorization. General authorization may contain limits and prohibitions.

Items that cannot be acquired using general authorization require *specific authorization*. Specific authorization would require an individual to get written permission to override the general authorization policies.

Proper authorization is required for many things in addition to spending. For example, some employees can sign contracts committing the organization to provide specific services. Some employees can represent the organization with respect to legal matters. The ultimate source of authority rests with the Board of Directors. The Board provides letters of delegation to senior managers, providing them with the authority to undertake a variety of functions on behalf of the organization. These senior managers can, in turn, delegate authority to specific individuals who report to them.

Adequate Documentation

The audit trail discussed earlier requires an ability to provide detailed documentation of what was spent and why it was spent. Documents, however, do not have to be on paper. The computer age is pushing us more and more toward electronic record keeping.

For example, at one time, organizations maintained files with all canceled checks. If a discrepancy arose concerning whether a payment had been made or not, the organization could find the canceled check in its files and use the check to prove that payment had been made. More and more often, payments are made by electronic transfer rather than by check. In many organizations, for example, very few payroll checks are issued. Instead, payments to employees are deposited directly into the employees' bank accounts.

In light of such dramatic changes, it is essential that organizations carefully think out what documentation will be available to them to allow them to trace back, explain, and prove that transactions have occurred. It is also important to recognize that loss of electronic data (such as the loss or erasure of a computer hard drive) can be as devastating as a fire that destroys all of an organization's paper records.

Proper Procedures

Control systems rely heavily on standard operating procedures, often in the form of a procedures manual. Doing things "by the book" may seem rigid to some employees; but if we follow clearly documented procedures, we are likely to reduce the number of errors. Less time will have to be spent correcting those errors.

By the same token, the "book" should be current and relevant. Internal control procedures should be reviewed and updated on a regular basis. New approaches for increasing efficiency and protecting resources should be adopted.

Physical Safeguards

Common sense dictates the need for physical safeguards. Cash and blank checks should obviously be kept locked when not in use. Backup copies of computer records should be maintained in a separate location. Controls should be put in place to protect valuable inventory.

Bonding, Vacations, and Rotation of Duties

If individuals are in positions in which it would be possible for them to steal significant amounts from the organization, it is appropriate to bond them. *Bonding* means that the organization purchases insurance to protect itself against theft by the employee. Many organizations fail to bond, being reluctant to give the impression that they don't trust their employees. However, bonding is similar to fire insurance. You don't expect your building to burn down—you may even have a sprinkler system—but the potential loss is too great to risk. Just as it would be foolish to not buy fire insurance, it is foolish to fail to bond key employees.

What other controls go hand in hand with the bonding of employees? One approach is mandated vacations and rotation of staff. Many types of defalcation require constant supervision by the embezzler. If money is being stolen from the accounts receivable cash stream, checks received later are often used to cover the cash that has been taken.

By requiring vacations, we move another employee into each role periodically. That provides an opportunity for discrepancies to be uncovered. Similarly, a formal rotation system establishes the fact that no employee will be doing exactly the same job year after year. If it is well known that all employees must take vacations and that rotation in duties will occur from time to time with little advance notice, these controls can serve not only to discover problems, but to prevent them as well.

Performance Audits

Performance audits, sometimes called *operational audits*, are systems reviews that should take place on a regular basis. They generally are divided into two subcategories, *economy and efficiency audits* and *program audits*. Economy and efficiency audits are reviews that determine if the organization is acquiring, protecting, and using its resources efficiently. Essentially they check for waste. Program audits check for effectiveness. They determine whether the organization's programs are accomplishing their objectives.

Larger organizations have internal audit departments. These departments work year-round on performance audits that review the financial and operating systems of the organization. They seek out weaknesses in controls that might allow for theft of resources. They also try to improve systems to reduce the chances that errors will occur in the recording or reporting of financial information. At the same time, internal auditors focus their performance audits on trying to find ways that the organization can better achieve its mission. This will at times require them to evaluate the role and functioning of each unit or department of the organization.

Outside independent auditors also serve a crucial role. Independent auditors have the benefit of experience from reviewing control systems in many different organizations. As a result, these external auditors can often offer suggestions for improvement in internal controls. From an outsider's perspective, they are more likely to see flaws in the system that most insiders might not notice.

Cost-Benefit Analysis

Management control systems can be quite simple or quite elaborate. The more careful we are to ensure that the organization's system catches all potential problems, the more it costs. Systems should be cost-effective. The organization should not spend more on the systems than they are worth. For example, one wouldn't spend $1,000 to prevent someone from possibly stealing $10. We should also be aware that no matter how careful we are with our control systems, fraud, embezzlements, and some inefficiencies can still take place.

KEY TERMS

Fraud—an intentional deception for the purpose of a financial gain.

Business fraud—in addition to the typical frauds that the lay person is likely to be aware of, business frauds include the overstatement of revenue, understatement of expenses, overstatement of assets, and understatement of liabilities.

Ethics programs to prevent fraud—a well-designed ethics program to prevent fraud generally includes a written statement, top management support, disclosure of actions management has taken re ethics, discussion of ethics in seminars on ethics and in other forums, a system for monitoring compliance, and clearly stated consequences.

The Sarbanes-Oxley Act (SOX)—requires rigorous internal control systems, reporting of financial transactions, and disclosure of conflicts of interest in an effort to prevent fraudulent activities.

Management or internal control systems (MCS)—a set of policies and procedures designed to keep operations going according to plan. MCS' deter fraud by making it difficult to commit the fraud and by making it more likely that the person committing the fraud will be caught.

QUESTIONS FOR REVIEW

1. What is fraud?
2. In addition to the types of fraud common to a lay person, what are the four main classes of fraud that take place in businesses? Focus on the financial reporting of the firm.
3. What are the three main approaches for preventing fraud discussed in the chapter?
4. What are the characteristics of a well-developed corporate ethics program?
5. What are some examples of the greater level of responsibility that the SOX legislation imposes on senior executives?
6. Do you think the SOX legislation was adequate to prevent fraud such as the Madoff scandal?
7. What is a management control system?
8. What is the difference between general and specific authorization?
9. What elements of a control system can be used to safeguard resources? Explain.

Chapter 19

The Role of the Outside Auditor

Organizations make plans, implement them, and then take actions to keep operations going according to plan. From time to time, at least annually, the organization stops to take stock of where it is and how well it has done. Financial statements are used to present that information. However, the stock market crash of 1929 brought to light substantial inadequacies in financial reporting. Investigations of bankrupt companies showed that financial statements contained numerous arithmetic errors, cases of undetected fraud, and a wide variety of accounting practices. A principal outcome of those investigations was the formation of the Securities and Exchange Commission (SEC).

The SEC requires companies under its jurisdiction to issue a financial report to stockholders annually. The report must contain financial statements prepared by the firm's management and audited by an outside independent auditor who is a Certified Public Accountant (CPA). To ensure consistency over time and comparability across organizations, the SEC requires that the information contained in the statements comply with a set of Generally Accepted Accounting Principles (GAAP) established by the accounting profession. The SEC's desire is that a reliable set of financial statements, one that presents a "fair representation" of the results of operations and the organization's financial position, is given to the users of the financial statement information. Those users include stockholders, bankers, suppliers, and other individuals.

A set of financial statements that has been audited by a CPA is referred to as the audited financials or the organization's annual financial report. Sometimes these annual reports are called certified reports or certified statements. However, it is the auditor or Certified Public Accountant who is certified, rather than the financial statements themselves. Each state licenses CPAs certifying them as experts in accounting and auditing. CPAs in turn provide an expert opinion on the information contained in the financial statements, and whether that information complies with GAAP. However, the CPA is just giving an expert opinion, and is not providing a certification that the financial statements are correct.

GENERALLY ACCEPTED ACCOUNTING PRINCIPLES (GAAP)

Achieving a result that everyone would consider to be a fair representation is quite difficult, especially because accounting represents more of an art than a science. In many instances, strong arguments can be posed for alternative accounting treatments. Selection of one uniform set of rules for all firms is not a simple exercise.

For example, consider a firm drilling for oil. The firm buys a tract of land intending to drill 100 exploratory wells. Hypothetically, suppose that statistically for every 100 wells drilled, the industry average is to find one well with commercially producible quantities.

The firm expects to spend $100,000 on each well it drills and expects to recover $20,000,000 worth of oil from the successful well. After one year, 50 wells have been drilled at a cost of $5,000,000 and no oil has been discovered. Consider how the firm might present this on its financial statements. Exhibit 19-1 provides income statements under three alternative accounting methods. Putting parentheses around a number is an accountant's indication of a negative number.

EXHIBIT 19-1
Alternative Accounting Methods for Oil Exploration

	YEAR ONE	YEAR TWO	
	ACTUAL RESULT	IF OIL FOUND	IF NO OIL
Method One			
Revenue	$ 0	$20,000,000	$ 0
Less Expense	5,000,000	5,000,000	5,000,000
Net Income	$(5,000,000)	$15,000,000	$ (5,000,000)
Method Two			
Revenue	$ 0	$20,000,000	$ 0
Less Expense	0	10,000,000	10,000,000
Net Income	$ 0	$10,000,000	$(10,000,000)
Method Three			
Revenue	$10,000,000	$10,000,000	$(10,000,000)
Less Expense	5,000,000	5,000,000	5,000,000
Net Income	$ 5,000,000	$ 5,000,000	$(15,000,000)

In all three methods, the net income will be the same for the two-year period. If the firm finds oil, it will receive $20,000,000 in return for a two-year cost of $10,000,000, leaving a profit of $10,000,000. If the firm doesn't find oil, then the combined two years must indicate an expenditure of $10,000,000 with no revenue, or a loss of $10,000,000.

Although the two-year totals are the same under all three methods, oil or no oil, the income reported in each year varies substantially depending on the method chosen. Method One takes things as they come. In Year One no oil is found, so the $5,000,000 spent is down the drain, so to speak. The firm reports a loss of $5,000,000 for the year.

Method Two argues that the $5,000,000 was an investment in a two- year project rather than being a loss. On the basis of the hypothetical oil industry statistics, the firm will likely find oil next year, and it gives an unduly harsh picture of the firm's results to show it as a loss. This method records no revenue or expense for Year One.

Method Three argues that because statistically the firm expects to find oil, and because half of the work is completed by the end of Year One, the firm should report half the profits by the end of Year One. In this method, $10,000,000 of revenue is recorded in Year One, even though oil has not yet been found. If no oil is found in Year Two, the Year One revenue must be eliminated by showing negative revenue in Year Two. Comparing the three methods at the end of Year One leaves the user of financial statements with the information that the firm either lost $5,000,000, or broke even, or made a profit of $5,000,000 during the year.

You may have a favorite among the three methods. Accountants will not allow use of Method Three. It is considered to be overly optimistic, because for a small number of holes drilled, such as 100, there may well be no oil at all. Methods One and Two, however, each have strong proponents and substantial theoretical support. Accountants frequently prefer a conservative approach and Method One provides it. On the other hand, accountants like to "match" expense with the revenue it causes to be generated. This preference would support Method Two.

This particular example highlights a major controversy in accounting. It represents only one of a number of situations in which the accounting profession has difficulty selecting one consistent rule and saying that it should be applied across the board to all firms in all situations. There is no true theory of accounting to resolve these dilemmas. The only way to achieve a logical order is by agreement on an arbitrary set of rules.

Comparison of different firms would be simplified if the set of rules selected permitted very little leeway for the firm. However, politically, accountants have not always been able to accomplish this because selection of one method over another will usually help one set of firms and hurt another set. In most instances firms have no choice, but there are a substantial number of situations where alternative accounting rules are allowed.

Then how does that make readers of financial statements any better off now than they were before 1929 and the subsequent establishment of the SEC? First, there are substantial tests of arithmetical accuracy that weren't previously required. Inventory is checked to see that the proper amounts have been recorded. Other audit tests are conducted to verify all of the firm's resources and obligations.

Second, and of equal importance, are the accountants' rules of disclosure. In 1929, a firm choosing from among alternative methods didn't necessarily disclose which method it had used. Today the firm can choose from only a relatively narrow set of alternative rules. Whenever the firm makes a choice, that choice must be explicitly stated somewhere in the financial statements.

Who makes the rules that firms must follow in their accounting practices? There is a rule-making body called the Financial Accounting Standards Board (FASB) (pronounced faz-B). The Governmental Accounting Standards Board (GASB) (pronounced gaz-B) makes GAAP for governmental organizations. The pronouncements of these boards carry the weight of competent authority, according to the American Institute of Certified Public Accountants (AICPA). The AICPA is a body much like the physicians' AMA and has substantial influence with its membership, so much influence that all CPAs look to it to specify the rules their clients must follow. If the CPA chooses not to follow one of the rules, he or she is subject to strong sanctions, including suspension or loss of the license to practice.

GAAP (pronounced gap) constitute a large number of pages of detailed technical rulings. FASB has grouped all of their rulings into one comprehensive "codification." Following are just a few of the most universally applicable rules.

Going Concern

In valuing a firm's assets, it is assumed that the firm will remain in business in the foreseeable future. If it appears that a firm may not remain a going concern, the auditor is required to indicate that in his or her report on the financial statements. The rationale is that if a firm does go bankrupt, its resources may be sold at forced auction. In that case, the resources may be sold for substantially less than their value as indicated on the firm's financial statements.

Conservatism

The principle of conservatism requires that sufficient attention and consideration be given to the risks taken by the firm. In practice this results in asymmetrical accounting. There is a tendency to anticipate possible losses, but not to anticipate potential gains.

There has been considerable argument over whether this rule actually protects investors. There is the possibility that the firm's value will be understated as a result of the accountant's extreme efforts not to overstate its value. From an economic perspective, we could argue that one could lose as much by failing to invest in a good firm as by investing in a bad one.

Matching

In order to get a fair reflection of the results of operations for a specific period of time, we should attempt to put expenses into the same period as the revenues that caused them to be generated. This principle of matching provides the basis for depreciation. If we buy a machine with an expected ten-year life, can we charge the full amount paid for the machine as an expense in the year of purchase? No, because that would make the firm look like it had a bad first year followed by a number of very good years. The machine provides service for ten years; it allows us to make and sell a product in each of the years. Therefore its cost should be spread out into each of those years for which it has helped to generate revenue.

Sometimes these principles can conflict with each other. The conservatism principle lends support to using the first method in the earlier oil drilling example. However, the matching principle lends support to the second method. Some of the most difficult reporting problems faced by CPAs arise when several of the generally accepted accounting principles come into conflict with each other.

Cost

The cost of an item is what was paid for it, or the value of what was given up to get it.

Objective Evidence

This rule requires accountants to ensure that financial reports are based on such evidence as reasonable individuals could all agree on within relatively narrow bounds.

For example, if we had bought a piece of property for $50,000 and we could produce a cancelled check and deed of conveyance showing that we paid $50,000 for the property, then reasonable people would probably agree that the property cost $50,000. Our cost information is based upon objective evidence. Twenty years after the property is purchased, management calls in an appraiser who values the property at $500,000. The appraisal is considered to be subjective evidence. Different appraisers might vary substantially as to their estimate of the property's value. Three different appraisers might well offer three widely different estimates for the same property.

In such a case, the rules of objective evidence require the property to be valued on the financial statements based on the best available objective evidence. This is the cost—$50,000! Consider the implications of this for financial reporting. If you thought that financial statements give perfectly valid information about the firm, this should shake your confidence somewhat. Financial statements provide extremely limited representations of the firm. Without an understanding of GAAP, the reader of a financial statement may well draw unwarranted conclusions.

Materiality

The principle of materiality requires the accountant to correct errors that are "material" in nature. Material means large or significant. Insignificant errors may be ignored. But how does one define significance? Is it $5, or $500, or $5,000,000? Significance depends substantially on the size and particular circumstances of the individual firm.

Rather than set absolute standards, accountants define materiality in terms of effects on the users of financial statements. If there exists a misstatement so significant that reasonable, prudent users of the financial statements would make a different decision than they would if they had been given correct information, then the misstatement is material and requires correction.

Thus, if an investor can say, "Had I known that, I never would have bought the stock," or a banker can say, "I never would have lent the money to them if I had known the correct total assets of the firm," then we have a material misstatement. The implications of this are that accountants do not attempt to uncover and correct every single error that has occurred during the year. In fact, to do so would be prohibitively expensive. There is only an attempt to make sure errors that are material in nature are uncovered.

Consistency

In a world in which alternative accounting treatments frequently exist, users of financial statements can be seriously misled if a firm switches back and forth among alternative treatments. Therefore, if a firm has changed its accounting methods, the auditor must disclose the change in his or her report. A note must be included along with the statements to indicate the impact of the change.

Full Disclosure

Accountants, being a cautious lot, feel that perhaps there may be some relevant item that users of financial statements should be aware of, but for which no rule exists that explicitly requires disclosure. So, to protect against unforeseen situations that may arise, there is a catchall generally accepted accounting principle called full disclosure. This rule requires that if there is any other information that would be required for a fair representation of the results of operations and financial position of the firm, then that information must be disclosed in a note that accompanies the financial statements.

INTERNATIONAL FINANCIAL REPORTING STANDARDS

There has been a growing movement to have one worldwide set of accounting standards. That would have great benefits for multi-national organizations. Rather than preparing financial statements in different countries using different accounting methods and principles, there could be a level of uniformity and consistency that would both save money and improve comparability and understandability of financial statements. It could lead to integrated information technology systems, help corporations understand the finances of international suppliers, customers, and subsidiaries, and make it easier to evaluate the finances of potential takeover candidates. However, if such a set of standards is adopted in the United States, it will have significant impacts not only on multinational organizations but also on those that operate only within the United States.

The International Accounting Standards Board (IASB) has developed a set of International Financial Reporting Standards (IFRS). Those standards, or a modified version of them, are either permitted or required in over 120 countries as of the writing of this book. The IFRS is a much newer system than US GAAP. As such it tends to be more general with fewer specific rules providing detailed guidance. For example, IFRS provides minimal guidance for specific industries, in contrast to US GAAP which has many rules aimed at dealing with issues of concern to different specific industries.

In 2010 the United States' Securities and Exchange Commission (SEC) reiterated its support for a single set of high-quality global accounting standards. The SEC made clear its intent to move the United States to the IFRS system, and it would appear that all that is left to decide is the exact final form of the IFRS system to be adopted and the dates when its use will be mandated. There are some, however, who would argue that ultimately, like the metric system, IFRS will never be implemented in the United States. It is too early in the process to know for sure, although it seems more likely than not that we will move to IFRS.

A joint convergence commission that is made up of members from the FASB and the IASB, is currently working on reconciling the differences between the GAAP in the United States (US GAAP) and the IASB's IFRS. In some cases the convergence commission's proposed changes are moving IFRS toward US GAAP and in other cases proposed changes are moving US GAAP toward IFRS. The aim to is reach one uniform set of standards. If total convergence is not reached, it is possible that a version of IFRS with some amendments might be adopted in the United States. A number of countries do use a modified version of IFRS.

While some firms may be allowed to use IFRS for their financial reporting in the near future, it is not likely that it will be required before 2016 at the earliest. While a uniform set of standards may save multi-national companies money in the long run, in the nearer term (from 2012 to 2017), adoption of IFRS would require collection and reporting of some information not previously required under US GAAP.

What About Companies that Operate Only in the United States?

Certainly, however, the cost of shifting to a new set of standards will not impact firms that are only domestic, will it? Yes, it will. Because we are not keeping US GAAP intact and allowing or requiring firms to use IFRS if they are multi-national. We are undergoing a convergence process. In that process many US GAAP are being modified. So ultimately all firms that report their financial results in accordance with US GAAP will have to undergo a wide range of changes. And this is likely to be the case even if IFRS ultimately is not adopted.

What is the Same and What is Different?

US GAAP and IFRS have a great deal in common, but as they say, the devil is in the details. On a technical level there are many differences between current US GAAP and IFRS. What exact elements of US GAAP are the same as IFRS and what elements differ? This is a difficult question to respond to because both IFRS and GAAP are currently moving targets. Both are changing at a rapid rate as the two bodies (FASB and IASB) race to achieve a convergence as quickly as possible. However, there are some elements that are becoming clear.

Both US GAAP and IFRS strive for financial statements that are understandable, reliable, comparable, relevant, and provide a fair presentation of the organization's results of operations and financial position. Users of financial statements—owners, lenders, employees, vendors, regulators, and others should receive information that provides a true picture of the financial situation of the organization.

Both systems rely on the accrual basis of accounting, rather than cash flow, as the primary measure of revenues and expenses. Both systems embrace the going concern concept. Both systems rely on monetary units of measurement. That is, assets are reported in terms of currency, rather than listing each physical asset.

However, we can already determine that there will be many differences from current US GAAP—some of them will have a dramatic impact on the numbers

reported on financial statements. We will discuss just a few of the likely prominent changes that will result from the adoption of IFRS.

US GAAP does not have any allowance for the impact of inflation. No
adjustments are made for lost purchasing power during periods of high inflation.
IFRS, however, does have provisions for adjusting numbers for the impact of
inflation during periods of hyperinflation (defined as 26% per year or more for
three consecutive years).

US GAAP treats some leases as operating leases (*see* Chapter 14). Such leases
do not appear on the balance sheet. But under IFRS all leases would show up as
both an asset (the valuable right to use the item being leased) and a liability (the
obligation to make payments under the lease) on the balance sheet.

LIFO (*see* Chapter 16) would probably disappear as an inventory option
under IFRS. This has major implications. A firm which has been using LIFO for
decades would have to report as expense the cost of inventory purchased many
years ago when prices were much lower. The Internal Revenue Service (IRS) is
tracking this closely and would possibly eliminate LIFO for tax purposes if IFRS
is adopted. However, payment of the large resulting tax obligation could be
spread out over a four year period.

Under current US GAAP, all research and development costs are treated as
an expense in the year they are incurred. We don't wait and charge these as
expenses in the future years when revenues related to these efforts are recorded,
since there is no assurance that the research and development efforts will lead to
any future revenues. However, while IFRS also treats research costs are expenses
as soon as they are incurred, IFRS allows development costs to be treated as an
asset rather than an expense under certain circumstances.

Implications of Changing to IFRS

There are many implications of changes in the accounting principles that a firm
uses for financial reporting. Rule changes can impact how and when assets and
liabilities are recorded. They can cause sometimes dramatic shifts in the amount
of profit an organization reports. And, since in some countries income taxes are
based on reported income, they can affect the amount of tax a company pays.

Changes in financial statement values will change how we interpret the
financial health of an organization. For example, IFRS allows for revaluation of
some nonfinancial assets to fair value (*see* Chapter 21). Imagine if a piece of land
that was purchased for $100,000 and recorded for the last 50 years on your
balance sheet at $100,000 were suddenly revalued on the balance sheet at $50
million. Key numbers on the balance sheet, such as total assets could change
dramatically overnight. The numbers that analysts use as benchmarks for strong
or weak financial performance (*see* Chapter 24) would have to be reassessed.

Contracts may be affected. Often contracts call for financial statement relationships to be maintained. For example, when a bond is issued, often the
borrower will be required to maintain a minimum amount of assets relative to
their liabilities. But changing accounting reporting requirements could cause
significant enough changes in the reported assets and liabilities to change those

relationships. In some cases this could create default situations. Such contracts would likely have to be renegotiated before adoption of the new standards.

Compensation may be affected. Many firms provide some compensation based on the firm's profits. If implementation of IFRS reporting rules result in different levels of profit being reported, that would impact compensation. All profit-sharing plans would have to be revisited and possibly revised.

This provides just a small sampling of some of the extensive differences between current US GAAP and IFRS and the implications of a shift from US GAAP to IFRS. There is no question that moving a company's reporting over to a new set of accounting standards will be a time-consuming and costly process. Some companies will feel the benefits outweigh the costs, but many others are likely to see relatively little direct benefit to offset the costs involved. If companies in the United States do adopt IFRS, the implementation process will be guided by the organization's financial managers, and in many cases consultants. While non-financial managers should be aware of this possible coming change, they will not have to take a lead position in the process of conversion.

THE AUDIT

The Management Letter and Internal Control

In performing an audit, the CPA checks for arithmetic accuracy as previously mentioned. In performing this check, the external auditor focuses on the system rather than the individual.

Consider a system in which an individual is issuing invoices to customers based on a shipping document. The individual takes a copy of the shipping document from the in-box, records the amount, issues the invoice, and places the shipping document in the out-box. Again and again, over and over, this same mechanical process is repeated. Occasionally the clerk takes the shipping document, sips some coffee, and puts the document in the out-box without having issued an invoice. Errors do happen.

The auditor will not try to discover every such error. The cost of reexamining every financial transaction would be prohibitive. Instead, by sampling some fraction of the documents processed, the auditor attempts to determine how often errors are occurring and how large they tend to be. The goal is to see if a material error may exist.

What if the accountant feels that the clerk is making too many errors and the potential for a material misstatement may exist? The clerk must be fired and replaced with a more conscientious individual, right? No, wrong. Humans will all make errors and the accountant wants the system to acknowledge that fact. The focus is on what accountants call the *internal control* of the accounting system. Basically, adequate internal control means that the system is designed in such a way as to catch and correct the majority of errors automatically, before the auditor arrives on the scene.

In our example with the clerk, the solution to the problem may be to have the clerk initial each shipping document immediately after he or she processes the invoice. A second individual would then review the shipping documents to see that all have been initialed. Those that haven't been initialed would be sent back for verification of whether an invoice was issued and for correction if need be. Errors can still occur—initialing the document after sipping the coffee, even though the invoice hasn't been processed—but they are less likely and should occur less frequently.

The auditor issues an internal control memo, often called a management letter, which points out the internal control weaknesses to management. Although there may be some expense involved for the firm to follow some of the recommendations, the inducement is that of reduced audit fees. Internal control weaknesses require an expanded audit so that the CPA can ascertain whether a material misstatement does exist. If the internal control is improved, the auditor will feel more comfortable relying on the client's system and less audit testing will be required. The management letter is given to the firm's top management and is not ordinarily disclosed to the public.

Fraud and Embezzlement

In a firm with good internal control, fraud and embezzlement are made difficult through a system of checks and balances as discussed in Chapter 18. The auditor does not consider it to be a part of his or her job to detect all frauds. In fact, many cases of embezzlement are virtually impossible to uncover.

The Auditor's Report

In addition to the management letter, the auditor issues a letter to the top management of the corporation and to its stockholders. This opinion letter generally has three standard paragraphs that are reproduced almost verbatim in most auditors' reports. Alternatively, some auditors combine the information from these three paragraphs into one longer paragraph. You might compare the auditor's letter in your firm's audited financial statements to the sample letter in Exhibit 19-2.

These three paragraphs are the standard clean opinion report. The first paragraph is referred to as the *opening* or *introductory* paragraph. The second paragraph is the *scope* paragraph. The third paragraph is the *opinion* paragraph. If there are any additional paragraphs, they represent unusual circumstances which require further explanation.

The opening paragraph serves to inform the users of the financial statements that an audit was performed by the auditor. In some cases auditors perform consulting or other services aside from audits. The opening paragraph indicates explicitly that the company's management bears the ultimate responsibility for the contents of the financial statements.

Exhibit 19-2—REPORT OF THE INDEPENDENT AUDITORS

To the Directors and Stockholders of Executive Corporation:

We have audited the accompanying balance sheets of Executive Corporation as of December 31, 2012 and 2011, and the related statements of income, retained earnings, and cash flow for the years then ended. These financial statements are the responsibility of the Company's management. Our responsibility is to express an opinion on these financial statements based on our audits.

We conducted our audits in accordance with generally accepted auditing standards. Those standards require that we plan and perform the audit to obtain reasonable assurance about whether the financial statements are free of material misstatement. An audit includes examining, on a test basis, evidence supporting the amounts and disclosures in the financial statements. An audit also includes assessing the accounting principles used and significant estimates made by management, as well as evaluating the overall financial statement presentation. We believe that our audits provide a reasonable basis for our opinion.

In our opinion, the financial statements referred to above present fairly, in all material respects, the financial position of Executive Corporation as of December 31, 2012 and 2011, and the results of its operations and its cash flows for the years then ended, in conformity with generally accepted accounting principles.

Steven A. Finkler, CPA

April 8, 2013

The scope paragraph describes the breadth or scope of work undertaken as a basis for forming an opinion on the financial statements. This paragraph explains the type of procedures auditors follow in carrying out an audit. Note that just as firms must follow generally accepted accounting principles in preparing their statements, CPAs must follow generally accepted auditing standards in auditing those statements.

The opinion paragraph describes whether the financial statements provide a fair representation of the financial position, results of operations, and cash flows of the company, in the opinion of the auditor. A clean opinion, such as this one, indicates that in the opinion of the auditor, exercising due professional care, there is sufficient evidence of conformity to GAAP, and there is no condition requiring further clarification. This paragraph does not contend that the financial statements are completely correct. It does not even certify that there are no material misstatements. The CPA does not give a guarantee or certification. The CPA merely gives an expert opinion.

Note that the opinion of the CPA is that the financial statements are a fair representation of the firm's financial position. This is a somewhat audacious remark. Considering the intangible assets that often are not recorded on the financial statements despite their potentially significant value, and considering that plant, property, and equipment are recorded on the balance sheet at their cost, even though their value today may be far in excess of cost, you have to have a lot of nerve to say the statements are fair.

The key is that the accountant merely says the statements are a fair presentation in accordance with generally accepted accounting principles. In other words, this *fairness* is not meant to imply fair in any absolute meaning of the word *fair*.

Certainly this creates a problem in that many users of the financial statements are unfamiliar with the implications of GAAP. Such individuals may interpret the word *fair* in a broader sense than is intended. This is why it is vital that in looking at an annual report an individual read the notes to the financial statements as well as the statements themselves. Later in the book we will discuss the notes to the financial statements in some detail.

The auditor may issue an *adverse, qualified,* or *disclaimer* opinion, if it is not possible to issue a clean opinion. An adverse opinion is a severe statement. It indicates that the auditor believes that the firm's financial statements are not presented fairly, in accordance with GAAP. A disclaimer indicates that the auditor was unable to compile enough evidence to form an opinion on whether or not the financial statements are a fair representation in accordance with GAAP. A qualified opinion indicates that the financial statements are a fair representation in conformity with GAAP, except as relates to a specific particular area.

In some cases the audit opinion letter will also contain additional paragraphs containing explanations. This is generally the case if there is a significant uncertainty, or a material change in the application of GAAP. Such paragraphs highlight special circumstances that might be of particular concern to the users of the financial statements. An example of a significant uncertainty is a lawsuit of such magnitude that, if the case is lost, it might cause the firm to become insolvent. A material change in GAAP must be reported because it makes the current financial statement no longer completely comparable to the previous ones for the same company. The presence of more than the standard opening, scope, and opinion paragraphs should alert the user to exercise special care in interpreting the numbers reported in the financial statements.

The COSO Opinion

The Sarbanes-Oxley Act (SOX) (discussed in Chapter 18) attempts to assure that public companies have adequate internal controls. As a result of the law, the Public Company Accounting Oversight Board (PCAOB) was established. A public company is a business that sells its securities (stock, bonds, etc.) that have been registered with the Securities and Exchange Commission (SEC) to the public, typically through a stock or bond exchange.

The PCAOB requires auditors of public companies to include disclosure regarding the internal controls of the firm being audited, as well as providing an opinion on the company's and auditor's assessment of the company's internal controls. This required disclosure is generally referred to as the COSO Opinion, derived from the Committee of Sponsoring Organizations of the Treadway Commission ("COSO") which established a framework for evaluation of the adequacy of internal control. The COSO Opinion can be incorporated into the Auditor's opinion letter, or may appear as a separate report.

The Management Report

It is common practice for the annual report of the firm to include not only the firm's financial statements, an auditors' report stating the auditor's opinion, the management letter on internal control written by the CPA, and the COSO opinion, but also a management report. In contrast to the management letter written by the CPA and given to the firm's management, the management report is written by the firm's management, and is addressed to readers of the annual report.

The management report explains that while the financial statements have been audited by an independent CPA, ultimately they are the responsibility of the firm's management. The report also discusses the organization's system of internal control, and the role of its audit committee. The audit committee, consisting of members of the Board of Directors, has the responsibility for supervising the accounting, auditing, and other financial reporting matters of the firm.

KEY TERMS

Audited financial statements—a presentation of the firm's financial position and its results of operations, in accordance with generally accepted accounting principles.

Generally accepted accounting principles (GAAP)—a set of rules used as a basis for financial reporting. Some key GAAP:

   a. *Going concern*—financial statements are prepared based upon the assumption that the firm will remain in business for the foreseeable future.

   b. *Conservatism*—in reporting the financial position of the firm, sufficient consideration should be given to the various risks the firm faces.

   c. *Matching*—expenses should be recorded in the same accounting period as the revenues that they were responsible for generating.

   d. *Cost*—the value of what was given up to acquire an item.

   e. *Objective evidence*—financial reports should be based on such evidence as reasonable individuals could all agree upon within relatively narrow bounds.

   f. *Materiality*—an error is material if any individual would make a different decision based upon the incorrect information resulting from the error than if he or she possessed the correct information.

   g. *Consistency*—to avoid misleading users of financial reports, firms should generally use the same accounting methods from period to period.

   h. *Full disclosure*—financial reports should disclose any information needed to assure that the reports are a fair presentation.

The management letter—a report to top management that makes suggestions for the improvement of internal control to reduce the likelihood of errors and undetected frauds or embezzlements.

The auditor's report—a letter from the outside auditor giving an opinion on whether or not the firm's financial statements are a fair presentation of the firm's results of operations, cash flows, and financial position in accordance with GAAP.

The COSO Opinion—a letter from the auditor providing an opinion on the company's and auditor's assessement of the company's internal controls.

The management report—a letter from the organization's management that is part of the annual report.

QUESTIONS FOR REVIEW

1. What event precipitated the establishment of the Securities and Exchange Commission and the requirement for publicly traded companies to issue audited financial statements to stockholders?

2. What is the role of the Certified Public Accountant in the audit process?

3. Does the auditor attempt to identify all accounting errors?

4. What is the auditor's management letter focused on and who is it submitted to?

5. What is the opinion letter and what are the different opinions that can be rendered?

6. Why are Generally Accepted Accounting Principles needed and what organization established them?

7. Explain the following Generally Accepted Accounting Principles:

   a. Going Concern

   b. Conservatism

   c. Matching

   d. Cost

   e. Objective Evidence

   f. Materiality

   g. Consistency

   h. Full Disclosure

8. What are IFRS? Will the movement toward IFRS impact companies that are not multi-national?

9. What is the COSO Opinion concerned with?

Chapter 20

Recording and Reporting Financial Information

Financial accounting consists largely of keeping the financial history of the firm. In performing financial accounting, the accountant attempts to keep close track of each event that has a financial impact on the firm. This is done in order to facilitate financial statement preparation. By keeping track of things as they happen, the accountant can periodically summarize and report the firm's financial position and the results of its operations.

DOUBLE ENTRY AND THE ACCOUNTING EQUATION

In order to keep track of the firm's financial history, the accountant has chosen a very common historical device. In the navy one keeps a chronological history of a voyage by daily entries into a log. For a personal history, individuals make entries in their diaries. Explorers frequently record the events of their trip in a journal. Accountants follow in the tradition of the explorers, each day recording the day's events in a journal, often referred to as a *general journal*. The entries the accountant makes in the journal are simply called *journal entries*. An event is first entered into the firm's official history via a journal entry.

In recording a journal entry, we need adequate information to describe an entire event. To be sure that all elements of a financial event (more commonly referred to as a "transaction") are recorded, accountants use a system called *double-entry bookkeeping*. In order to understand double entry, we should think in terms of the basic equation of accounting, that is:

ASSETS (A) = LIABILITIES (L) + STOCKHOLDERS' EQUITY (SE)

Any event having a financial impact on the firm affects this equation because the equation summarizes the entire financial position of the firm. Furthermore, by definition this equation must always remain in balance. Absolutely nothing can happen (barring a mathematical miscalculation) that would cause this equation not to be in balance, because stockholders' equity has been defined in such a way that it is a residual value that brings the equation into balance.

If the equation must remain in balance, then a change of any one number in the equation must change at least one other number. We have great latitude in which other number changes. For example, we might begin with the equation looking like:

A	=	L	+	SE
$150,000	=	$100,000	+	$50,000

If we were to borrow $20,000 from the bank, we would have more cash, so assets would increase by $20,000 and we would owe money to the bank. Our liabilities would increase by $20,000. Now the equation would be:

A	=	L	+	SE
$170,000	=	$120,000	+	$50,000

The equation is in balance. Compare this equation to the previous one. Two numbers in the equation have changed. The term double entry merely signifies that it is not possible to change one number in an equation without changing at least one other number.

However, the two numbers that change need not be on different sides of the equation. For example, what if we now buy some raw materials inventory for $15,000 and paid cash for it? Our asset cash has decreased while our asset inventory has increased. The equation now is:

A	=	L	+	SE
$170,000	=	$120,000	+	$50,000

The equation appears as if it hasn't changed at all. That's not quite true. The left side of the equation has both increased and decreased by $15,000. Although the totals on either side are the same, our journal entry would have recorded the specific parts of the double-entry change that took place on the left side of the equation.

DEBITS AND CREDITS

Earlier an accountant's journal was compared to a navy logbook. That's not the only nautical similarity. Sailors use the terms *port* and *starboard*. Many a time you've watched an old seafaring movie, and in the middle of a fierce storm, with the skies clouded and the winds blowing, the seas heaving and the rains pouring, someone yells out, "Hard to the port!" The sailor at the large oaken wheel, barely able to stand erect in the gusts of wind and the torrential downpour, struggles hard to turn the ship in the direction ordered. Perhaps you thought they were heading for the nearest port—ergo, "Hard to the port." Not at all. The shouted command was to make a left turn.

It seems that port simply stated means left and starboard really means right. Of course, it's more sophisticated than that; port means the left-hand side as you face toward the front of the boat or ship and starboard means the right-hand side as you face the front. Really what port means is debit, and starboard means credit. Certainly we can drape the terms *debit* and *credit* in vague definitions and esoteric uses, but essentially debit means left (as you face the accounting document in front of you) and credit means right.

Perhaps you had figured that out on your own, perhaps not. If you had, then you are potentially threatening to take away the jobs of your accountants and bookkeepers. To prevent that, some rather interesting abbreviations have been introduced to common accounting usage. Rarely will the accountant write out the words *debit* or *credit*. Instead, abbreviations are used. The word *credit* is abbreviated Cr. Got it? Then you can guess the abbreviation for debit: Dr. If you didn't guess that, it's not too surprising given the absence of the letter "r" from the word debit. How did this abbreviation come about? Accounting as we know it today has its roots in Italy during the 1400s. Italy is the home of Latin, and were we to trace the word debit back to its Latin roots, the "r" would turn up.

The terms *debit* and *credit* deserve a little more clarification. Prior to actually using the terms debit and credit, accountants perform a modification to the accounting equation (that is, Assets (A) equal Liabilities (L) plus Stockholders' Equity (SE)). Essentially, this modification requires examination of what causes stockholders' equity to change. Chapter 4 said that stockholders' equity (SE) equaled contributed capital (CC) plus retained earnings (RE). So we could think of our basic equation as assets equal liabilities plus contributed capital plus retained earnings, or:

$$A = L + CC + RE$$

In order to find out where we are at the end of a year, we would need to know where we started and what changes occurred during the year. The changes in assets are equal to the change in liabilities, plus the change in contributed capital, plus the change in retained earnings, or:

$$\Delta A = \Delta L + \Delta CC + \Delta RE$$

where the delta symbol "Δ" indicates a change in some number: For example, ΔA represents the change in assets.

Moving a step further, retained earnings increase as a result of net income and decrease when dividends are paid. Net income consists of revenues (R) less expenses (E). Revenues make owners better off and expenses make owners worse off. Dividends (D) are a distribution of some of the firm's profits to its owners. Therefore, our basic equation of accounting now indicates that the change in assets is equal to the change in liabilities, plus the change in contributed capital, plus the revenues, less the expenses and dividends. In equation terms:

$$\Delta A = \Delta L + \Delta CC + \Delta R - \Delta E - \Delta D$$

We can add the change in expenses and the change in dividends to both sides of the equation. Doing so produces the following equation:

$$\Delta A + \Delta E + \Delta D = \Delta L + \Delta CC + \Delta R$$

Having made these changes in the basic equation, we can return to our discussion of debits and credits. When we say that debit means left, we are saying that debits are increases in anything on the left side of this equation. When we say that credit means right, we are saying that credits increase anything on the right side of this equation. Of course, that leaves us with a slight problem. What do we do if something on either side decreases? We will have to reverse our terminology. An account on the left is decreased by a credit and an account on the right is decreased by a debit.

Debits and credits are mechanical tools that aid bookkeepers. Debits and credits have no underlying theoretical or intuitive basis. In fact, the use of debits and credits as explained here may seem counterintuitive. Cash, which is an asset, is increased by a debit. Cash is decreased by a credit.

If you think about this, it may not quite tie in with the way you've been thinking about debits and credits until now. In fact, what we've said here may seem to be downright wrong. Most individuals who are not financial officers have relatively little need to use the terms *debit* and *credit* in a business setting. We come upon the terms much more often in their common lay usage.

Most of us have come into contact with the terms *debit* and *credit* primarily from such events as the receipt of a debit memo from the bank. Perhaps we have a checking account and we are charged 30 cents for each check we write. If we write twenty checks one month, we will receive a notice from the bank that it is debiting our account by $6.00. Something here doesn't tie in with the earlier discussion of debits and credits.

If a debit increases items on the left, and assets are on the left, our assets should increase with a debit. But when the bank debits our account, it takes money away from our account. When we make a deposit, the bank credits, or increases, our account. The discrepancy results from the entity concept of accounting discussed in Chapter 3. Under the entity concept, each entity must view financial transactions from its own point of view. In other words, the firm shouldn't worry about the impact on its owners, or managers, or customers; it should only consider the impact of a transaction on itself.

When the bank debits your account, it is not considering your cash balance at all! The bank is considering its own set of books. To the bank, you are considered a liability. You gave the bank some money and it owes that amount of money to you. When the bank debits your account, it is saying that it is reducing an item on the right. The bank is reducing a liability. To you as an entity, there is a mirror image. While the bank is reducing its liability, on your records you must reduce your cash. Such a reduction is a credit. Therefore, receipt of a debit memo should cause you to record a credit on your books or financial records.

Consider returning merchandise to a store. The store issues you a credit memo. From the store's point of view, it now owes you money for the returned item. The store's liability has risen so it has a credit. From your point of view, you have a receivable from that store and receivables are assets. Thus you have an increase in an asset, or a debit.

You'll have to reflect on this new way of thinking about debits and credits for a while if you're not accustomed to it, and if you wish to become fluent in the use of debits and credits. Unfortunately, because the items on one side of the equation increase with debits and the items on the other side decrease with debits, and vice versa for credits, it can take a while before it becomes second nature.

If you still find debits and credits to be somewhat confusing, don't be overly concerned. Trying to look at things from a mirror image of what you've been used to all your life isn't easy. Fortunately, debits and credits are simply bookkeeping tools, and you don't need to use them extensively to understand the concepts of accounting and finance.

The Appendix to this chapter provides an example of the recording process for those readers who want a more detailed look at the process.

LEDGERS

When we get to the end of an accounting period (typically a month, quarter, or year), we want to report what has occurred. We need some method of summarizing the massive quantity of information we've recorded using journal entries into a format concise enough to be useful to those who desire financial information about the firm.

Financial statements are used to present the firm's financial position and results of operations to interested users of financial information. As we learned in Chapter 4, the financial statements themselves are only several pages long. How can we process our journal entry information in such a way as to allow for such a substantial summarization? We do it via use of a ledger. A ledger is a book of *accounts*. An account is simply any item that we would like to keep track of. Every account that might be affected by a journal entry is individually accounted for in a ledger.

Although today many firms have computerized their bookkeeping systems so that they no longer have a ledger book, you can think of a ledger as if it were simply a book. Each page in the ledger book represents one account. For instance, there is a page for the cash account, and one for the inventory account, and one for retained earnings. Every time we make a journal entry, we are changing the amount that we have in at least two ledger accounts in order to keep the basic equation of accounting in balance.

An immediate benefit of the ledger system is that it allows us to determine how much we have of any item at any point in time. For example, suppose that someone asked us on May 4th how much cash we currently have. One way to provide that information would be to review each and every journal entry that we made since the beginning of the year, determine which ones affected cash, and calculate by how much the cash total has changed. That presents an enormous amount of work.

Using a ledger approach, immediately after making a journal entry, we update our ledger for each account that has changed as a result of that entry. For example, suppose that the first thing that happened to Executive Corporation in 2012 was a purchase of insurance for $3,000, which was paid for in cash. We would first record this event as a journal entry. Then we would go to the ledger account for cash and show a decrease of $3,000, and go to the ledger account for prepaid insurance and show an increase of $3,000. At the same time, we could update the balance in each account.

The ledger is, in some respects, a more complete picture of the firm than the journal is. Each year the journal indicates what happened or changed during that year. The ledger not only contains this year's events, but also tells us where we were when we started out at the beginning of the year. For instance, assume that Executive Corporation had $52,000 in cash at the end of 2011. Our cash account in the ledger would show $52,000 as the opening balance at the beginning of 2012. Thus, when we purchased our insurance on January 2, 2012, we would be able to determine that our initial balance of $52,000 was decreased by $3,000, and that there is a remaining cash balance of $49,000. This gives a better overall picture of the firm than the $3,000 change alone does.

Essentially, the ledger combines account balances from the beginning of the year with the journal entries that were recorded during the year. All of the beginning balances for this year can be found by looking at last year's ending balance sheet. The balance sheet is the statement of financial position. The firm's financial position at the beginning of the year will be identical to its financial position at the end of the previous year. Therefore, the ledger accounts start the year with balances from the year-end balance sheet of the previous year. During the year, the changes that occur and are recorded as journal entries are used to update the ledger accounts. The year-end balance in each account is simply the sum of the opening balance plus the changes recorded in that account during the year. Those year-end balances provide the information needed to prepare financial statements at the end of the year.

The Appendix to this chapter presents an example of how financial statements can be derived from ledger balances.

CHART OF ACCOUNTS

Up to this point we have always referred to accounts by their names, such as cash or inventory. In practice, most organizations find it helpful to assign code numbers to each account. This facilitates the process of recording journal entries in the computer systems widely used for accounting.

Typically, a company will use a fairly systematic approach to assigning numbers. All asset code numbers might begin with a 1, liabilities with a 2, revenues with a 3, and expenses with a 4, for example. A second and third digit would give more specific information. For example, cash might be represented by 100, while accounts receivable would be represented by 110. Most companies have receivables from many customers. A second set of numbers might provide that detailed information. For example, 110-12850 might refer to accounts receivable from customer number 12850. The company might therefore sell $5,000 of its product to customer 12850 on account. It would record a $5,000 increase in its account number 110-12850.

Charts of accounts can be quite flexible. If a company has five divisions, it can set aside one digit for each division. That digit might come at the beginning or end of the entire account code used for each transaction. Also, the company may choose to use the chart to identify specific programs, projects, departments, or other information. Thus, an account number might look something like 4-110-12850-028. This might indicate that the consulting division (division 4 of the company's five divisions) has an account receivable (110) from customer 12850 related to new venture consulting services (028). This allows the organization to easily sort data and prepare reports by client, project, department, etc.

Although this may appear to be complicated, it actually keeps things clear and simple once you know how the company's chart of accounts is set up. The official chart of accounts provides the guide to the system of accounts used by any organization. It will first define the intended purpose of each digit and the meaning of each number contained in each digit. So the first thing you would learn would be that the first digit represents the division of the company, and the specific number associated with each of the five divisions would be listed. Next you would learn the meaning of the second digit, which in this case indicates whether we are looking at an asset, liability, revenue, or expense. If the second digit is 1 in this system, it means we are looking at an asset. The next two digits indicate the specific asset, liability, revenue, or expense. Thus, the 110 after the first hyphen tells us that we are looking at an asset, specifically accounts receivable. And so on.

Generally, in addition to defining the meaning of each digit and providing all data needed to interpret an account number, a complete chart is also maintained. This allows a user to look up any specific account number. Bear in mind, however, that the chart of accounts is a dynamic document. New accounts are frequently added to an accounting system, and it is important to keep the chart of accounts up to date.

KEY TERMS

Double-entry accounting—Each financial event affects the basic equation of accounting. In order for the equation to remain in balance, the event must affect at least two items in the equation, therefore the "double" entry.

Journal—a book (or computer memory file) in which all financial events are recorded in chronological sequence.

Debits—increases in assets, expenses, and dividend accounts; decreases in liability, revenue, and contributed capital accounts.

Credits—increases in liability, revenue, and contributed capital accounts, and decreases in asset, expense, and dividend accounts.

Ledger—a book (or computer memory file) in which we keep track of the impact of financial events on each account. The ledger can provide us with the balance in any account at any point in time.

QUESTIONS FOR REVIEW

1. The place that financial transactions are first recorded is called the _____.
2. Double-entry bookkeeping makes sure that the fundamental equation of accounting is always kept _____ _____.
3. How many accounts will be impacted when a journal entry is recorded?
4. A debit would be an increase in what types of accounts?
5. A debit would be a decrease in what types of accounts?
6. What primary benefit do we get from a ledger that we don't get from a journal?
7. What is a chart of accounts?
8. Balance Sheet and Income Statement (Appendix)

Coffin Corporation had the following highly summarized financial events during the current year:

1. Jan. 2—Ordered new equipment with a 10-year life, for $80,000. No payment was made and the equipment has not been delivered.

2. Feb. 19—Bought $35,000 of inventory. Only $20,000 was paid for the inventory on that date, and the balance is owed to the suppliers. Coffin expects to be able to sell the inventory for $60,000.

3. July 12—Received the equipment ordered January 2, and mailed a check for the balance due.

4. Dec. 28—Coffin paid its employees $68,000 of wages. Wage expense for the year is $66,000. The payment included the $2,000 wages payable balance outstanding from the previous year plus some payment for work done this year.

5. Dec. 30—Sales for the year totaled $123,000. All but $3,000 of that amount has been collected. The entire $6,000 balance in accounts receivable from beginning of the year was also collected. The cost of the inventory sold was $32,000.

6. Dec. 31—Coffin makes a payment of $34,000 on its long-term note. This is an interest free business development loan.

7. Dec. 31—Coffin's building and equipment are now one year older. Depreciation for the year is $15,000.

Assume that Coffin began the year with the following dollar balances (shown in alphabetical order) in their accounts:

Accounts Payable	2,000
Accounts Receivable	6,000
Cash	180,000
Equipment, Net	150,000
Notes Payable	150,000
Contributed Capital	130,000
Retained Earnings	52,000
Wages Payable	2,000

Prepare:

a. An income statement.

b. A comparative statement of financial position (balance sheet).

APPENDIX—RECORDING AND REPORTING THE FINANCIAL INFORMATION

Recording Financial Events

Let's consider an example in which we will actually record a series of transactions for a hypothetical firm, Executive Corporation, for 2012. The purpose of this example is to give you a feel for the way that financial information is recorded, and to show the process by which millions of transactions occurring during a year can be summarized into several pages of financial statements. At the same time, we will use the specific transactions in the example to highlight a number of accounting conventions, principles, and methods.

EXHIBIT 20-A-1
Executive Corporation
Balance Sheet
As of December 31, 2011

ASSETS

Current Assets:	
Cash	$ 52,000
Accounts Receivable	18,000
Inventory	20,000
Total Current Assets	$ 90,000
Fixed Assets:	
Plant and Equipment	60,000
TOTAL ASSETS	$150,000

EQUITIES

LIABILITIES	
Current Liabilities:	
Accounts Payable	$ 17,000
Wages Payable	10,000
Total Current Liabilities	$ 27,000
Long-Term Liabilities:	
Mortgage Payable	40,000
TOTAL LIABILITIES	$ 67,000
STOCKHOLDERS' EQUITY	
Common Stock	$ 10,000
Retained Earnings	73,000
TOTAL STOCKHOLDERS' EQUITY	$ 83,000
TOTAL LIABILITIES & STOCKHOLDERS' EQUITY	$150,000

Exhibit 20-A-1 presents the balance sheet for Executive Corporation as of December 31, 2011. From this balance sheet, we can obtain information about assets, liabilities, and stockholders' equity for the beginning of 2012. Year-end closing balances will be identical to opening balances for the following year. Our basic equation at the start of 2012 is as follows:

A	=	L	+	SE
$150,000	=	$67,000	+	$83,000

In order to examine financial events during the year, we are interested in the change in this equation. As previously explained, the change in the equation may be stated as follows:

$$\Delta A + \Delta E + \Delta D = \Delta L + \Delta CC + \Delta R$$

The way that accountants actually record journal entries assures that the equation remains in balance at all times. Each journal entry first lists all accounts that have a debit change, and then lists all accounts that have a credit change. The account names for accounts with a debit change are recorded in a column on the left, and the account names for accounts with a credit change are recorded in a column indented slightly to the right. Similarly, the actual dollar amounts appear in two columns, with the debit column to the left of the credit column.

For example, suppose that we buy inventory and pay $5 cash for it. One asset, inventory, goes up by $5, and another asset, cash, goes down $5. In journal entry form this would appear as:

	Dr.	Cr.
Inventory	$5	
Cash		$5
To record purchase of inventory for cash		

Notice that the word Inventory appears to be somewhat to the left, and the dollar amount on that line appears in the Dr. column. As noted earlier, an increase in an asset is a debit. The word Cash is indented to the right, and the dollar amount on that line is in the Cr. column. A decrease in the asset, cash, is a credit. A brief explanation is often recorded for each journal entry. In this example the explanation is that the purpose of the journal entry was "To record purchase of inventory for cash." The total of all numbers in the Dr. column must equal the total of all numbers in the Cr. column, or the fundamental equation of accounting will not be in balance.

In the example that follows, we will indicate the impact of each transaction on the fundamental equation of accounting, and then show how it would appear in journal entry form.

Executive Corporation 2012 Financial Events

1. January 2. Purchased a three-year fire insurance policy for $3,000. A check was mailed. The starting point for making a journal entry is to determine what has happened. In this case, we have $3,000 less cash than we used to and we have paid in advance for three years worth of insurance. Any item that we would like to keep track of is called an account, because we want to account for the amount of that item. Here, the balance in our cash account (an asset) has gone down, and our prepaid insurance (P/I) account (also an asset) has increased. This

results in offsetting changes on the left side of the equation, so there is no net effect or change to the equation.

$$\Delta A \quad + \quad \Delta E + \Delta D \quad = \quad \Delta L + \Delta CC + \Delta R$$

Cash – 3,000 = No change on right side

P/I + 3,000

	Dr.	Cr.
Prepaid Insurance	$3,000	
Cash		$3,000

2. January 18. The firm mails a check to its supplier for $15,000 of the $17,000 it owed them at the end of last year. (Refer to Exhibit 20-A-1 for the accounts payable liability balance at the end of the previous year.) This requires a journal entry showing a decrease in the cash balance and a reduction in the accounts payable (A/P) liability to our supplier.

$$\Delta A \quad + \quad \Delta E + \Delta D \quad = \quad \Delta L \quad + \Delta CC + \Delta R$$

Cash – 15,000 = A/P – 15,000

	Dr.	Cr.
Accounts Payable	$15,000	
Cash		$15,000

Notice that when we look at the impact on the equation, both cash and accounts payable are negative numbers. Each decreases by $15,000. In the journal entry format, negative signs are never needed or used. The decrease in cash is a credit, and appears as $15,000 in the credit column. The decrease in accounts payable results in a debit, and appears in the debit column.

3. February 15. The firm places an order with an equipment manufacturer for a new piece of machinery. The new machine will cost $10,000, and delivery is expected early next year. A contract is signed by both Executive Corporation and the equipment manufacturer. In this case there is no journal entry, even though there is a legally binding contract.

In order for there to be a journal entry, three requirements must be fulfilled. The first is that we know how much money is involved. In this case, we do know the exact amount of the contract. Second, we must know when the transaction is to be fulfilled. Here, we know that delivery will take place early the following year. Finally, the accountant requires that there must have been some exchange, and that the transaction be recorded only to the extent that there has been an exchange. From an accounting point of view, Executive has not yet paid anything, nor has it received anything. There is no need to record this into the financial history of the firm via the formal process of a journal entry.

This doesn't mean that the item must be totally ignored. If an unfilled contract involves an amount that is material, then the principle of full disclosure would require that a note to our financial statements disclose this future commitment. However, the balance sheet itself may not show the machine as an asset, nor show a liability to pay for it.

4. March 3. Executive purchases inventory on account for $15,000. It will be able to sell the inventory for $30,000. The effect of this transaction is to increase the amount of inventory (Inv.) asset that we have and to increase a liability, accounts payable (A/P). Do we record the newly purchased inventory at $15,000 or the amount for which we can sell it? According to the cost principle, we must value inventory at what it cost, even though we might be able to sell it for more than that amount.

$$\Delta A \quad + \quad \Delta E + \Delta D \quad = \quad \Delta L \quad + \Delta CC + \Delta R$$
$$\text{Inv} + 15{,}000 \qquad\qquad = \quad \text{A/P} + 15{,}000$$

	Dr.	Cr.
Inventory	$15,000	
Accounts Payable		$15,000

5. April 16. Cash of $14,000 is received from customers for purchases from last year. This increases one asset, cash, while reducing another asset, accounts receivable (A/R).

$$\Delta A \quad + \quad \Delta E + \Delta D \quad = \quad \Delta L + \Delta CC + \Delta R$$
$$\text{Cash} + 14{,}000 \qquad\qquad = \quad \text{No change on right side}$$
$$\text{A/R} - 14{,}000$$

	Dr.	Cr.
Cash	$14,000	
Accounts Receivable		$14,000

6. May 3. Executive sells inventory that had cost $28,000 for a price of $56,000. The customers have not yet paid for the goods, although they have received them. This is an income-generating activity. Executive has revenues of $56,000 from the sale. It also has an expense of $28,000, the cost of resources used to generate the sale. We can treat this as two transactions. The first transaction relates to the revenue and the second to the expense.

First, we have had a sale of $56,000, so we have to record revenue of $56,000 (Sales). We haven't been paid yet, so we have an account receivable of $56,000. This leaves the accounting equation in balance.

The second transaction concerns inventory and expense. In order to make the sale, we shipped some of our inventory. Thus, we have less inventory on hand. This reduction in inventory represents the cost of the sale, so in addition to reducing the inventory account, we record a cost of goods sold expense (CGS) equal to the decrease in inventory. Once again, this transaction leaves the accounting equation in balance.

$$\Delta A \quad + \quad \Delta E \quad + \Delta D \ = \Delta L + \Delta CC \quad + \Delta R$$

A/R + 56,000 $\quad\quad\quad\quad\quad\quad\quad\quad\quad\quad =$ Sales + 56,000

Inv − 28,000 $\quad$ CGS + 28,000 $\quad\quad$ = No change on right side

	Dr.	Cr.
Accounts Receivable	$56,000	
Cost of Goods Sold	28,000	
Inventory		$28,000
Sales		56,000

7. June 27. Executive places a $9,000 order to resupply its inventory. The goods have not yet been received. In this case there will be no formal journal entry. Our purchasing department undoubtedly keeps track of open purchase orders. However, as in the case of the equipment contract previously discussed, there is no journal entry until there is an exchange by at least one party to the transaction. We haven't paid for the goods and the supplier has not yet supplied them.

8. November 14. Workers were paid $18,000. This payment included all balances outstanding from the previous year. Because we are paying $18,000, cash will decrease by $18,000. Is this all an expense of the current year? No. We owed workers $10,000 from work done during the previous year. Thus, only $8,000 is an expense of the current year. Our journal entry will show that labor expense (Labor) rises by $8,000 and that wages payable (W/P) decline by $10,000. Note that three accounts have changed. Double-entry accounting requires that at least two accounts change. The equation would not be in balance if only one account changed. However, it is perfectly possible that more than two accounts will change. Here we can see that although three accounts have changed, in net, the equation is in balance.

$$\Delta A \quad + \quad \Delta E \quad + \Delta D \ = \Delta L \quad\quad + \Delta CC + \Delta R$$

Cash − 18,000 $\quad$ Labor + 8,000 $\quad\quad\quad$ = W/P − 10,000

	Dr.	Cr.
Labor Expense	$ 8,000	
Wages Payable	10,000	
Cash		$18,000

9. December 31. At year-end, Executive makes its annual mortgage payment of $10,000. The payment reduces the mortgage balance by $4,000. It doesn't quite seem correct to pay $10,000 on a liability but only reduce the obligation by $4,000. Actually, mortgage payments are not merely repayment of a debt. They also include interest that is owed on the debt. If Executive is making mortgage payments on its plant and equipment just once a year, then this payment includes interest on the $40,000 balance outstanding at the end of last year (see Exhibit 20-A-1).

If the mortgage is at a 15 percent annual interest rate, then we owe $6,000 of interest for the use of the $40,000 over the last year. Thus the transaction lowers cash by $10,000, but increases interest expense (IE) (also on the left side of the equation) by $6,000. The reduction of $4,000 on the right side to reduce the mortgage payable (M/P) account leaves the equation exactly in balance.

$$\Delta A \quad + \quad \Delta E \quad + \Delta D \; = \Delta L \quad\quad + \Delta CC + \Delta R$$
$$\text{Cash} - 10{,}000 \quad \text{IE} + 6{,}000 \quad\quad = \text{M/P} - 4{,}000$$

	Dr.	Cr.
Interest Expense	$ 6,000	
Mortgage Payable	4,000	
Cash		$10,000

10. December 31. A dividend of $3,000 is declared and paid to Executive's stockholders. This creates two changes on the left side of the equation. Cash decreases and dividends (Div) increase. Recall that a dividend is not an expense, but rather a distribution of some of the firm's profits to its owners.

$$\Delta A \quad + \quad \Delta E + \quad\quad \Delta D \quad\quad = \Delta L + \Delta CC + \Delta R$$
$$\text{Cash} - 3{,}000 \quad\quad\quad \text{Div} + 3{,}000 \quad = \text{No change on right side}$$

	Dr.	Cr.
Dividends	$3,000	
Cash		$3,000

11. December 31. At year-end, Executive makes an adjustment to its books to indicate that one year's worth of prepaid insurance has been used up. Many financial events happen at a specific moment in time. In those cases, we simply record the event when it happens. Some events, however, happen over a period of time. Technically one could argue that a little insurance coverage was used up each and every day, so the accountant should have recorded the expiration of part of the policy each day, or for that matter, each minute.

There is no need for that degree of accuracy. The accountant merely wants to make sure that the books are up to date prior to issuing any financial reports based on them. Therefore, a number of adjusting entries are made at the end of the accounting period.

One might ask why the accountant bothers to make such an entry even then. Why not wait until the insurance is completely expired? The matching principle would not allow that. In each case of an adjusting entry, the overriding goal is to place expenses into the correct period— the period in which revenues were generated as a result of those expenses.

In the case of the insurance, we have used up one-third of the $3,000, three-year policy, so we must reduce our asset, prepaid insurance (P/I) by $1,000, and increase our insurance expense (Ins) account by $1,000.

ΔA	+	ΔE	+ ΔD	= ΔL + ΔCC + ΔR
P/I − 1,000		Ins + 1,000		= No change on right side

	Dr.	Cr.
Insurance Expense	$1,000	
Prepaid Insurance		$1,000

12. December 31. Executive also finds that it owes office employees $3,000 at the end of the year. These wages will not be paid until the following year. This requires an adjusting entry in order to accrue this year's labor expenses. The entry increases labor expense and, at the same time, increases the wages payable liability account.

ΔA	+	ΔE	+ ΔD	= ΔL	+ ΔCC + ΔR
		Labor + 3,000		= W/P + 3,000	

	Dr.	Cr.
Labor Expense	$3,000	
Wages Payable		$3,000

13. December 31. The plant and equipment that the firm owns are now one year older. In order to get a proper matching of revenues for each period with the expenses incurred to generate those revenues, the cost of this plant and equipment was not charged to expense when it was acquired. Instead we allocate some of the cost to each year in which the plant and equipment helps the firm to provide its goods and services. The journal entry increases an expense account called depreciation expense (Depr) to show that some of the cost of the asset is becoming an expense in this period. In this year the expense amounts to $6,000. The calculation of annual depreciation expense is discussed in Chapter 13.

The other impact (recall that the double-entry system requires at least two changes) is on the value of the plant and equipment (P&E). Because the plant and equipment are getting older, we wish to adjust their value downward by the amount of the depreciation.

ΔA	+	ΔE	+ ΔD	= ΔL + ΔCC + ΔR
P/E − 6,000		Depr + 6,000		= No change on right side

	Dr.	Cr.
Depreciation Expense	$6,000	
Plant and Equipment		$6,000

These transactions for Executive Corporation give a highly consolidated view of the thousands, millions, or tens of millions of transactions that are recorded annually by a firm. These few transactions cannot hope to have captured every individual transaction or type of transaction that occurs in your particular firm. However, in this brief glance you can begin to understand that there is a systematic approach for gathering the raw bits of data that make up the financial history of the firm.

There may be an enormous number of individual journal entries for a firm during the year. The next step is to summarize these numerous individual journal entries to provide useful summarized information to interested users of financial statements.

Deriving Financial Statements

Exhibit 20-A-2 presents the information from which we can prepare a set of financial statements for Executive Corporation. This exhibit represents a highly abbreviated ledger for the entire corporation for the whole year. All of the journal entries for the year have been recorded. Each column represents one ledger account. The opening balance is recorded for each account, based on information from Exhibit 20-A-1, Executive Corporation's December 31, 2011 Balance Sheet. The horizontal lines represent the individual numbered journal entries from earlier in this appendix.

A number of the ledger accounts in Exhibit 20-A-2 start with a zero balance. This occurs for one of two reasons. The first reason is simply that there was no balance at the end of last year, so there is no balance at the beginning of this year. Such is the case with prepaid insurance. The second reason is that some items are kept track of year by year rather than cumulatively. The income statement accounts relate specifically to the accounting period. We kept track of our income for 2011. Once 2011 was over and its results reported in our financial statements, we wish to keep track of 2012's income separately from 2011's. Therefore, all of the revenue and expense accounts start 2012 with a zero balance. When we get to the end of this year and ask, "What was our revenue this year?" we want to know the revenue of this year separate and apart from any revenue we made in earlier years.

The revenue and expense accounts are called *temporary accounts* because we will start them over each year with a zero balance. The dividends declared account is also a temporary account. It keeps track of how much in dividends we declared during the entire year. There is a separate permanent account, dividends payable, which would keep track of any dividends we've declared but not yet paid.

The key to conveying financial information is the ending balance of each ledger account. As long as we are using a system in which each journal entry is *posted*, or recorded in the individual ledger accounts involved, we are able to determine the ending balance in each ledger account. Those ending balances provide the information needed for a complete set of financial statements.

EXHIBIT 20-A-2
Executive Corporation
Ledger for 2012 (000's omitted)
Ledger Accounts

Transaction	Assets: Cash	Prepaid Insurance	Accounts Receivable	Inventory	Plant & Equipment	Expenses: Cost of Goods Sold	Labor	Interest	Insurance	Depreciation	Div.: Dividends	=	Liabilities: Accounts Payable	Wages Payable	Mortgage Payable	Stockholder's Equity: Common Stock	Retained Earnings	Rev.: Revenue
Beginning Balance	$52	$0	$18	$20	$60	$0	$0	$0	$0	$0	$0	=	$17	$10	$40	$10	$73	$0
1	-3	3										=						
2	-15											=	-15					
3												=	15					
4	14		-14									=						
5				15								=						
6			56	-28		28						=						56
7								6				=						
8	-18						8					=		-10				
9	-10											=			-4			
10	-3										3	=						
11		-1							1			=						
12							3					=		3				
13					-6					6		=						
Ending Balance	$17	$2	$60	$7	$54	$28	$11	$6	$1	$6	$3	=	$17	$3	$36	$10	$73	$56

Excel Exercise

Use Template 18 to record journal entries, post them to ledger accounts, and calculate ending balances that can be used to prepare financial statements. This template is on the CD that accompanies this book.

The Income Statement

Exhibit 20-A-3 presents the 2012 Income Statement for Executive Corporation. The income statement for any firm consists merely of a comparison of its revenues and expenses. In order to prepare this statement, we would have to look at the ending balance in each revenue and expense ledger account. The ending balance in the revenue account at the bottom of Exhibit 20-A-2 shows revenue of $56,000, which is exactly the same as the revenue in the income statement in Exhibit 20-A-3. You can compare each of the expenses between Exhibits 20-A-2 and 20-A-3 as well, and will find them to be the same. This must be so, because the way that the income statement was prepared was to simply take the ending balances from each of the revenue and expense ledger accounts.

EXHIBIT 20-A-3
Executive Corporation
Income Statement
For the Year Ending December 31, 2012

Revenue		$56,000
Less Expenses:		
Cost of Goods Sold	$28,000	
Labor	11,000	
Interest	6,000	
Insurance	1,000	
Depreciation	6,000	
Total Expenses		52,000
Net Income		$ 4,000

The Balance Sheet

The retained earnings ledger account in Exhibit 20-A-2 has the same balance at the end of the year as it had at the beginning of the year. The retained earnings of a firm increase when it has income, and decrease when dividends are declared. In fact, every revenue will increase retained earnings, while expenses and dividends will decrease it. We have had all of these items, but the retained earnings account hasn't changed. The reason for this is that we have simply been keeping track of the specific changes in revenues, expenses, and dividends, instead of showing their impact on the retained earnings account.

By keeping track of revenues and expenses in detail rather than directly indicating their impact on retained earnings, we have generated additional information. This information has been used to derive an income statement. If we simply changed retained earnings directly whenever we had a revenue or expense, we would not have had the information needed to produce an income statement.

Nevertheless, we cannot produce a balance sheet without updating the information in our retained earnings account. Exhibit 20-A-4 provides a statement that updates both of the stockholders' equity accounts.

EXHIBIT 20-A-4
Executive Corporation
Analysis of Changes in Stockholders' Equity
For the Year Ending December 31, 2012

	COMMON STOCK	RETAINED EARNINGS
Beginning Balance 1/1/12	$10,000	$73,000
Capital Contributions during 2012	0	
Net Income for 2012		4,000
Dividends Declared 2012		(3,000)
Ending Balance 12/31/12	$10,000	$74,000

In Exhibit 20-A-4, we can see that the common stock balance did not change this year. Possible changes would include additional issuance of common stock through a private offering or a general offering to the public, issuance of stock as part of employee incentive plans, or retirement of stock. Retained earnings, as noted above, increase as a result of a positive net income (they decrease as a result of losses), and decrease when dividends are declared. (The parentheses around the $3,000 of dividends indicate that the $3,000 is being subtracted.)

All of the information used in Exhibit 20-A-4 comes either directly or indirectly from the ledger accounts in Exhibit 20-A-2 The common stock balance did not change during the year. Had there been changes to the common stock account, we could have determined what they were from the ledger account. Entries into ledger accounts are dated, allowing easy reference to the journal to review any transaction in its entirety. The dividend figure in Exhibit 20-A-4 is the ending balance in the dividends ledger account from Exhibit 20-A-2. The net income figure in Exhibit 20-A-4 does not appear anywhere in Exhibit 20-A-2. It is, however, merely a summary of the year-end revenue and expense items from the income statement, Exhibit 20-A-3. All of the Exhibit 20-A-3 items came directly from Exhibit 20-A-2. We now have all of the information we need to produce a balance sheet.

The balance sheet for Executive Corporation for 2012 appears in Exhibit 20-A-5. The asset and liability balances came directly from Exhibit 20-A-2 and the stockholders' equity balances came from our derivation in Exhibit 20-A-4. The preparation of this financial statement is really quite simple, given the ledger account balances. The balances are simply transferred to the financial statement, with the main work involved being the determination of which accounts are short-term and which accounts are long-term.

Excel Exercise

Template 19 uses the journal entry information from Template 18 to derive an Income Statement and Balance Sheet. This template is included on the CD that accompanies this book.

EXHIBIT 20-A-5
Executive Corporation
Balance Sheet
As of December 31, 2012

ASSETS

Current Assets:		
Cash	$17,000	
Prepaid Insurance	2,000	
Accounts Receivable	60,000	
Inventory	7,000	
Total Current Assets		$ 86,000
Fixed Assets:		
Plant and Equipment, net		54,000
TOTAL ASSETS		$140,000

EQUITIES

LIABILITIES		
Current Liabilities:		
Accounts Payable	$17,000	
Wages Payable	3,000	
Total Current Liabilities		$ 20,000
Long-Term Liabilities:		
Mortgage Payable		36,000
TOTAL LIABILITIES		$ 56,000
STOCKHOLDERS' EQUITY		
Common Stock		$ 10,000
Retained Earnings		74,000
TOTAL STOCKHOLDERS' EQUITY		$ 84,000
TOTAL LIABILITIES & STOCKHOLDERS' EQUITY		$140,000

The Statement of Cash Flows

The one remaining financial statement that is widely used to report the results of operations is the statement of cash flows. As discussed in Chapter 4, this statement focuses on the firm's sources and uses of cash. This statement also provides insight about the firm's liquidity, or its ability to meet its current obligations as they come due for payment. The statement of cash flows is divided into three major sections: cash from operating activities; cash from investing activities; and cash from financing activities.

The operating activities are those that relate to the ordinary revenue- and expense-producing activities of the firm. Firms tend to be particularly interested in how their day-to-day revenues and expenses affect cash balances. These activities include items such as payments to employees and suppliers and collections of cash from customers.

The investing activities of the firm relate to the purchase and sale of fixed assets and securities. It is clear that the purchase of stocks and bonds represents an investing activity. The accounting rule-making body determined that the purchase of property, plant, and equipment also represents an investment, and should be accounted for in this category. Lending money (and receiving repayments) also represents an investing activity.

The financing activities of the firm are concerned with borrowing money (or repaying it), issuance of stock, and the payment of dividends. Note that when a firm lends money, it is investing. However, borrowing money relates to getting the financial resources the firm needs to operate. Thus, borrowing is included in the financing category, along with issuance of stock. Dividends paid are considered to be a financing activity because they are a return of financial resources to the firm's owners. They are not included in operating activities because dividends paid are not classified as an expense, but rather as a distribution to the firm's owners of income earned.

There are two different approaches to calculating and presenting the statement of cash flows. These are the direct and the indirect methods. Exhibit 20-A-6 presents an example of the Statement of Cash Flows, prepared using the direct method. The direct method lists each individual type of account that resulted in a change in cash.

Looking at Exhibit 20-A-2, we can see that cash was affected by transactions 1, 2, 5, 8, 9, and 10. Review of each of those journal entries provides the information needed to prepare Exhibit 20-A-6. For example, transaction 1 consisted of a $3,000 payment for insurance. Therefore, the decrease in cash was for an operating activity, specifically payment for insurance.

This may be a cumbersome task when there are a large number of individual transactions. For example, how much cash was collected from customers during 2012? By looking at transaction 5 from Exhibit 20-A-2, we know that the answer is $14,000. We can see the increase in cash and the reduction in accounts receivable. Typically, however, there would be an extremely large number of individual journal entries related to receipts from customers.

Rather than review each transaction, accountants usually prepare the cash flow statement by making general inferences from the changes in the balances of various accounts. Note that accounts receivable at the beginning of the year were $18,000, and revenues from sales to customers during the year were $56,000. Combining what was owed to us at the beginning of the year with the amount customers purchased this year indicates that there was a total of $74,000 that we would hope to eventually collect from customers. At the end of the year the accounts receivable balance was $60,000. Therefore we can infer that $14,000 must have been collected (the $74,000 total due us, less the $60,000 still due at the end of the year).

Let's consider another example. The mortgage payable account started with a balance of $40,000 and ended with a balance of $36,000 (Exhibit 20-A-2). Rather than reviewing all of the journal entries related to mortgage payments, accountants would infer that $4,000 was spent on the financing activity of repaying debt. However, this inference process requires care. It is possible, for instance that $20,000 was paid on the mortgage principal, but a new mortgage of $16,000 was taken on a new piece of equipment. The statement of cash flows must show both the source of cash from the new mortgage, as well as the payment of cash on the old mortgage. Therefore, preparation of the statement requires at least some in-depth knowledge about changes in the accounts of the firm.

EXHIBIT 20-A-6
Executive Corporation
Statement of Cash Flows (Direct Method)
For the Year Ending December 31, 2012

Cash Flows from Operating Activities		
Collections from Customers	$ 14,000	
Payments to Employees	(18,000)	
Payments to Suppliers	(15,000)	
Payments for Insurance	(3,000)	
Payments for Interest	(6,000)	
Net Cash Used for Operating Activities		$ (28,000)
Cash Flows from Investing Activities		
None		
Net Cash Used for Investing Activities		0
Cash Flows from Financing Activities		
Payment of Mortgage Principal	$ (4,000)	
Payment of Dividends	(3,000)	
Net Used for Financing Activities		(7,000)
NET INCREASE/(DECREASE) IN CASH		$ (35,000)
CASH, DECEMBER 31, 2011		52,000
CASH, DECEMBER 31, 2012		$ 17,000

An alternative approach for developing and presenting the statement of cash flows is referred to as the indirect method. The indirect method starts with net income as a measure of cash from operations. It then makes adjustments to the extent that net income is not a true measure of cash flow. Exhibit 20-A-7 was prepared using the indirect method.

One of the most common adjustments to income is for depreciation. When buildings and equipment are purchased, there is a cash outflow. Each year, a portion of the cost of the buildings or equipment is charged as a depreciation expense. That expense does lower net income, but it does not require a cash outflow. Therefore, the amount of the depreciation expense is added back to net income to make net income more reflective of true cash flows. In Exhibit 20-A-7 we see that the $6,000 depreciation expense is added to net income.

There are a variety of other items that cause net income to over- or under-state the true cash flow. For example, if customers buy our product or service, but don't pay for it before the end of the year, then revenue, and therefore net income, will overstate cash inflow. Therefore, in Exhibit 20-A-7, there is a negative adjustment for the increase in accounts receivable.

Many of the adjustments to net income that are needed to determine cash flow from operating activities are quite confusing. Therefore many people prefer use of the direct method. However, because net income is considered essential to the process of generating cash, the net income reconciliation is required. If the direct method is used, the Cash Flows from Operating Activities portion of the indirect method (Exhibit 20-A-7) must be included as a supporting schedule.

EXHIBIT 20-A-7
Executive Corporation
Statement of Cash Flows (Indirect Method)
For the Year Ending December 31, 2012

Cash Flows from Operating Activities		
Net Income		$ 4,000
Adjustments		
Depreciation Expense	$ 6,000	
Decrease in Inventory	13,000	
Increase in Accounts Receivable	(42,000)	
Increase in Prepaid Insurance	(2,000)	
Decrease in Wages Payable	(7,000)	
Total Adjustments to Net Income		(32,000)
Net Cash Used for Operating Activities		$ (28,000)
Cash Flows from Investing Activities		
None		
Net Cash Used for Investing Activities		0
Cash Flows from Financing Activities		
Payment of Mortgage Principal	$ (4,000)	
Payment of Dividends	(3,000)	
Net Cash Used for Financing Activities		(7,000)
NET INCREASE/(DECREASE) IN CASH		$ (35,000)
CASH, DECEMBER 31, 2011		52,000
CASH, DECEMBER 31, 2012		$ 17,000

The information contained in the statement of cash flows is quite dramatic in this example. Although Exhibit 20-A-3 indicated that there was a positive net income of $4,000, the firm is using substantially more cash than it is receiving. In some cases this might reflect recent spending on buildings and equipment. A decline in cash is not necessarily bad. However, in this case, we note from the statement of cash flows (Exhibit 20-A-6 or 20-A-7) that no money was used for investing activities. The largest decline in cash came from operations. What was the single largest cause of the decline? Exhibit 20-A-6 would seem to indicate that payments to employees were the largest item. They caused the largest cash outflow.

However, this is an example in which the net income reconciliation provides particularly useful information. Looking at the cash flows from operating activities section of Exhibit 20-A-7, the most striking number is the $42,000 increase in receivables. A growing company is likely to have growing receivables. In this case, however, the growth in receivables seems to be unusually large. What does this mean? It could mean that the firm needs to make a stronger effort to collect payment from its customers on a timely basis. Or it could mean that sales were made to buyers who can't pay. The statement of cash flows highlights the receivables problem for the user of the statement. If receivables continue to grow at this rate, the firm will run out of cash, probably before the end of the next year. Although there is no crisis yet, there may be unless we take this situation into account in managing the firm and in planning for cash inflows and outflows for the coming year.

Key Concepts

Timing for recording transactions—Journal entries can be made only if we know with reasonable certainty the amount of money involved and the timing of the event, and if there has been exchange by at least one party to the transaction.

Adjusting entries—Most financial events occur at one specific point in time and are recorded as they occur. Some financial events occur continuously over time, such as the expiration of insurance or the accumulation of interest. Adjusting entries are made immediately prior to financial statement preparation to bring these accounts up to date.

Income statement preparation—The income statement is directly prepared from the year-end ledger balances of the revenue and expense accounts.

Balance sheet preparation—Ledger account balances can be used to provide an analysis of changes in stockholders' equity accounts. This analysis, together with other ledger account balances, is used to prepare the balance sheet.

Statement of cash flows—This statement shows the sources and uses of the firm's cash. It specifically shows cash from operating, investing, and financing activities. It can be prepared under two alternative methods:

    a. *the direct method*—Lists the change in cash caused by each account.

    b. *the indirect method*—Starts with net income as an estimate of cash flow, and makes a series of adjustments to net income to determine cash flow from operating activities.

Chapter 21

Valuation of Assets, Liabilities and Stockholders' Equity

In the last chapter we focused on how financial transactions are recorded and reported. In the next chapter we will take a closer look at financial statements. But first, in this chapter we will consider some issues related to how assets and liabilities that appear on the balance sheet are valued.

One would not expect there to be much controversy over the valuation of balance sheet items. Wouldn't they simply be recorded at what they're worth? Unfortunately, it isn't as easy as that. Consider having bought a car three years ago for $20,000. Today it might cost you $24,000 to buy a similar car. Is your car worth $20,000 or $24,000?

Wait, it's more complicated than that. Your old car is no longer new and so its value has gone down with age. Because the old car is three years old, and generally cars are expected to have a five-year useful life, your car has lost 60 percent of its value, so it's only worth $8,000. However, due to inflation, you could sell the car for $14,000 and you'd have to pay $16,000 to buy it on a used car lot.

What is the value of your car? Is it $20,000 or $24,000, or $8,000, $14,000, or $16,000? Obviously valuation is a complex issue. This chapter looks at how accountants value assets, liabilities, and stockholders' equity for inclusion in financial statements. In addition, several other useful valuation methods that are not allowed for financial statement reporting will be discussed.

ASSET VALUATION

Historical Cost or Acquisition Cost

Financial statements generally value assets based on their historical or acquisition cost. This is done in order to achieve a valuation based on the GAAP of objective evidence. If the firm values all of its assets base on what was paid for them at the time it acquired them, there can be no question as to the objectivity of the valuation.

For example, let's suppose that some number of years ago a railroad company bought land at a cost of $10 an acre. Suppose that 1,000 acres of that land runs through the downtown of a major city. Today, many years after the acquisition, the firm has to determine the value at which it wishes to show that land on its current financial statements. The historical cost of the land is $10,000

($10 per acre multiplied by 1,000 acres). By historical cost, we mean the historical cost to the firm as an entity. The firm may have bought the land from previous owners who paid $1 per acre. Their historical cost was $1 per acre, but to our entity the historical or acquisition cost is $10 per acre.

Accountants are comfortable with their objective evidence. If the land cost $10,000 and the firm says it cost $10,000, then everyone gets a fair picture of what the land cost. However, one might well get the impression from the balance sheet that the property is currently worth only $10,000.

In fact, today that land might be worth $10,000,000 (or even $100,000,000). The strength of using the historical cost approach is that the information is objective and verifiable. However, the historical cost method also has the weakness of providing outdated information. It doesn't give a clear impression of what assets are currently worth. Despite this serious weakness, historical or acquisition cost is the method that generally accepted accounting principles require for most assets reported on audited financial statements.

For assets that wear out, such as buildings and equipment, the historical cost is adjusted each year to recognize the fact that the asset is being used up. Each year the asset value is reduced by an amount that is referred to as depreciation expense. Depreciation is discussed in Chapter 13.

Fair Value or Mark-to-Market Accounting

Given the limitations of historical cost in providing a reasonable current measure of asset value, GAAP has been moving away from that historical cost approach. Financial assets (e.g. stocks and bonds), are now reported on the balance sheet based on the current *fair value* of the assets. These fair values are often based on trading that takes place in an active market-place, such as a stock exchange, where similar assets are traded. For example, if your organization purchased 100 shares of Google for $400 a share a number of years ago, and at the end of your most recent fiscal year the last trade of Google stock on the New York Stock Exchange was at $600 a share, then the fair value at your annual reporting date would be $60,000 (i.e. 100 shares x $600). The fair value is based on the selling price if the price at which you could buy that asset is different from the amount you could sell it for. The process of updating the value of assets to their current fair or market value in a process called *mark-to-market*.

GAAP creates a hierarchy of fair values that must be used when asset values are reported in audited financial statements. Level 1 fair values are based on the most reliable information such as direct observation of the prices at which trades of the identical stock took place. So if two people or companies (unrelated to your company) traded Google stock on your balance sheet date, that would create a Level 1 (the highest level) fair value. Level 2 would include assets whose fair value is based on similar, but not identical assets (e.g. bonds issued by one organization may be considered to be similar to bonds that were traded that had the same maturity, bond rating, and other characteristics, but were issued by another organization). Level 2 data is not as reliable as Level 1. For example, other bonds may be similar to the one you hold, but no two bonds issued by different companies could be considered to be exactly the same, and therefore the value of the bond you hold may not be exactly the same as the one used to obtain the fair value estimate. Level 3 in the hierarchy is reserved for assets whose fair value is based on indirect measurements that involve a significantly greater amount of assumption and estimates. This is considered to be the least reliable information in the hierarchy.

Despite the potential weaknesses of assigning fair values using less than totally reliable information, under normal conditions mark-to-market generally results in a better reporting of an asset at its true current value than historical cost does. However, if market values differ from the true underlying value of the asset, the valuations can be distorted. Such distortions might occur if there is great uncertainty about the underlying asset value or if current market conditions have created an irrational swing toward over-exuberance or over-pessimism, as might occur during financial crises.

The Subprime Crisis of 2008

Some argue that the subprime mortgage crisis of 2008 was caused by mark-to-market accounting. Under the fair-value accounting rules, banks were required to mark their financial assets to their market value. In the case of mortgage backed securities (MBS) this created a particular problem. Many banks owned a large amount of MBS. These are securities that consist of a large number of mortgages that have been bundled together. Every month the owner of MBS receives the interest and principal payments that have been collected from the homeowners as they pay off their mortgages.

As housing prices started to plunge in 2007 and 2008, and foreclosures started to rise, the value of MBS became uncertain. Although only a minority of homeowners actually stopped making payments on their mortgages, investors had no way of knowing how bad the housing crisis would become, and therefore how much of the underlying value of MBS might be lost.

With great uncertainty in the marketplace, buyers became risk averse and did not want to buy these securities until they could better assess how bad the housing crisis would get. Without buyers, market prices plunged. Given the fact that most home-owners did keep paying their mortgages, one could argue that the dramatic drop in market value of the MBS was irrational, or at least overly pessimistic.

This put banks in a bind. Suppose a bank originally bought some MBS at 95% of the face value of the mortgages in the MBS portfolio. That meant that if 95% of the mortgages paid off, the bank would not incur losses. But suddenly 15% of the mortgages in some MBS stopped paying interest and principal. From the bank's perspective, 85% of the homeowners were still paying, and the security should be worth 85% of its face value (actually more that than, considering that once the non-paying loans went through foreclosure, some value would be realized on the sale of the foreclosed homes). But with almost no market for these distressed MBS assets, they were forced by their auditors to mark the securities down to perhaps 20% or 30% of face value. While this recognizes the value they could currently sell the MBS for, it ignores the cash flows still being generated by the majority of mortgages in the MBS that were still delivering interest and principal payments on a normal basis. Some would argue that although the goal of the mark-to-market is to provide better information about the value of the asset, this in fact produced misleading information.

The consequences were devastating for a lot of banks. Some banks had borrowed money to buy the MBS. As the reported market value of the MBS fell, the lenders called for the banks to provide more collateral or repay the loans, often forcing the banks to sell the MBS at extremely distressed prices, thus locking in losses that would likely have mostly reversed themselves once the market stabilized.

Banks are also required to keep reserves. That is, there must be a certain amount of assets on the balance sheet, relative to the amount of debt the bank has. Mark-to-market rules caused the balance sheet value of the MBS to fall so much that many banks fell below their legal reserve requirements. Banks needed to raise capital, often being forced to sell off the MBS at severe losses, or even forcing the banks into bankruptcy.

Some argue that mark-to-market magnified the crisis. If the assets were not marked down so much, the banks would not have fallen below reserve requirements and would not have been forced to make sales at the very worst time, taking enormous losses. Others argue that you shouldn't blame accountants for simply making banks report the true current market value of their investments, and take the consequences of having made risky investments.

If banks had been allowed to determine a value for their MBS based on the cash flow that was being generated by the majority of homeowners who were still making payments on their mortgages, banks wouldn't have had to record such severe asset markdowns. Fewer banks would have been below their required reserves and been forced to sell off assets at extreme low points in the market. In late 2008 the FASB and SEC issued a "clarification" of GAAP indicating that forced liquidations are not indicative of fair value and that expected cash flows from investments can be used to make estimates of fair value. In 2009 the FASB further eased mark-to-market rules in periods when markets are unsteady or inactive, thus allowing for the valuation to be based on a price that would be received in an orderly market rather than a forced liquidation.

Despite the problems with mark-to-market that led to easing of fair value requirements, it is unlikely that mark-to-market will be eliminated. Many feel it is a better approach than historical cost measurement, and there are some who would like to eliminate historical cost completely in favor of fair value measurement, even for assets such as land, buildings, and equipment.

Price-Level Adjusted Historical Cost

Accountants are ready to admit that the ravages of inflation have played a pretty important part in causing the value of assets to change substantially from their historical cost. The longer the time between the purchase of the asset and the current time, the more likely it is that a distortion exists between the current value of an item and its historical cost. Fair value, or mark-to-market accounting only affects financial assets such as stocks and bonds. Buildings, land, and equipment are not adjusted to current market values. One proposed solution to the problem is price-level adjusted historical cost or PLAHC (pronounced plack). This method is frequently referred to as *constant dollar valuation*.

The idea behind constant dollar valuation is that most of the change in value of assets over time has been induced by price-level inflation. Thus, if we use a price index such as the Consumer Price Index (CPI) to adjust the value of all assets based on the general rate of inflation, we would report each asset at about its current worth. While this approach may sound good, it has some serious flaws.

Unfortunately, not everything increases at the same rate of inflation. The land in the railroad example may have increased in value much faster than the general inflation rate. There is no way to easily adjust each asset for the specific impact that inflation had on that particular asset, using price indexes such as the CPI.

Where does that leave us? Well, PLAHC gives an objective measurement of assets. However it might allow an asset worth $10,000,000 to be shown on the balance sheet at only $110,000. Perhaps it is better to leave the item at its cost and inform everyone that it is the cost and is not adjusted for inflation, rather than to say that it has been adjusted for inflation when the adjustment may be a poor one.

Net Realizable Value

Another alternative for the valuation of assets is to measure them at what you could get if you were to sell them. This concept of valuation makes a fair amount of sense. If you were a potential creditor, be it banker or supplier, you might well wonder, "If this firm were to sell off all of its assets, would it be able to raise enough cash to pay off all of its creditors?"

The term *net* is used in front of *realized value* to indicate that we wish to find out how much we could realize net of any additional costs that would have to be incurred to sell the asset. Thus, commissions, packing costs, and the like would be reductions in the amount we could expect to obtain. This would be similar to a fair value approach for all assets.

Is this a useful method? Certainly. Does it give a current value for our assets? Definitely. Then why not use it on financial statements instead of historical cost? The big handicap of the net realizable value method is that it is based on someone's subjective estimate of what the asset could be sold for. There is no way to determine the actual value of each of the firm's assets unless they are sold. Another problem occurs if an asset that is quite useful to the firm does not have a ready buyer. In that case, the future profits method discussed below provides a more reasonable valuation.

The Level 1 to Level 3 hierarchy for fair value reporting has only been in place for a few years. It is possible that if Level 3 valuations are well accepted, it would pave the way for net realizable value to be used for reporting the value of most assets.

Future Profits

The main reason a firm acquires most of its assets is to use them to produce the firm's goods and services. Therefore, a useful measure of their worth is the profits they will contribute to the firm in the future. This is especially important in the case where the assets are so specialized that there is no ready buyer. If the firm owns the patent on a particular process, the specialized machinery for that process may have no realizable value other than for scrap.

Does that mean that the specialized machinery is worthless? Perhaps yes, from the standpoint of a creditor who wonders how much cash the firm could generate if needed to meet its obligations. From the standpoint of evaluating the firm as a going concern, a creditor may well be more interested in the ability the firm has to generate profits. Will the firm be more profitable because it has the machine than it would be without it?

Under this relatively sensible approach, an asset's value is set by the future profits the firm can expect to generate because it has the asset. However, once again the problem of dealing with subjective estimates arises.

Replacement Cost

The replacement cost approach is essentially the reverse of the net realizable value method. Rather than considering how much we could get for an asset were we to sell it, we consider how much it would cost us to replace that asset. While this might seem to be a difference that splits hairs, it really is not.

Suppose that last year you could buy a unit of merchandise for $5 and resell it for $7. This year you can buy the unit for $6 and sell it for $8. You have one unit remaining that you bought last year. Today, its historical cost is $5, the amount you paid for it; its net realizable value is $8, the amount you can sell it for; and its replacement cost is $6, the amount you would have to pay to replace it in your inventory. Three different methods result in three different valuations.

Replacement cost (often referred to as current cost) is another example of a subjective valuation approach. Unless you actually go out and attempt to replace an asset, you cannot be absolutely sure what it would cost to do so.

Which Valuation is Right?

Unfortunately, none of these methods is totally satisfactory for all information needs. Different problems require different valuations. The idea that there is a different appropriate valuation depending on the question being asked may not seem to be quite right. Why not simply say what it's worth and be consistent?

From the standpoint of financial statements, we have little choice. GAAP requires the use of historical cost information for some asset types and fair value for others. That restricts options substantially in providing financial statements. You might say, "Okay, the financial statements must follow a certain set of rules, but just among us managers, what is the asset's real value?" We respond, "Why do you want to know?" We really are not avoiding the question. Let's consider a variety of possible examples.

First, assume that one of your duties is to make sure the firm has adequate fire insurance coverage. The policy is currently up for renewal and you have obtained a copy of your firm's annual report. According to the balance sheet, your firm has $40,000,000 of plant and equipment. You don't want to be caught in the cold, so you decide to insure it for the full $40 million. Nevertheless, you may well have inadequate insurance. The $40 million merely measures the historical cost of your plant and equipment.

Which valuation method is the most appropriate? In this case, the answer is replacement cost. If one of the buildings were to burn down, then our desire would be to have enough money to replace it. Other measures, such as net realizable value, are not relevant to this decision.

Suppose we are considering the acquisition of a new machine. What measure of valuation is the most appropriate? We could value the machine at its historical cost—that is, the price we are about to pay for it. This method cannot possibly help us to decide if we should buy the asset. Looking at an asset's value from the point of view of its cost would lead us to believe that every possible asset should be bought, because by definition it would be worth the price we pay for it.

How about using the net realizable value? What would the net realizable value of the machine be the day after we purchase it? Probably less than the price we paid because it is now used equipment. In that case, we wouldn't ever buy the machine. How about using replacement cost? On the day we buy a machine, the replacement cost will simply be the same as its historical cost.

Logically, why do we wish to buy the machine? Because we want to use it to make profits. The key factor in the decision to buy the machine is whether or not the future profits from the machine will be enough to more than cover its cost. So the appropriate valuation for the acquisition of an asset is the future profits it will generate.

Finally, consider the divestiture of a wholly owned subsidiary that has been sustaining losses and is projected to sustain losses into the foreseeable future. What is the least amount that we would accept in exchange for the subsidiary? Historical cost information is hopelessly outdated and cannot possibly provide an adequate answer to that question. Replacement cost information can't help us. The last thing in the world we want to do is go out and duplicate all of the assets of a losing venture. If we base our decision on future profits, we may wind up paying someone to take the division because we anticipate future losses, not profits.

The appropriate valuation in this case would be net realizable value. Certainly we don't want to sell the entire subsidiary for less than we could get by auctioning off each individual asset.

As you can see, it is essential that you be flexible in the valuation of assets. As a manager, you must do more than simply refer to the financial statements. In order to determine the value of assets, you must first assess why the information is needed. Based on that assessment, you can determine which of the methods discussed here provides the most useful information for the specific decision to be made.

VALUATION OF LIABILITIES

Valuation of liabilities does not cause nearly as many problems as valuation of assets. With liabilities, if you owe Charlie fifty bucks, it's not all that hard to determine exactly what your liability is; it's fifty bucks. In general, our liability is simply the amount we expect to pay in the future.

Suppose we purchase raw materials for our production process at a price of $580 on open account with the net payment due in thirty days. We have to pay $580 when the account is due. Therefore, our liability is $580. The crucial aspects are that our obligation is to be paid in cash and it is to be paid within one year. Problems arise if either of these aspects does not hold.

For instance, suppose we borrow $7,000 from a bank today and have an obligation to pay $10,000 to the bank three years from today. Is our liability $10,000? No, it isn't. Banks charge interest for the use of their money. The interest accumulates as time passes. If we are to pay $10,000 in three years, that implies that $3,000 of interest will be accumulating over that three-year period. We don't owe the interest today, because we haven't yet had the use of the bank's money for the three years. As time passes, each day we will owe the bank a little more of the $3,000 of interest. Today, however, we owe only $7,000, from both a legal and an accounting point of view.

You might argue that legally we owe the bank $10,000. That really isn't so, although the bank might like you to believe that it is. Let's suppose that you borrowed the money in the morning. That very same day, unfortunately, your rich aunt passes away. The state you live in happens to have rather fast processing of estates and around one o'clock in the afternoon you receive a large inheritance in cash. You run down to the bank and say that you don't need the money after all. Do you have to pay the bank $10,000?

If you did, your interest for one day would be $3,000 on a loan of $7,000. That is a rate of about 43 percent per day, or over 15,000 percent per year. Perhaps there would be an early payment penalty, but it would be much less than $3,000. Generally, accountants ignore possible prepayment penalties and record the liability at $7,000.

Another problem occurs if the liability is not going to be paid in cash. For example, perhaps we have received an advance payment for an order of widgets that we intend to fill over the coming year. What we owe is widgets, but we have to make some attempt to value that liability. Take the example one step further. We have received $18,000 for the widgets, but they will only cost us $9,000 to make. Is our liability $18,000 or $9,000?

In cases in which the obligation is nonmonetary in nature, we record the obligation as the amount received, not the cost of providing the nonmonetary item. What if for some reason we cannot provide the widgets? Will the customer be satisfied to receive a refund of $9,000 because that's all it would have cost us to make the widgets? No, the customer needs to get the full $18,000 back, so we must show that amount as the liability. If, over time, we make partial shipments, we can reduce the liability in a pro rata fashion.

VALUATION OF STOCKHOLDERS' EQUITY

The valuation of stockholders' equity is relatively easy. Recall that assets are equal to liabilities plus stockholders' equity. Once the value of assets and liabilities has been determined, the stockholders' equity is whatever it must take to make the equation balance. Remember that the stockholders' equity is, by definition, a residual of whatever is left after enough assets are set aside to cover liabilities. Thus, given the rigid financial statement valuation requirements for assets and liabilities, there is little room left for interpreting the value of stockholders' equity.

On the other hand, might there not be another way to determine the value of the firm to its owners? For a publicly held firm the answer is clearly yes. The market value of the firm's stock is a measure of what the stock market and the owners of the firm think it's worth. If we aggregate the market value of the firm's stock, we have a measure of the total value of the owners' equity.

Is the market value of the firm likely to equal the value assigned by the financial statements? Probably not. The financial statements tend to substantially undervalue a wide variety of assets. Intangible assets that may be quite valuable are not always included in financial statements. Further, historical cost asset valuation causes the tangible assets to be understated in many cases. Thus, the assets of the firm may be worth substantially more than the financial statements indicate. If the public can determine that to be the case (usually with the aid of the large number of financial analysts in the country), the market value of the stock will probably exceed the value of stockholders' equity indicated on the financial statements. Furthermore, stock prices are often dictated by the firm's ability to earn profits. In some cases companies with few assets can still be quite profitable, and therefore have a market value well in excess of the stockholders' equity shown on the balance sheet.

This discussion of valuation of assets and equities has left us in a position to better interpret the numbers that appear in financial statements. Financial statements are the end product of the collection of information regarding a large number of financial transactions. Each transaction is recorded individually into the financial history of the firm using the valuation principles of this chapter.

KEY TERMS

Asset valuation—There are a variety of asset valuation methods. The appropriate value for an asset depends on the intended use of the asset valuation information.

    a. *Historical cost*—the amount an entity paid to acquire an asset. This amount is the value used as a basis for tax returns and financial statements.

    b. *Fair value or mark-to-market*—a valuation method that is used to record financial assets (such as stocks and bonds) at the current value we could sell them for. Similar to *net realizable value* but with a greater focus on objective data.

c. *Price-level adjusted historical cost*—a valuation method that adjusts the asset's historical cost, based on the general rate of inflation.

d. *Net realizable value*—valuation of an asset based on the amount we would receive if we sold it, net of any costs related to the sale.

e. *Future profits*—This valuation method requires each asset to be valued on the basis of the amount of additional profits that can be generated because we have the asset.

f. *Replacement cost*—Under this method each asset is valued at the amount it would cost to replace that asset.

Liability valuation—The value of liabilities depends on whether they are short-term or long-term and whether or not they are to be paid in cash.

a. *Short-term cash obligations*—Amounts to be paid in cash within a year are valued at the amount of the cash to be paid.

b. *Long-term cash obligations*—Amounts to be paid in cash more than a year in the future are valued at the amount to be paid, less the implicit interest included in that amount.

c. *Nonmonetary obligations*—for obligations that require you to provide goods or services rather than cash, the liability is generally valued at the amount received, rather than the expected costs of providing the goods or services.

Stockholders' equity valuation—Given a value for each of the assets and liabilities, stockholders' equity is the residual amount that makes the fundamental equation of accounting balance.

QUESTIONS FOR REVIEW

1. What are the benefits of historical cost or acquisition cost as a basis for valuing assets?

2. What adjustment is made to historical cost for assets that wear out?

3. What types of assets use fair value or mark-to-market valuation?

4. What crisis may have been exacerbated by fair value accounting? Why?

5. What does PLAHC try to adjust for?

6. What is the primary way that net realizable value differs from fair value accounting?

7. If you are buying fire insurance, what valuation method should you use?

8. If you borrow money from the bank, is your liability the day you take out the loan equal to the amount you borrowed or the amount you are obligated to repay?

9. Suppose you collect payment for your services, but you haven't provided your service yet. What is the basis for valuing the liability?

10. Does the stockholders' equity we see on a balance sheet provide a good sense of the true ownership value of the company?

Chapter 22

A Closer Look at Financial Statements

We now turn our attention to trying to get as much useful information as possible from a set of financial statements. There are a variety of reasons for wanting to be able to do this. First and foremost is to enable us to manage our firm better. Second, we want to be able to review the financial statements of close competitors to evaluate our performance as compared to theirs. Third, we may want to evaluate the financial statements of a firm in which we wish to invest. Fourth, we want to evaluate the financial statements of firms we are considering extending credit to.

We may be looking for different types of information in each case. Before extending credit, we want to assess a firm's liquidity and solvency. Before investing in a firm, we wish to know about its potential profitability. The goal of financial statement analysis is to derive from financial statements the information needed to make informed decisions.

We do this primarily through examination of the financial statements themselves, the notes that accompany the financial statements, and through the use of a technique called ratio analysis. Generally accepted accounting principles (GAAP), in recognition of many of the limitations of financial numbers generated by accounting systems, require that clarifying notes accompany financial statements. The information contained in these notes may be more relevant and important than the basic statements themselves. Ratio analysis is a method for examining the numbers contained in financial statements to see if there are relationships among the numbers that can provide us with useful information.

Chapter 23 focuses on the notes to the financial statements. Chapter 24 discusses ratio analysis. In the remainder of this chapter we will present a hypothetical set of financial statements to use as a basis of discussion for Chapters 22-24.

THE BALANCE SHEET

Exhibit 22-1 presents the balance sheet for the hypothetical Pacioli Wholesale Corporation (PW) that will be the subject of our analysis. The information is provided for two years. In recognition of the fact that information in a vacuum is not very useful, accountants generally provide comparative data. In the case of PW, the financial statements present the current fiscal year ending June 30, 2012 and the previous fiscal year ended June 30, 2011. Many financial reports contain the current year and the two previous years for comparison.

EXHIBIT 22-1
Pacioli Wholesale Corporation
Statement of Financial Position
As of June 30 2012 and June 30, 2011

ASSETS

	2012	2011
Current Assets		
Cash	$ 8,000	$ 7,000
Marketable Securities	12,000	9,000
Accounts Receivable, Net of Uncollectible Accounts	22,000	30,000
Inventory	49,000	40,000
Prepaid Expenses	3,000	2,000
Total Current Assets	$ 94,000	$ 88,000
Fixed Assets		
Buildings and Equipment	$150,000	$120,000
Less Accumulated Depreciation	40,000	30,000
Net Buildings and Equipment	$110,000	$ 90,000
Land	50,000	50,000
Total Fixed Assets	$160,000	$140,000
Goodwill	$ 45,000	$ 50,000
TOTAL ASSETS	$299,000	$278,000

LIABILITIES AND STOCKHOLDERS' EQUITY

	2012	2011
Current Liabilities		
Wages Payable	$ 3,000	$ 2,000
Accounts Payable	29,000	25,000
Taxes Payable	15,000	12,000
Total Current Liabilities	$ 47,000	$ 39,000
Long-Term Liabilities		
Mortgage Payable	$ 45,000	$ 50,000
Bond Payable	100,000	100,000
Deferred Taxes	39,000	35,000
Total Long-Term Liabilities	$184,000	$185,000
Stockholders' Equity		
Common Stock, $1 Par, 1000 Shares	$ 1,000	$ 1,000
Common Stock—Excess over Par	24,000	24,000
Preferred Stock, 10%, $100 Par, 100 Shares	10,000	10,000
Retained Earnings	33,000	19,000
Total Stockholders' Equity	$ 68,000	$ 54,000
TOTAL LIABILITIES & STOCKHOLDERS' EQUITY	$299,000	$278,000

The accompanying notes are an integral part of these statements.

All the numbers on the PW financial statements are rounded to the nearest thousand dollars. For large corporations, it is not uncommon to round numbers to the nearest hundred thousand or even million dollars.

Current Assets

The first assets listed on the balance sheet are the current assets. These are the most liquid of the firm's resources. The current assets are presented on the balance sheet in order of liquidity. Cash, the most readily available asset for use in meeting obligations as they become due, is listed first. Cash includes amounts on deposit in checking and savings accounts as well as cash on hand. The next item is marketable securities that are intended to be liquidated in the near term. They can be converted to cash in a matter of a few days. Marketable securities that the firm intends to hold as long-term investments shouldn't be listed with current assets, but instead under a long-term investment category, after fixed assets.

The next current asset listed is accounts receivable, net of uncollectible accounts. It is usually the case that we do not expect to collect what is due us from all of our customers. Credit policies, discussed in Chapter 15, may have an impact on the level of bad debts.

Inventory is not as liquid as receivables because we first have to sell the goods in order to generate receivables. Prepaid expenses are generally small, relative to the rest of the balance sheet. They include such items as prepaid rent or insurance. Prepaid expenses are grouped with current assets even though they will not usually generate any cash to use for paying current liabilities.

Long-Term Assets

All assets the firm has that are not current assets fall into the general category of long-term assets. Prominent among the long-term assets are fixed assets, which include the property, plant, and equipment used to process or produce the firm's product or service. A variety of other long-term assets may appear on the balance sheet. There would be a category for investments if we had marketable securities that we anticipated keeping for more than one year.

In the case of PW, there is an asset called goodwill. Goodwill is an intangible asset that may arise through the acquisition of another company. Most firms have some goodwill: They have customer loyalty and a good relationship with their suppliers. However, goodwill is an intangible asset that accountants usually leave off the balance sheet because of the difficulty in measuring it. When one company takes over another, if it pays more for the company it is acquiring than can reasonably be assigned as the fair market value of the specific identifiable assets that it is buying, then the excess is recorded on the balance sheet of the acquiring company as goodwill. This follows the accountant's philosophy that people are not fools. If we pay more for a company than its other assets are worth, then there is a presumption that the various intangibles we are acquiring that can't be directly valued must be worth at least the excess amount we paid.

Liabilities

The firm's current liabilities are those that exist at the balance sheet date, which have to be paid in the next operating cycle—usually considered to be one year. Common current liabilities include wages payable, accounts payable, and taxes payable. The taxes payable include only the portion to be paid in the near term, not the taxes that have been deferred more than one year beyond the balance sheet date.

Long-term liabilities include any recorded liabilities that are not current liabilities. There may be a variety of commitments that the firm has made that will not be included with the liabilities. For example, if the firm has operating leases (see Chapter 14), they will not appear on the balance sheet, even though they may legally obligate the firm to make large payments into the future. The notes to the financial statements are especially important in disclosing material commitments.

Stockholder' Equity

The stockholders' equity section of the balance sheet contains a number of elements. Instead of simply having contributed capital and retained earnings, there are a number of separate items that comprise contributed capital. There are two general classes of stock—common stock and preferred stock. Both types of stock were discussed in Chapter 5. In addition, there is a distinction between amounts paid in exchange for stock that represent *par value* and amounts in excess of par.

Par value is a legal concept. In many states, firms are required to set an arbitrary amount as the par value of their stock. As was discussed in Chapter 5, one of the primary reasons many firms incorporate is to achieve a limited liability for their owners. Limited liability assumes that the corporation's stock was originally issued for at least its par value. If stock is issued below the par value—let's say that $10 par value stock is issued for $7—then the owner would be liable for the difference between the issue price and the par value should the firm go bankrupt. Given that situation, the par value of a corporation's stock is generally set low enough so that all stock is issued for at least the par value. Par value is an arbitrary value set by the firm.

There is no connection between the par value and any underlying *value* of the firm. There is no reason to believe that the arbitrarily selected par value is a good measure of what a share of stock is worth. In fact, because most firms are very careful to set par low enough so that there is no extra liability for the corporation's owners, par value has become almost meaningless. Therefore, some states now allow corporations to issue stock without assigning a par value.

From an accounting perspective, we wish to be able to show the user of financial statements whether there is some potential additional liability to the stockholders. To accomplish this, the accountant will have one account to show amounts received for stock up to the par value amount. Anything paid above par for any share will go into a separate account with a name such as "excess paid over par" or "additional paid-in capital."

In the case of PW, we see that it has 1,000 shares of $1 par value common stock. The balance in the common stock par account is $ 1,000, meaning that all 1,000 shares were issued for at least $1 each, the par value. There are 100 shares of $100 par value preferred stock and the balance in the preferred stock par account is $10,000, indicating that each of the 100 shares was issued for at least $100. Therefore, we know that the stockholders of PW have limited liability. They can lose everything they've paid for their stock, but if the firm goes bankrupt, the creditors cannot attempt to collect additional amounts from the stockholders personally.

As is quite commonly the case, PW's stockholders have paid more than the par value for at least some of the stock issued by the corporation. The common stock excess over par account has a balance of $24,000. Together with the $1,000 in the common stock par account, this indicates the investors paid $25,000 (or gave the firm resources worth $25,000) for 1,000 shares of stock. On average, investors have paid $25 per share for the common stock. There is no excess over par account for the preferred stock. Therefore, we know that the preferred stockholders each paid exactly $100 per share for the preferred stock.

The preferred stock is referred to as 10 percent, $100 par stock, indicating that the annual dividend rate on the preferred stock is 10 percent of the $100 par value. Each preferred share must receive a $10 dividend before the firm can pay any dividend to the common stock shareholders.

The retained earnings, as discussed earlier in the book, represent the profits that the firm earned during its existence that have not been distributed to the stockholders as dividends, and therefore have been retained in the firm. Remember that this category, like the others on the liability and owners' equity side of the balance sheet, represents claims on assets. There is no pool of money making up the retained earnings. Rather, the profits earned over the years and retained in the firm have likely been invested in a variety of fixed and current assets.

Excel Excercise

You may use Template 20 to prepare a Balance Sheet for your organization. The template is on the CD that accompanies this book.

THE INCOME STATEMENT

The income statement of PW (Exhibit 22-2) does not overtly raise as many new concepts and issues as the balance sheet did. PW uses the common multiple-step statement in which various expenses are shown separately. For instance, product costs are all grouped under the heading "Cost of Goods Sold." The gross profit or gross margin provides information about the margin of profitability when sales are compared to the direct product costs of the firm.

Subtracting the various other day-to-day operating costs from the gross profit results in operating income. By operating costs, we mean the various selling, administrative, and general costs of the firm. These costs include everything except product costs, financing costs, and taxes. Financing costs are isolated as a separate figure because of the specific financial leverage decisions (*see*

Chapter 9) the firm makes. There is a much greater degree of control over whether interest expense exists than, say, selling expenses. Management can decide whether money is to be borrowed, thus generating interest expense, or whether money should be raised through the issuance of stock.

Management can choose to use a single-step statement in which far less information is given about individual types of expenses. In this latter case, less information is provided to stockholders and creditors. On the other hand, less information is also given to competitors. The single-step approach cannot be used if it would mask information that the auditor believes is necessary for a fair representation of the firm's position and results of operations.

EXHIBIT 22-2
Pacioli Wholesale Corporation
Income Statement and Analysis of Retained Earnings
For the Years Ending June 30, 2012 and June 30, 2011

		2012		2011
Sales		$297,000		$246,000
Less Cost of Goods Sold		162,000		143,000
Gross Profit		$135,000		$103,000
Operating Expenses				
Selling Expenses	$30,000		$25,000	
General Expenses	12,000		10,000	
Administrative Expenses	49,000		40,000	
Total Operating Expenses		$ 91,000		$ 75,000
Operating Income		$ 44,000		$ 28,000
Interest Expense		12,000		10,000
Income Before Taxes		$ 32,000		$ 18,000
Income Taxes		13,000		7,000
Net Income		$ 19,000		$ 11,000
Earnings Per Share Common	$ 18.00		$ 10.00	
Less Dividends 2012 and 2011		5,000		3,000
Addition to Retained Earnings		$ 14,000		$ 8,000
Retained Earnings July 1, 2011 and 2010		19,000		11,000
Retained Earnings June 30, 2012 and 2011		$ 33,000		$ 19,000

The accompanying notes are an integral part of these statements.

The line following net income in Exhibit 22-2 contains earnings per share data. GAAP require inclusion of information on a per-share basis for common stock. It is felt that this type of information may be more relevant than net income for many users of financial information. Consider an individual who owns 100 shares of common stock of a large corporation. The corporation reports that its profits have risen from $25,000,000 to $30,000,000. On the surface, we would presume that the stockholder is better off this year. What if, however, during the year the firm issued additional shares of stock, thereby creating additional owners. Although total profits have risen $5,000,000 or 20 percent, because of the additional shares of stock outstanding, investors will find that their share of earnings increased by less than 20 percent. In fact, it is quite possible that the profits attributable to each individual share may have fallen, even though the total profit for the firm has increased.

Therefore, we must show not only net income for the firm, but also net income per share of common stock. Although there are 1,000 shares of common stock for PW, and the net income was $19,000, the earnings or income (the two terms are used interchangeably) per share is $18.00, rather than the expected $19.00. This is because $1,000 has to be paid as a 10 percent dividend to the preferred shareholders. This portion of the income of the firm doesn't belong to the common shareholders. The remaining $18,000 does.

Many corporations have outstanding securities that can be converted to common stock. For example, convertible debt represents loans that give the lender the option of taking shares of common stock instead of a cash repayment. This potential increase in the number of common shares outstanding can reduce the portion of total earnings owned by each of the current shareholders. If PW had such potential conversions, the earnings per share (EPS) of $18.00 would have been called *basic* EPS and the potential lower amount would also be shown and would be called *diluted* EPS.

For PW, the balance in the common and preferred stock accounts didn't change during the year (Exhibit 22-1). However, upon looking at the stockholders' equity section of the balance sheet, we see that the retained earnings has changed. Furthermore, the change is not exactly equal to the firm's income for the year. Somewhere in the financials we need some way of reconciling this change. In PW's case it has chosen one of the most common approaches—retained earnings are reconciled as part of the income statement.

In order to accomplish this reconciliation, the first step is to subtract any of this year's dividends from this year's net income. The difference is the amount of this year's earnings that are being retained in the firm. This year's earnings that are retained in the firm plus the balance of retained earnings at the start of the year gives us the retained earnings balance at year-end. This number should, and does, reconcile directly with the number that appears on the balance sheet as the year-end retained earnings.

Excel Excercise

You may use Template 21 to prepare an Income Statement and Analysis of Retained Earnings for your organization. The template is on the CD that accompanies this book.

THE STATEMENT OF CASH FLOWS

The statement of cash flows focuses on financial rather than operating aspects of the firm. Where did the money come from, and how did the firm spend it? While the major concern of the income statement is profitability, the statement of cash flows is very concerned with viability. Is the firm generating and will it generate enough cash to meet both short-term and long-term obligations?

The statement of cash flows shows where the firm got its cash and how it used it over the entire period covered by the financial statement. This feature is similar to the income statement, which shows revenues and expenses for the entire accounting period, and is different from the balance sheet that shows the firm's financial position at a single point in time. The statement of cash flows is divided into three major sections: cash from operating activities, cash from investing activities, and cash from financing activities.

The operating activities are those that relate to the ordinary revenue- and expense-producing activities of the firm. Firms tend to be particularly interested in how their day-to-day revenues and expenses affect cash balances. These activities include items such as payments to employees and suppliers and collections of cash from customers.

The investing activities of the firm relate to the purchase and sale of fixed assets and securities. It is clear that the purchase of stocks and bonds represents an investing activity. The accounting rule-making body determined that the purchase of property, plant, and equipment also represents an investment, and should be accounted for in this category. Lending money (and receiving repayments) also represents an investing activity.

The financing activities of the firm are concerned with borrowing money (or repaying it), issuance of stock, and the payment of dividends. Note that when a firm lends money, it is investing. However, borrowing money relates to getting the financial resources the firm needs to operate. Thus, borrowing is included in the financing category, along with issuance of stock.

PW's statement of cash flows is presented in Exhibit 22-3. The first element of the statement is cash flows from operating activities. This is a key focal point, because it provides information on whether the routine operating activities of the firm generate cash, or require a cash infusion. If the operating activities generate a surplus of cash, the firm is more financially stable and viable than if they consume more cash than they generate. This does not mean that negative cash from operating activities is bad. It may be indicative of a growing, profitable firm that is expanding inventories and receivables as it grows. However, it does provide a note of caution. Overly rapid expansion, without other adequate cash sources, can cause financial failure.

EXHIBIT 22-3
Pacioli Wholesale Corporation
Statement of Cash Flows
For the Years Ending June 30, 2012 and June 30, 2011

	2012	2011
Cash Flows from Operating Activities		
Net Income	$ 19,000	$ 11,000
Add Expenses Not Requiring Cash:		
Depreciation	10,000	8,000
Impairment of Goodwill	5,000	0
Increase in Taxes Payable and Deferred Taxes	7,000	8,000
Other Adjustments:		
Add Reduction in Accounts Receivable	8,000	1,000
Add Increase in Wages Payable	1,000	0
Add Increase in Accounts Payable	4,000	0
Subtract Decrease in Accounts Payable	0	(3,000)
Subtract Increase in Inventory	(9,000)	(2,000)
Subtract Increase in Prepaid Expenses	(1,000)	0
Net Cash from Operating Activities	$ 44,000	$ 23,000
Cash Flows from Inventory Activities		
Increase in Marketable Securities	$ (3,000)	
Sale of Fixed Assets	0	$ 2,000
Purchase of New Equipment	(30,000)	(20,000)
Net Cash Used for Investing Activities	$(33,000)	$(18,000)
Cash Flows from Financing Activities		
Payment of Mortgage Principal	$ (5,000)	$ (5,000)
Payment of Dividends	(5,000)	(3,000)
Net Cash from Financing Activities	$(10,000)	$ (8,000)
NET INCREASE/(DECREASE) IN CASH	$ 1,000	$ (3,000)
CASH, BEGINNING OF YEAR	7,000	10,000
CASH, END OF YEAR	$ 8,000	$ 7,000

The accompanying notes are an integral part of these statements.

The cash flows from operating activities are first approximated by the net income of the firm. Revenue activities are generally generators of cash, and expenses generally consume cash. That is not always the case, however, and a number of adjustments are needed. First of all, there are certain expenses that do not consume cash. In Exhibit 22-3, note that there are several expenses that are added to net income. Depreciation reflects a current year expense for a portion of fixed assets that are being used up during the year. These assets were mostly purchased in earlier years, and paid for at that time. The income statement charges part of their cost as an expense in the current year. However, that does not necessarily require any cash. Similarly, a reduction in the value of goodwill (called Impairment of Goodwill) will often occur only years after payment was made to acquire that goodwill. Therefore, net income is an imperfect measure of cash flow. It treats all expenses as if they consumed cash. Since depreciation and impairment did not consume cash, they are added back. To the extent that cash was actually spent this year on fixed asset purchases, it will show up in the investing activity portion of the statement of cash flows.

Taxes are another expense that do not necessarily require cash. As noted earlier (Chapter 13), some tax expense may be deferred for a number of years into the future, requiring no current cash payment, even though they are currently recorded as an expense. Additionally, some taxes that are due for the current year may not actually be paid until the tax return is filed, several months after the end of the year. These taxes also show up as an expense, even though the cash payment has not yet been made. Thus, these increases in taxes that are recorded as expenses but don't require cash payments must be added back to net income to arrive at a clearer picture of actual cash flows.

In addition to these expense items, there are a variety of other activities related to operations that consume or provide cash, but are not adequately approximated by net income. For example, when the firm purchases more inventory than it uses, the extra inventory is not an expense. Nevertheless, we must pay for it, so there is a cash flow. Increases in inventory must therefore be subtracted to show that they consume cash. On the other hand, if wages payable increase, that indicates that less cash was currently paid than we would expect based on the labor expenses we had for the year.

These adjustments can become complicated. However, for the non-financial manager it is not necessary to be able to make the various adjustments. Nonfinancial managers should focus on interpretation of the numbers. It is more important to be aware of the fact that these components show us what is affecting cash from operating activities. For instance, increases in accounts receivable require a subtraction from net income on the cash flow statement. This is because net income assumes that all revenues have been received. If accounts receivable are rising, the firm is not collecting all of its revenues from the current year. If we note a large increase in accounts receivable, it warns the managers that perhaps greater collections efforts are in order.

The second part of the statement of cash flows is cash from investing activities. We note here that PW increased its marketable securities, using $3,000 of cash, and purchased new equipment for $30,000. In the prior year, some equipment had been purchased and some equipment had been sold.

The third section of the statement is cash flows from financing activities. In this case there were no cash inflows from financing activities in either year. The corporation issued no new stock, nor were there increases in debt. The only financing activities relate to paying off an existing mortgage to creditors and paying dividends to shareholders.

Combining the cash flows from operating, investing, and financing activities yields the net increase or decrease in cash for the year. Added to the cash balance at the beginning of the year, this provides the cash balance at the end of the year. This is the same balance as that appearing on the balance sheet (Exhibit 22-1).

For PW the final cash balance has not been varying substantially. At the end of 2012 the balance is $8,000. The prior year it was $7,000. More important than the stability in the closing balance each year is the fact that the investments made by PW are being financed from operating activities. Not only are operations generating a positive cash flow, but further this cash flow is generally sufficient, or nearly sufficient, to cover the firm's investing and financing needs.

Right now, PW is relatively stable. It is growing and profitable, has twice as much in current assets as current liabilities, and has sustained its cash balance. On the other hand, as growth continues it must carefully monitor this statement. Increases in fixed assets, inventory, and receivables that normally accompany growth may prevent the firm from remaining in balance. Managers should consider whether the cash being generated from activities will be sufficient to sustain planned growth. If not, they should start to plan for either increases in long-term debt or the issuance of additional stock. A specific focus on the statement of cash flows can be a tremendous aid to management in preparing an orderly approach to meeting the financial needs of the firm.

Excel Exercise

You may use Template 22 to prepare a Statement of Cash Flows for your organization. The template is on the CD that accompanies this book.

KEY TERMS

Financial statement analysis—techniques of analyzing financial statement information to find out as much about the firm's financial position and the results of its operations and its cash flows as possible. The focus is on the financial statements, the notes to the financial statements, and ratio analysis.

Par value—a legal concept related to limited liability of stockholders. There is no relationship between par value and a fair or correct value of the firm's stock.

Earnings per share—Rather than focus simply on net income or total earnings, GAAP require disclosure of the earnings available to common shareholders on a per-share basis.

QUESTIONS FOR REVIEW

1. What is the main purpose of the Statement of Cash Flows and what are the three categories used within the statement?

2. What are some of the benefits of a thorough review of the financial statements?

3. Are financial statements usually presented with one year of data or more? Why?

4. What does "000 omitted" mean?

5. Assets are listed in order of liquidity. What does that mean?

6. What does "accounts receivable, net" mean?

7. Why is a Statement of Cash Flows needed, if we can see the change in cash by looking at the amount of cash on the balance sheet at the beginning and end of the year?

8. Should each of the sections of the cash flow statement show an increase in cash for a healthy organization?

Chapter 23

Notes to the Financial Statements

The financial statements for Pacioli Wholesale (PW) Corporation tell a great deal about the company. We have information about the firm's resources, obligations, net worth (stockholders' equity), profitability, and cash flows. Yet financial statements are extremely limited in their ability to convey information. Therefore, audited financial statements must be accompanied by a set of *notes*. These notes explain the company's significant accounting policies and provide disclosure of other information not contained in the balance sheet, income statement, and statement of cash flows, but that is necessary for the statements to be a fair representation of the firm's financial position and the results of its operations.

This chapter presents a hypothetical set of notes for the financial statements of PW. We will first present each note and then discuss it before moving on to the next note. This discussion will not be exhaustive. Each firm has notes that apply to its own unique circumstances.

SIGNIFICANT ACCOUNTING POLICIES

The notes section generally begins with a statement of accounting policies. This is particularly important because of the alternative choices of accounting methods allowed, even within the constraints of generally accepted accounting principles (GAAP). In cases in which the firm has a choice of methods, that choice will likely have an impact on both the balance sheet and the income statement and possibly on the statement of cash flows. The financial statement figures are not meaningful unless we know what choices the firm has made.

NOTE A: Significant Accounting Policies

1. *Sales—Sales are recorded when title passes; for most sales this is at the time of shipment.*

   For some businesses, revenue can be recorded prior to the final sale. For example, a construction company can record some revenue on a partially completed building if it has a sales contract. Even though the title has not yet passed to the buyer, some revenue and expense might be reported in that situation. On the other hand, for some sales for which there is great uncertainty about the collection of the sales price, revenue recognition is deferred until the time of cash receipt. For example, if a company sells swampland in Florida for a vacation or retirement home, it can generally only record revenue as cash installments are received, because of the uncertainty surrounding receipt of future installments. For PW, which is a wholesale company, the normal rules of accrual accounting require revenue recognition when title passes, which is normally when the goods are shipped.

2. *Short-term investments—Short-term investments are stated at their fair market value.*

   PW has $12,000 of marketable securities at the end of fiscal year 2012 (*see* Exhibit 22-1). Many assets are valued at the amount we paid for them, based on the *cost* principle of accounting. However, objective market prices for stocks and bonds are available from many sources. We can determine the price at which identical securities were actually sold. Therefore, marketable securities are generally shown on the balance sheet at their fair market value.

3. *Inventories—Inventories are stated at cost, not to exceed market. Cost is calculated using the last-in, first-out (LIFO) method.*

   Here the principle of recording at cost (based on objective evidence) conflicts with that of conservatism (adequate consideration of relevant risks). In this case, GAAP requires use of lower of cost or market value (LCM). If the market value exceeds cost, we use the cost. If the cost exceeds market value, we use the market value. Essentially, we are willing to value inventory below its cost, but not above it.

   So, inventories are stated using LCM because of the GAAP of conservatism. But how does PW measure the cost of its inventory? This note tells us that PW uses the LIFO method to determine inventory cost. LIFO/ FIFO is a choice the firm is allowed under GAAP. Note that if International Financial Reporting Standars (IFRS) are adopted, LIFO may no longer be allowed. *See* Chapter 19.

4. *Property, plant, and equipment—Property, plant, and equipment are recorded at cost, less depreciation. Depreciation taken over the useful lives of plant and equipment is calculated on the straight-line basis.*

   For tax purposes, law largely mandates our depreciation choices. For financial reporting, however, we have a fair degree of latitude. We could use a declining balance or sum-of-the-years-digits approach as an alternative to straight-line depreciation. For PW in 2012, operating costs included $10,000 of depreciation calculated on a straight-line (STL) basis. Suppose that the double-declining balance (DDE) depreciation would have been $18,000, and that the sum-of-the-years-digits (SYD) depreciation would have been $14,000.

   The firm's reported net income can be greatly affected by the choice of accounting methods. Disclosure of choices, such as the inventory and depreciation methods used, provides users with a greater ability to understand the firm's financial situation.

5. *Taxes on income—Income taxes reported on the income statement differ from taxes paid as a result of deferred income taxes. Deferred income taxes arise when there are differences between the year in which certain transactions, principally depreciation, affect taxable income and the year they affect net income.*

This note discusses deferred taxes. Based on our discussion in Chapter 13, we are already familiar with that issue. See Note B (below) for additional discussion.

OTHER NOTES

In addition to a summary of accounting policies, the annual report contains other notes that provide additional disclosure of information needed for the financial statements to provide a fair representation of the financial position of the firm and the results of its operations.

Part 5 of Note A above was concerned with the calculation of the amount of tax expense reported on the financial statements. Note B concerns the difference between taxes actually paid and the tax rate. PW is assumed to be in a 41 percent and 39 percent combined federal and state average tax bracket for 2012 and 2011, respectively, after adjusting for the federal tax benefit. This benefit arises from the tax deductibility of state and local income taxes on the federal tax return. Because our 2012 pretax income is $32,000 (Exhibit 22-2), we would expect tax payments of $13,000. However, PW did not pay $13,000 in 2012. Note B explains why.

NOTE B: Tax Payments

Differences between the effective tax rate and the statutory federal income tax rate are reconciled as follows:

IMPACT ON PRETAX INCOME	2012	2011
Statutory federal income tax rate	34%	34%
State and local income taxes net of the federal income tax benefit	7%	5%
Deferred tax increase	(13%)	(17%)
Taxes Paid as a percentage of pretax income (effective tax rate)	28%	22%

We note from Exhibit 22-1 that deferred taxes increased by $4,000 in 2012. Based on Note A, Part 5, this must be attributed primarily to the use of accelerated depreciation for tax return purposes. In other words, only $9,000 of the $13,000 tax expense was paid or payable for 2012. $9,000 is only 28 percent of pretax income. This note makes it clear that the effective tax rate for PW for 2012 was not the statutory combined federal and state rate of 41 percent that was reported on the income statement as tax expense, but instead was only 28 percent.

NOTE C: Inventory

If the first-in first-out (FIFO) method of inventory had been used, inventories would have been $9,000 and $5,000 higher at June 30, 2012 and June 30, 2011, respectively.

The Internal Revenue Service (IRS) allows a firm to use LIFO on its tax return only if it uses LIFO for its income statement and balance sheet, which are included in its annual report to its stockholders. However, the Securities and Exchange Commission (SEC) requires publicly held firms to disclose their inventory on a FIFO basis if it differs significantly from inventory on a LIFO basis. This practice allows a financial analyst to convert income calculated on a LIFO basis to what it would have been if the firm were on a FIFO basis.

NOTE D: Commitments and Contingent Liabilities

Lease commitments and contingent liabilities stemming from pending litigation are not considered to be material in the opinion of management.

The firm is required to disclose any material obligations under non-cancelable long-term leases, or other potential liabilities that are significant in amount. Recall that a financial transaction is not recorded unless there has been exchange. If PW has signed a contract raising its president's salary from $50,000 to $500,000 and guaranteeing that new salary for the next ten years, there would be no journal entry to record the new $5,000,000 total obligation. However, if that amount is material, disclosure would be required as a commitment or contingent liability.

NOTE E: Goodwill

The goodwill recorded on the balance sheet arose as a result of the acquisition of another company for more than the fair market value of the identifiable assets of that company. It has been determined that due to permanent changes in market conditions, the goodwill has permanently lost 10 percent of its value during 2012. Therefore, goodwill has been reduced from $50,000 to $45,000 on the balance sheet and a $5,000 expense has been charged.

When one firm acquires another for more than the value of the specific identifiable resources, the excess is grouped under the category of goodwill. It is very common for goodwill to arise when acquisitions occur. If the ongoing firm being acquired wasn't worth more than its specific assets, the purchaser might simply buy similar assets rather than acquiring the firm. Many intangibles arise over a firm's life, such as reputation for quality products and creditworthiness. Goodwill remains as an asset on the balance sheet indefinitely under current GAAP. Goodwill is only reduced when there is a clear impairment to its value. At such time the entire impairment is treated as a one-time reduction in the value of goodwill. This differs from tax treatment that allows the organization to deduct the cost of goodwill as an expense over a fifteen-year period.

NOTE F: Industry Segment Information

The firm has only one major type of operation—that of selling consumer goods to retail outlets. All of the firm's operations are domestic.

One of the requirements of financial reporting is industry segment information. A major reason for this requirement is that many firms have diversified substantially, making it difficult for stockholders and other users of financial information to determine just what business the company is in. Therefore, firms are required to disclose financial information about components of a business for which separate financial information is available and is used for making decisions. While the intent is to protect and inform stockholders, the information provided can, in fact, hurt stockholders.

The type of information disclosed for a business with multiple types of operations includes not only a description of each type of business, but also sales, operating profit, net earnings, and assets for each segment. This means that a competitor can examine your financial statements (or for that matter, you can examine a competitor's financial statements) to determine which segments are the most profitable. This information can be a tremendous aid in planning competitive strategy. The same is true of geographic data. If it is disclosed that our growth is occurring primarily in Latin America, our competitors may use that information to decide that it is time for a push in Asia.

Management is far more answerable to the firm's stockholders about its mistakes if the mistakes aren't buried among the successes. If the firm is losing some money in Latin America or in one major line of business, it is harder to hide that fact from the firm's owners when disclosure is required by the line of business and geographic location. Therefore this disclosure is required for the benefit of stockholders and creditors, despite the potentially negative impact on the firm's competitive position.

SUMMARY

This chapter does not present an all-inclusive listing of required notes to the financial statements. Depending on the exact circumstances of different companies, a wide variety of disclosures are required by GAAP and by requirements of the SEC. The most important learning issue in this chapter is not the information contained in the notes discussed here. Rather, it is that the reader should have an awareness of the importance of the information that is contained in the notes to the financial statements.

The notes to the financial statements may at first seem both overwhelming and boring. They certainly don't make for light reading. You have to work through them slowly and carefully to understand the information that each note is trying to convey. Exactly which choices has the firm made, and what are the implications of each choice? Is the company reliant on one key customer? If so, that fact would have to be disclosed somewhere in the notes. Can the company use all of its cash, or does it have a "compensating balance" agreement with its bank that requires it to maintain a minimum balance? If the latter, the firm's liquidity is somewhat overstated in the balance sheet. Compensating balance arrangements must be disclosed. Are there securities outstanding, such as convertible bonds that can be converted into common stock? If so, then the firm's net income might have to be shared among more stockholders. Such potential dilution, if significant, is discussed in the notes.

We could continue with examples of the types of information relevant to creditors, investors, and internal management contained only in the notes to the financials. Not all notes are relevant to all readers. Some items are of more concern to employees than to stockholders. Some items help creditors more than internal managers. Whatever your purpose in using a financial report, the key is that the financial statements by themselves are incapable of telling the full story. To avoid being misled by the numbers, it is necessary to supplement the information in the statements with the information in the notes that accompany the statements.

KEY TERMS

Significant accounting policies—Whenever GAAP allow a firm a choice in accounting methods, the firm must disclose the choice that it made. This allows the user of financial statements to better interpret the numbers, such as net income, contained in the financial statements.

Other notes—The firm must disclose any information that a user of the financial statements might need in order to have a fair representation of the firm's financial position and the results of its operations in accordance with GAAP. This information should be included in either the financial statements themselves or the notes that accompany the financial statements.

QUESTIONS FOR REVIEW

1. Notes are a required part of audited financial statements. The two main types of disclosure contained in the notes are: _____ and _____.

2. What are three types of policies that would typically be disclosed in the first note that accompanies financial statements?

3. What are some types of additional disclosure that you might see in the notes?

Chapter 24

Ratio Analysis

One of the most widely used forms of financial analysis is the use of ratios. Ratios can provide information that is useful for investment decisions such as, "Should we acquire XYZ Corporation?" Ratios can provide information regarding whether we should sell to XYZ or lend money to XYZ. They can also help internal management of an organization gain an awareness of their company's strengths and weaknesses. And, if we can find weaknesses, we can move to correct them before irreparable damage is done.

What is a ratio? Basically, a ratio is simply a comparison of any two numbers. In financial statement analysis, we compare numbers taken from the financial statements. For instance, if we want to know how much Pacioli Wholesale Corporation (PW) had in current assets as compared to current liabilities at the end of fiscal 2012, we would compare its $94,000 in current assets (Exhibit 24-1) to its $47,000 in current liabilities. Or more briefly, it had $94,000 compared to $47,000. Mathematically, we could state this as $94,000 divided by $47,000, which is equal to two. This means that there are two dollars of current assets for every one dollar of current liabilities. This would be referred to either as a ratio of 2 or a ratio of 2 to 1. This particular ratio is called the current ratio. In this chapter, we discuss many widely used ratios, but the discussion is not all-inclusive. Each industry may have many ratios specially suited to its needs.

BENCHMARKS FOR COMPARISON

Is the PW current ratio of 2 good or bad? Is it high enough? Is it too high? We don't want to have too little in the way of current assets, or we may have a liquidity crisis—that is, insufficient cash to pay our obligations as they become due. We don't want to have too much in the way of current assets because this implies that we are passing up profitable long-term investment opportunities. But there is no correct number for the current ratio. We can only assess the appropriateness of our ratios on the basis of some benchmark or other basis for comparison.

There are three principal benchmarks. The first is the firm's history. We always want to review the ratios for the firm this year, as compared to what they were in the several previous years. This enables us to discover favorable or unfavorable trends that are developing gradually over time, as well as pointing up any numbers that have changed sharply in the space of time of just one year.

EXHIBIT 24-1
Pacioli Wholesale Corporation
Statement of Financial Position
As of June 30, 2012 and June 30, 2011

	2012		2011	
ASSETS				
Current Assets				
Cash	2.7%	$ 8,000	2.5%	$ 7,000
Marketable Securities	4.0%	12,000	3.2%	9,000
Accounts Receivable, Net of Uncollectible Accounts	7.4%	22,000	10.8%	30,000
Inventory	16.4%	49,000	14.4%	40,000
Prepaid Expenses	1.0%	3,000	.7%	2,000
Total Current Assets	31.4%	$ 94,000	31.7%	$ 88,000
Fixed Assets				
Buildings and Equipment	50.2%	$150,000	43.2%	$120,000
Less Accumulated Depreciation	13.4%	40,000	10.8%	30,000
Net Building and Equipment	36.8%	$110,000	32.4%	$ 90,000
Land	16.7%	50,000	81.0%	50,000
Total Fixed Assets	53.5%	$160,000	50.4%	$140,000
Goodwill	15.1%	$ 45,000	18.0%	$ 50,000
TOTAL ASSETS	100.0%	$299,000	100.0%	$278,000
LIABILITIES AND STOCKHOLDERS' EQUITY				
Current Liabilities				
Wages Payable	1.0%	$ 3,000	.7%	$ 2,000
Accounts Payable	9.7%	29,000	9.0%	25,000
Taxes Payable	5.0%	15,000	4.3%	12,000
Total Current Liabilities	15.7%	$ 47,000	14.0%	$ 39,000
Long-Term Liabilities				
Mortgage Payable	15.1%	$ 45,000	18.0%	$ 50,000
Bond Payable	33.4%	100,000	36.0%	100,000
Deferred Taxes	13.0%	39,000	12.6%	35,000
Total Long-Term Liabilities	61.5%	$184,000	66.5%	$185,000
Stockholders' Equity				
Common Stock $1 Par,	.3%	$ 1,000	.4%	$ 1,000
Common Stock—Excess over Par	8.0%	24,000	8.6%	24,000
Preferred Stock, 10%, $100 Par, 100 Shares	3.3%	10,000	3.6%	10,000
Retained Earnings	11.0%	33,000	6.8%	19,000
Total Stockholders' Equity	22.7%	$ 68,000	19.4%	$ 54,000
TOTAL LIABILITIES & STOCKHOLDERS' EQUITY	100.0%	$299,000	100.0%	$278,000

The accompanying notes are an integral part of these statements.

The second type of benchmark is to compare the firm to other individual organizations. We would like to obtain financial information for one or more of our specific competitors. Using that information, we can compute a set of ratios and compare our ratio values to theirs. In an effort to make it easier for companies and financial analysts to get comparable information about specific companies, the Securities and Exchange Commission (SEC) requires that all United States public companies reporting on a GAAP basis provide their financial statements to the Commission and on their corporate websites in an interactive data format using XBRL.

XBRL, or eXtensible Business Reporting Language, is a tool for electronic communication of financial data. It was developed by a not-for-profit international consortium of companies, governments, and other organizations, and is gaining widespread use worldwide. Using the XBRL system, each element of a financial statement is coded using an identifying tag. Once financial data has been stored electronically in XBRL format, it can be selected and analyzed without any manual data entry. This means that someone seeking comparable financial data can go either to the SEC's online Interactive Data Electronic Applications (IDEA) system or to a company's website, and download the information in XBRL format. Once downloaded, using the XBRL tags, data can easily be selected for use in developing ratios for comparison. This system substantially simplifies the process of getting and analyzing comparable financial data.

The third type of benchmark is industrywide comparison. Dun and Bradstreet and the Risk Management Association (RMA) are a few examples of firms that collect financial data, compute ratios by industry, and publish the results. Not only are industry averages available, but the information is often broken down both by size of firm and in a way that allows determination of relatively how far away from the norm you are.

EXHIBIT 24-2

AGRICULTURE—Wheat Farming NAICS 111140

Comparative Historical Data columns: 4/1/07-3/31/08 ALL, 4/1/08-3/31/09 ALL, 4/1/09-3/31/10 ALL.
Current Data Sorted by Sales — 26 statements (4/1-9/30/09); 101 statements (10/1/09-3/31/10).

	4/1/07-3/31/08 ALL	4/1/08-3/31/09 ALL	4/1/09-3/31/10 ALL	0-1MM	1-3MM	3-5MM	5-10MM	10-25MM	25MM & OVER
Type of Statement									
Unqualified	35	24	21	4	2	2	2	3	8
Reviewed	24	21	16	1	4	3	2	1	5
Compiled	16	15	17	3	5	1	4	4	
Tax Returns	19	26	22	11	6	1	2	2	6
Other	70	53	51	8	16	6	10	5	
NUMBER OF STATEMENTS	164	139	127	27	33	13	20	15	19
	%	%	%	%	%	%	%	%	%
ASSETS									
Cash & Equivalents	12.3	12.3	13.8	19.4	13.6	10.4	17.6	6.0	10.9
Trade Receivables (net)	20.5	18.0	14.5	1.3	13.0	13.3	15.3	30.8	22.6
Inventory	15.4	18.3	10.3	1.2	8.2	4.6	14.8	15.1	22.4
All Other Current	4.3	3.5	4.8	6.1	5.9	.9	4.1	3.7	5.1
Total Current	52.6	52.0	43.4	28.1	40.7	29.3	51.8	55.7	61.1
Fixed Assets (net)	35.9	35.1	46.4	62.7	47.9	56.0	39.3	30.9	33.9
Intangibles (net)	4.4	4.7	3.6	3.2	4.5	3.9	.7	9.8	.8
All Other Non-Current	7.1	8.2	6.6	6.1	6.9	10.8	8.2	3.6	4.2
Total	100.0	100.0	100.0	100.0	100.0	100.0	100.0	100.0	100.0
LIABILITIES									
Notes Payable-Short Term	15.6	13.9	12.9	4.3	25.8	11.6	7.5	13.9	8.3
Cur. Mat.-L.T.D.	3.7	2.9	4.0	5.1	5.7	3.7	2.1	3.2	2.2
Trade Payables	10.1	11.7	9.3	9.0	8.9	5.0	6.2	9.7	16.0
Income Taxes Payable	.5	.4	.3	.0	.5	.4	.1		.3
All Other Current	8.6	8.6	13.2	16.5	11.9	11.5	9.4	18.7	11.6
Total Current	38.5	37.5	39.6	35.0	52.8	32.1	25.2	45.8	38.4
Long-Term Debt	25.0	21.2	32.6	83.1	21.6	16.2	17.8	15.9	19.6
Deferred Taxes	.3	.4	.4	.0	.3	.3	1.2	.9	.2
All Other Non-Current	7.1	5.9	3.8	1.2	2.3	.3	1.5	12.6	8.1
Net Worth	29.2	35.0	23.7	-19.3	23.3	51.1	54.2	24.7	33.7
Total Liabilities & Net Worth	100.0	100.0	100.0	100.0	100.0	100.0	100.0	100.0	100.0
INCOME DATA									
Net Sales	100.0	100.0	100.0	100.0	100.0	100.0	100.0	100.0	100.0
Gross Profit									
Operating Expenses	86.5	88.1	89.6	82.5	88.0	93.2	93.9	92.4	92.9
Operating Profit	13.5	11.9	10.4	17.5	12.0	6.8	6.1	7.6	7.1
All Other Expenses (net)	4.6	3.6	3.5	9.9	2.3	3.9	.8	1.0	1.1
Profit Before Taxes	8.9	8.4	6.9	7.6	9.7	2.9	5.3	6.6	6.0
RATIOS									
Current	2.4	2.3	2.6	5.7	2.3	2.0	4.2	2.2	2.1
	1.4	1.4	1.3	1.1	1.2	.9	2.3	1.3	1.7
	1.0	.9	.7	.2	.4	.6	1.1	.9	1.2
Quick	1.8	1.7	1.9	3.7	1.2	1.3	3.5	1.6	1.8
	.8	.8	.8	.4	.6	.2	1.8	.9	.9
	.4	.4	.2	.1	.1	.2	.7	.5	.3
Sales/Receivables	0 999.8	2 152.3	0 UND	0 UND	0 UND	0 UND	2 230.6	0 UND	19 19.1
	28 13.1	28 13.0	19 19.2	0 UND	1 302.4	22 16.9	31 11.9	21 17.1	34 10.6
	53 6.9	47 7.8	44 8.4	4 90.2	46 7.9	38 9.7	64 5.7	64 5.7	51 7.1

	Col 1	Col 2	Col 3	Col 4	Col 5	Col 6	Col 7	Col 8	Col 9
Sales/Working Capital	4.7 / 16.8 / -114.5	5.4 / 16.2 / -67.8	4.9 / 16.5 / -16.2	4.6 / 161.3 / -4.6	4.8 / 19.8 / -5.2	27.6 / -32.2 / -9.5	2.4 / 6.6 / 32.1	6.8 / 15.7 / -59.1	5.7 / 13.7 / 28.7
EBIT/Interest	(133) 7.6 / 3.4 (111) / 1.5	16.0 / 4.0 (109) / 1.4	9.8 / 2.6 / .5	(16) 11.3 / 3.4 (29) / -.2	6.9 / 2.1 (12) / .9	5.1 / 1.8 (18) / .4	29.8 / 4.0 / .8	10.9 / 3.5 / 1.1	22.5 / 2.2 / -.6
Net Profit + Depr., Dep., Amort./Cur. Mat. L/T/D	(25) 5.9 / 2.5 (22) / .8	8.6 / 3.2 (18) / 1.6	2.3 / 1.5 / 1.0						
Fixed/Worth	.3 / 1.2 / 4.8	.2 / .8 / 2.3	.4 / 1.2 / 5.4	.9 / 2.3 / -3.9	.6 / 1.2 / NM	.6 / 1.3 / 2.5	.2 / .7 / 1.6	.3 / 1.1 / -4.0	.4 / .8 / 1.9
Debt/Worth	.8 / 2.5 / 11.0	.7 / 1.9 / 6.7	.6 / 2.0 / 15.2	.4 / 4.4 / -3.6	.7 / 2.3 / -18.1	.3 / 1.1 / 3.6	.3 / .7 / 4.9	1.7 / 2.0 / -10.5	.9 / 3.2 / 6.2
% Profit Before Taxes/Tangible Net Worth	(134) 53.1 / 20.3 (118) / 6.3	48.5 / 16.6 (101) / 4.1	32.3 / 8.7 / -1.1	(18) 26.9 / -.3 (24) / -13.9	33.1 / 9.0 (11) / 1.5	5.6 / 2.2 (11) / -.5	70.8 / 9.9 (11) / -.6	49.8 / 25.4 (17) / -15.2	36.1 / 11.0 / -9.5
% Profit Before Taxes/Total Assets	15.8 / 6.6 / 2.0	15.4 / 5.6 / 1.0	12.0 / 2.3 / -.7	20.2 / 1.5 / -1.6	10.7 / 2.6 / .6	2.8 / 1.3 / -1.7	12.0 / 5.9 / -.4	12.0 / 8.0 / .6	14.0 / 2.3 / -3.8
Sales/Net Fixed Assets	31.0 / 7.7 / 2.5	48.0 / 7.6 / 2.3	20.8 / 3.7 / .8	16.8 / 1.1 / .2	19.5 / 3.7 / .7	6.5 / 3.9 / 1.3	12.6 / 3.9 / 1.3	37.4 / 15.1 / 3.7	32.4 / 6.4 / 2.3
Sales/Total Assets	3.3 / 1.7 / .9	3.1 / 2.0 / .8	2.7 / 1.4 / .5	1.8 / .8 / .2	2.6 / 1.6 / .4	1.7 / 1.5 / .6	2.4 / 1.5 / .6	3.6 / 2.7 / 1.0	3.5 / 2.3 / 1.3
% Depr., Dep., Amort./Sales	(126) .8 / 2.0 (109) / 5.5	.8 / 2.5 (99) / 6.3	1.9 / 5.1 / 12.1	(18) 2.5 / 11.9 (24) / 20.6	2.8 / 5.6 / 18.1	(18) 1.1 / 4.4 (14) / 7.6	.7 / 2.6 (16) / 7.8		.8 / 2.6 (16) / 4.5
% Officers', Directors' Owners' Comp/Sales	(42) 3.1 / 3.1 (29) / 7.0	1.3 / 3.3 (37) / 5.5	1.6 / 3.9 / 7.1		(12) 1.2 / 3.0 / 5.0				
Net Sales ($)	5938124M	8189597M	36371165M	11213M	59421M	48142M	135253M	234293M	3148843M
Total Assets ($)	3618296M	3930356M	1792627M	31698M	1171185M	72947M	139603M	195695M	1235499M

M = $ thousand   MM = $ million

© RMA 2010

For example, if your current ratio is 2, and the industry average is 2.4, is that a substantial discrepancy? Published industry data may show that 25 percent of the firms in the industry have a current ratio below 1.5. In this case, we may not be overly concerned that our ratio of 2.0 is too low. We are still well above the bottom quartile of firms in our industry. On the other hand, what if only 25 percent of the firms in the industry have a current ratio of less than 2.1? In this case, over three-quarters of the firms in the industry have a higher current ratio than we do. This might be a cause for some concern. At the very least, we might want to investigate why our ratio is particularly low, compared to our industry. Exhibit 24-2 presents one page from the *RMA's eStatement Studies 2010/2011*. Note that this page provides information about the balance sheet and income statement as well as a variety of ratios for firms in one industry. The firms are broken down by size, and ratio values are given for the mean firm and also the 25th and 75th percentiles.[1]

There are five principal types of ratios that we examine in this chapter. They are 1) common size ratios, 2) liquidity ratios, 3) efficiency ratios, 4) solvency ratios, and 5) profitability ratios.

COMMON SIZE RATIOS

Common size ratios are used as a starting point in financial statement analysis. Suppose that we wished to compare our firm to another. We look to our cash balance and see that it is $10,000, while the other firm has cash of $5,000. Does this mean we have too much cash? Does the other firm have too little cash? Before we can even begin to consider such questions, we need more general information about the two firms. Are we twice as big as the other firm? Are we smaller than the other firm? The amount of cash we need depends on the size of our operations compared to theirs. Comparing our cash to their cash does not create a very useful ratio.

However, we can "common size" cash by comparing it to total assets. If our cash of $ 10,000 is one-tenth of our total assets and their cash of $5,000 is one-tenth of their total assets, then relative to asset size, both firms are keeping a like amount of cash. This is much more informative. Therefore, the first step in ratio analysis is to create a set of common size ratios. Usually common size ratios are converted to percentages. Thus, rather than referring to cash as being one-tenth of total assets, we would refer to it as being 10 percent of total assets.

To find our common size ratios, we need a key number for comparison. On the balance sheet, the key number is total assets or total equities (that is, liabilities plus stockholders' equity). We calculate the ratio of each asset on the balance sheet as compared to total assets. We calculate the ratio of each liability and

---

[1] It should be noted by the reader that (i) the Data contained in Exhibit 24-2 was compiled by RMA from a sample not necessarily statistically representative and reliance thereon should be limited accordingly; (ii) the Data has been obtained from or is based upon sources believed by RMA to be reliable, however, the Data is provided without warranty of any kind and RMA makes no representations or warranties, express or implied, to licensee or any other person or entity as to the accuracy, timeliness, completeness, merchantability or fitness for any particular purpose of any of the Data; and (iii) the Data is provided without warranty on the understanding that any person or entity that acts upon it or otherwise changes position in reliance thereon does so entirely at such person's or entity's own risk.

stockholders' equity account as compared to the total equities. For the income statement, all numbers are compared to total sales. Once we have calculated the common size ratios, we can use them to compare our firm to itself over time, to specific competitors, and to industrywide statistics.

The common size ratios for PW's balance sheet and income statement are presented in Exhibits 24-1 and 24-3. Exhibit 24-2 also provides common size balance sheet and income statement ratios.

EXHIBIT 24-3
Pacioli Wholesale Corporation
Income Statement
For the Years Ending June 30, 2012 and June 30, 2011

	2012		2011	
Sales	100.0%	$297,000	100.0%	$246,000
Less Cost of Good Sold	54.5%	162,000	58.1%	143,000
Gross Profit	45.5%	$135,000	41.9%	$103,000
Operating Expenses				
Selling Expenses	10.1%	$ 30,000	10.2%	$ 25,000
General Expenses	4.0%	12,000	4.1%	10,000
Administrative Expenses	16.5%	49,000	16.3%	40,000
Total Operating Expenses	30.6%	$ 91,000	30.5%	$ 75,000
Operating Income	14.8%	$ 44,000	11.4%	$ 28,000
Interest Expense	4.0%	12,000	4.1%	10,000
Income before Taxes	10.8%	$ 32,000	7.3%	$ 18,000
Income Taxes	4.4%	13,000	2.8%	7,000
Net Income	6.4%	$ 19,000	4.5%	$ 11,000

The Balance Sheet: Assets

Looking at the balance sheet (Exhibit 24-1), we can begin to get a general feeling about PW by comparing the common size ratios for two years. Note that there will typically be some rounding errors in ratio analysis. We could eliminate them by being more precise. For example, in 2012 the ratio of cash to total assets really is 2.6756 percent. We generally don't bother with such precision. Ratios can't give their users a precise picture of the firm. They are meant to serve as general conveyors of broad information. Our concern is if a number is particularly out of line—either unusually high or low. It is virtually impossible to interpret minor changes.

For PW, current assets have remained relatively stable, falling from 31.7 percent to 31.4 percent of total assets. Note, however, that accounts receivable have fallen while inventory has risen. Is this good or bad? If accounts receivable have fallen because sales are down this year or because there are more bad debts, and inventory has risen because PW is left with a lot of unsold goods, then this is bad. On the other hand, if accounts receivable are down because the firm has been successful in its efforts to collect more promptly, and inventory is up because it is needed to support growing sales, then this is a good sign.

Clearly, ratios can't be interpreted in a vacuum. The ratio merely points out what needs to be investigated. The ratio doesn't provide answers in and of itself. In the case of PW, the income statement (Exhibit 24-3) shows us that sales did indeed rise during the fiscal year ending June 30, 2012. It would appear that the changes in accounts receivable and inventory represent a favorable trend.

Fixed assets (Exhibit 24-1) for PW have increased, not only in absolute terms, but also as a percentage of total assets. After accounting for depreciation that has accumulated on buildings and equipment over their lifetime, we see a rise in net buildings and equipment from 32.4 percent to 36.8 percent of total assets. Reinvestment in buildings and equipment is generally a good sign for a firm.

The Balance Sheet: Equities

The current liability common size ratios have remained fairly constant over time (Exhibit 24-1). Each has risen slightly, which might well have been anticipated given the rise in sales and inventory noted earlier. As our operations grow and become more profitable, we might expect some growth in current liabilities to match the increases in inventory. In any case, the changes here appear to be modest.

Long-term liabilities (Exhibit 24-1) have fallen as a percentage of total equities. This is primarily because the firm has not needed to raise funds from the debt market to finance its fixed asset growth. Deferred taxes have risen modestly, an indication that we are taking advantage of the Modified Accelerated Cost Recovery System, which in effect creates interest-free government loans as we acquire additional equipment (*see* Chapter 13).

The common size ratio for stockholders' equity (Exhibit 24-1) has risen from 19.4 percent for 2011 to 22.7 percent for 2012. This is not surprising considering the absolute growth in profits retained in the firm (Exhibit 22-2).

Excel Excercise

Template 23 may be used to calculate common size ratios for your organization's Balance Sheet. The template is on the CD that accompanies this book.

The Income Statement

For the income statement (Exhibit 24-3), sales is the key figure around which all common size ratios are calculated. This year the cost of goods sold has fallen in relation to sales. Assuming that quality has been maintained, this is a favorable trend. By keeping production costs down relative to the selling price, profits should rise. Internal management of a firm should, nevertheless, be very interested in determining why this occurred. If the causes were related to improved efficiency, we want to know that so we can reward the individuals responsible and maintain the higher level of efficiency. On the other hand, if the improvement is caused by use of poorer quality raw materials, the long-run impact may be to hurt our reputation and long-run profits.

Therefore, even favorable trends such as reduced cost of goods sold should be viewed with caution. Investigation is needed to determine why that change occurred.

For PW, other operating expenses have remained fairly stable, increasing in relative proportion to the dollar increase in overall sales. Gross profit has risen from 41.9 percent to 45.5 percent, and operating income has risen from 11.4 percent to 14.8 percent, both as a result of the change in the cost of goods sold expense. The firm is making more profit on each dollar of sales than it had in the prior year. Of course, greater profits are associated with greater taxes. Because the pretax profit per dollar of sales has risen from 7.3 percent to 10.8 percent, the tax per dollar of sales has also risen from 2.8 percent to 4.4 percent.

Excel Excercise

Template 24 may be used to calculate common size ratios for your organization's Income Statement. The template is on the CD that accompanies this book.

Common Size Ratios: Additional Notes

The common size ratios give a starting point. You can quickly get a feel for any unusual changes that have occurred, adjusted for the overall size of assets and the relative amount of sales. Comparison with specific and industrywide competition would point out other similarities and differences. For example, our firm has 31.4 percent of its assets in the current category. (*See* Exhibit 24-1). Is that greater or less than the industry average? If it's substantially greater or less, then you might want to investigate why. Are we in a peculiarly different situation relative to other firms in our industry? From Exhibit 24-2 we see that the agriculture—wheat farming industry had about 43 to 53 percent of total assets in the current category for the three reported years. For some industries that is a very high proportion. In other industries, that might be considered low. As mentioned earlier, the key to interpretation of ratios is benchmarks. Without a basis for comparison, it is impossible to reasonably interpret the meaning of a ratio.

LIQUIDITY RATIOS

Liquidity ratios attempt to assess whether a firm is maintaining an appropriate level of liquidity. Too little liquidity raises the possibility of default and bankruptcy. Too much liquidity implies that long-term investments with greater profitability have been missed. Financial officers have to walk a tightrope to maintain enough, but not too much, liquidity.

The most common of the liquidity ratios is the current ratio (*see* Exhibit 24-4), discussed earlier in the chapter. This ratio compares all of the firm's current assets to all of its current liabilities. A common misleading rule of thumb is that the current ratio should be 2. A manufacturing industry needs inventories and receivables. Both of those items result in significant amounts of current assets. An airline, on the other hand, collects most payments in advance of providing service, so its receivables are low. Its product isn't inventoriable, so except for spare parts and supplies, its inventory is low. You should expect the airline industry to have a very low current ratio.

A second liquidity ratio exists that places even more emphasis on the firm's short-term viability—its ability to stay in business. This ratio is called the quick ratio. It compares current assets quickly convertible into cash to current liabilities (*see* Exhibit 24-4). The concept here is that while not all current assets become cash in the very near term, most current liabilities have to be paid in the very near term. For example, prepaid rent is a current asset, but it is unlikely that we could cash in that prepayment to use to pay our debts. Inventory, while salable, takes time to sell.

EXHIBIT 24-4
Liquidity Ratios

$$\text{Current Ratio} = \frac{\text{Current Assets}}{\text{Current Liabilities}}$$

$$\text{Quick Ratio} = \frac{\text{Cash} + \text{Marketable Securities} + \text{Receivables}}{\text{Current Liabilities}}$$

The quick ratio compares the firm's cash, plus marketable securities, plus accounts receivable to its current liabilities. Accounts receivable are considered to be "quick" assets because there are factoring firms that specialize in lending money on receivables or actually buying them outright, so they can be used to generate cash almost immediately. For PW, the quick ratio fell from 1.2 in 2011 to .9 in 2012.

Both of these ratios have commonly been used as measures of the firm's risk—how likely it is to get into financial difficulty. However, you should be extremely cautious in using these ratios. No one or two ratios alone can tell the entire story of a firm. They should be used like clues or pieces of evidence for the financial analyst who is really acting as a detective. Any one clue can point in the wrong direction.

For example, suppose a firm has large balances in cash and marketable securities, and its current ratio is 4 or 5. Is this an extremely safe company? The current ratio by itself leads us to believe that it is. The quick ratio might be 3. This ratio also leads us to believe that the firm is very safe. However, what if the company is losing money at a rapid rate, and the only thing that staved off bankruptcy was the sale of a major plant or investment? The sale generated enough cash to meet immediate needs and left an excess, resulting in the high current and quick ratios. How long will this excess last? If the cash and securities are large relative to current liabilities, but small relative to operating costs or long-term liabilities, then the firm may still be extremely risky.

On the other hand, a profitable firm, with careful planning, may be rapidly expanding. Due to cash payments related to the expansion, perhaps the current ratio falls to 1.5 and the quick ratio to .6 at year-end. However, within a month or two after the year-end, the firm may be receiving cash from the issuance of stock or debt that has already been arranged. This firm is probably stable. The point is that all of the ratios when taken together can supplement the financial statements and the notes to the financial statements. They can point out areas for specific additional investigation. No one or two ratios by themselves can, in any way, replace the information in the financial statements, the notes to the financial statements, and the other information possessed by management.

Excel Excercise

Template 25 may be used to calculate liquidity ratios for your organization. The template is on the CD that accompanies this book.

EFFICIENCY RATIOS

The firm wants to maximize its profits for any given level of risk. This requires the firm to operate efficiently. A number of ratios exist that can help a firm to assess how efficiently it is operating and allow for comparison between firms and over time. These ratios are sometimes referred to as *activity ratios*. The principal efficiency or activity ratios measure the efficient handling of receivables, inventory, and total assets.

Receivables Ratios

One problem faced by most firms is the timely collection of receivables. Once receivables are collected, the money received can be used to pay off loans or it can be invested. This means that once the money is received, either we would be paying less interest, or we would be earning more interest. Therefore, we want to collect our receivables promptly.

The receivables turnover ratio (Exhibit 24-5) is a very common indicator of efficiency in collecting receivables. It measures how many times during the year our receivables are generated and then collected. To measure the turnover of receivables, we compare our sales on credit to our average accounts receivable balance. The average accounts receivable is simply the balance in accounts receivable at the beginning and the end of the year divided by two. In the case of PW, the average accounts receivable is $22,000 plus $30,000 divided by two, or $26,000. The turnover ratio for 2012 is sales of $297,000, divided by $26,000, which equals 11.4. This number by itself is not very meaningful.

EXHIBIT 24-5
Efficiency Ratios

$$\text{Receivables Turnover Ratio} = \frac{\text{Credit Sales}}{\text{Average Receivables Balance}}$$

$$\text{Days Receivable} = \frac{365}{\text{Receivables Turnover}}$$

$$\text{Inventory Turnover Ratio} = \frac{\text{Costs of Good Sold}}{\text{Average Inventory Balance}}$$

$$\text{Days of Inventory} = \frac{365}{\text{Inventory Turnover}}$$

$$\text{Total Asset Turnover Ratio} = \frac{\text{Total Sales}}{\text{Total Assets}}$$

We often think of receivables in terms of how long it takes from the sale to the collection. A useful aid in analysis is to convert our receivables turnover into a statistic referred to as "days receivable," or more simply, the average age of receivables (Exhibit 24-5). We arrive at this statistic by dividing the 365 days in a year by the receivables turnover ratio. For PW, the average age of receivables is thirty-two days (365/11.4).

This is much easier to relate to. Consider whether thirty-two days is a reasonable average length of time to wait for collection of receivables. If the industry average is forty days we might be pleased with ourselves. If the industry average is twenty days we may be concerned. However, like the current ratio, we want the turnover of receivables or the average age to be neither too low nor too high. We are really striving for a middle ground, rather than as far to one extreme as possible.

The problem is that, in order to keep the age of receivables low, our credit manager may attempt to deny credit to any firm that typically pays slowly. This is not necessarily in the best interests of the company. The sales may create enough profits that we benefit even if the customer is slow to pay.

Therefore, we not only want to calculate the receivables turnover and age of receivables, but we also need to investigate that ratio to see if a short average age of receivables indicates too restrictive a credit policy on whom we sell to, or if a long age indicates too loose a credit policy or a lack of sufficient efforts to collect on a timely basis.

Inventory Ratios

The same type of ratios calculated for receivables can also be calculated with respect to inventory (Exhibit 24-5). The inventory turnover ratio is the cost of goods sold divided by the average inventory (beginning plus ending inventory divided by two). For PW for 2012, the inventory turnover ratio is $162,000 (cost of goods sold from Exhibit 24-3) divided by the average of $49,000 and $40,000 (2012 and 2011 ending inventory balances from Exhibit 24-1), which is equal to 3.6. The average age of PW's inventory is 100.3 days, calculated by dividing 365 days in a year by the inventory turnover.

If we keep inventory on hand for too long a period, we are wasting money through lost interest that could have been earned, or through extra interest paid on money borrowed to maintain the inventory. Excessively large inventories also result in unnecessarily high warehousing costs, property taxes, and spoilage. On the other hand, if we don't maintain a sufficiently large inventory, we may lose sales or have production-line stoppages due to stock-outs of finished goods or raw materials, respectively.

Industrywide statistics are usually available for total inventory turnover. However, it is especially useful to compute the turnover and age of inventory separately for raw materials, work in process, and finished goods for manufacturing concerns. For example, a common response to why inventory turnover is slow is that the business is seasonal, and the firm must stockpile *finished goods* for the busy season, often Christmas. On the other hand, if we examine the inventory ratios on a more detailed basis, we may find it is, in fact, *raw materials* that are being held for excessive periods of time.

Total Asset Turnover

A final efficiency ratio is the total asset turnover ratio. This ratio compares sales to total assets. The more sales an organization can generate per dollar of assets, the more efficient it is, other things being equal. If we divide 2012 sales of $297,000 (from Exhibit 24-3) by total assets of $299,000 (from Exhibit 24-1) the ratio of .99 indicates nearly $1 of sales for each dollar invested in assets. This is an improvement compared to the .88 ratio for the prior year.

Excel Excercise

Template 26 may be used to calculate efficiency ratios for your organization. The template is included in the CD that accompanies this book.

SOLVENCY RATIOS

One of the primary focuses on the firm's riskiness occurs through examination of its solvency ratios. Unlike the liquidity ratios that are concerned with the firm's ability to meet its obligations in the very near future, solvency ratios take more of a long-term view. They attempt to determine if the firm has overextended itself through the use of financial leverage. That is, does the firm have principal and interest payment obligations exceeding its ability to pay, not only now, but into the future as well? These ratios are sometimes referred to as *leverage* or *capital structure* ratios.

Two of the most common of the solvency ratios are the interest coverage ratio and the debt to equity ratio (Exhibit 24-6). The former focuses on the ability to meet interest payments arising from liabilities. The latter focuses on the protective cushion owners' equity provides for creditors. If a bankruptcy does occur, creditors can share in the firm's assets before the owners can claim any of their equity. The more equity that the owners have in the firm, the greater the likelihood that the firm's assets will be great enough to protect the claims of all the creditors.

EXHIBIT 24-6
Solvency Ratios

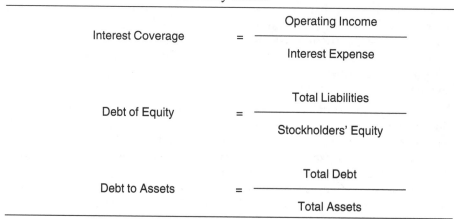

$$\text{Interest Coverage} = \frac{\text{Operating Income}}{\text{Interest Expense}}$$

$$\text{Debt of Equity} = \frac{\text{Total Liabilities}}{\text{Stockholders' Equity}}$$

$$\text{Debt to Assets} = \frac{\text{Total Debt}}{\text{Total Assets}}$$

The interest coverage ratio compares funds available to pay interest to the total amount of interest that has to be paid. The funds available for interest are the firm's profits before interest and taxes. As long as the profit before interest and taxes (the operating income) is greater than the amount of interest, the firm will have enough money to pay the interest owed. Therefore operating income is divided by interest expense to calculate this ratio. The higher this ratio is, the more comfortable creditors feel. For PW in 2012, the operating income is $44,000, and the interest is $12,000 (Exhibit 24-3). The interest coverage ratio therefore is 3.7. This is a relative improvement from 2011 when the operating profit was $28,000 and interest was $10,000. In that year, the interest coverage was 2.8.

However, we should be careful in our use of the term *improvement*. From a creditor's point of view, this is an improvement because profits are up relative to interest, creating a greater cushion of safety. From the firm's point of view, whether this is an improvement or not depends on its attitude toward risk and profits. If the firm desires to be highly leveraged, this rise in the interest coverage ratio indicates that the firm could have paid more dividends to its owners and financed more of its expansion through increased borrowing. This would have increased the rate of return earned by the owners, although they would have incurred a greater risk because of the increased leverage. (Review Chapter 9 for a discussion of financial leverage and its implications.)

There are several different debt/equity ratios. For example, we can compare long-term liabilities to stockholders' equity, or total liabilities to stockholders' equity. We can also compare total debt (i.e. liabilities) to the firm's total assets. The greater the debt relative to total assets, the more risky the firm.

For example, at the end of fiscal 2012, PW has $299,000 of total assets (Exhibit 24-1). These assets are available to repay our liabilities. The total liabilities of PW are $231,000, which consists of $47,000 of current liabilities and $184,000 of long-term liabilities. The debt to assets ratio of $231,000 to $299,000 is .77. If PW were to have financial difficulty, and perhaps even go bankrupt and sell off all of its assets, it would have to realize, on average, 77 cents on every dollar of assets in order to fully pay its creditors.

It is important to bear in mind that the nature of the firm and its industry have a lot to do with what is an acceptable level of debt, relative to equity, and what level of interest payments can be considered reasonably safe. For a business with very constant sales and earnings, more debt is relatively safer than for a firm that has wide swings in profitability. Therefore, any arbitrary rules of thumb commonly used, such as a debt to equity ratio of .5, are not terribly valuable.

Excel Excercise

Template 27 may be used to calculate solvency ratios for your organization. The template is on the CD that accompanies this book.

PROFITABILITY RATIOS

When all is said and done, the key focus of accounting and finance tends to be on profits. Profitability ratios attempt to show how well the firm did, given the level of risk and types of risk it actually assumed during the year.

If we compare a firm's net income to that of the competition, it is an inadequate measure. Suppose that the chief competitor of PW had earnings of $57,000 this year, while PW made only $19,000. Did the competitor have a better year? Not necessarily. It earned three times as much money, but perhaps it required four times as much in resources to do it. Even earnings per share is inadequate. Suppose that PW's earnings per share of $18.00 were only one-third of the competitor's $54.00. If the investors in PW's competitor invested four times as much to buy each of their shares, they would have been better off investing an equal total amount of money in PW. Therefore, a number of profitability ratios exist to help in evaluating the firm's performance.

Margin Ratios

Margin ratios are one common class of profitability ratios. Firms commonly compute their gross margin, operating margin, and profit margin as a percentage of sales (sometimes referred to as *Return on Sales*). These ratios (Exhibit 24-7) are nothing more than common size ratios we calculated earlier in the chapter. For PW in 2012, the gross margin was 45.5 percent, the operating margin was 14.8 percent, and the profit margin was 6.4 percent. These margins are often watched closely, as changes can be early warning signals of serious problems. A slacking off of a percentage or two in the gross margin can mean the difference between healthy profits or a loss in many industries. For instance, in the supermarket industry the profit margin is rarely more than 1 or 2 percent. A 2 percent change in the gross margin can totally wipe out the supermarket's profit.

EXHIBIT 24-7
Profitability Ratios

MARGIN RATIOS

$$\text{Gross Profit} = \frac{\text{Gross Profit}}{\text{Sales}} \times 100\%$$

$$\text{Operating Margin} = \frac{\text{Operating Income}}{\text{Sales}} \times 100\%$$

$$\text{Profit Margin} = \frac{\text{Net Income}}{\text{Sales}} \times 100\%$$

RETURN ON INVESTMENT (ROI) RATIOS

$$\text{Return on Assets (ROA)} = \frac{\text{Net Income}}{\text{Total Assets}} \times 100\%$$

$$\text{Return on Equity (ROE) or Return on Net Assets (RONA)} = \frac{\text{Net Income}}{\text{Stockholders' Equity}} \times 100\%$$

Return on Investment (ROI) Ratios

Another broad category of profitability measures falls under the heading of return on investment (ROI). There are many definitions for return on investment, although individual firms usually select one definition and use that as a measure of both individual and firm performance. Because we cannot know the specific definition a firm has chosen, we will discuss a variety of ROI measures in this section. Even if none of the ones discussed here is exactly the same as that chosen by your firm, you should gain enough from the discussion to understand the strengths and weaknesses of whatever ROI measure(s) your firm uses.

Return on assets (ROA) is an ROI measure that evaluates the firm's return or net income relative to the asset base used to generate the income. If we could invest $100 in each of two different investments, and one generated twice as much income as the other, we would prefer the investment generating twice as much income (assuming the levels of risk had been the same).

Therefore, the firm that generates more income, relative to the amount of investment, is doing a better job, other things equal. If we divide the profit earned by the amount of assets employed to generate that profit, we get the ROA. A high ROA is better than a small one. The ROA measure is particularly good for evaluating division managers. It focuses on how well they used the assets entrusted to them.

Is that what the firm's owners want to know? Not really. They are not as interested in the use of assets as they are with the return on their investment. They want to focus on how well the firm did in earning a return on the stockholders' equity. This is commonly called the return on equity (ROE) or the return on net assets (RONA). (*See* Exhibit 24-7.) Note that net assets are defined as being the assets less the liabilities. Net assets are equivalent to the firm's book value or net worth or stockholders' equity.

While ROA is good for evaluating managers but inadequate for evaluating the firm, ROE is good for evaluating overall firm performance but not for manager evaluation. Except for the very top officers of the firm, managers don't control whether the firm borrows money or issues stock to raise funds. Most managers are simply trying to use the funds that the finance officers have provided them most efficiently. If two managers operated their firms exactly the same, except that one firm was financed substantially with debt, while the other was financed almost exclusively with equity, the firms would have substantially different ROEs for two reasons. First of all, the stockholders' equity will be different for the two firms, because one firm issued more stock than the other, so the denominator of the ratio will be different. Second, the interest expense will differ because one firm borrowed less than the other, so the net income will not be the same. Therefore, the numerator of the ratio would be different. How can we evaluate what part of the firm's results was caused by reasons other than the leverage decision, and what part was caused by the specific decision regarding financial leverage?

ROE is a useful measure of the income that the firm was able to generate relative to the amount of owners' investment in the firm. ROE includes the effect caused by the firm's degree of leverage. To remove the impact of leverage from our evaluation, we should use ROA. This eliminates the problem with respect to the denominator of the ROE ratio. The asset base or denominator of the ROA ratio is the same whether the source of the money used to acquire the assets is debt or equity. However, ROA leaves a problem with the numerator. The return, or numerator (that is, the net income) is affected by the amount of interest the firm pays. For this reason, the measure of ROA often used for evaluation avoiding the impact of the leverage decision is calculated using something called delevered net income.

Delevered net income means recalculating the firm's income by assuming that it had no interest expense at all. In doing this, we can put firms with different decisions regarding the use of borrowed money vs. owner-contributed funds all on a comparable basis. We can see how profitable each firm was relative to the assets it used regardless of their source. We have completely separated any profitability (or loss) created by having used borrowed money instead of owner-invested capital. The way we delever net income is to take the firm's operating margin (income before interest and taxes) and calculate taxes directly on that amount, ignoring interest. The result is a net income based on the assumption that there had been no interest expense.

This should not lead the reader to believe that all firms calculate ROA in exactly the same way. Some firms use assets net of depreciation as the basis for comparison. This is how the assets appear on the balance sheet. Some firms ignore depreciation and use gross assets as a base. The reason for this is to avoid causing a firm or division to appear to have a very high return on assets simply because its assets are very old and fully depreciated. Such fully depreciated assets cause the base of the ratio to be very low and, therefore, the resulting ratio to be very large. Along the same lines, some firms use replacement cost instead of historical cost to place divisions in an equal position.

Despite any of these adjustments, use of any of the ROA measures for evaluation of managers creates undesired incentives. Suppose the firm and its owners are happy to accept any project with an after-tax rate of return of 20 percent. One division of the firm currently has an ROA of 30 percent, and a proposed project that would have a 25 percent ROA is being evaluated. The manager of the division wants to reject the project entirely if he or she is evaluated based on ROA. The 25 percent project, even though profitable, and perhaps better than anything else the firm's owners could do with their money, will bring down that division's weighted average ROA, which is currently 30 percent. Even though the project is good for the firm and its owners, it would hurt the manager's performance evaluation.

For this reason we recommend an ROI concept called residual income (RI). Under this approach, the firm specifies a minimum required ROA rate, using one of the various approaches previously discussed. For each project being evaluated, we would multiply the amount of asset investment required for the project by the required ROA rate. The result would be subtracted from the profits anticipated from the project. If the project is expected to earn more than the proposed investment multiplied by the required rate, then there will be a residual left over after the subtraction. A division manager would be evaluated on the residual left over from all his or her projects combined.

For example, suppose that 20 percent was considered to be an acceptable rate to the firm. Currently all projects for the division earn 30 percent. Suppose further that a project requiring an investment of $100,000 of assets was proposed. If this new project would earn a profit of $25,000, or 25 percent ROA, it would be rejected by a manager evaluated on an ROA basis and accepted by a manager evaluated on an RI basis. From an ROA basis, the 25 percent would lower the currently achieved 30 percent average. For RI, we would multiply the $100,000 investment by the 20 percent ROA required rate, getting a result of $20,000. When the $20,000 is subtracted from the profit of $25,000, there is a $5,000 residual income. The manager is considered to have increased his or her RI by $5,000.

The advantage of this method is that if the firm would like to undertake any project earning a return of more than 20 percent, division managers will have an incentive to accept all such projects. This is because all projects earning more than 20 percent will cover the minimum desired 20 percent ROA and have some excess left over. This excess adds to the manager's total residual income. Thus, RI motivates the manager to do what is also in the best interests of the firm.

The reader can readily see that ROI is not a simple topic. The finance officers of most firms spend a fair amount of time considering the implications of various forms of ROI for both motivation and evaluation. Unfortunately, many firms use just one ROI measure for the firm and its managers. In attempting to make the measure serve multiple roles, the ROI measures used often are so complex that they are difficult to understand. The net result often is that ROI measures do not motivate the way they are intended to and do not provide fair measures of performance.

Excel Excercise

Template 28 may be used to calculate profitability ratios for your organization. The template is on the CD that accompanies this book.

KEY TERMS

Ratio—any number compared to another number. Ratios are calculated by dividing one number into another.

Benchmarks—a firm's ratios can be compared to ratios for the same firm from prior years and to ratios of a specific competitor and to ratios for the entire industry.

XBRL—eXtensible Business Reporting Language, is a tool for electronic communication of financial data which assigns an identifying electronic tag to each element of a financial statement.

Common size ratios—all numbers on the balance sheet are compared to total assets or total equities, and all numbers on the income statement are compared to total sales. This makes intercompany or interperiod comparison of specific numbers such as cash more meaningful.

Liquidity ratios—assess the firm's ability to meet its current obligations as they become due.

Efficiency ratios—assess the efficiency with which the firm manages its resources, such as inventory and receivables.

Solvency ratios—assess the firm's ability to meet its interest payments and long-term obligations as they become due.

Profitability ratios—assess how profitable the firm was and how well it was managed by comparing profits to the amount of resources invested in the firm and used to generate the profits earned.

QUESTIONS FOR REVIEW

1. What are some of the benefits or uses of ratio analysis?
2. When common size ratios are prepared, each asset is compared to _____ and each expense is compared to _____.
3. There is no "correct" value for ratios, so an organization generally will compare ratios for a specific year to what?

4. What are the problems of too much or too little liquidity?

5. Using Exhibits 24-1 and 24-3, calculate the current ratio, days in accounts receivable, total asset turnover, interest coverage, long-term debt to stockholders' equity, profit margin, and return on equity for 2012. Show your work.

Chapter 25

A Primer on Taxes

HOW MUCH DO YOU NEED TO KNOW?

Taxation in the United States is incredibly complicated. Starting from a fairly simple basic framework of a graduated income tax, our government has added rules and regulations that have created an intricately complex web. Some of the complexity exists to respond to policy goals. For example, allowing individuals to deduct donations encourages people to make charitable contributions. This is something the government feels it should provide incentives for individuals to do. Similarly, a number of "tax breaks" exist for corporations, to encourage them to undertake activities society sees as being beneficial. Each tax break adds to the complexity of the system.

Not all tax breaks are designed to meed specific policy goals. Sometimes special interest groups lobby for advantageous tax treatment. As a result, some complexity exists because of the loopholes that have been created to lower the taxes paid by some taxpayers. On the other hand, taxpayers can be very creative in making existing rules work to their advantage. As a result, sometimes the tax code becomes even more tortuous as efforts are made to close unintended loopholes.

Providing a full understanding of tax rules and regulations is well beyond the scope of this book. On the other hand, managers must always keep in mind the fact that taxes exist, and that their decisions may result in taxes being higher or lower. Since financial decisions affect taxes, you need to have at least a bare-bones understanding of the tax system. We will focus here on issues related to federal income tax. There are many other types of taxes that managers need to be aware of as well.

Often companies are subject to state and local income or franchise taxes, sales tax, Social Security tax, and real estate tax, in addition to a wide variety of charges and user fees such as sewer levies, motor vehicle charges, and excise fees. These various taxes and fees vary tremendously from one area of the country to another. All companies should seek the assistance of a qualified tax expert who, at a minimum, can review all issues related to compliance with all tax laws. In addition, tax consultants can provide valuable assistance in minimizing your tax obligations.

PERSONAL VS. CORPORATE TAXES

The first and perhaps most important distinction to be made is the difference between personal income taxes and corporate income taxes.

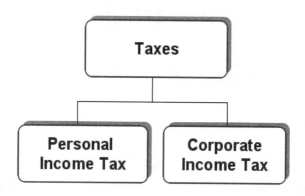

The personal income tax is levied on U.S. citizens and residents. The corporate income tax is levied on entities that have incorporated in the United States. This dual structure affects the decision of whether to run a business as an incorporated or unincorporated business. Businesses can be formed as *sole proprietorships, partnerships, limited liability companies (LLCs),* or *corporations.*

Sole proprietorships, partnerships, and LLCs are unincorporated businesses. A sole proprietorships is owned and run by one person. The profits of the business are directly profits of the individual and are reported to the government on the individual's own federal tax return. Partnerships are similar to sole proprietorships, but the business is owned by more than one person. Partners report their share of the business income on their personal tax returns.

Corporations pay federal income tax on their profits. After paying these taxes, when corporations distribute their earnings to their owners, the owners must also pay personal income taxes. This creates an effective *double taxation*. The same profits are taxed twice!

Corporations may temporarily avoid the second layer of taxes, the personal taxes, by retaining their profits rather than distributing them in the form of taxable dividends. A downside of this is that the owners do not receive current distributions from the corporation. A potential benefit, however, is that the retained profits from those activities make the corporation more valuable. That drives up the value of the stock.

If the owners sell some of their stock at these higher prices, they earn a profit called a *capital gain*. For individuals, capital gains on investments owned for more than one year are taxed at substantially lower rates than ordinary income. Double taxation still exists, but its impact is thus first deferred for a period of time while the profits are retained, and then partially offset due to the lower capital gains tax rate when the stock is sold.

Limited Liability without Double Taxation

Clearly, it would be the best of both worlds to have the benefits of limited liability, while paying taxes only once. There are several options that allow companies to gain these benefits. The options are S corporations (Sub-S), limited liability companies (LLCs), and limited liability partnerships (LLPs).

An S corporation is often referred to as an "S corp" or as a "Sub-S" because the rules related to these corporations are contained in Subchapter S of the Internal Revenue Code, which allows corporations to be treated as if they were partnerships for tax purposes. The primary benefit is that the owners have the limited liability benefit of corporate form while avoiding the corporate income taxes. There are a variety of restrictions related to the number and type of shareholders and the need for shareholders to all agree to S corporation treatment.

Note that there may be reasons that some shareholders would prefer not to have such treatment. For example, the owners of an S corp will be taxed on their share of the year's profits each year, the same as if it were a partnership. But if the corporation does not declare a dividend and distribute those profits, some owners may not have the cash they need to pay the taxes on their share of the profits. Also, partnerships, corporations, and foreign investors may not invest in an S corp.

Limited liability companies (LLCs) are neither partnerships nor corporations. They are a types of organization that has the benefits of limited liability for all their owners. They may elect to be taxed as if they were corporations or partnerships, and they may have an unlimited number of owners, something that in not possible for an S corp. However, in some states LLCs may have their own negative aspects, such as being subject to gross receipts taxes.

The last type of organization that combines these features is a limited liability partnership (LLP). LLPs are partnerships and are taxed as such. In this type of organization partners are liable for their own acts and those of individuals under their direction. However, they are not liable for acts of other partners. This is a common business form for professional organizations, such as public accounting firms. There may be state laws that prevent a professional organization from incorporating or becoming an LLC. In such a case, the LLP form affords some limited liability for the partners.

THE TAX RATE AND THE TAX BASE

For both the personal and corporate income tax, the most essential elements are the *tax base* and the *tax rate*. The tax base defines what is subject to the tax. For individuals, their federal income tax base is their *taxable income*. This taxable income is calculated by applying tax regulations that indicate what must be included in taxable income. For example, wages and most interest are included, but some types of interest (e.g., interest on a municipal bond) may be tax-exempt. Such tax-exempt interest is not part of taxable income. The tax rate is the percentage that is multiplied by the tax base to calculate the tax.

PROGRESSIVE, PROPORTIONAL, AND REGRESSIVE TAX RATES

Tax systems can be *progressive, proportional,* or *regressive.*

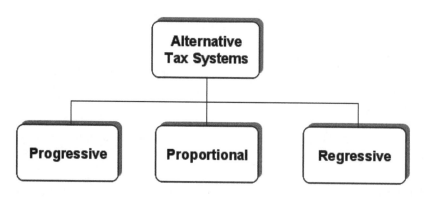

A progressive system has increasing rates as the tax base increases. A proportional tax would maintain one tax rate for all payers regardless of their tax base. A regressive tax is on that has declining rates as the tax base grows.

Our personal income tax structure is based primarily on a progressive basis. This approach is deemed to have a greater degree of equity, because those most able to afford taxes are called upon to pay a larger share.

Proponents of the flat tax support the notion of a proportional tax. They would argue that even under a flat tax, those with a greater tax base pay more taxes. For example, if we had an across-the-board proportional flat tax of 20 percent, someone earning $10,000 might pay $2,000 while someone earning $1,000,000 would pay $200,000. The rich would pay more than the poor. Opponents argue that the rich wouldn't be paying at a progressive or increasing rate. They would argue that, to the person earning $10,000, a tax of just 15 percent or $1,500 might be much harder to bear than a tax of 40 percent of $400,000 for a person earning $1,000,000.

Under the existing progressive tax rates, a person earning $10,000 pays less than $2,000, and the person earning $1,000,000 pays considerably more than $200,000. Or do they? Flat tax proponents argue that rich Americans can afford to spend a fair amount of money on strategies to avoid taxes. They find loopholes to substantially reduce their taxes. It is possible that some taxpayers earning $1,000,000 would pay more taxes with a flat 20 percent tax with no loopholes than they currently pay, even though tax rates currently are graduated to a higher level than 20 percent. Further, flat tax proponents argue that there could be a floor at a level such as $50,000. Individuals with a tax base below that floor would not be subject to tax at all. They argue that the simplicity of taxes under such a system (they envision a postcard tax return) and the reduction of efforts to avoid taxes would make the system much more equitable in the long run.

Regressive taxes place the heaviest burden squarely on the shoulders of those least able to pay. Your first reaction may be that we certainly would never enact such a tax. However, currently the FICA tax for Social Security and Medicare is 5.65 percent paid by the employee and 7.65 percent paid by the employer on wages up to $106,800, and then 1.45 percent on wages above that amount. This a regressive tax, as the rate is lower for wages over $106,800.

MARGINAL, AVERAGE, AND EFFECTIVE TAX RATES

You should not assume that the taxes paid are all paid at the highest rate the taxpayer might fall into. The lowest portion of a taxpayer's taxable income is taxed at the lowest rate. For example, for a married couple filing a joint return in April 2012, for their taxable income earned during 2011, the tax rate was 10% on the first $17,000 of taxable income. The rate then rose to 15% on additional income up to $69,000, then 25% on additional income up to $139,500, then 28% on additional income up to $212,300, then 33% on additional income up to $379,150, and then 35% on income above that level. *See* Table 25-1.

This gives rise to the distinction between the *marginal, average,* and *effective tax rates.*

Suppose that you were married and filed a joint tax return for 2011, and you had taxable income of $100,000. Your marginal tax rate is the amount that you will have to pay on additional income that is earned. For example if you earned another $5,000, the marginal tax rate on that $5,000 would have been 25 percent, because your income fell into the $69,001 to $139,350 tax bracket. However, what if you earned an extra $50,000 rather than an extra $5,000. Part of that additional income would have been taxed at 25 percent. However, with your starting tax base of $100,000, the $50,000 of extra income would have pushed you over the $139,350 point, into a higher tax bracket. The amount earned above the $139,350 level would have been taxed at a rate of 28 percent. That would have become your new marginal tax rate. You can then anticipate that additional earnings will be taxed at that rate (or higher if you move into an even higher tax bracket).

TABLE 25-1
2011 Tax Rate Schedule for Married Individuals Filing a Joint Return

If Taxpayer's Income is At Least	But Not Over	Base Tax	+	Rate	On the Amount Over
$ 0	$ 17,000	$ 0		10%	$ 0
$ 17,001	$ 69,000	$ 1,700		15%	$ 17,000
$ 69,001	$139,350	$ 9,500		25%	$ 69,000
$139,351	$212,300	$ 27,087		28%	$139,350
$212,301	$379,150	$ 47,513		33%	$212,300
$379,151	—	$102,573		35%	$379,150

Would the $50,000 of additional income have resulted in your paying an average of 28 percent on all of your taxable income? No. Even though you were moved into the 28 percent tax bracket, that rate is just paid on the amount above $139,350. The first $17,000 would still have been taxed at 10 percent, the next $52,000 at 15 percent, and so on. All together the tax would have been $30,069 on $150,000 of taxable income. If we compare this total tax to the base of $150,000 we find that the average rate paid would have been 20.0 percent ($30,069 tax ÷ $150,000 tax base = 20.0 percent average tax rate). We can see this average rate is less than the marginal tax rate assessed on the highest portion of taxable income.

Note further that the tax rate is only applied to the tax base. Part of a taxpayer's income is not included in the tax base. For example, taxpayers may not have to pay tax on tax-exempt interest. If we divide the tax of $30,069 by the total income of the taxpayer including the income that is not taxable, the rate would fall further. That rate is referred to as the effective tax rate.

Tax Brackets

There are separate tax rate structures for corporations and individuals. The corporate tax rate structure was designed to ease the tax burden on small corporations. This encourages individuals to incorporate to get the benefits of limited liability, without creating a tremendous tax burden. The corporate tax structure at the time of this writing appears in Table 25-2.

TABLE 25-2
Corporate Tax Brackets

Taxable Income Over	But Not Over	Tax Rate
$ 0	$ 50,000	15%
$ 50,000	$ 75,000	25%
$ 75,000	$ 100,000	34%
$ 100,000	$ 335,000	39%
$ 335,000	$10,000,000	34%
$10,000,000	$15,000,000	35%
$15,000,000	$18,333,333	38%
$18,333,333	.....	35%

Even though the rates start out fairly low, this still can pose a substantial burden for a small business owner. Suppose that a business earns $45,000 of profit. The owner may well need all of this money to live on. Retaining it in the business to avoid double taxation may not be a feasible option. Further, there is an "excess accumulated earnings tax" designed to prevent corporations from retaining earnings to avoid double taxation.

A corporation would have to pay 15 percent tax on the $45,000 of profit, and then the remaining profit could be paid to the owner as a dividend. The owner would then pay tax on the dividend. However, there is a solution to this problem. The owner can also be an employee of the corporation and can be paid a reasonable salary. If $45,000 is reasonable, then the profits of the business would drop to zero after incurring the employee wage expense of $45,000. The owner will have effectively gained limited liability with no increase in taxes. Corporations can also avoid double taxation on payments to pension plans.

The tax rate for very profitable corporations is 35 percent. Notice from Table 25-2, however, that there is a range where the marginal rate is 39 percent and another where it is 38 percent. The purpose of these rates in excess of 35 percent is to eliminate the benefit that corporations with low profits receive. The structure is designed so that for corporations with profits in excess of $100,000 the benefits of the 15 percent and 25 percent brackets are phased out, and by $355,000 the corporation is paying 34 percent on *all* of its taxable income, not just on the marginal portion. For corporations with profits in excess of $15,000,000, the benefit of the 34 percent bracket is phased out. By the time we reach $18,333,333 or above, the corporation winds up paying 35 percent on all of its taxable income, rather than just on the income in the top bracket. The marginal and average tax rate would both be 35 percent.

Individual tax brackets are even more complicated. There are separate rate schedules for single individuals, for heads of household, for married filing joint returns, and for married filing separate returns. In addition, tax rates are complicated by capital gains tax rules. As noted earlier, if investments are held more than one year, they often qualify for long-term capital gains tax treatment. The maximum long-term capital gains rate is generally at a lower rate.

CALCULATING FEDERAL INCOME TAX

The calculation of federal income tax is complicated by a variety of deductions, exemptions, and other factors related to the Internal Revenue Service's rules and regulations. Table 25-3 summarizes the calculation for both individuals and corporations.

TABLE 25-3
Calculation of Federal Income Tax

Total Income from All Sources	$XXX
Less: Exclusions (items specifically excluded such as interest on some municipal bonds)	– XX
Gross Income	$XXX
Less Deductions (itemized deductions for individuals or expenses for businesses)	– XX
Less: Exemptions (for individuals only)	– XX
Taxable Income	$XXX
Tax on Taxable Income (computed using Tax Rate Schedules)	$XXX
Less: Tax Credits	– XX
Tax Obligation	$XXX
Less: Prepayments	– XX
Balance Due to Government or Refund Due to Taxpayer	$XXX

Taxpayers must first determine their total income. This includes income on items that may be exempt from tax for some reason. The items that are specifically exempt are then excluded. However, if the exclusions become too great, they are subject to the alternative minimum tax (AMT). The AMT is designed to ensure that all taxpayers (whether individuals or businesses) pay at least some minimum percent of tax on their income. Total income, less exclusions, is referred to as gross income. From this gross income, deductions and exemptions are subtracted. For a business, this refers to the basic expenses of running the business. For an individual this refers to itemized or standard deductions and personal exemptions. The net result is taxable income.

The tax rate schedules are then applied to the taxable income to determine the income tax before consideration of tax credits. Credits are allowed for a variety of reasons. For example, if taxes are paid to a foreign country, the taxpayer is allowed in some circumstances to subtract that foreign tax as a credit.

In some cases foreign taxes can be subtracted as a deduction rather than a credit. Does it matter which way you subtract the foreign tax? Tremendously. A credit is subtracted after the tax has been computed. A one-dollar credit reduces federal taxes by $1. A deduction is subtracted before taxes are calculated. A one-dollar deduction reduces federal taxes based on the marginal tax rate. For example, if your marginal rate is 35 percent, a one-dollar deduction save you 35 cents, while a one-dollar credit saves you $1. Whenever a choice is available, other things equal, a credit is always preferred to a deduction.

Once credits have been subtracted, the result is the tax obligation to the government. If prepayments of taxes have already been made, those amounts are subtracted to find out the remaining amount that the taxpayer owes to the government or the government owes the taxpayer.

Excel Excercise

Template 29 provides an opportunity to try experimenting with tax calculations. The template is included on the CD that accompanies this book.

OTHER CONCERNS FOR CORPORATIONS

Although the tax brackets may seem straightforward, corporations do not always pay the rate in the table, which is referred to as the *statutory* rate. There are many factors that affect the actual rate paid. Two of the most prominent of these relate to operating loss carryovers and to dividends received.

Operating Loss Carryovers

When a corporation's deductions are greater than its gross income, it has a loss, referred to as a *net operating loss (NOL)*. Corporations are allowed to use this loss to offset profits in other years, thus lowering the tax for those years. The corporation may first carry back the NOL to offset income from two years before the current tax year, then the year before the current tax year; then any remaining balance may be carried forward for up to twenty years until the full NOL is used to offset profits. After twenty years any remaining NOL expires.

Corporations may choose not to carry back the NOL, but instead to only carry it forward. This election would be made if taxes in earlier years were at low marginal tax rates and the corporation expects to be in a higher tax bracket in future years.

Dividends Received

Think double taxation is bad? How about triple taxation? At times corporations invest in the stock of other corporations. If they receive dividends from those corporations, those dividends will be taxable income. The result is that one corporation earns profits and pays tax on the profit. It pays dividends to a second corporation that owns some of its stock. That second corporation must pay tax on that dividend income. When this second corporation pays dividends to its stockholders, the stockholders will pay tax on that same income.

To lessen the impact of this triple taxation, corporation are allowed, subject to some limitations, a dividends-received deduction. The dividends-received deduction works as follows: if a corporation owns less than 20 percent of the corporation paying the dividend, it may deduct 70 percent of the dividends received from that corporation. If the corporation receiving the dividend owns 20 percent or more, but less than 80 percent of the stock of the corporation paying the dividend, 80 percent of the dividend may be deducted. If a corporation owns 80 percent or more of the corporation that is paying the dividend, it may deduct the entire dividend received.

CONCLUSION

This chapter has served as no more than a brief introduction to the complicated world of taxation. It is important for readers to always bear in mind that their actions often have tax implications. There are many opportunities for controlling your tax liability, and it is often worth the cost to have a tax specialist provide input as decisions are made.

KEY TERMS

Limited liability—legal protection of personal assets from creditors.

Business form

> *Sole proprietorships* and *general partnerships* generally have unlimited liability.

> *Corporations* have an unlimited lifetime, ownership can be transferred easily, and they have limited liability.

> *S corporations, limited liability companies*, and *limited liability partnerships* have the benefit of at least some limited liability and the ability to avoid double taxation.

Tax base—defines what is subject to the tax.

Tax rate—the percentage that is multiplied by the tax base to calculate the tax.

Tax rate schedule—a chart that shows the percentage of tax that must be paid on different amounts of taxable income.

Marginal tax rate—the percentage of an extra dollar of taxable income that must be paid in tax.

Net operating loss (NOL)—a corporation's loss that may be used to offset income in other years, to lower taxes in those years.

Dividends-received deduction—to reduce the impact of triple taxation, corporations may deduct some or all of the dividends that they receive from other corporations.

QUESTIONS FOR REVIEW

1. What is double taxation?
2. Why do we need to distinguish capital gains separately from other income?
3. What is the primary benefit of an S-corp.?
4. What is the primary limitation of an S-corp.?
5. What is the difference between the tax rate and the tax base?
6. Proponents of a flat tax support what type of tax system?
7. What is the difference between marginal, average, and effective tax rates?
8. How much federal income tax would be paid by a corporation with $8 million of taxable income, assuming that tax rates have not changed from those shown in Table 25-2?

Chapter 26

Summary and Conclusion

This book has covered quite a bit of ground. In completing this book, you should have gained an improved understanding of the nature of accounting and finance. You should have a wealth of vocabulary and should be aware of many concerns of financial managers, as well as some of the tools they use to manage their concerns. For example, by now you are well aware of the emphasis on profitability, but should also have an awareness of the risks that go along with profits, and the fact that financial managers are attempting to balance the level of profit with the level of risk.

You should be aware of the financial manager's concern for liquidity, and the many measures of liquidity that the accountant builds into financial statements. This information helps the financial officer compute ratios on liquidity and solvency to monitor the firm's viability and to enable adjustments to be made if problems arise.

Accounting and finance go hand in hand in the financial process of the firm. The accountant provides information, both historical and prospective, and the finance officer uses that information to make crucial decisions regarding how much the firm will invest and from where the invested resources will come.

This book is not a comprehensive handbook on all the issues of accounting and finance. Such completeness in all detail was not the goal of this book. What the author hopes is that you have been taught a vocabulary, a language—the language of business. Obviously a book such as this one can't answer all the specific questions of all the many readers of the book. But if it helps you formulate specific questions for further exploration, that in itself is an accomplishment. You should now also be in a better position to understand your financial managers' answers to your questions.

A final caveat: You are not a financial analyst after having read this book. Don't think of this book as a how-to-do-it book. Don't attempt to do your own tax planning based on the tax discussions contained in this book. Accounting and finance are highly complex areas.

This doesn't mean that they should simply be left to the experts. Nonfinancial managers have a need to be able to understand the basic goals and techniques of financial officers. You should be able to understand what is going on and what is being said. Don't, however, gain an overconfidence that, "That's all there is to financial management." Rather, think of it this way: Hopefully someone soon will write a book on operating management for staff and financial managers. It won't teach them all there is to know about line management, but they certainly could use it—communication, after all, is a two-way street.

GLOSSARY

accelerated depreciation: techniques that allocate a higher portion of a long-term asset's cost as an expense in the earlier years of its useful lifetime and a smaller portion in the later years.

accounting: system for keeping track of the financial status of an organization and the financial results of its activities.

accounts payable: amounts owed to suppliers.

accounts receivable: money owed to an **entity** for goods and services it has provided.

accrual accounting: a system of recording financial events that recognizes revenue when goods and services have been provided and eventual receipt of payment is expected, and recognizes expenses when resources are consumed.

accrual basis: accounting system that records revenues in the year in which they become earned (whether received or not).

accumulated depreciation: total amount of depreciation related to a fixed asset that has been taken over the years the organization has owned that asset.

acid test: see **quick ratio**.

aging schedule: management report that shows how long receivables have been outstanding since an invoice was issued

allowance for uncollectible accounts: estimated portion of total **accounts receivable** that is not expected to be collected because of **bad debts**; also called allowance for bad debts.

amortization: allocation of the cost of an asset over its lifetime.

annuity: series of payment or receipts, each in the same amount and spaced at even time periods.

assets: tangible or **intangible** resources.

audit: examination of the financial records of the organization to evaluate the internal control system and to determine if financial statements have been prepared in accordance with **GAAP**.

auditor's report: a letter from a Certified Public Accountant providing an expert opinion about whether an organization's financial statements provide a fair representation of its financial position and the results of its operations, in accordance with **GAAP**.

audit trail: a set of references that allows an individual to trace back through accounting documents to the source of any number.

bad debts: amounts that are owed to the organization that are never collected.

balance sheet: financial report that indicates the financial position of the organization at a specific point in time; officially referred to as the **statement of financial position**.

bond or bond payable: formal borrowing arrangement whereby a transferable certificate represents the debt.

bond holder: creditor of the organization who owns one of the organization's **bonds payable**.

bonding of employees: insurance policy protecting the organization against embezzlement and fraud by employees.

break-even analysis: technique for determining the minimum volume of services or goods that must be provided to be financially self-sufficient.

break-even volume: the volume just needed to break even. Losses would generally be incurred at lower volumes and profits at higher volumes; sometimes called the break-even point.

budget: a formal, quantitative expression of management's plans and intentions or expectations.

budgeted cost of work performed (BCWP): the budgeted total cost of the work that has been completed.

budgeted cost of work scheduled (BCWS): the budgeted total cost of the work that has been scheduled.

business plan: detailed plan for a proposed program, project, or service, including information to be used to assess financial feasibility.

call provision: a clause in a **bond** agreement that allows the borrower to repay the bond early.

capital acquisitions: see **capital assets**.

capital assets: assets with useful lives extending beyond the year in which they are purchased or put into service; also referred to as long-term investments, capital items, capital investment, or capital acquisitions.

capital budgeting: process of proposing and analyzing the purchase of **capital assets**.

capital cost: see **cost of capital**.

capital lease: form of long-term financing in which a long-term, noncancelable contractual arrangement is made to lease a **capital asset**.

carrying costs of inventory: capital (interest) costs and out-of-pocket costs related to holding inventory. Out-of-pocket costs include such expenses as insurance on the value of inventory and obsolescence of inventory.

cash accounting: a system of recording financial events that recognizes revenue when cash is collected and expenses when cash is paid.

cash basis: accounting system under which revenues are recorded when cash is received and expenses are recorded when cash is paid.

cash budget: plan for the cash receipts and disbursements of the organization.

cash equivalents: items that are quickly and easily convertible into cash, such a checking accounts and **commercial paper**.

cash flow statement: financial statement that examines the organization's sources and uses of cash.

cash management: active process of planning for borrowing and repayment of cash or investing excess cash on hand.

certificate of deposit: bank deposit with a fixed maturity term.

charts of accounts: accounting document that defines an identifying number for each possible element of a financial transaction.

collateral: specific asset pledged to a lender as security for a loan.

collection period: amount of time from when a bill is issued until the cash payment for that bill is collected.

commercial paper: form of short-term borrowing in which the borrower issues a financial security that can be traded by the lender to someone else.

common size ratio: class of ratios that allows one to evaluate each number on a financial statement relative to the size of the organization.

compound interest: method of calculating interest in which interest is earned not only on the original investment but also on the interest earned in interim periods.

conservatism principle: GAAP stating that financial statements must give adequate consideration to the risks faced by the organization.

contingent liabilities: obligations that will exist in the future if certain events occur, such as if the organization loses a lawsuit.

contra asset: an asset that is used to offset or reduce another asset.

contributed capital: amounts that individuals have paid directly to the firm in exchange for share of ownership such as common or preferred stock; also called **paid-in capital**.

contribution margin: amount by which the revenue exceeds the variable cost.

corporation: business form in which the owners (shareholders or stockholders) have limited liability—they are not liable for more than the amount they invested in the firm.

cost accounting system: any coherent system designed to gather and report cost information.

cost allocation: the process of taking costs from one area or cost objective and allocating them to others.

cost convention: GAAP that requires most assets to be valued at their cost at the time of acquisition.

cost driver: an activity that causes costs to be incurred.

cost-effectiveness: a measure of whether costs are minimized for the desired outcome.

cost of capital: the cost to the organization of its long-term debt and equity financing.

cost variance: any difference between the earned value and the actual cost.

credit (cr.): bookkeeping term for an increase in an item on the right side of the **fundamental equation of accounting** or a decrease in an item on the left side.

creditors: entities to whom the organization owes money.

critical path: a set of activities which total to the longest overall time to complete a project. A delay in the critical path will delay project completion. Speeding up any task on the critical path can speed completion of the project.

current: within one year; short-term or near-term.

current assets: resources the organization has that are cash, that can be converted to cash within on year, or that will be used up within one year. Often referred to as short-term or near-term assets.

current liabilities: obligations due to be paid within one year.

current ratio: current assets divided by **current liabilities**; this **liquidity ratio** assesses the ability of the organization to meet its current obligations as they come due.

days of inventory on hand: 365 divided by the **inventory turnover** ratio; this **efficiency ratio** assesses how many days' supply of inventory is kept on hand.

days receivable: 365 divided by the **receivables turnover** ratio; this **efficiency ratio** indicates the average number of days from the issuance of an invoice until a receivable is collected.

debit (dr.): bookkeeping term for an increase in an item on the left side of the **fundamental equation of accounting** or a decrease in an item on the right side.

debt: liability; an amount owed by one **entity** to another.

debt service: required interest and principal payments on money owed.

debt to equity: leverage ratio that considers the relative magnitude of debt to equity to assess the risk created by the use of **leverage**.

decision package: all information and analysis related to a **zero-based budgeting** review.

deficit: the excess of cash spending over cash receipts or of **expenses** over **revenues**.

defined-benefit plan: pension plan in which the organization is required to make specific defined payments to participants during their retirements.

defined-contribution plan: pension plan in which the employer's only obligation is to put into the plan a set amount of money each year.

depreciation expense: the portion of the original cost of a **capital asset** allocated as an expense each year.

derivatives: securities whose value is derived from the value of something else.

direct costs: a) costs incurred within the organizational unit for which the manager has responsibility; b) cost of resources used for direct provision of goods or services.

disbursement: cash payment.

discount: the amount a bond sells for below its face value because the market demands a higher interest rate than the bond pays.

discounted cash flow: method that compares amounts of money paid at different points of time by **discounting** all amounts to the present.

discounting: reverse of **compound interest**; a process in which interest that could be earned over time is deducted from a future payment to determine how much the future payment is worth at the present time.

discount rate: interest rate used in **time value of money** analysis.

dividend: distribution of profits to owners of the **entity**.

double-entry accounting: whenever a change is made to the **fundamental equation of accounting,** at least one other change must be made to keep the equation in balance.

earned value management: a technique that assures that projects are adequately planned and resources appropriately used by evaluating progress during the life of a project.

earned value (EV): the budgeted total cost of the work that has been completed.

economic order quantity (EOQ): technique that determines the optimal amount of inventory to order at one time.

efficiency ratios: ratios that examine the efficiency with which the organization uses its resources. Examples are **receivables turnover, days of inventory on hand,** and **total asset turnover**.

efficiency variance: see **quantity variance**.

electronic spreadsheet: a software program that allows for automatic re-computations when one number in the **spreadsheet** changes.

employee benefits: compensation provided to employees in addition to their base salary; for example, health insurance, life insurance, vacation, and holidays.

entity: specific individual, organization, or part of an organization for which we are accounting.

equities: liabilities and owners' equity; the right-hand side of the balance sheet.

equity: ownership; e.g. the share of a house that is owned by the homeowner free and clear of any mortgage obligation is the homeowners' equity in the house.

expected value: the weighted average of the value of each possible outcome taking into account the likelihood of each outcome.

expense: the cost of services provided; expired cost.

external accountant: accountant who is not an employee of the organization, often hired to perform an audit.

face value: see **maturity value**.

factoring: selling the organization's accounts receivable.

fair value: see **mark-to-market**.

favorable variance: variance in which less money was spent or more money was earned than the budgeted amount.

finance: field that focuses on the alternative sources and uses of the organization's financial resources such as cash, marketable securities, and debt.

financial accounting: system that records historical financial information, summarizes it, and provides reports of what financial events have occurred and of what the financial impact of those events has been.

financial management: the subset of management that focuses on generating financial information to improve decision making.

financial statement analysis: analysis of the financial condition of an entity by reviewing financial statements including the accompanying notes and **auditor's report**, performing **ratio analysis**, and using comparative data.

financial statements: reports that convey information about the entity's financial position and the results of its activities.

financing accounts receivable: using the organization's accounts receivable as security or collateral for a loan.

first-in, first-out (FIFO): inventory-costing method that assumes the oldest inventory is used first.

fiscal: financial.

fiscal year: one-year period defined for financial purposes. A fiscal year may start at any point during the calendar year and finish one year later. Fiscal year 2013 with a June 30 year-end refers to the period from July 1, 2012, through June 30, 2013.

fixed assets: those assets that will not be used up or converted to cash within one year.

fixed costs: costs that do not change in total as volume of goods or services changes with the **relevant range**.

flexible budget: budget that is adjusted for volume of output.

flexible budgeting: process of developing a budget based on different workload levels.

flexible budget variance: difference between actual results and the flexible budget.

float: the interim period from when a check is written until the check is cashed and clears the bank.

fraud: an intentional deception for the purpose of a financial gain.

fringe benefits: see **employee benefits**.

full disclosure: GAAP that requires notes to financial statements to convey all information necessary for the user to have a fair understanding of the financial position of the organization and the results of its operations.

fundamental equation of accounting: assets equal liabilities plus owners' equity.

fungible: interchangeable.

future value (FV): the amount that a sum of money paid or received will grow to be worth at some point in the future.

GAAP: see **Generally Accepted Accounting Principles**.

general journal: first place that financial transactions are entered into the accounting records.

general ledger: book of accounts, listing the balances and all changes in each account.

Generally Accepted Accounting Principles (GAAP): set of rules that must be followed for the organization's financial statements to be deemed a fair presentation of the organization's financial position and results of operations.

goal congruence: bringing together the goals, desires, and wants of the organization with those of its employees.

goal divergence: natural differences between the goals, desires, and needs of the organization and those of its employees.

goals: broad, timeless ends of the organization meant to aid the organization in accomplishing its **mission**.

going-concern principle: GAAP that requires an explicit note in the auditor's opinion letter if there is a significant possibility that the organization will not be able to continue operations for the entire coming year.

goodwill: the value of the organization above the value of its specific physical assets.

hurdle rate: see **required rate of return**.

income: excess of revenues over expenses.

income statement: financial statement that reports the results of operations over a period of time.

incremental budgeting: an approach to resource allocation that simply adds an additional percentage or amount onto the prior year's budget allocation.

incremental costs: additional costs that will be incurred if a decision is made that would not otherwise be incurred.

indirect costs: a) costs assigned to an organizational unit from elsewhere in the organization; b) costs within a unit that are not incurred for direct provision of goods or services.

indirect expenses: see **indirect costs**.

inputs: resources used for producing the organization's output. Examples are labor and supplies.

intangible asset: asset without physical substance or form.

interest coverage ratio: operating income divided by interest expense; a measure of the organization's ability to meet its required interest payments.

interim statements: financial statements covering a period of time less than one year.

internal accountant: accountant who works as an employee of the organization.

internal control: a system of accounting checks and balances designed to minimize clerical errors and the possibility of fraud or embezzlement.

internal rate of return (IRR): discounted cash-flow technique that calculates the rate of return earned on a specific project or program.

International Financial Reporting Standards (IFRS): a set of generally accepted accounting principles developed by the International Accounting Standards Board (IASB) and used worldwide in over 120 countries.

inventory: materials and supplies held for use in providing services or making a product.

inventory-carrying costs: see **carrying costs of inventory**.

inventory costing: the process of determining the cost to be assigned to each unit of **inventory**.

inventory management: refers to the appropriate ordering and storage of supplies.

inventory-ordering costs: see **ordering costs**.

inventory turnover: efficiency ratio that evaluates the relative number of times that the organization's inventory has been consumed and replaced during the year.

investments: primary stocks and bonds that the organization does not intend to sell within one year.

IRR: see **internal rate of return**.

journal entry: entry into the **general journal** or a **subsidiary journal**.

just-in-time (JIT) inventory: an approach to inventory management that calls for the arrival of inventory just as it is needed, resulting in zero inventory levels.

last-in, first-out (LIFO): inventory valuation method that accounts for inventory as if the most recent acquisitions are used first.

lease: agreement providing for the use of an asset in exchange for rental payments.

leasehold asset: the **balance sheet** title for the asset on a **capital lease**.

leasehold liability: the **balance sheet** title for the liability on a **capital lease**.

ledger: accounting record that tracks changes in each asset, liability, revenue, expense, and equity account.

leverage: a) the use of debt as a source of financing, increasing risk because of the requirement to make interest payments; b) the use of fixed costs to increase profits if the volume of goods or services sold is high.

leverage ratios: ratios that examine the relative amount of debt the organization has; sometimes referred to as **solvency** ratios.

liabilities: legal financial obligations the organization has to outsiders.

line item: any item listed as a separate line on a budget.

line of credit: prearranged loan to be made when and if needed by the **entity** in an amount up to an agreed limit.

liquid: able to be quickly converted to cash.

liquidate: convert into cash, by sale if necessary.

liquidity ratios: class of ratios that examine the ability of the entity to meet its obligations in the coming year.

lockbox: post office box that is emptied directly by the bank, with receipts immediately deposited into the organization's account.

long-range plan: plan that covers a period longer than one year, focusing on general objectives to be achieved by the organization.

long-term: period longer than one year.

long-term assets: see **capital assets**.

long-term financing: the various alternatives available to the organization to get the money needed to acquire **capital assets.**

long-term investment: see **capital assets.**

long-term liabilities: obligations that are not due until more than one year has passed.

management control system: complete set of policies and procedures designed to keep operations going according to plan.

management letter: letter from the CPA to the management of the **entity** discussing weaknesses in the internal control system that were revealed as part of an audit.

management's discussion: section of an annual report in which the organization's management discusses the organization's performance.

management's accounting: subset of accounting that generates financial information that can help managers to manage better.

marginal cost analysis: process for making decisions based on the costs that change as a result of the decision rather than on the full or average costs.

marginal costs: variable costs plus any change in fixed costs incurred because of a change in activity.

mark-to-market: a valuation method that is used to record financial assets (such as stocks and bonds) at the current market value we could sell them for.

marketable securities: investments in stocks and bonds that the organization intends to sell within one year.

master budget: set of all the major budgets in the organization; generally includes the operating, long-range, program, capital, and cash budgets.

matching: recording the revenues from the sale of a unit in the same period as the expenses incurred to generate the revenue.

material: amount substantial enough that an error of that magnitude in the financial statements would affect a decision made by a user of the statements.

maturity: due date or end date of a loan arrangement.

maturity value: the principal amount of a loan to be repaid at the ending date or maturity date of the loan.

mission statement: statement of the purpose or reason for existence of an **entity.**

monetary denominator: **GAAP** that requires resources be stated on financial statements in terms of an amount of money.

money market: the market for short-term marketable securities or the market for short-term debt instruments.

mortgage payable: a loan secured by specific **real property.**

near term: within one year; current or short-term.

negotiable certificate of deposit: certificate of deposit that can be transferred from one party to another.

net book value: the original cost of the asset less the total **accumulated depreciation** for that asset.

net cash flow: difference between cash receipts and payments.

net income: revenue less expense; profit.

net present value (NPV): present value of a series of receipts, less the present value of a series of payments.

net working capital: current assets less **current liabilities**.

net worth: owners' equity.

network analysis: a management tool that finds the **critical path** to achieve the least amount of time to complete a project.

network cost budgeting: a technique that combines **network analysis** and cost accounting to generate the most cost-effective approach to a project, often recommending extra spending in order to reduce the time required for the **critical path**.

note payable: written document representing a loan.

NPV: see **net present value**.

objective evidence: GAAP that requires assets to be valued based on objective, rather than subjective, information.

objectives: specific targets to be achieved to attain goals.

operating: related to the normal routine revenue and expense activities of the organization.

operating budget: plan for the day-in and day-out operating revenues and expenses of the organization.

operating expenses: costs of the organization related to its general operations.

operating lease: lease that is either short-term or cancelable.

operating margin: profitability ratio that compares operating profit to operating revenue.

operating revenues: revenues earned in the normal course of providing the organization's goods or services.

operating statement: compares the **entity's revenues** and other **support** to its **expenses** for a period of time. Also called the income statement, activity statement, profit and loss (P&L) statement, or earnings report.

operations: routine activities of the organization related to its **mission** and the provision of goods or services.

opinion letter: letter providing a CPA's expert opinion as to whether a set of financial statements are a fair presentation of the financial position and results of operations of the organization, in accordance with **GAAP**.

ordering cost: those costs associated with ordering inventory, such as clerical time to prepare a purchase order.

output: the number of units of service or product produced.

overhead: indirect costs allocated to a unit or department from elsewhere in the organization.

owners' equity: residual value, owned by the owners, left over when the liabilities of an organization are subtracted from its assets.

paid-in capital: see **contributed capital**.

partnership: type of business form in which a group of people (partners) have unlimited liability.

payback: evaluation approach that calculates how long it takes for a project's revenues to exceed all costs including the initial cash outlay.

payroll payable: amounts owed to employees.

period costs: costs that are treated as expense in the accounting period when they are incurred, regardless of when the organization's goods or services are sold.

periodic inventory: inventory method under which the organization uses a count of inventory to determine how much has been sold and how much is left on hand.

perpetual inventory: inventory method under which the organization keeps a record of each unit removed from inventory.

planned value (PV): the budgeted total cost of the work that has been scheduled.

planning: selecting a course of action from a range of possible alternatives.

plant: building.

posting: process of recording all parts of a journal entry in the specific ledger accounts affected by the entry.

premium: the amount a bond sells for in excess of its face value because the market is willing to accept a lower rate than the bond pays.

prepaid expenses: assets that have been paid for, but not yet used, e.g., rent paid in advance.

present value: value of future receipts or payments **discounted** to the present.

price variance: variance caused by spending a different amount per unit of resource than had been anticipated.

principal: the amount of money borrowed on a loan.

product costs: expenses that are directly related to the production of goods and services.

profit: excess of revenues over expenses.

profit center: responsibility unit that is accountable for both revenues and expenses.

profit margin: see **return on sales**.

profitability ratios: ratios that assess the profitability of the organization; examples are the **operating margin** and **total margin** ratios.

profit sharing plan: an incentive arrangement under which some or all employees receive a portion of an organization's profits that exceed a certain threshold.

pro forma financial statements: forecast of what financial statements will look like if results are as expected.

program audits: reviews of the organization's operations to check for effectiveness.

project: a limited effort by an organization, having a clear beginning and an end.

proprietorship: business owned by one individual, who has unlimited liability.

quantity variance: variance caused by using more input per unit of output than had been budgeted.

quick ratio: cash plus marketable securities plus accounts receivable, all divided by current liabilities. Sometimes called the **acid test**.

rate variance: **price variance** for labor inputs.

ratio analysis: comparison of one number to another in order to gain insight from the relationship.

real property: land and anything attached to it (such as a building)

receivables: see **accounts receivable**.

receivables turnover: revenues divided by **accounts receivable;** see **average collection period**.

registered bonds: bonds whose ownership is tracked by the borrower.

relevant range: that range of activity that might reasonably be expected to occur in the budget period.

repurchase agreements (repos): short-term investment collateralized by securities.

required rate of return: the rate of return that must be achieved for a capital project to be considered financially worthwhile. Also called the **hurdle rate**.

responsibility accounting: attempt to hold individuals or departments accountable for outcomes.

responsibility center: part of the organization for which a manager is assigned responsibility.

retained earnings: the portion of the profits of a for-profit corporation that have not been distributed to the owners in the form of dividends.

return on assets (ROA): a measure of the amount of profit earned for each dollar invested in the organization's assets.

return on investments (ROI): a ratio that assesses the profitability of the investment.

return on sales (ROS): a ratio that determines the amount of profit generated by each dollar of revenue.

revenue: amounts of money that the organization has received, or is entitled to receive, in exchange for goods and services that is has provided.

revenue to total assets: ratio measure of the amount of revenue generated per dollar of assets used.

revenue variances: variance resulting from changes in the total demand, an organization's share of total demand, mix of products or services, and the prices for each class of product or service.

safety stock: minimum level of inventory that an organization would always attempt to maintain on hand.

schedule variance: the difference between the **planned value** and the **earned value** at a point in time.

secured creditor: creditor whose loan to the organization is secured by **collateral**.

sensitivity analysis: recalculations using varying assumptions and predictions, often referred to as "what-if" analysis.

short-term: within one year; current on near term.

sinking fund: segregated assets to be used for replacement of plant and equipment or the repayment of a long-term loan.

solvency: ability to meet current and future obligations.

solvency ratios: class of ratios that evaluates the organization's ability to meet its obligations as they come due over a time frame longer than one year.

specific identification: inventory valuation method that identifies and tracks each unit of inventory.

spreadsheet: document with a grid of columns and row, often used for financial computations.

stated value of a bond: the amount that will be paid at the end of the loan period.

statement of financial position: financial report that indicates the financial position of the organization at a specific point in time.

straight-line depreciation: technique that allocates an equal portion of a long-term asset's cost as an expense each year.

strategic plan: a document that sets the direction the organization will take to achieve its underlying **mission.**

strategies: broad plans for the attainment of **goals.**

subsidiary journal: detailed journals in which original entries are first made, with only a summary total entry being made to the **general journal.**

subsidiary ledger: ledgers in which detailed information is recorded, with only a summary being posted to the **general ledger.**

tangible: having physical substance or form.

terms: refers to when an account payable is due and the discount for early payment.

time-series: forecasting approach that uses past trends and seasonal patterns as predictors for the future.

times interest earned: solvency ratio that assesses the ability of the organization to make interest payments.

time value of money: recognition of the fact that an amount of money in the future is less valuable than that same amount today.

total variance: difference between the actual results and the originally budgeted amount.

total asset turnover: efficiency ratio that assesses the number of dollars of revenue generated for each dollar invested in assets.

total margin: profitability ratio that determines profits per dollar of revenues.

trade credit: accounts payable.

uncollectibles: see **allowance for uncollectible accounts.**

unfavorable variance: variance in which more was spent than the budgeted amount.

unregistered bonds: bonds for which the borrowing organization does not have a record of whom the lenders are. Often called bearer bonds.

unsecured notes: loans that do not have any collateral.

use variance: quantity variance.

variable costs: costs that vary in direct proportion with volume.

variance: difference between the budget and actual results.

variance analysis: investigation by managers to determine why actual results varied from the budget.

vendor: supplier who sells to the organization.

viability: ability to continue in existence.

volume variance: variance caused by a change in the workload level.

wages payable: amounts owed to employees.

working capital: current assets less **current liabilities.**

workload level: volume of goods or services that the organization provides.

write-off: entry to eliminate as asset from the accounting records by treating it as an expense.

XBRL (eXtensible Business Reporting Language): tool for electronic communication of data by assigning an identifying electronic tag to each element of a financial statement.

zero balance accounts: a system in which automatic bank account transfers leave certain accounts with a zero balance at the end of each day.

zero-base budgeting (ZBB): budgeting approach that requires an examination and justification of all costs, rather than just the incremental costs, and that requires examination of alternatives rather than just one approach.

zero-coupon bonds: bonds that do not pay interest until the maturity date, when all accumulated interest and principal is paid.

ANNOTATED LIST OF WEB SITES RELATED TO FINANCE AND ACCOUNTING

Below is an extensive list of web sites related to finance and accounting. These sites have been specifically chosen for their relevance to nonfinancial managers.

Please note that we do not specifically endorse any products offered at any of these sites. Also note that, unfortunately, many web sites disappear over time. We apologize if any of the links below are no longer functioning.

1. GENERAL ACCOUNTING PORTALS

Portals are web sites that primarily provide links to other sites. The following are two of the best sites for accounting and finance links.

http://www.aicpa.org
The web site of the trade association for CPAs.

http://accounting.rutgers.edu/
Rutgers University is rapidly building an unsurpassed accounting web site infrastructure, with links to numerous accounting sources and resources.

2. BUSINESS NEWSPAPERS AND MAGAZINES

A number of business newspapers and magazines provide a variety of useful information on financial issues. Articles are often relevant for both business and personal finance. Although subscriptions are required for some services, the sites below all provide extensive information for free.

http://online.wsj.com/home-page
This is the home page for the *Wall Street Journal.*

http://news.ft.com/home/us/
This is the home page for the *Financial Times,* the leading international financial daily newspaper.

http://www.fortune.com
This is the home page for *Fortune* magazine.

http://www.businessweek.com
This is the home page for *BusinessWeek* magazine. It is one of the most popular sources for domestic and international business news.

http://www.barrons.com/
This is the home page for *Barron's* weekly business newspaper.

http://www.money.com/money/
This is the home page for *Money* magazine. It is of primary interest for personal finances.

http://www.smartmoney.com
This is the home page for *Smartmoney* magazine. It is of primary interest for personal finances.

http://www.kiplinger.com
This is the home site for *Kiplinger's*, a widely read source for personal finances and economic forecasts.

3. ACCOUNTING AND FINANCE ASSOCIATIONS

Although the primary purpose of a trade association is to serve its members, many finance and accounting associations have a wealth of useful information for nonmembers as well. Listed below are some of the most important sites.

http://www.imanet.org/
This is the home site for the Institute of Management Accountants, a professional organization devoted exclusively to management accounting and financial management.

http://aaahq.org/
This is the home site for the American Accounting Association, the primary association of accountants in academics.

http://www.afajof.org/
This is the home site for the American Finance Association, the primary association of finance academics.

http://afponline.org/
This is the home site for the Association of Finance Professionals.

4. TAX BASICS

The sites in this section provide tax information for personal and business taxes.

http://www.irs.gov/
This is the home page for the Internal Revenue Service. The site provides a wealth of useful information on all issues related to U.S. federal income taxes.

http://www.taxresources.com/
A source of up-to-date information on taxes, as well as a number of other useful tax links.

http://www.usnews.com/
This is the home page for *U.S. News and World Report*. It often contains articles on taxation geared to a nonfinancial audience.

http://www.moneycentral.com/
This MSN site often contains articles on taxation geared to a nonfinancial audience.

http://businessweek.findlaw.com/
At this site, *BusinessWeek On-Line* often provides articles on taxes for small businesses.

5. BUSINESS PLANS

A number of sites provide assistance in writing a business plan, as well as other information related to starting a new business. Some good site are:

http://www.sba.gov/category/navigation-structure/starting-managing-business/starting-business/writing-business-plan
The government's Small Business Administration site provides a wealth of information on starting a business and developing a business plan.

http://www.businessplans.org/
The Center for Business Planning provides resources to help in creating a business or managing a business.

http://www.business-plan.com/
OUT OF YOUR MIND...AND INTO THE MARKETPLACE is a publisher focusing on business plan books and software.

http://www.planware.org/salepwb.htm
Business Planning Software—sophisticated package of business plan tools.

http://www.bplans.com/
Bplans.com provides a wealth of information for starting a business and developing a business plan. Sample plans, books, articles, and software are available through this site.

http://morebusiness.com/
The motto of Morebusiness.com is that it is a web site by entrepreneurs for entrepreneurs. Chock full of articles, features, tools, templates, and other information for business plans and new businesses.

6. RAISING VENTURE CAPITAL

Raising venture capital is a difficult challenge for most new businesses. Listed below are web sites for a few venture capital organizations. We suggest that you also use a search engine and simply search for "venture capital" to identify additional organizations that are located in your geographic area. Also note that some venture capitalists will give you a better deal than others. It pays to shop around.

http://www.vcinstitute.org/
This is the home page for The Venture Capital Institute, a trade association for venture capitalists. Although not aimed at the general public, it does provide valuable information for someone starting out on the search for financing.

http://www.vfinance.com/
This web site features the Venture Capital Resource Directory, a broad listing of venture capital firms.

7. BUDGETING

A number of vendors provide software and other assistance to help in the budget process. An example is:

http://www.epssoftware.com/
EPS Software provides budgeting, planning, forecasting, and management reporting software.

8. GENERAL ACCOUNTING AND FINANCE

The two sites listed here provide a wide range of tutorials and information about general accounting and finance topics of interest to non-financial managers.

http://www.teachmefinance.com/
TeachMeFinance.com provides simple explanations of concepts: time value of money, present value, future value, annuites, bond valuation, internal rate of return, and more.

http://www.studyfinance.com
A brief on-line course in various finance concepts.

9. INVENTORY MANAGEMENT

There are numerous web sites offering inventory management services. A few examples are listed below:

http://www.simba.org/
Web site of the Society for Inventory Management Benchmarking Analysis.

http://www.effectiveinventory.com/
Effective Inventory Management provides articles, course, and software for inventory management.

10. RATIO ANALYSIS

http://www.ventureline.com/ratio-analysis-accounting-ratios/
VentureLine provides extensive discussions of ratio analysis at this site. Industry ratio analysis reports may be generated on-line.

Index

(References are to page numbers)